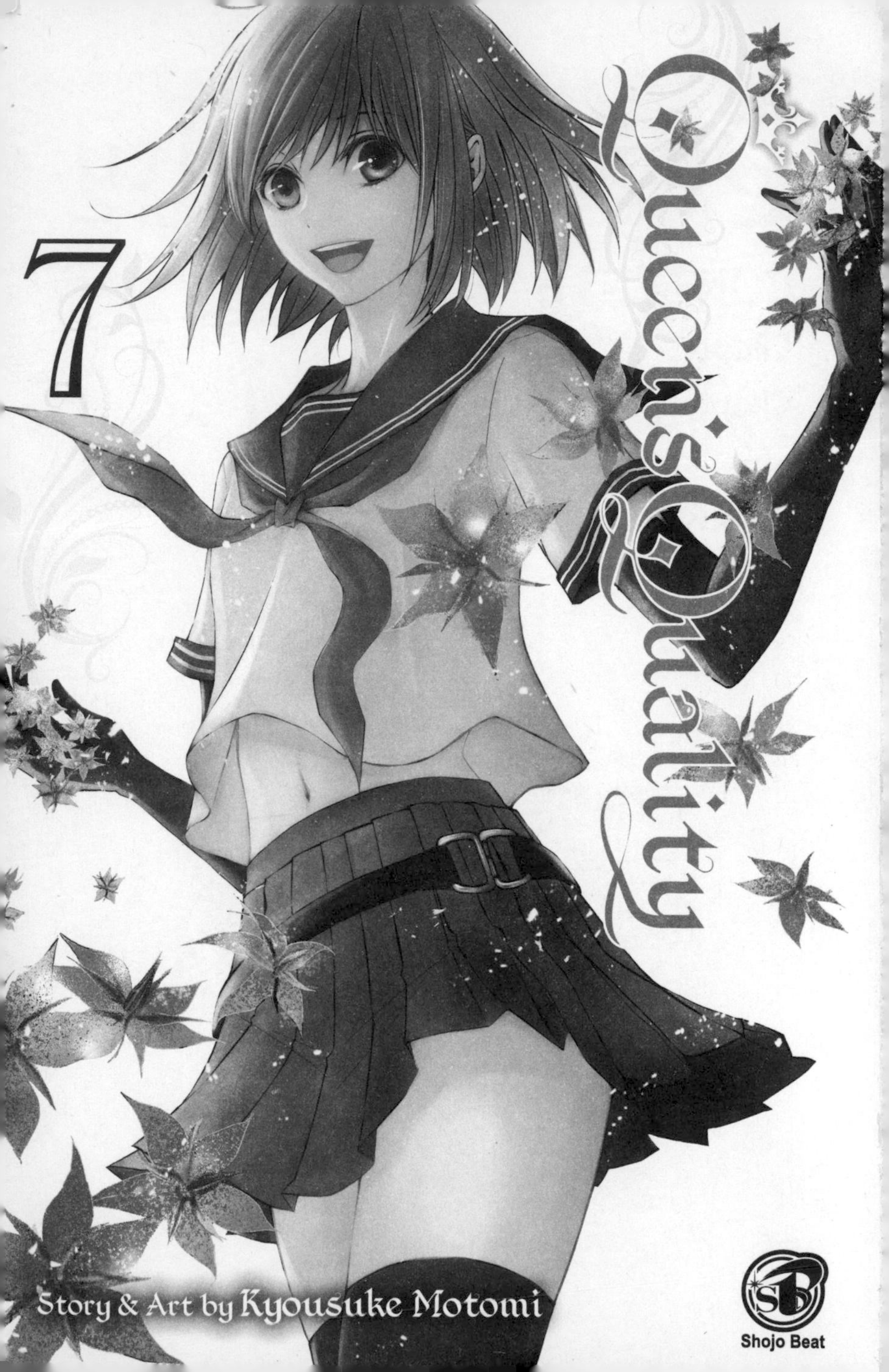
7
Queen's Quality
Story & Art by Kyousuke Motomi
Shojo Beat

Queen's Quality

CONTENTS

7

Cast of Characters

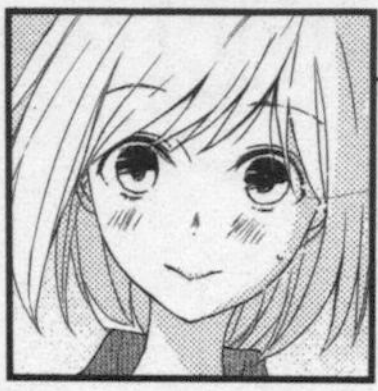

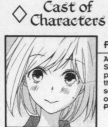

Fumi Nishioka

An apprentice Sweeper with the powers of a Queen, this second-year high school student dreams of finding her very own Prince Charming.

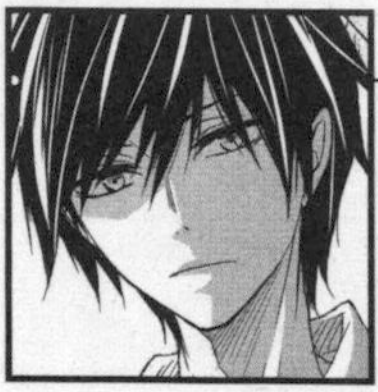

Kyutaro Horikita

A mind Sweeper who cleanses people's minds of dangerous impurities. He's incredibly awkward with people, but he has feelings for Fumi.

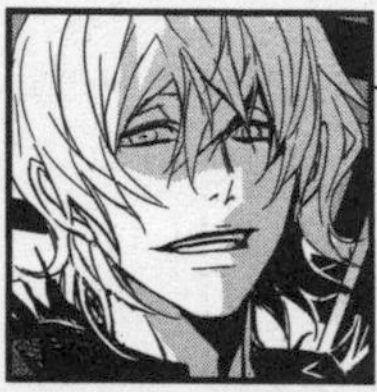

Ataru Shikata

A former bug handler who uses bugs to manipulate people. Saved by Fumi and Kyutaro, he has joined the Genbu Clan.

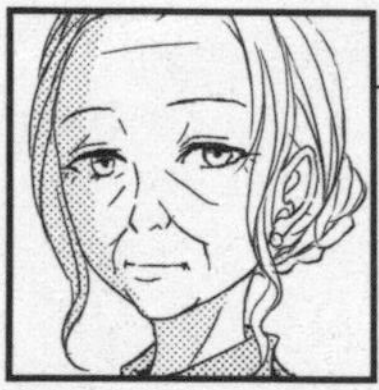

Miyako Horikita

The prior head of the Genbu Gate Sweepers. She can be both strict and kind, and she watches over and advises Fumi.

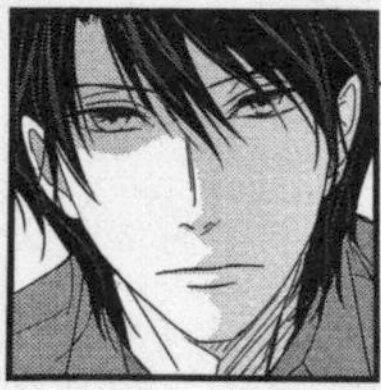

Koichi Kitagawa

The chairman of the school Fumi and Kyutaro attend. He's a Sweeper as well as being Kyutaro's brother-in-law.

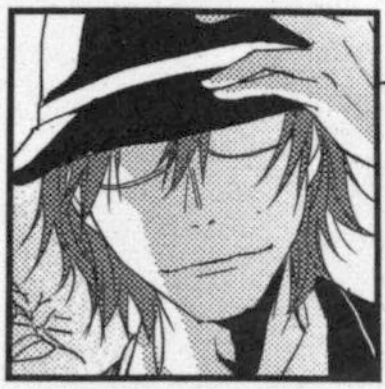

Takaya Kitahara

A psychiatrist who's related to the Genbu Gate Sweepers. He's an expert with suggestive therapy, and he counsels Fumi.

Story Thus Far

The Horikitas are a family of Sweepers—people who cleanse impurities from human hearts. After seeing Fumi's potential, they take her on as an assistant and trainee. However, Fumi has the untapped, immense power of a Queen, and she's awakened both the White Queen and the Black Queen inside of her.

The Black Queen, who is Fumi's self-esteem, fades away once she becomes one with Fumi—this produces the Dark-Gray Queen. Later, Fumi, Kyutaro and Ataru go to Seichi, the Holy Ground of the Old Byakko Clan, in order to train and get stronger. Kyutaro gets separated from the others and finds himself battling someone who looks exactly like him! Fumi is frantically looking for Kyutaro when a mystical cat appears before her...

MONTHLY BETSUCOMI SALE DATE NOTICE ON TWITTER

CHAPTER 31

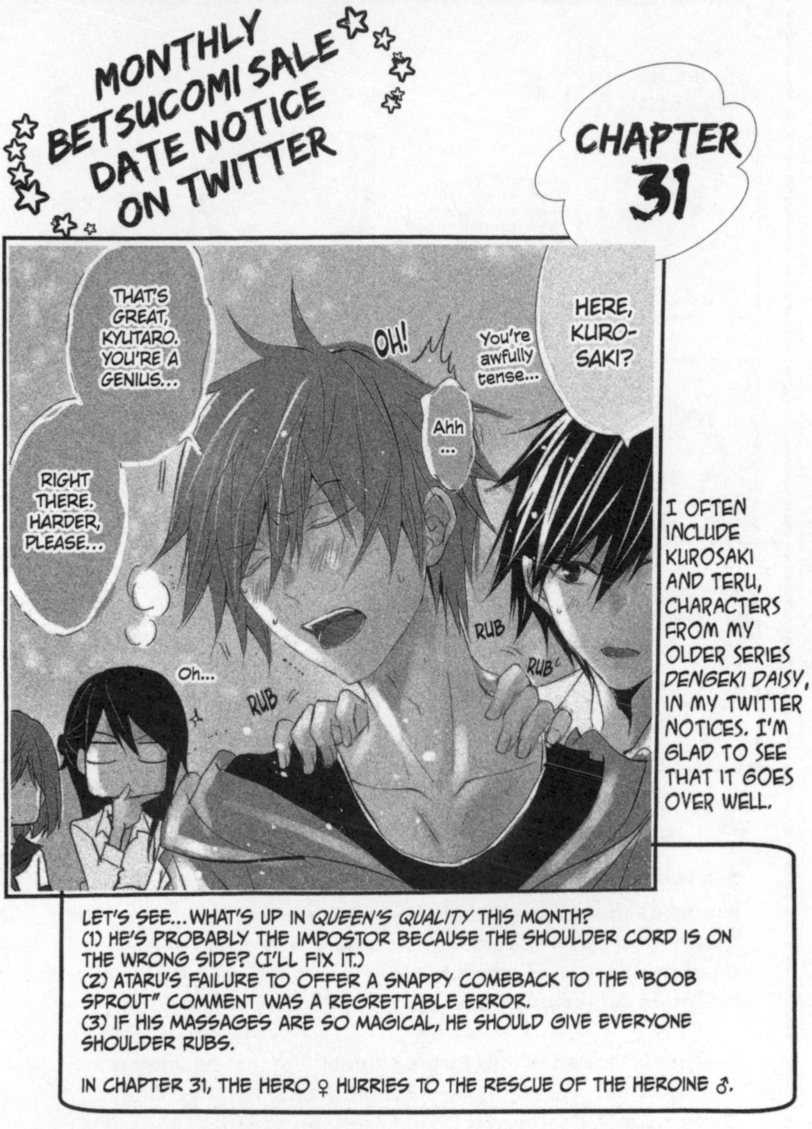
HERE, KURO-SAKI?
You're awfully tense...
OH!
Ahh ...
THAT'S GREAT, KYUTARO. YOU'RE A GENIUS...
RIGHT THERE. HARDER, PLEASE...
RUB
RUB
RUB
Oh...

I OFTEN INCLUDE KUROSAKI AND TERU, CHARACTERS FROM MY OLDER SERIES *DENGEKI DAISY*, IN MY TWITTER NOTICES. I'M GLAD TO SEE THAT IT GOES OVER WELL.

LET'S SEE...WHAT'S UP IN *QUEEN'S QUALITY* THIS MONTH?
(1) HE'S PROBABLY THE IMPOSTOR BECAUSE THE SHOULDER CORD IS ON THE WRONG SIDE? (I'LL FIX IT.)
(2) ATARU'S FAILURE TO OFFER A SNAPPY COMEBACK TO THE "BOOB SPROUT" COMMENT WAS A REGRETTABLE ERROR.
(3) IF HIS MASSAGES ARE SO MAGICAL, HE SHOULD GIVE EVERYONE SHOULDER RUBS.

IN CHAPTER 31, THE HERO ♀ HURRIES TO THE RESCUE OF THE HEROINE ♂.

I POST TWEETS LIKE THIS EVERY MONTH. YOU'LL FIND ME MUTTERING ABOUT OTHER SILLY STUFF TOO.

@motomikyosuke

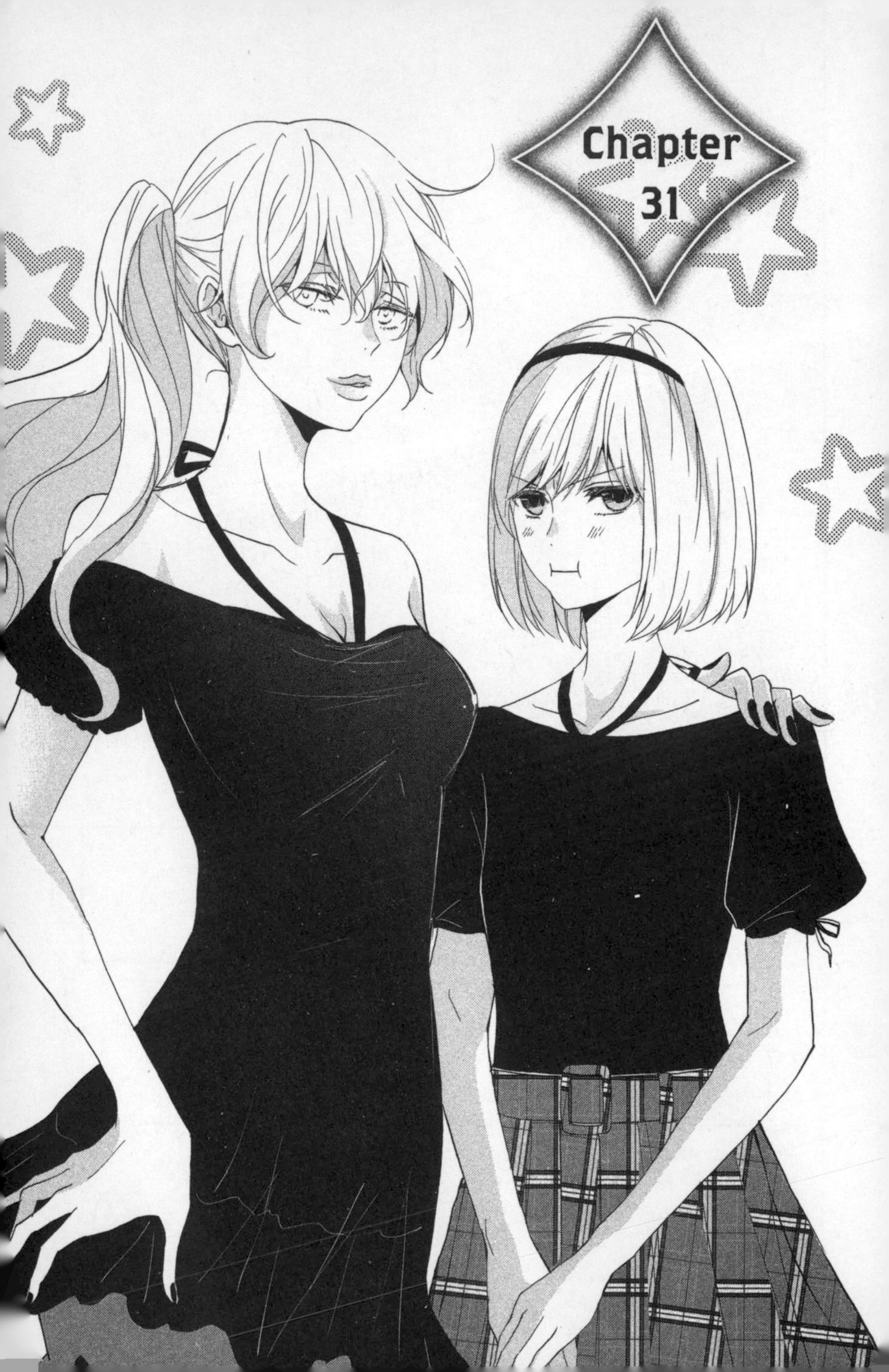
Chapter 31

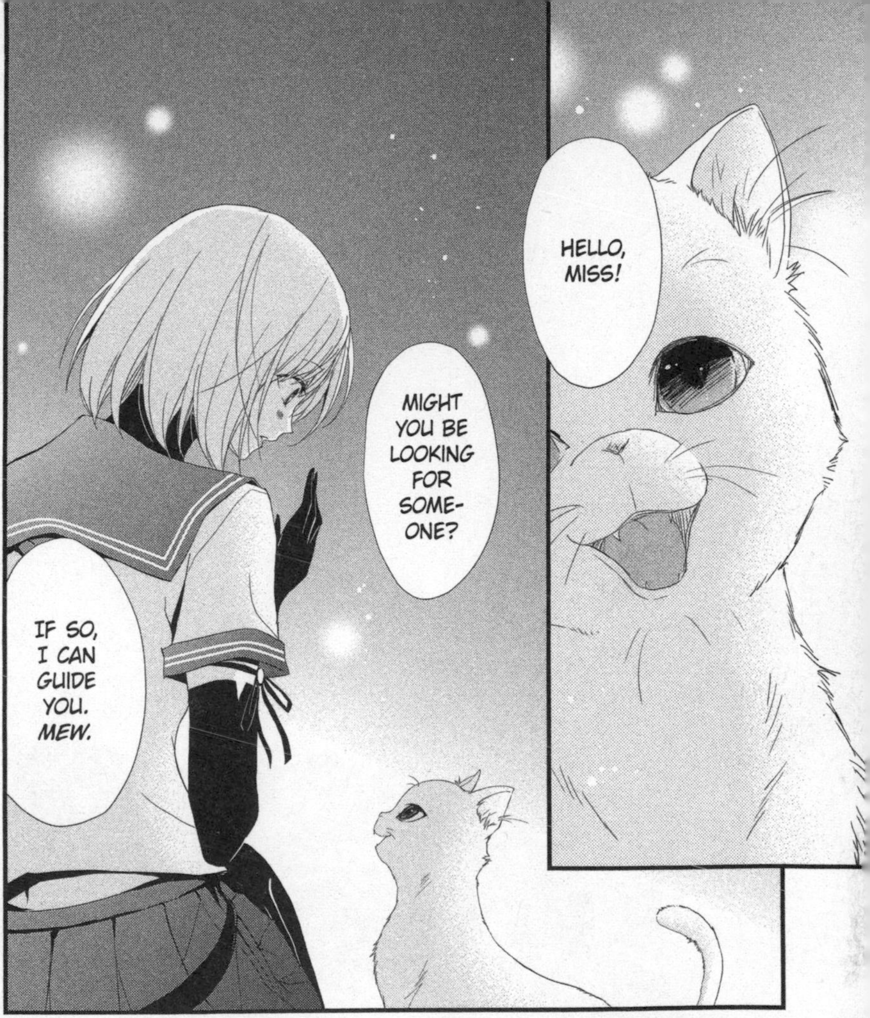
HELLO, MISS!
MIGHT YOU BE LOOKING FOR SOME-ONE?
IF SO, I CAN GUIDE YOU. MEW.

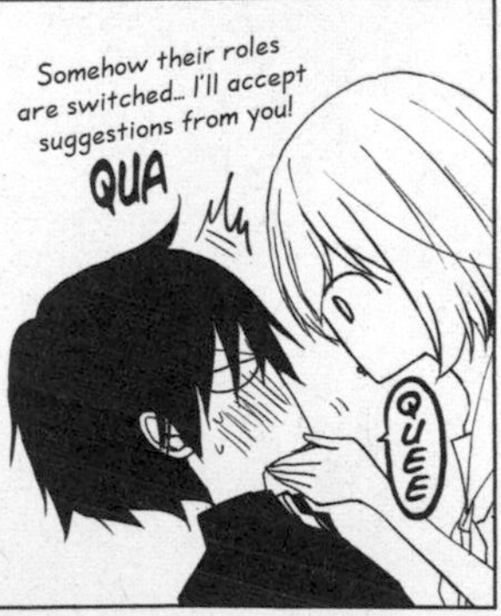
Somehow their roles are switched... I'll accept suggestions from you!
QUA
QUEE

Hello, everyone!
This is Kyousuke Motomi. Thank you so much for picking up *Queen's Quality* volume 7. If we include the volumes of *QQ Sweeper*, this is the tenth volume of the story! I feel so emotional about it! I hope you'll follow the story to its end.

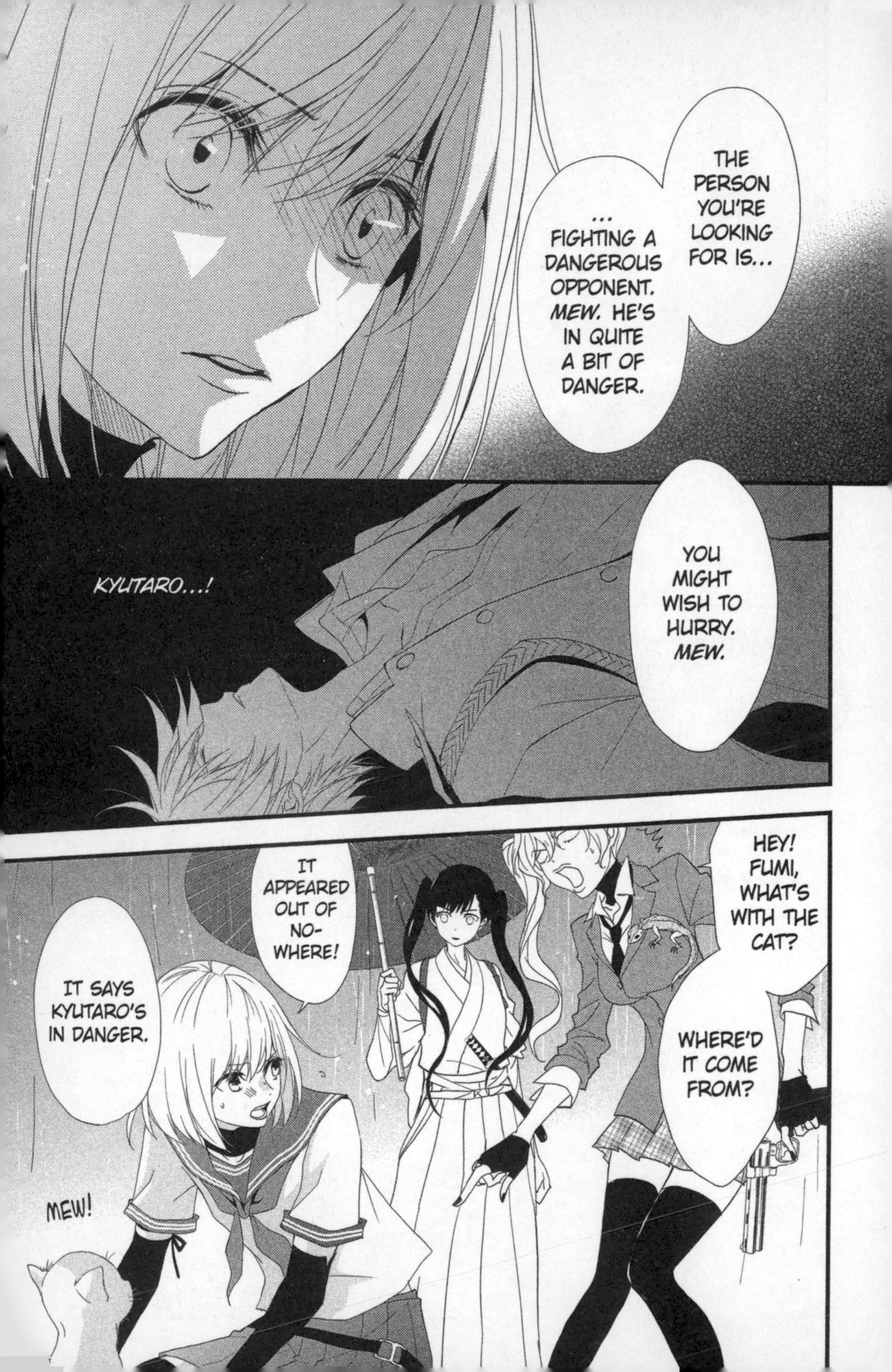
THE PERSON YOU'RE LOOKING FOR IS...
... FIGHTING A DANGEROUS OPPONENT. *MEW.* HE'S IN QUITE A BIT OF DANGER.
YOU MIGHT WISH TO HURRY. *MEW.*
KYUTARO...!
HEY! FUMI, WHAT'S WITH THE CAT?
WHERE'D IT COME FROM?
IT APPEARED OUT OF NO-WHERE!
IT SAYS KYUTARO'S IN DANGER.
MEW!

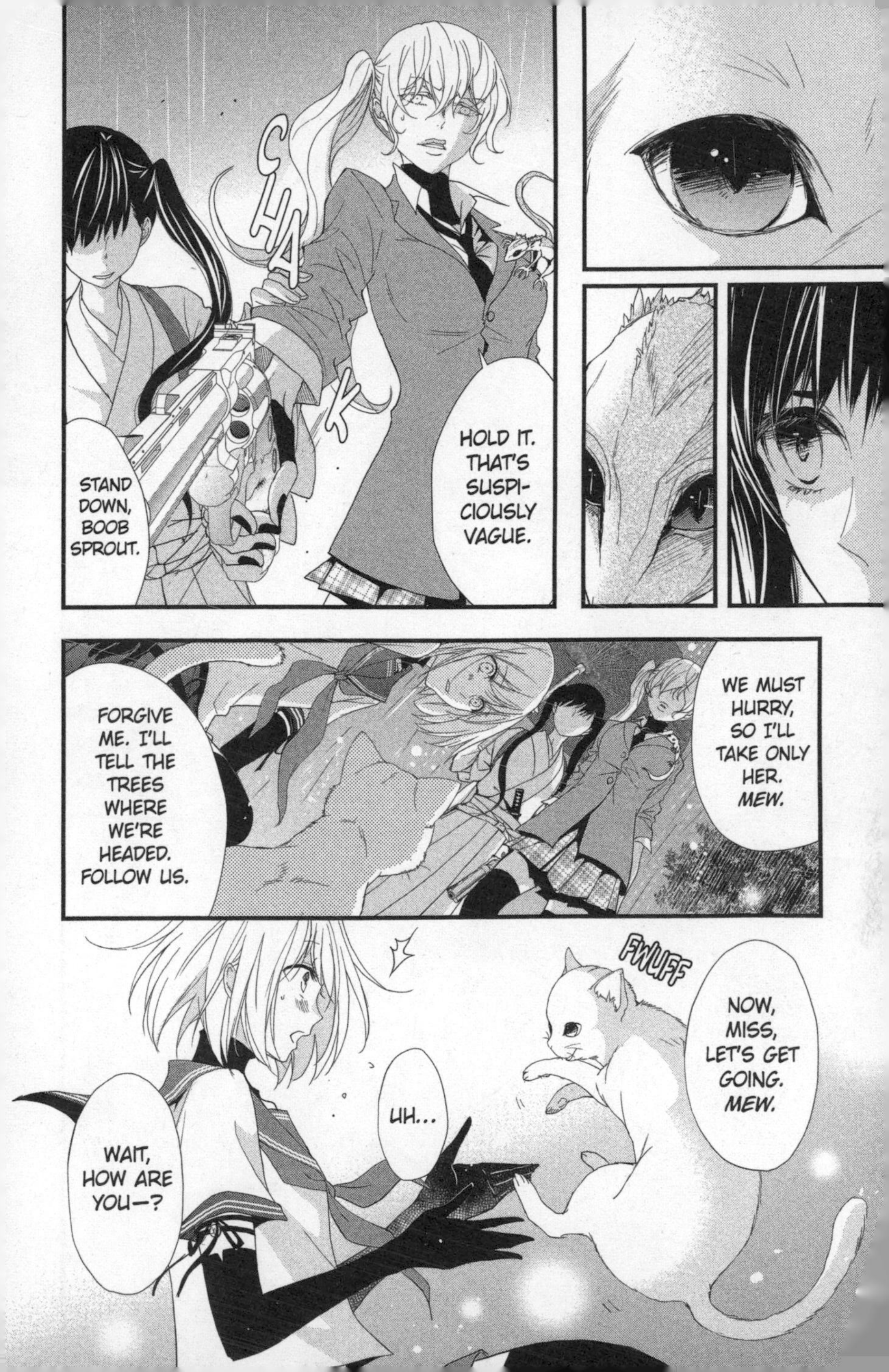
HOLD IT. THAT'S SUSPICIOUSLY VAGUE.
CHAK
STAND DOWN, BOOB SPROUT.
WE MUST HURRY, SO I'LL TAKE ONLY HER. MEW.
FORGIVE ME. I'LL TELL THE TREES WHERE WE'RE HEADED. FOLLOW US.
FWUFF
NOW, MISS, LET'S GET GOING. MEW.
UH...
WAIT, HOW ARE YOU—?

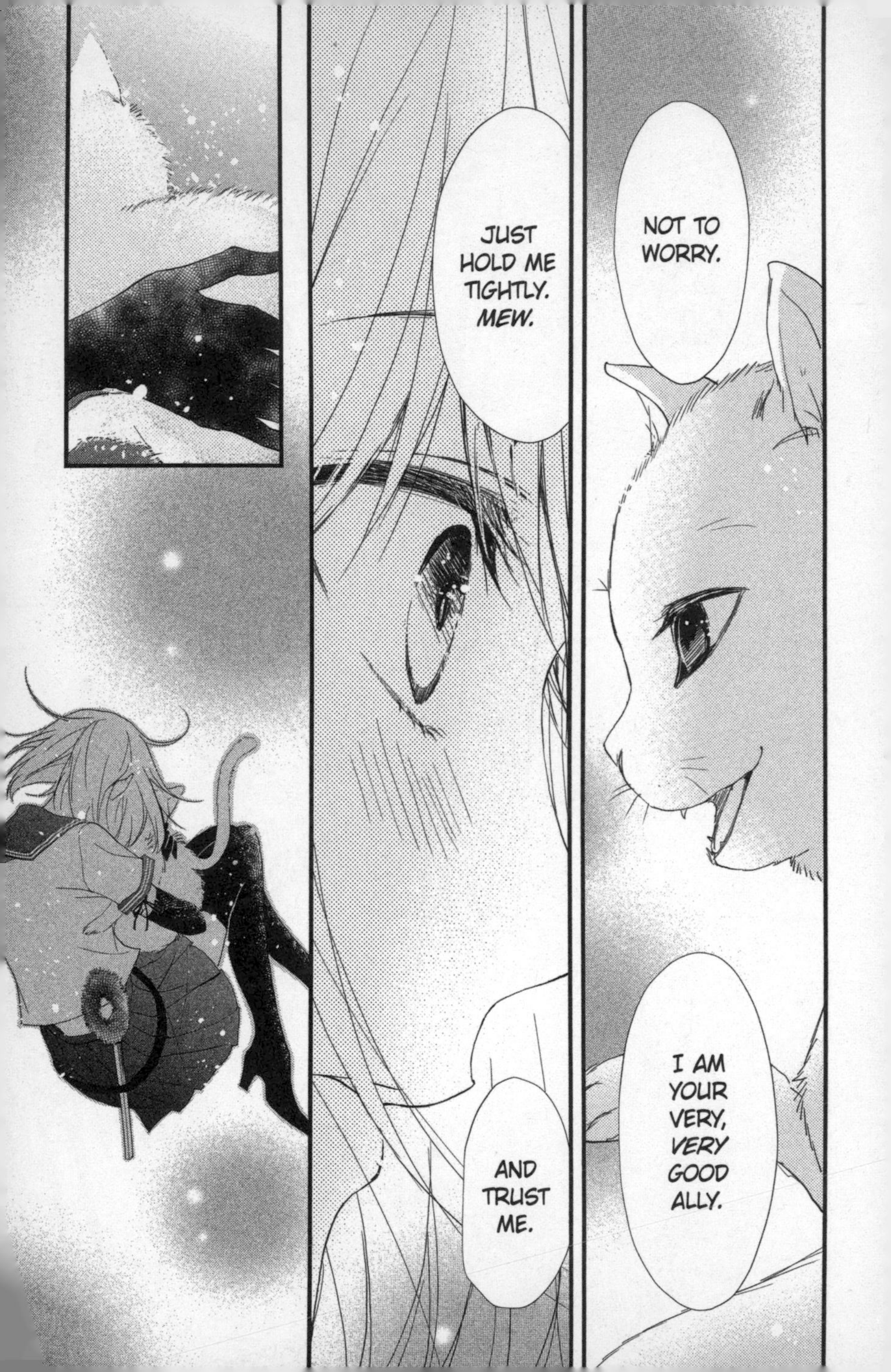
NOT TO WORRY.
I AM YOUR VERY, *VERY* GOOD ALLY.
JUST HOLD ME TIGHTLY. *MEW.*
AND TRUST ME.

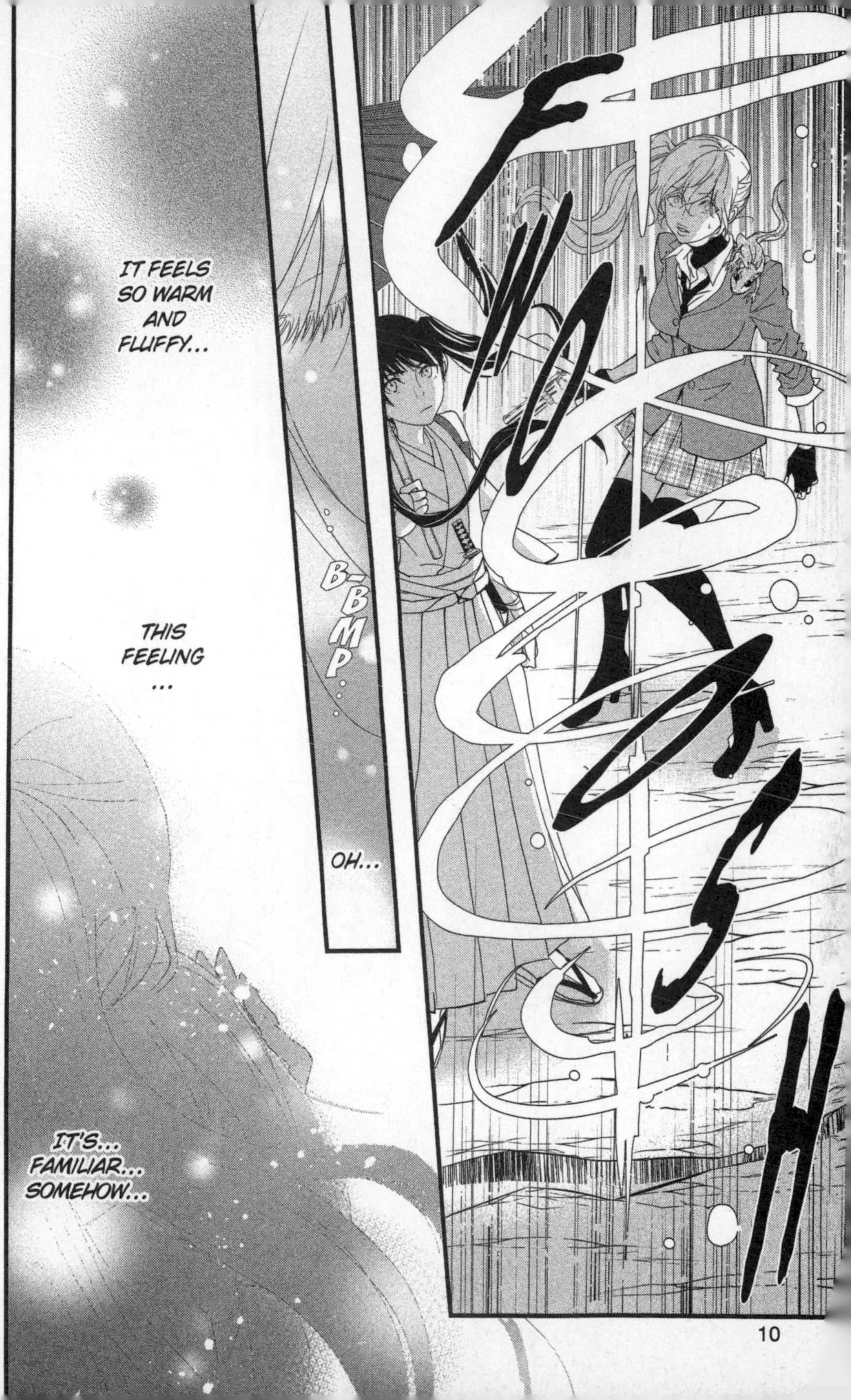
FWOOSH
B-BMP...
OH...
IT FEELS SO WARM AND FLUFFY...
THIS FEELING...
IT'S... FAMILIAR... SOMEHOW...

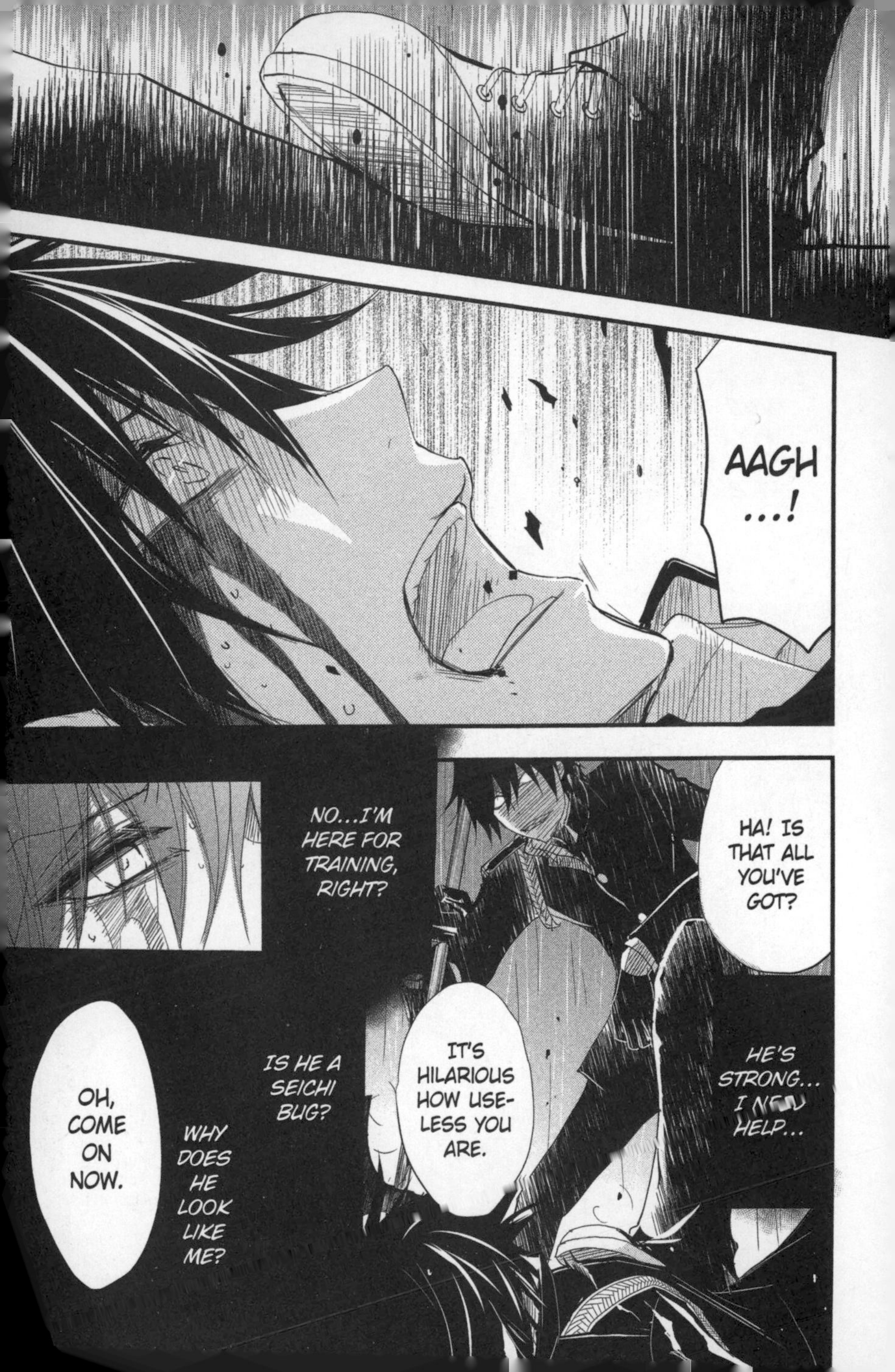

AAGH ...!
HA! IS THAT ALL YOU'VE GOT?
NO...I'M HERE FOR TRAINING, RIGHT?
HE'S STRONG... I NEED HELP...
IT'S HILARIOUS HOW USE-LESS YOU ARE.
IS HE A SEICHI BUG?
WHY DOES HE LOOK LIKE ME?
OH, COME ON NOW.

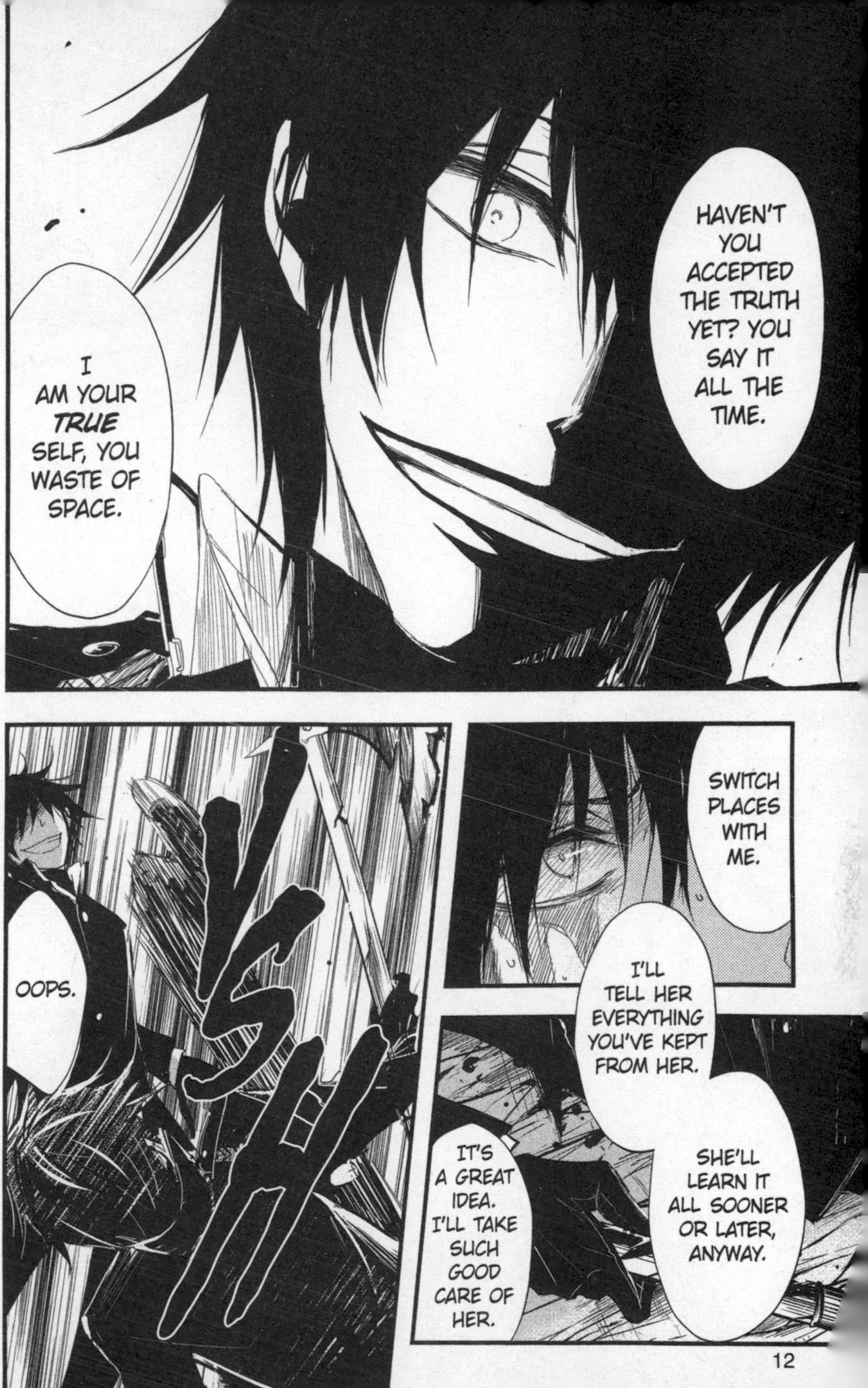
HAVEN'T YOU ACCEPTED THE TRUTH YET? YOU SAY IT ALL THE TIME.
I AM YOUR TRUE SELF, YOU WASTE OF SPACE.
SWITCH PLACES WITH ME.
I'LL TELL HER EVERYTHING YOU'VE KEPT FROM HER.
SHE'LL LEARN IT ALL SOONER OR LATER, ANYWAY.
IT'S A GREAT IDEA. I'LL TAKE SUCH GOOD CARE OF HER.
OOPS.

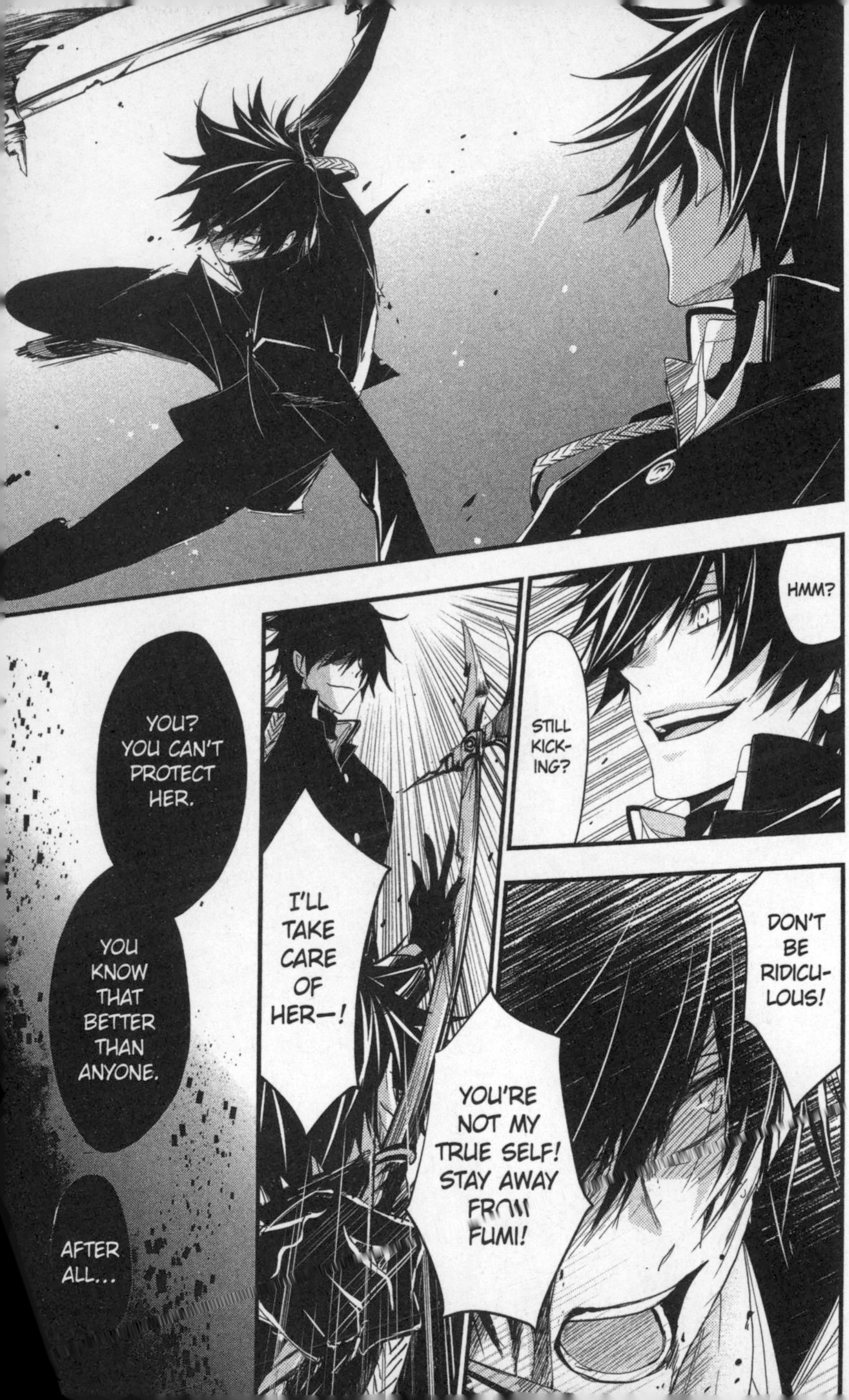
HMM?
STILL KICK-ING?
DON'T BE RIDICU-LOUS!
YOU'RE NOT MY TRUE SELF! STAY AWAY FROM FUMI!
I'LL TAKE CARE OF HER—!
YOU? YOU CAN'T PROTECT HER.
YOU KNOW THAT BETTER THAN ANYONE.
AFTER ALL...

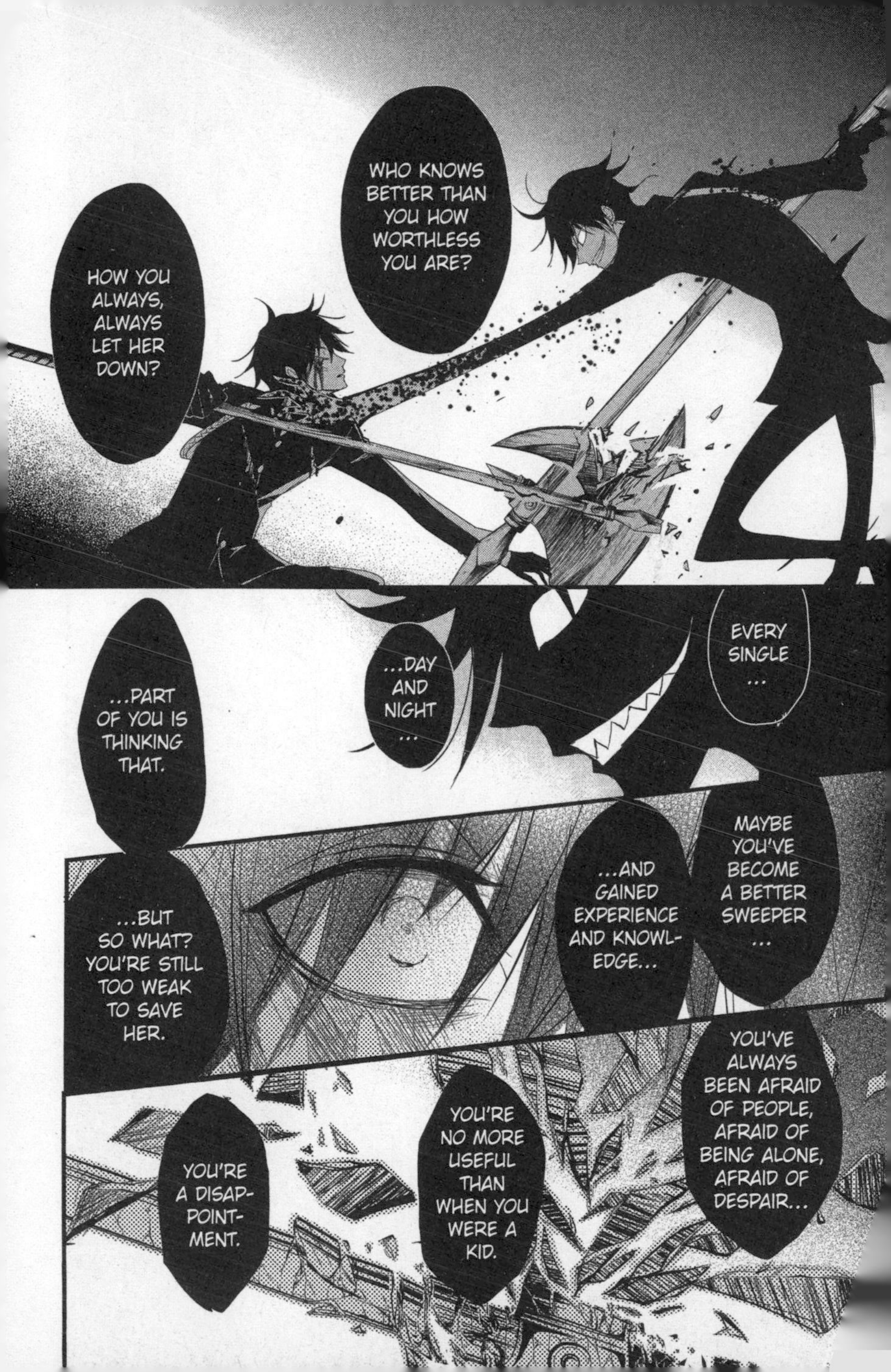
WHO KNOWS BETTER THAN YOU HOW WORTHLESS YOU ARE?
HOW YOU ALWAYS, ALWAYS LET HER DOWN?
EVERY SINGLE...
...DAY AND NIGHT...
...PART OF YOU IS THINKING THAT.
MAYBE YOU'VE BECOME A BETTER SWEEPER...
...AND GAINED EXPERIENCE AND KNOWL-EDGE...
...BUT SO WHAT? YOU'RE STILL TOO WEAK TO SAVE HER.
YOU'VE ALWAYS BEEN AFRAID OF PEOPLE, AFRAID OF BEING ALONE, AFRAID OF DESPAIR...
YOU'RE NO MORE USEFUL THAN WHEN YOU WERE A KID.
YOU'RE A DISAP-POINT-MENT.

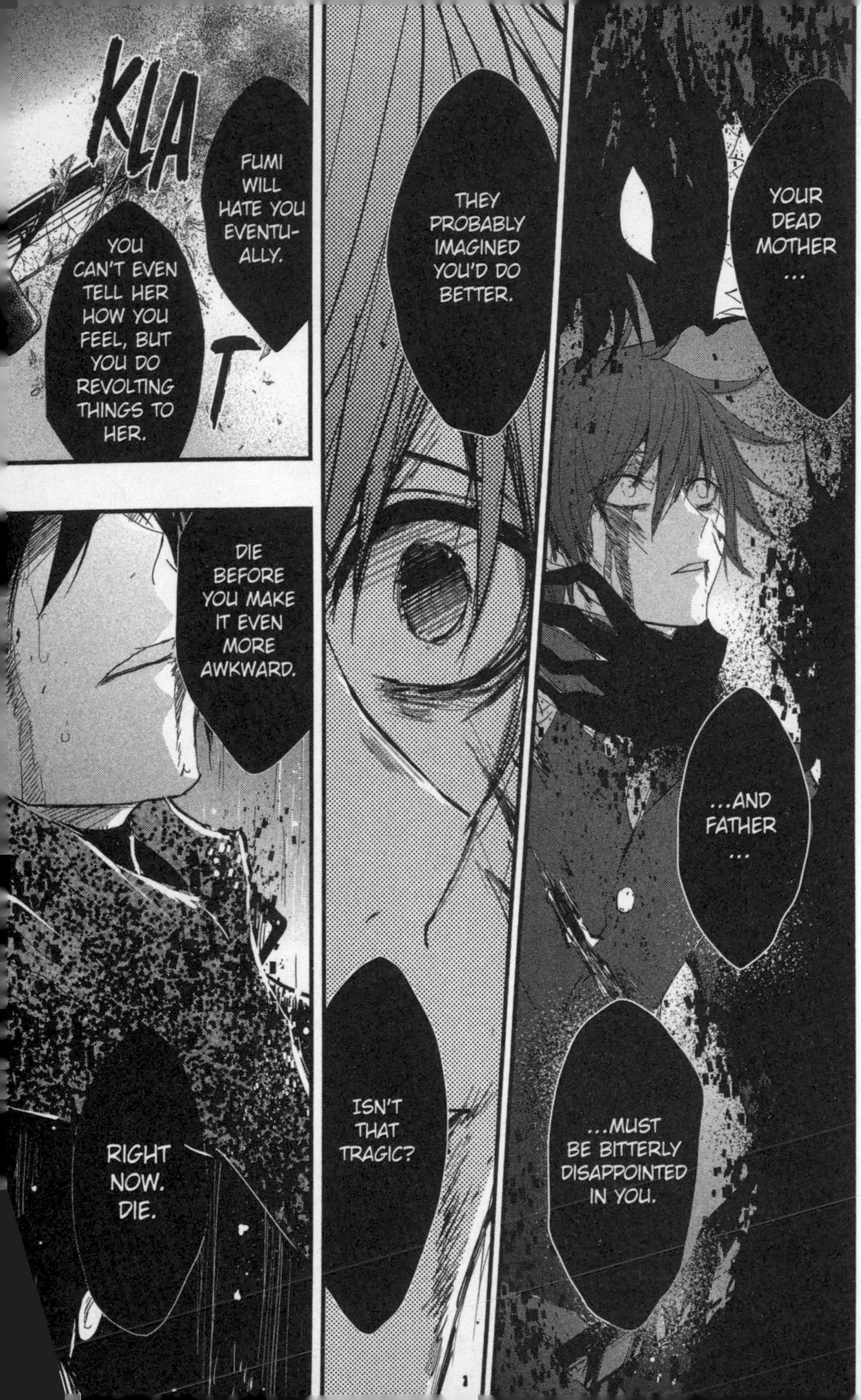
YOUR DEAD MOTHER ...
...AND FATHER ...
...MUST BE BITTERLY DISAPPOINTED IN YOU.
THEY PROBABLY IMAGINED YOU'D DO BETTER.
ISN'T THAT TRAGIC?
KLA
T
FUMI WILL HATE YOU EVENTU-ALLY.
YOU CAN'T EVEN TELL HER HOW YOU FEEL, BUT YOU DO REVOLTING THINGS TO HER.
DIE BEFORE YOU MAKE IT EVEN MORE AWKWARD.
RIGHT NOW. DIE.

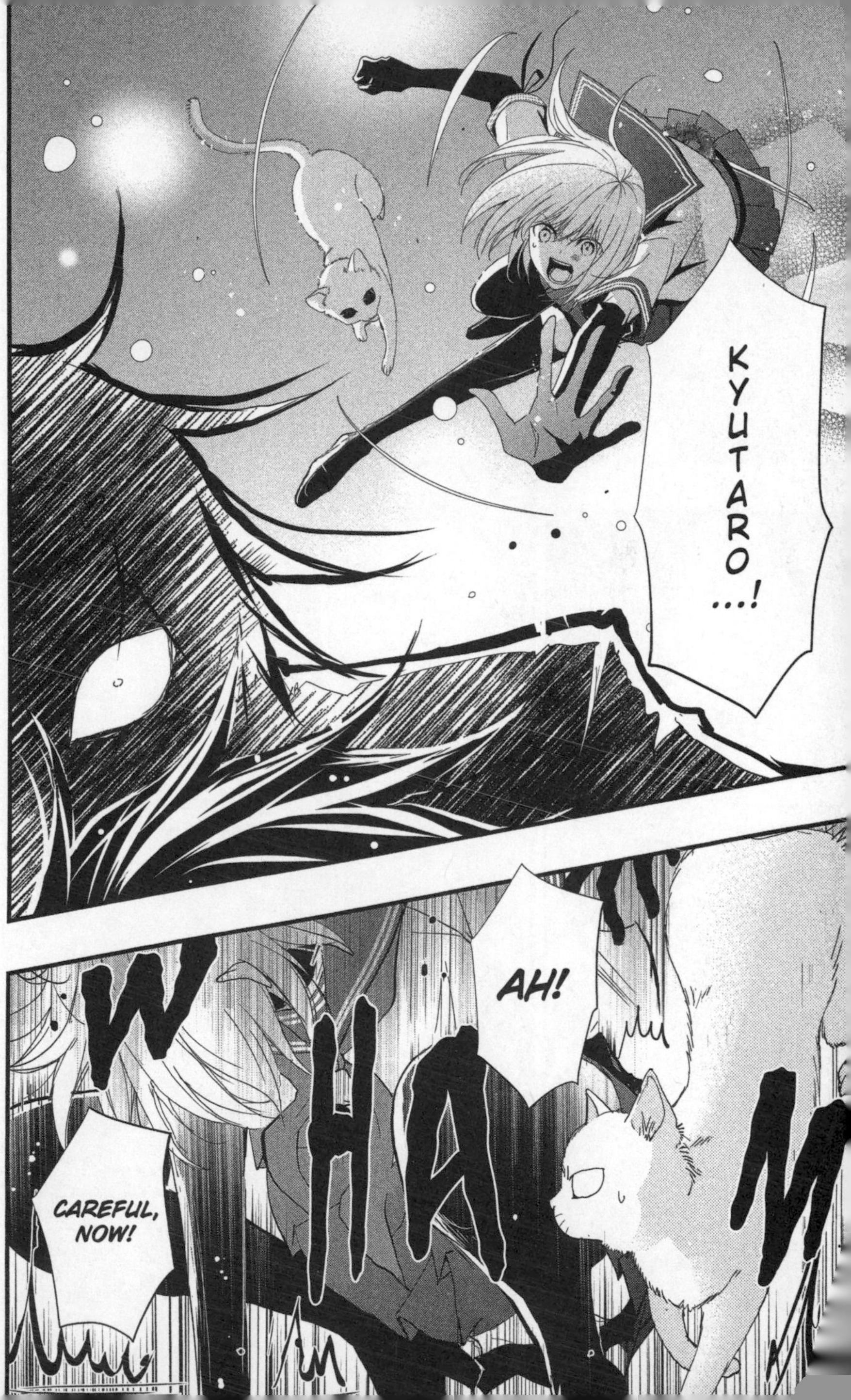
KYUTARO...!
AH!
WHAM
CAREFUL, NOW!

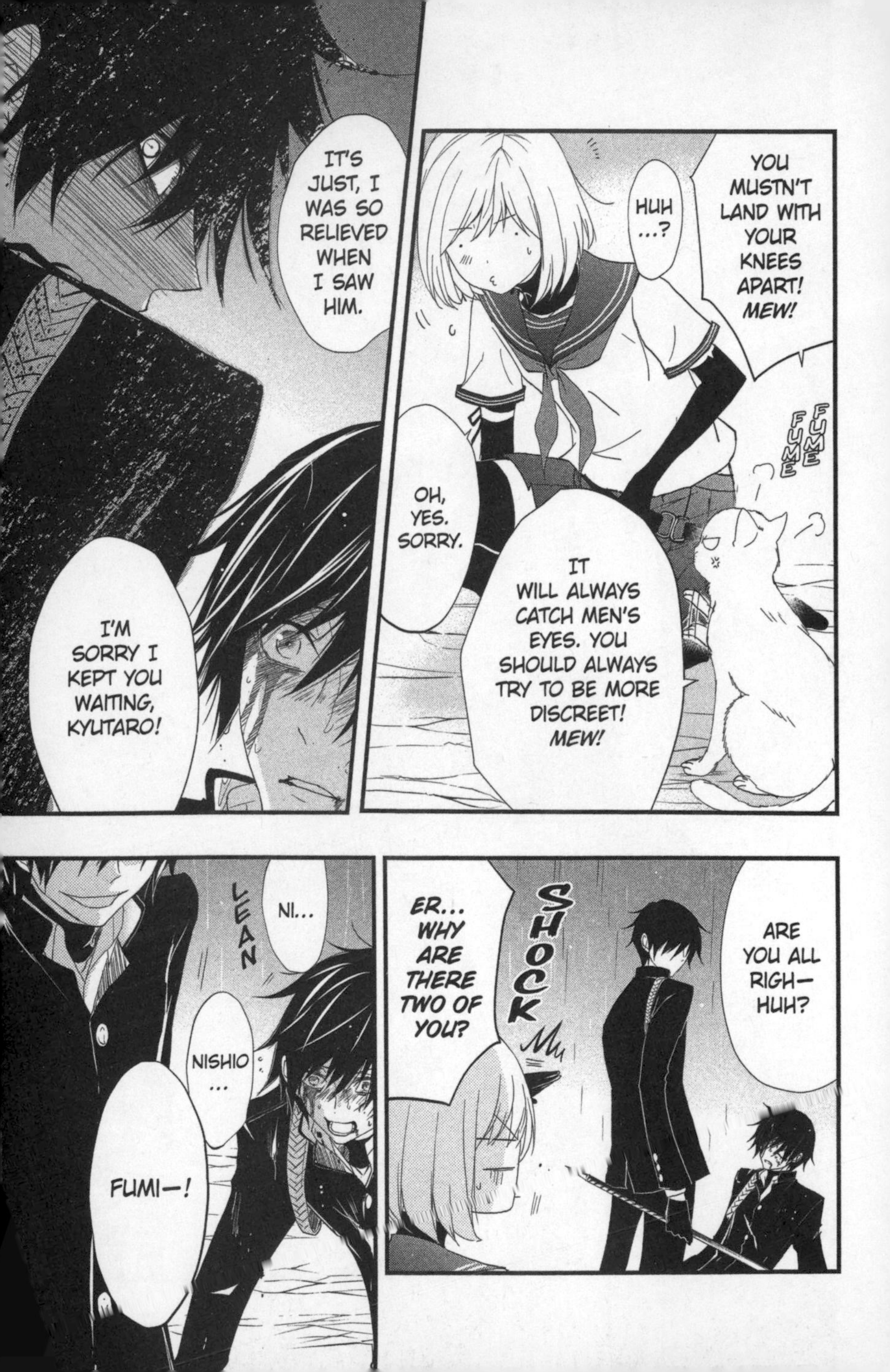

YOU MUSTN'T LAND WITH YOUR KNEES APART! MEW!
HUH ...?
FUME FUME
IT WILL ALWAYS CATCH MEN'S EYES. YOU SHOULD ALWAYS TRY TO BE MORE DISCREET! MEW!
OH, YES. SORRY.
IT'S JUST, I WAS SO RELIEVED WHEN I SAW HIM.
I'M SORRY I KEPT YOU WAITING, KYUTARO!
ARE YOU ALL RIGH— HUH?
SHOCK
ER... WHY ARE THERE TWO OF YOU?
NI...
LEAN
NISHIO ...
FUMI—!

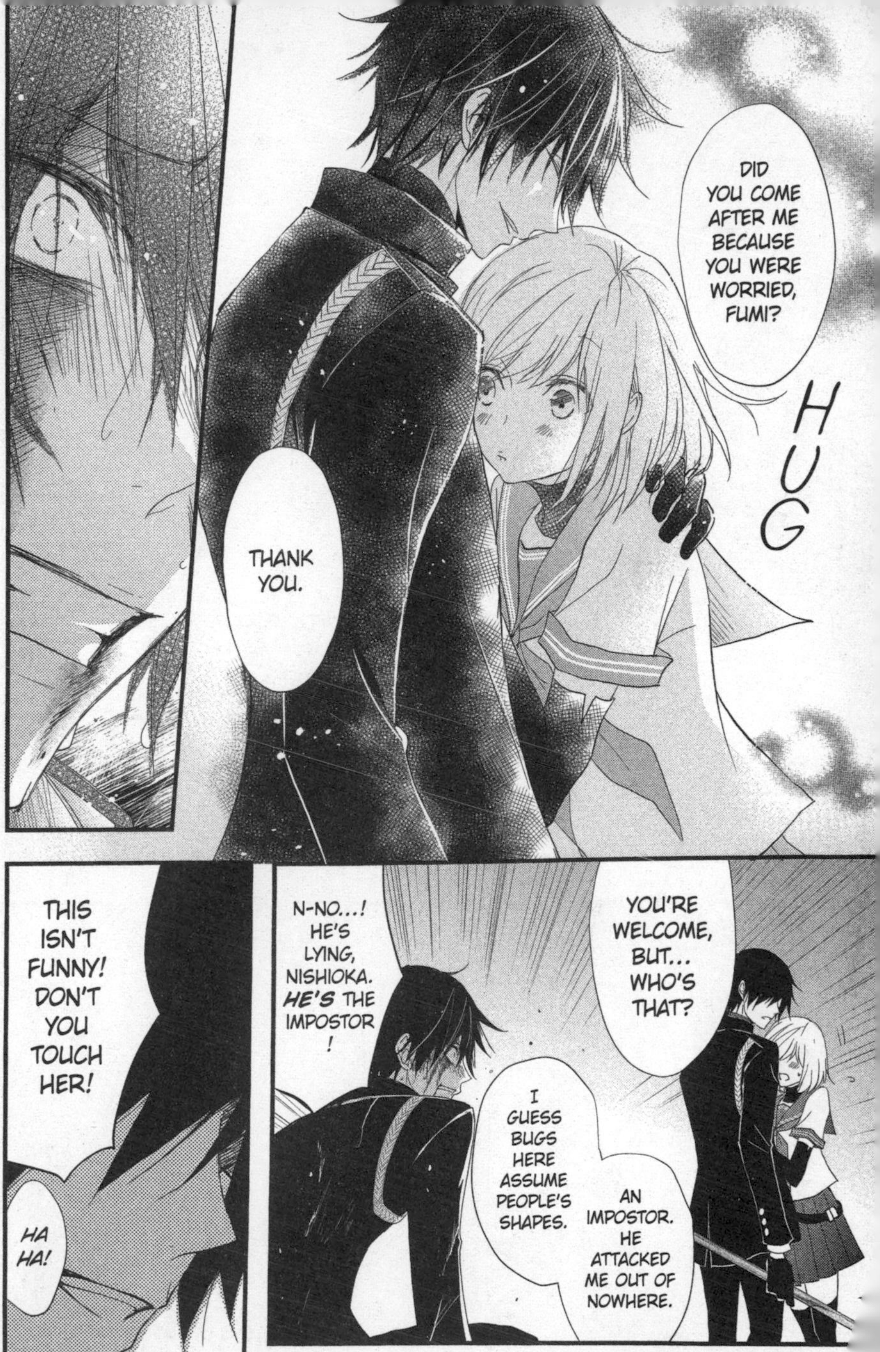
DID YOU COME AFTER ME BECAUSE YOU WERE WORRIED, FUMI?
HUG
THANK YOU.
YOU'RE WELCOME, BUT... WHO'S THAT?
AN IMPOSTOR. HE ATTACKED ME OUT OF NOWHERE.
I GUESS BUGS HERE ASSUME PEOPLE'S SHAPES.
N-NO...! HE'S LYING, NISHIOKA. HE'S THE IMPOSTOR!
THIS ISN'T FUNNY! DON'T YOU TOUCH HER!
HA HA!

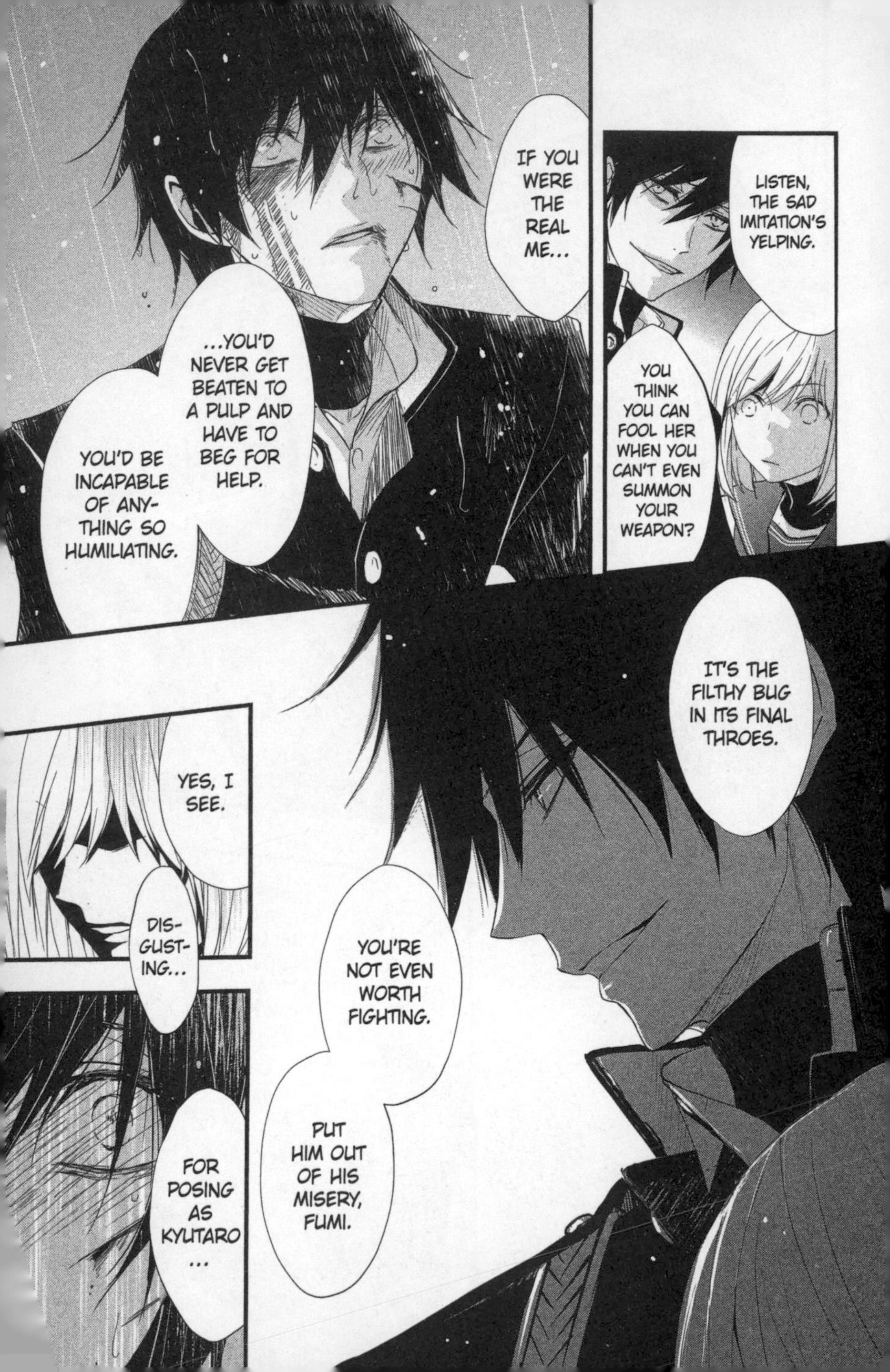
LISTEN, THE SAD IMITATION'S YELPING.
YOU THINK YOU CAN FOOL HER WHEN YOU CAN'T EVEN SUMMON YOUR WEAPON?
IF YOU WERE THE REAL ME...
...YOU'D NEVER GET BEATEN TO A PULP AND HAVE TO BEG FOR HELP.
YOU'D BE INCAPABLE OF ANY-THING SO HUMILIATING.
IT'S THE FILTHY BUG IN ITS FINAL THROES.
YOU'RE NOT EVEN WORTH FIGHTING.
PUT HIM OUT OF HIS MISERY, FUMI.
YES, I SEE.
DIS-GUST-ING...
FOR POSING AS KYUTARO...

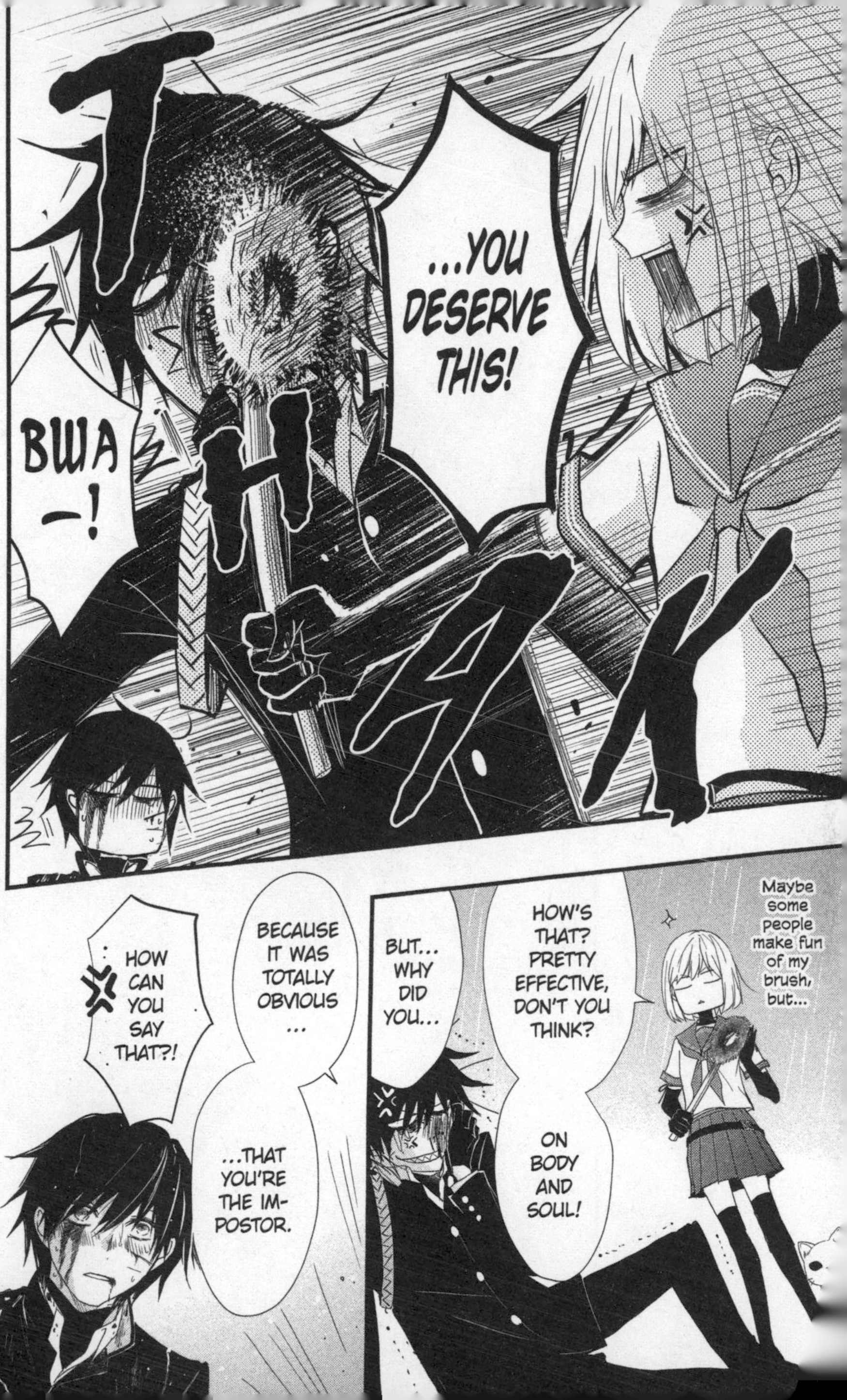
...YOU DESERVE THIS!
BWA—!
Maybe some people make fun of my brush, but...
HOW'S THAT? PRETTY EFFECTIVE, DON'T YOU THINK?
ON BODY AND SOUL!
BUT... WHY DID YOU...
BECAUSE IT WAS TOTALLY OBVIOUS...
...THAT YOU'RE THE IM-POSTOR.
HOW CAN YOU SAY THAT?!

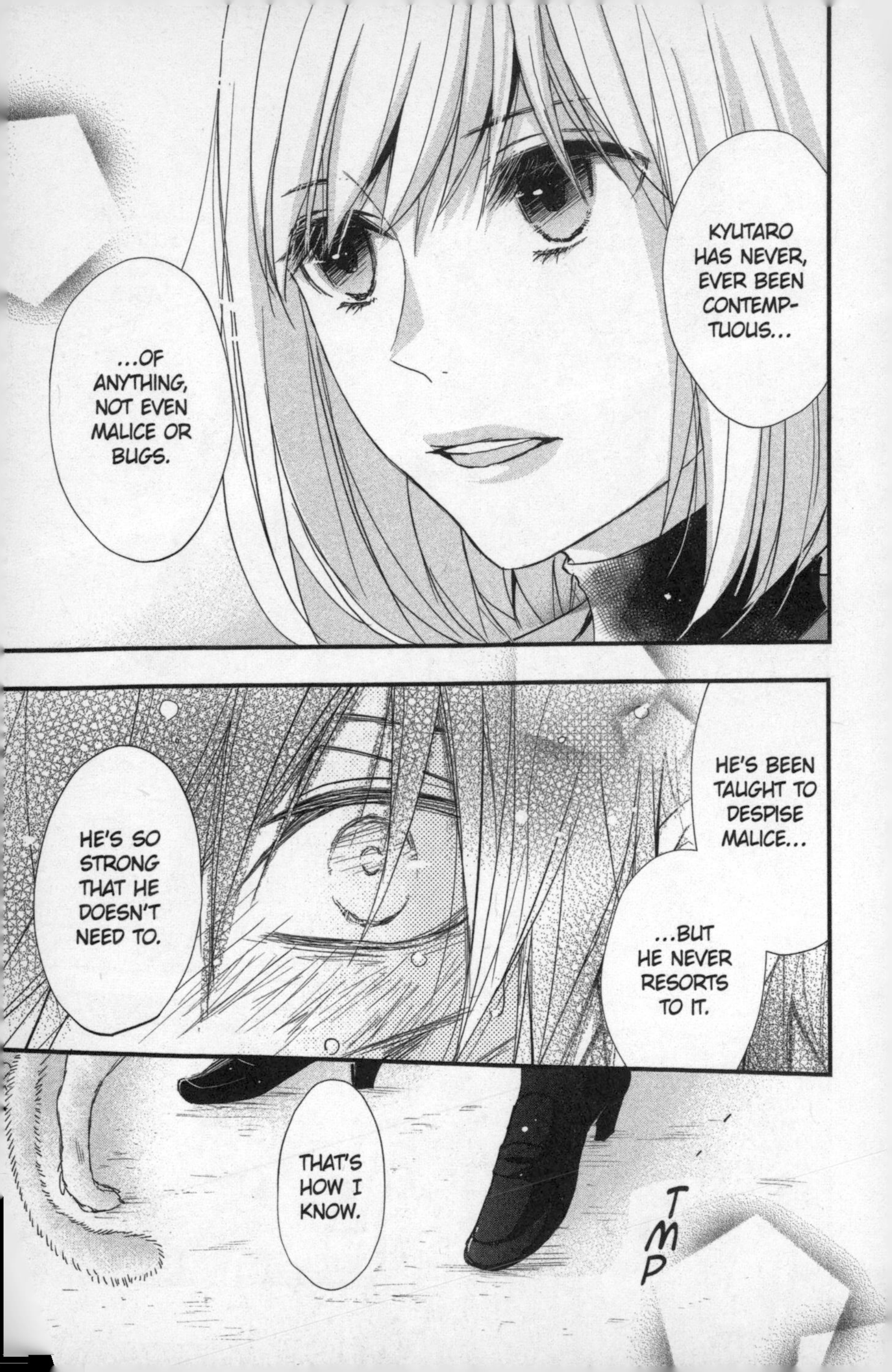
KYUTARO HAS NEVER, EVER BEEN CONTEMPTUOUS...
...OF ANYTHING, NOT EVEN MALICE OR BUGS.
HE'S BEEN TAUGHT TO DESPISE MALICE...
...BUT HE NEVER RESORTS TO IT.
HE'S SO STRONG THAT HE DOESN'T NEED TO.
THAT'S HOW I KNOW.
TMP

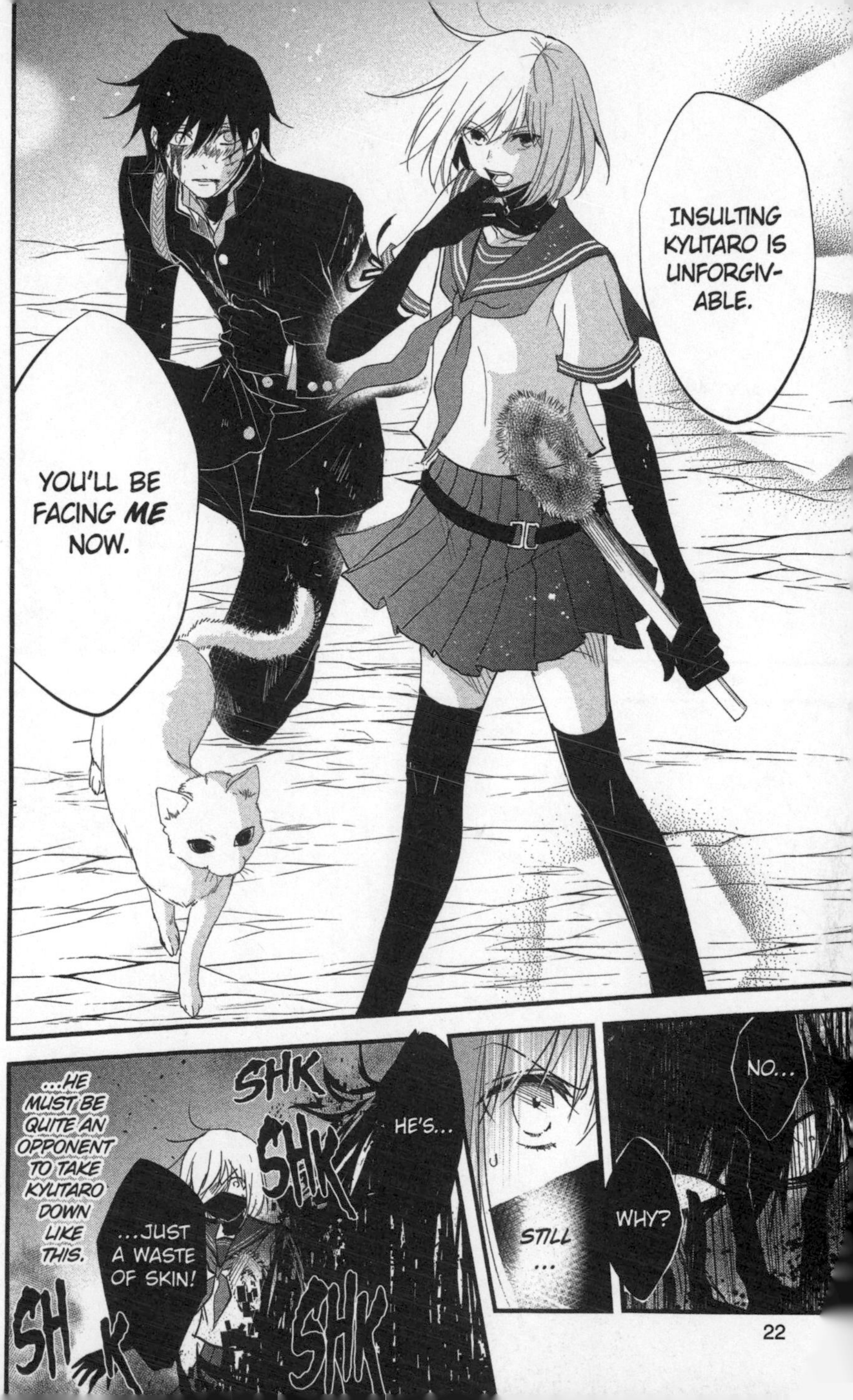
INSULTING KYUTARO IS UNFORGIV-ABLE.
YOU'LL BE FACING *ME* NOW.
NO...
WHY?
STILL ...
HE'S...
SHK
SHK
...HE MUST BE QUITE AN OPPONENT TO TAKE KYUTARO DOWN LIKE THIS.
...JUST A WASTE OF SKIN!
SHK
SH K

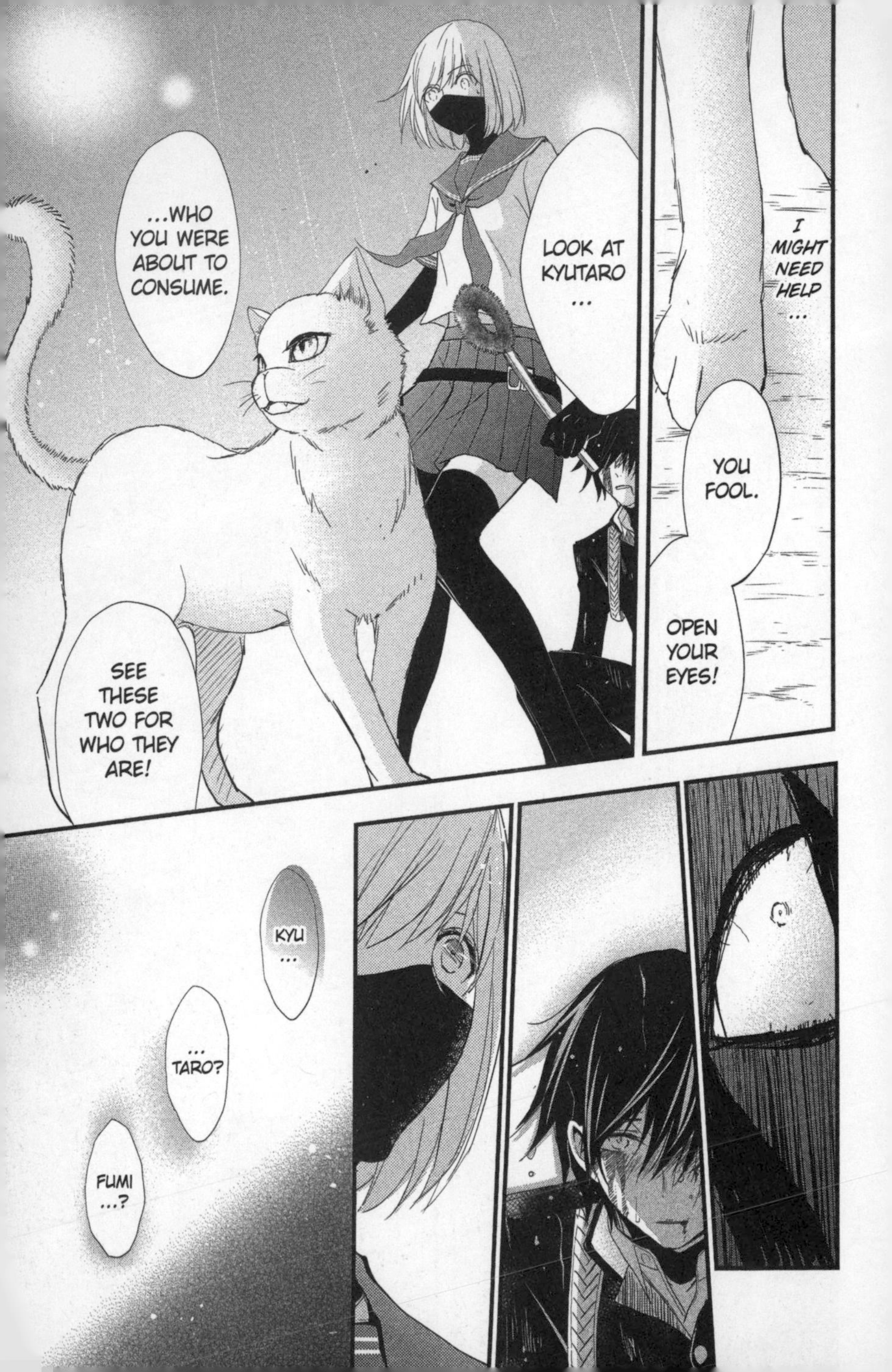

I MIGHT NEED HELP ...
YOU FOOL.
OPEN YOUR EYES!
LOOK AT KYUTARO ...
...WHO YOU WERE ABOUT TO CONSUME.
SEE THESE TWO FOR WHO THEY ARE!
KYU ...
... TARO?
FUMI ...?

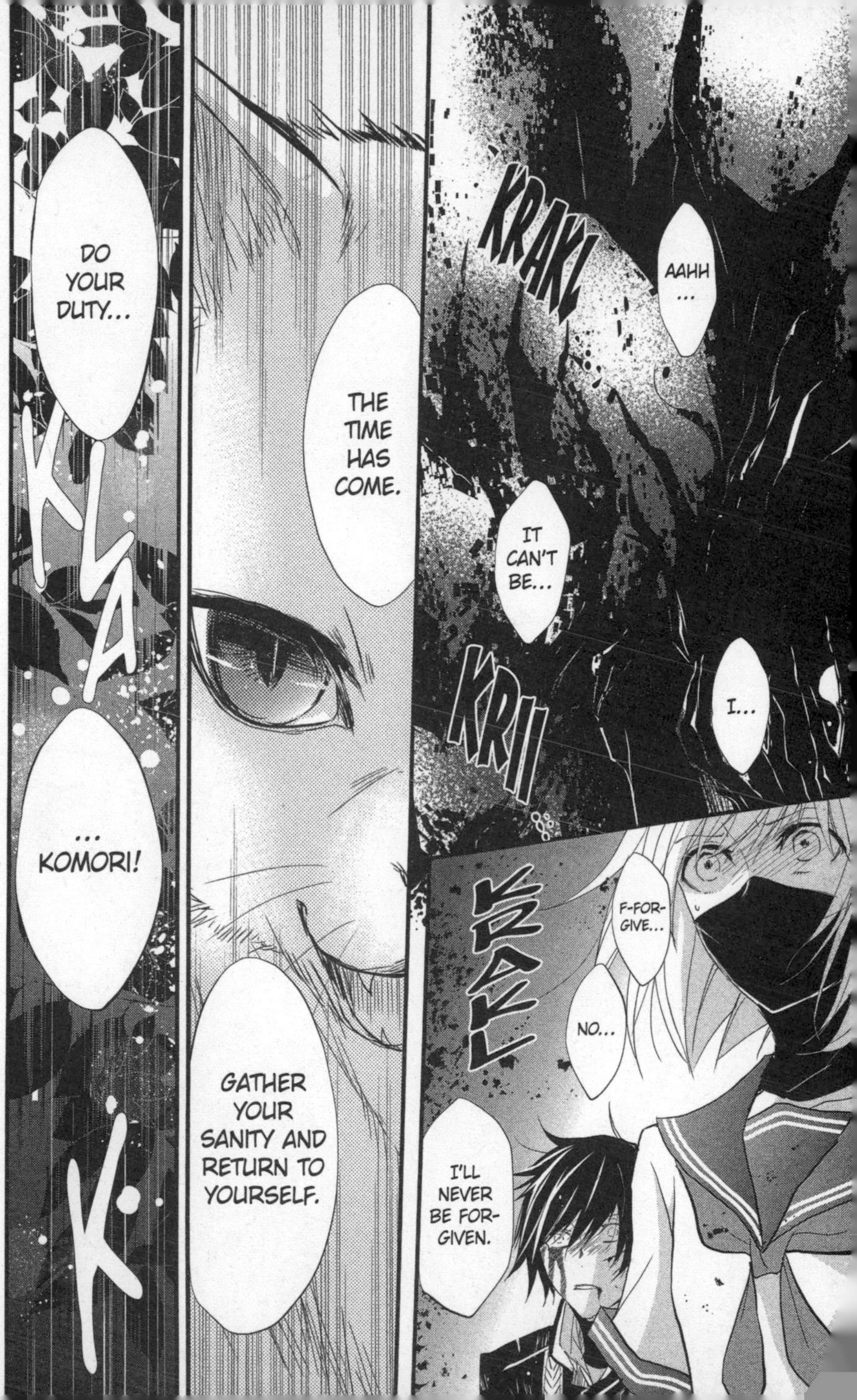
KRAK!
AAHH...
IT CAN'T BE...
KRII
I...
KRAK
F-FOR-GIVE...
NO...
I'LL NEVER BE FOR-GIVEN.
THE TIME HAS COME.
GATHER YOUR SANITY AND RETURN TO YOURSELF.
DO YOUR DUTY...
KLA
...KOMORI!
K

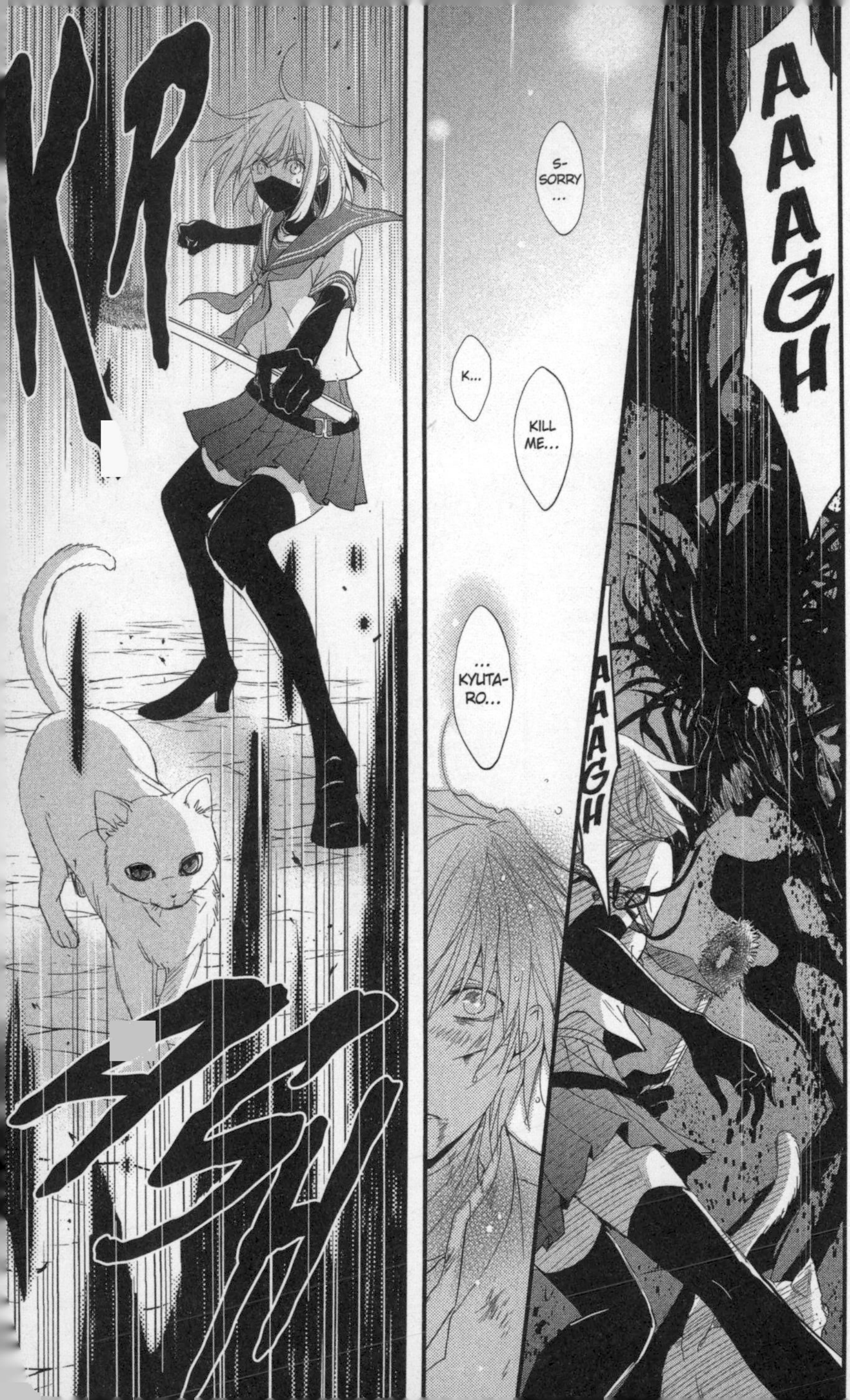
AAAAGH
S-SORRY...
K...
KILL ME...
AAAAGH
... KYUTA-RO...

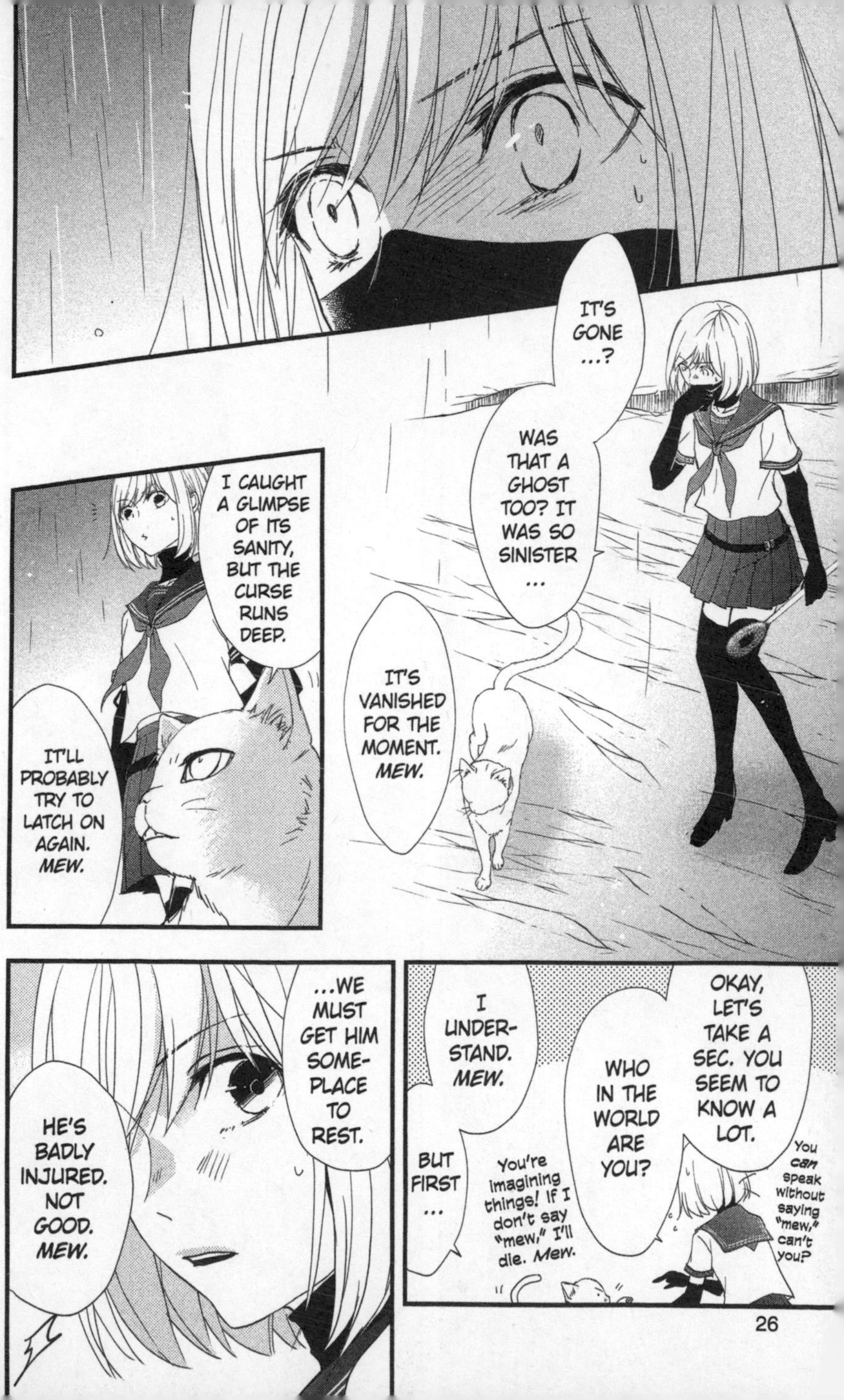
IT'S GONE ...?
WAS THAT A GHOST TOO? IT WAS SO SINISTER ...
IT'S VANISHED FOR THE MOMENT. *MEW.*
I CAUGHT A GLIMPSE OF ITS SANITY, BUT THE CURSE RUNS DEEP.
IT'LL PROBABLY TRY TO LATCH ON AGAIN. *MEW.*
OKAY, LET'S TAKE A SEC. YOU SEEM TO KNOW A LOT.
You *can* speak without saying "mew," can't you?
WHO IN THE WORLD ARE YOU?
You're imagining things! If I don't say "mew," I'll die. *Mew.*
I UNDER-STAND. *MEW.*
BUT FIRST ...
...WE MUST GET HIM SOME-PLACE TO REST.
HE'S BADLY INJURED. NOT GOOD. *MEW.*

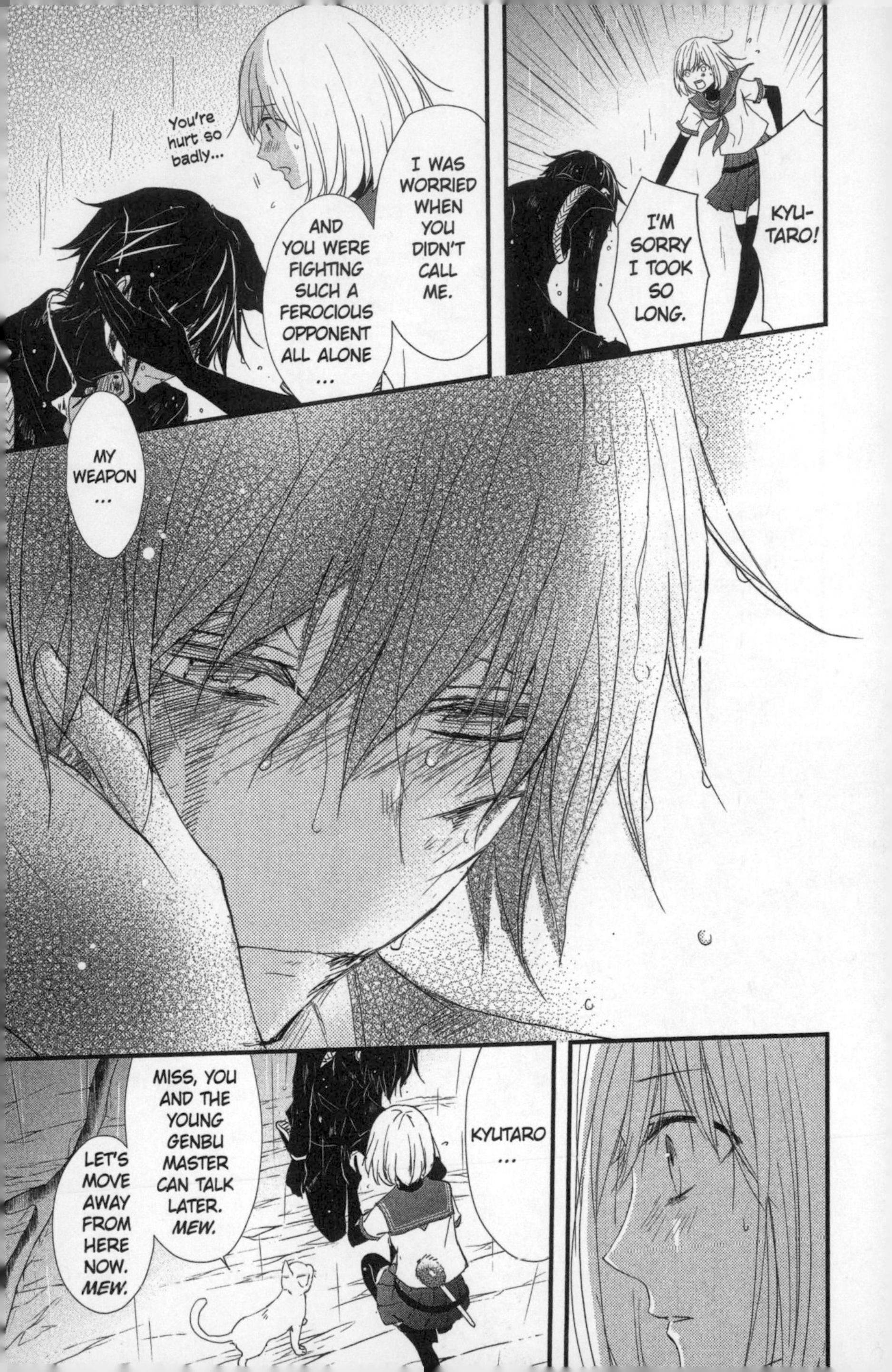
KYU-TARO!
I'M SORRY I TOOK SO LONG.
I WAS WORRIED WHEN YOU DIDN'T CALL ME.
AND YOU WERE FIGHTING SUCH A FEROCIOUS OPPONENT ALL ALONE...
You're hurt so badly...
MY WEAPON...
KYUTARO...
MISS, YOU AND THE YOUNG GENBU MASTER CAN TALK LATER. *MEW.*
LET'S MOVE AWAY FROM HERE NOW. *MEW.*

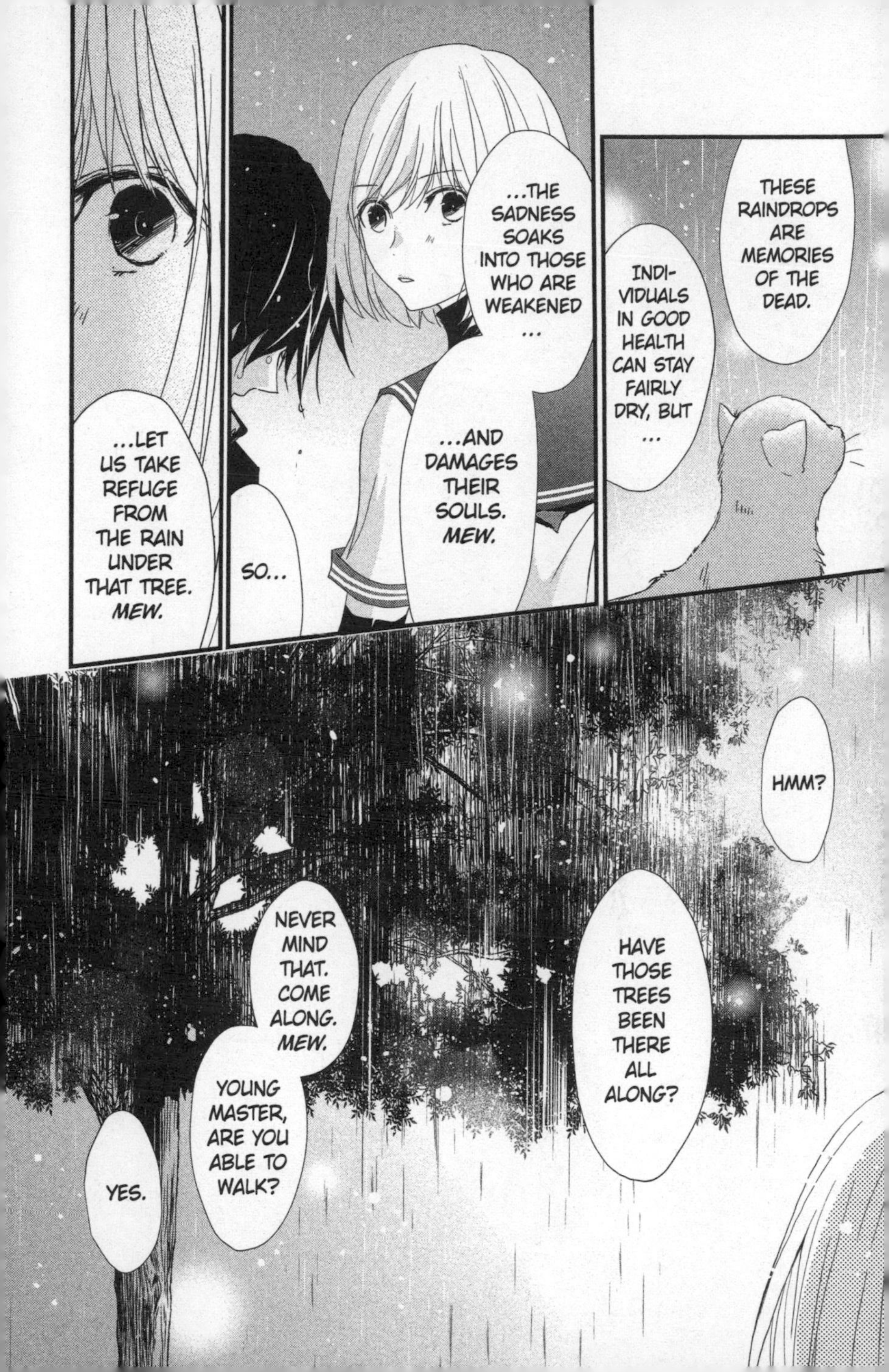
THESE RAINDROPS ARE MEMORIES OF THE DEAD.
INDI-VIDUALS IN GOOD HEALTH CAN STAY FAIRLY DRY, BUT ...
...THE SADNESS SOAKS INTO THOSE WHO ARE WEAKENED ...
...AND DAMAGES THEIR SOULS. *MEW.*
SO...
...LET US TAKE REFUGE FROM THE RAIN UNDER THAT TREE. *MEW.*
HMM?
HAVE THOSE TREES BEEN THERE ALL ALONG?
NEVER MIND THAT. COME ALONG. *MEW.*
YOUNG MASTER, ARE YOU ABLE TO WALK?
YES.

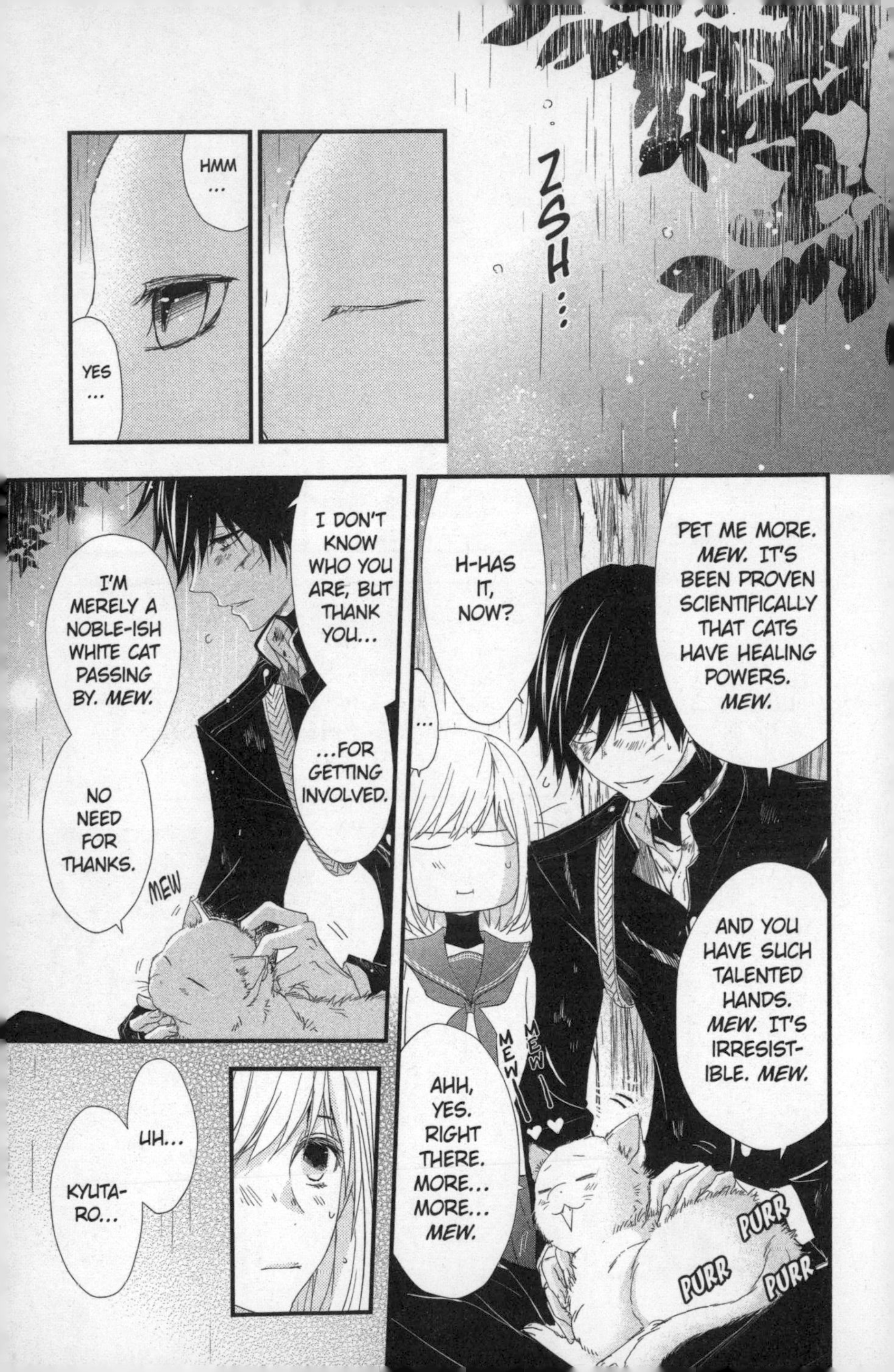
ZSH...
HMM...
YES...
H-HAS IT, NOW?
PET ME MORE. MEW. IT'S BEEN PROVEN SCIENTIFICALLY THAT CATS HAVE HEALING POWERS. MEW.
...
AND YOU HAVE SUCH TALENTED HANDS. MEW. IT'S IRRESIST-IBLE. MEW.
MEW MEW
AHH, YES. RIGHT THERE. MORE... MORE... MEW.
PURR PURR
PURR PURR
I DON'T KNOW WHO YOU ARE, BUT THANK YOU...
I'M MERELY A NOBLE-ISH WHITE CAT PASSING BY. MEW.
...FOR GETTING INVOLVED.
NO NEED FOR THANKS.
MEW
UH...
KYUTA-RO...

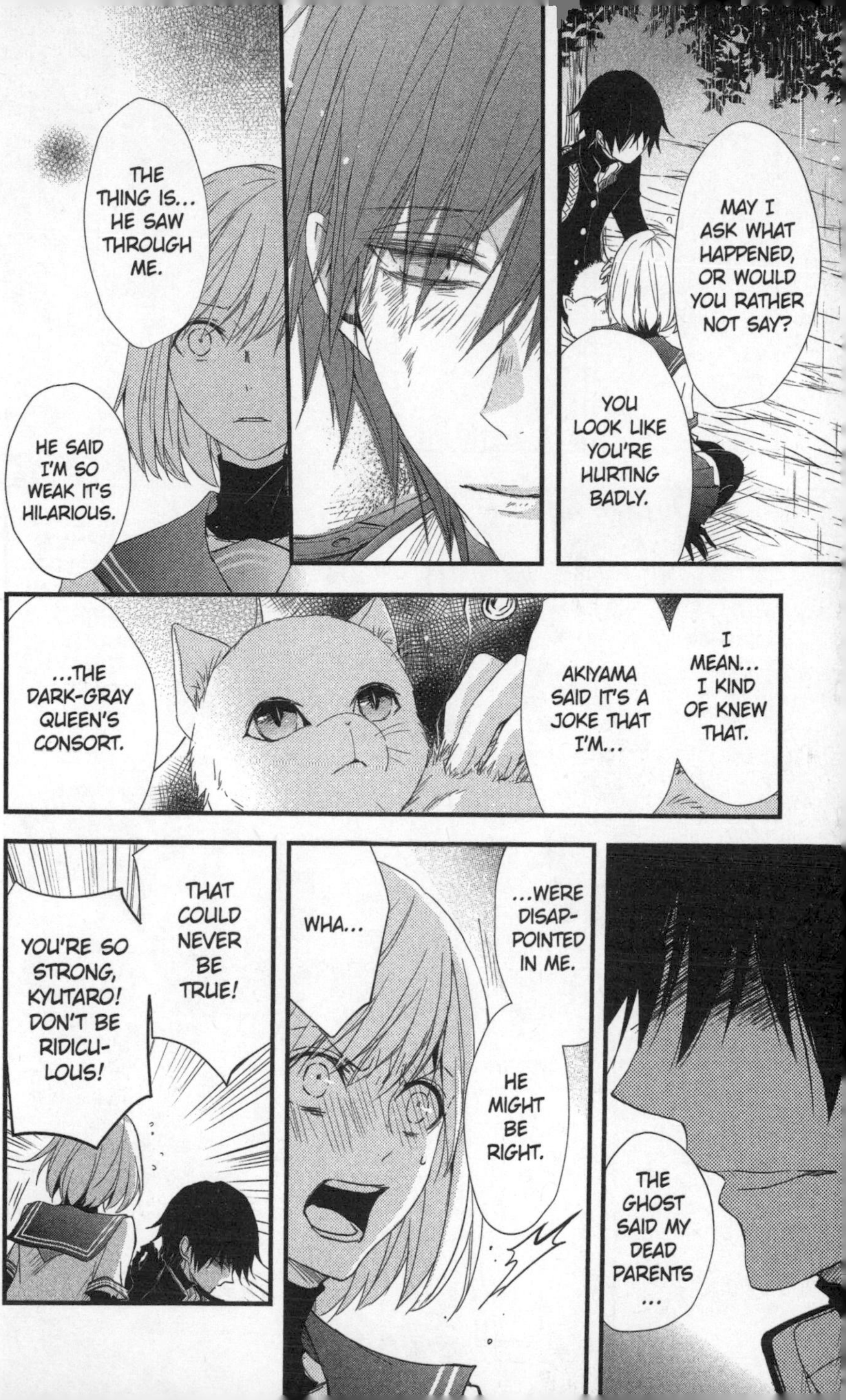
MAY I ASK WHAT HAPPENED, OR WOULD YOU RATHER NOT SAY?
YOU LOOK LIKE YOU'RE HURTING BADLY.
THE THING IS... HE SAW THROUGH ME.
HE SAID I'M SO WEAK IT'S HILARIOUS.
I MEAN... I KIND OF KNEW THAT.
AKIYAMA SAID IT'S A JOKE THAT I'M...
...THE DARK-GRAY QUEEN'S CONSORT.
THE GHOST SAID MY DEAD PARENTS ...
...WERE DISAPPOINTED IN ME.
HE MIGHT BE RIGHT.
WHA...
THAT COULD NEVER BE TRUE!
YOU'RE SO STRONG, KYUTARO! DON'T BE RIDICULOUS!

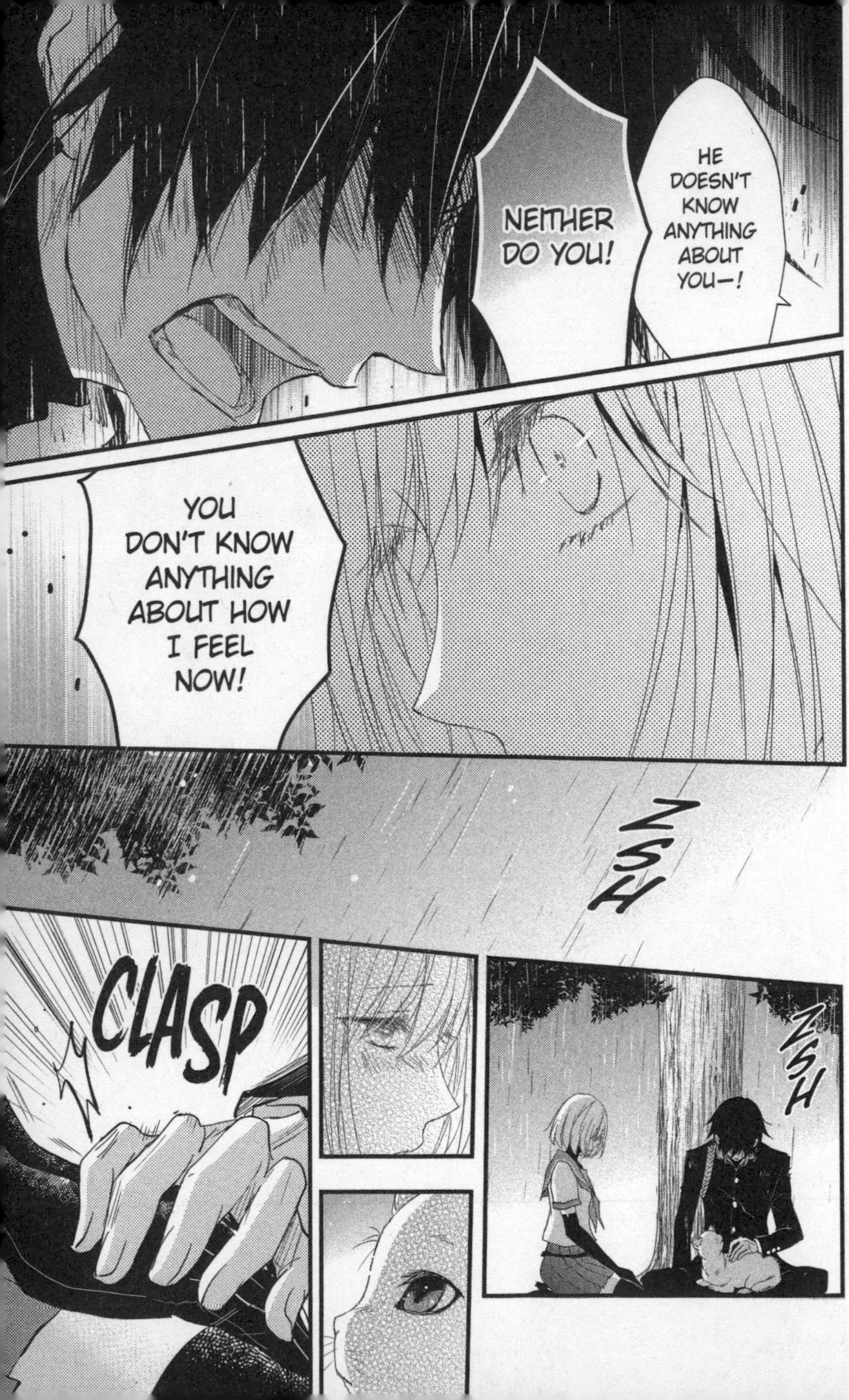
HE DOESN'T KNOW ANYTHING ABOUT YOU—!
NEITHER DO YOU!
YOU DON'T KNOW ANYTHING ABOUT HOW I FEEL NOW!
ZSH
ZSH
CLASP

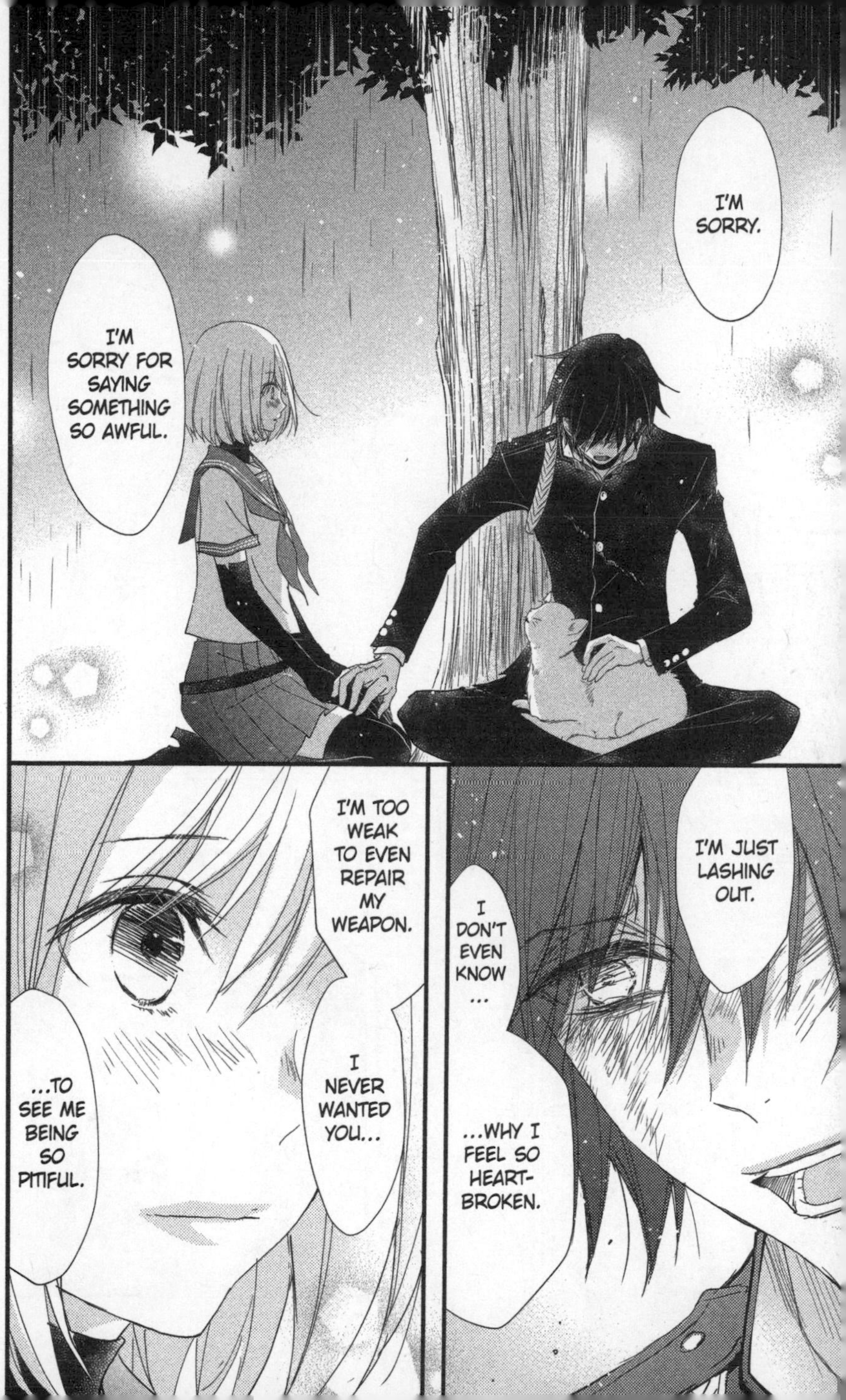
I'M SORRY.
I'M SORRY FOR SAYING SOMETHING SO AWFUL.
I'M JUST LASHING OUT.
I DON'T EVEN KNOW...
...WHY I FEEL SO HEART-BROKEN.
I'M TOO WEAK TO EVEN REPAIR MY WEAPON.
I NEVER WANTED YOU...
...TO SEE ME BEING SO PITIFUL.

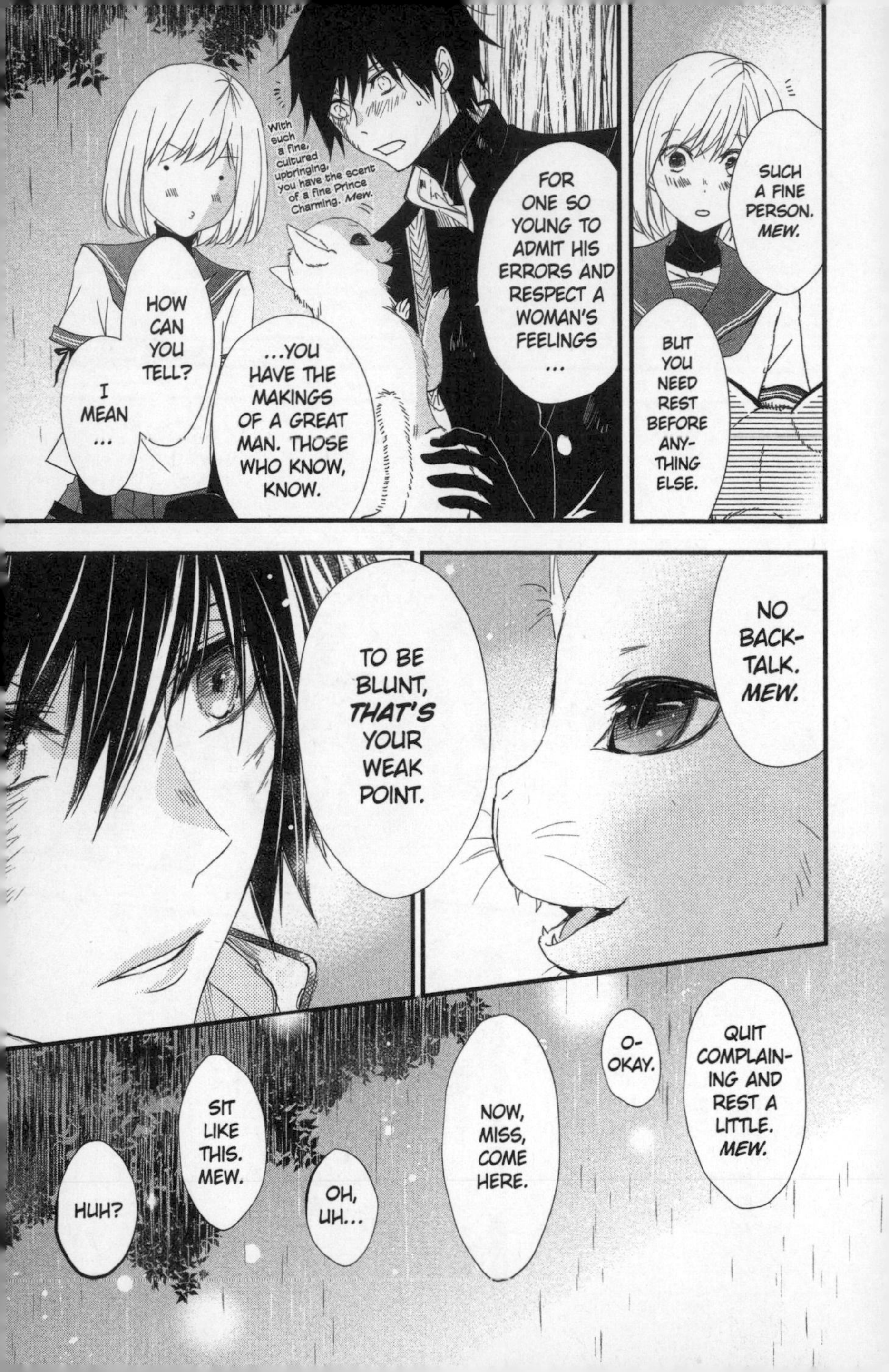
SUCH A FINE PERSON. *MEW.*
BUT YOU NEED REST BEFORE ANYTHING ELSE.
FOR ONE SO YOUNG TO ADMIT HIS ERRORS AND RESPECT A WOMAN'S FEELINGS...
...YOU HAVE THE MAKINGS OF A GREAT MAN. THOSE WHO KNOW, KNOW.
With such a fine, cultured upbringing, you have the scent of a fine Prince Charming. *Mew.*
HOW CAN YOU TELL?
I MEAN...
NO BACK-TALK. *MEW.*
TO BE BLUNT, *THAT'S* YOUR WEAK POINT.
QUIT COMPLAINING AND REST A LITTLE. *MEW.*
O-OKAY.
NOW, MISS, COME HERE.
OH, UH...
SIT LIKE THIS. MEW.
HUH?

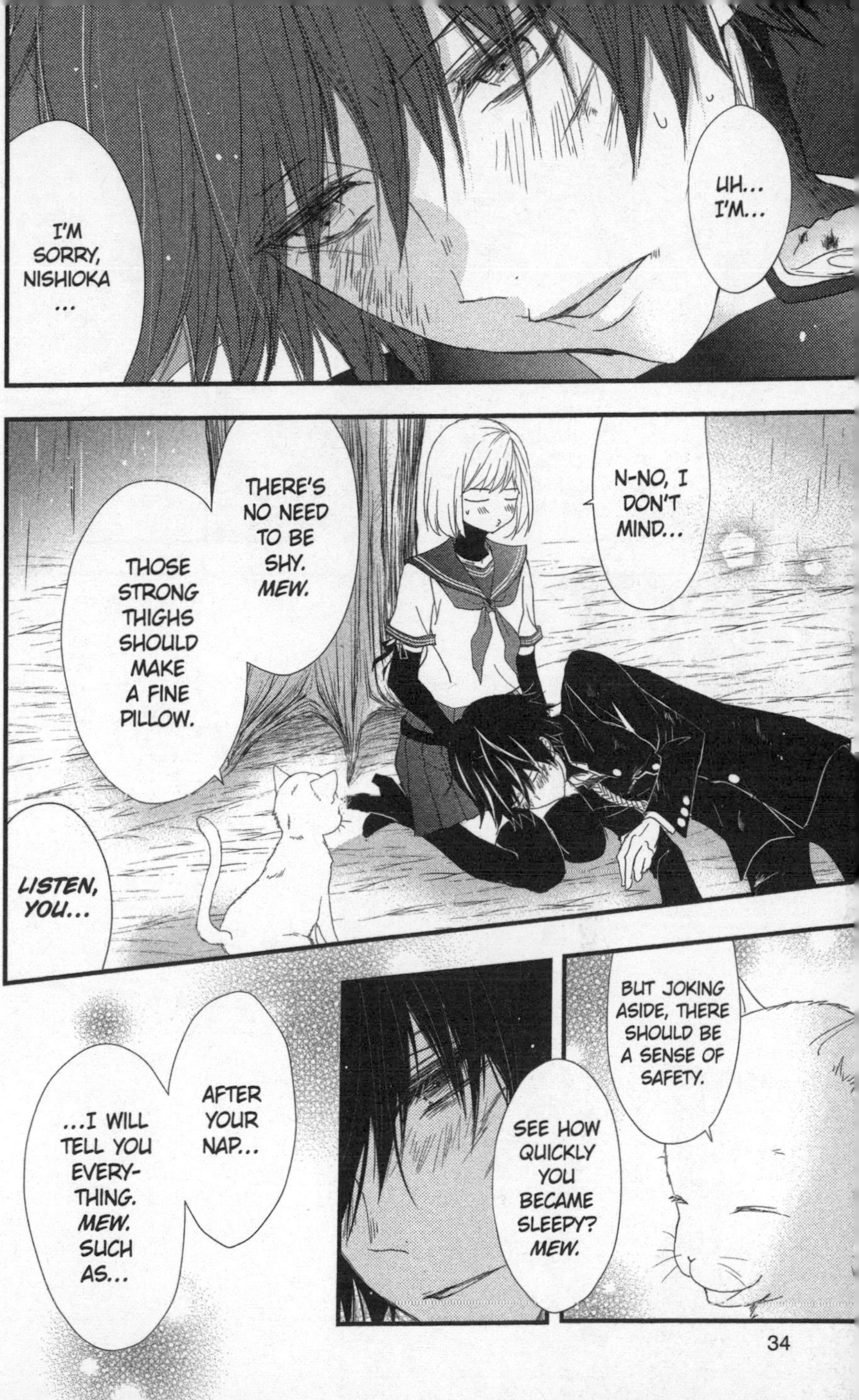
UH... I'M...
I'M SORRY, NISHIOKA...
N-NO, I DON'T MIND...
THERE'S NO NEED TO BE SHY. *MEW.*
THOSE STRONG THIGHS SHOULD MAKE A FINE PILLOW.
LISTEN, YOU...
BUT JOKING ASIDE, THERE SHOULD BE A SENSE OF SAFETY.
SEE HOW QUICKLY YOU BECAME SLEEPY? *MEW.*
AFTER YOUR NAP...
...I WILL TELL YOU EVERY-THING. *MEW.* SUCH AS...

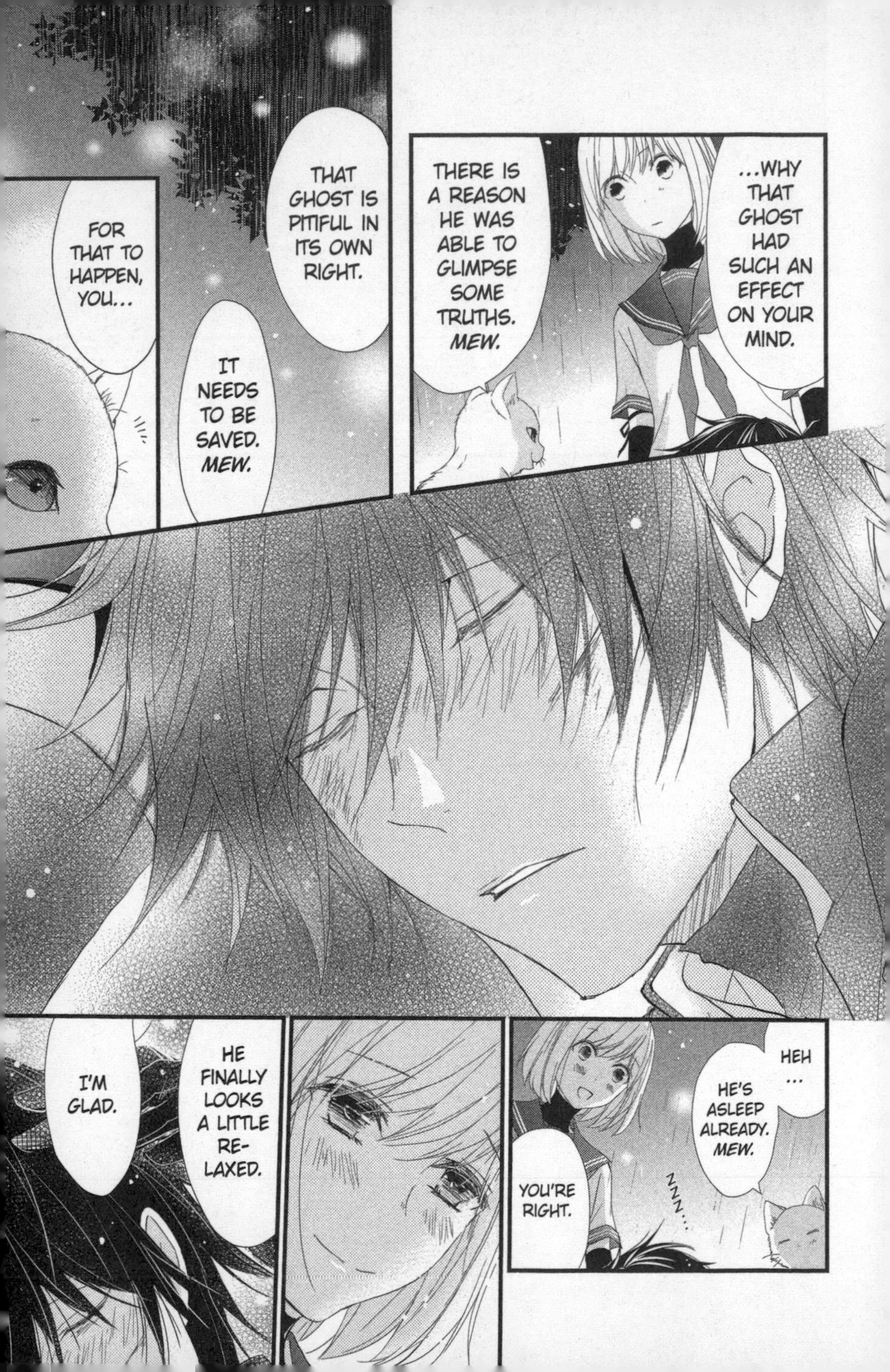
...WHY THAT GHOST HAD SUCH AN EFFECT ON YOUR MIND.
THERE IS A REASON HE WAS ABLE TO GLIMPSE SOME TRUTHS. *MEW.*
THAT GHOST IS PITIFUL IN ITS OWN RIGHT.
IT NEEDS TO BE SAVED. *MEW.*
FOR THAT TO HAPPEN, YOU...
HEH...
HE'S ASLEEP ALREADY. *MEW.*
ZZZ...
YOU'RE RIGHT.
HE FINALLY LOOKS A LITTLE RE-LAXED.
I'M GLAD.

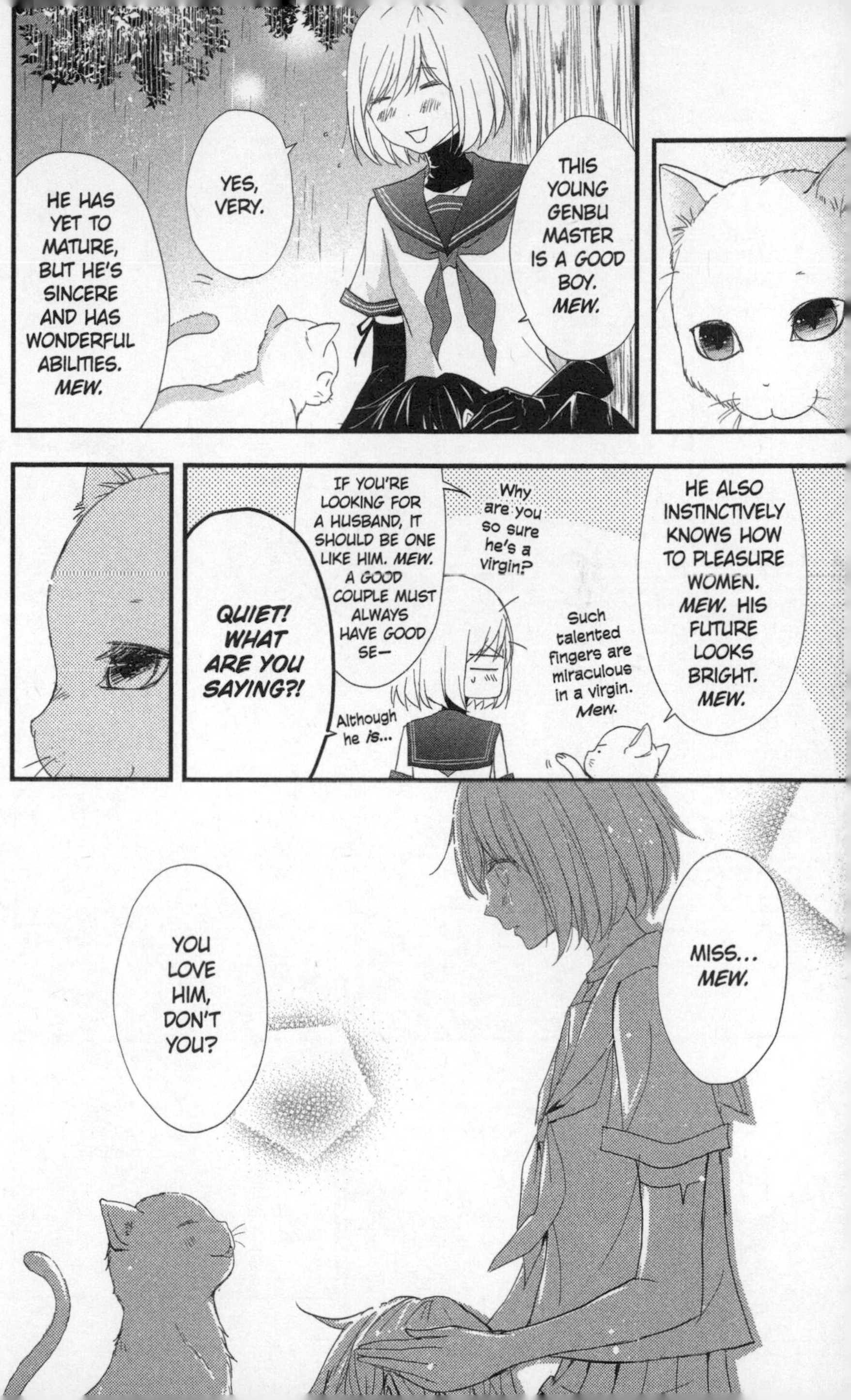
THIS YOUNG GENBU MASTER IS A GOOD BOY. *MEW.*
YES, VERY.
HE HAS YET TO MATURE, BUT HE'S SINCERE AND HAS WONDERFUL ABILITIES. *MEW.*
HE ALSO INSTINCTIVELY KNOWS HOW TO PLEASURE WOMEN. *MEW.* HIS FUTURE LOOKS BRIGHT. *MEW.*
Such talented fingers are miraculous in a virgin. *Mew.*
Why are you so sure he's a virgin?
IF YOU'RE LOOKING FOR A HUSBAND, IT SHOULD BE ONE LIKE HIM. *MEW.* A GOOD COUPLE MUST ALWAYS HAVE GOOD SE—
Although he *is*...
QUIET! WHAT ARE YOU SAYING?!
MISS... *MEW.*
YOU LOVE HIM, DON'T YOU?

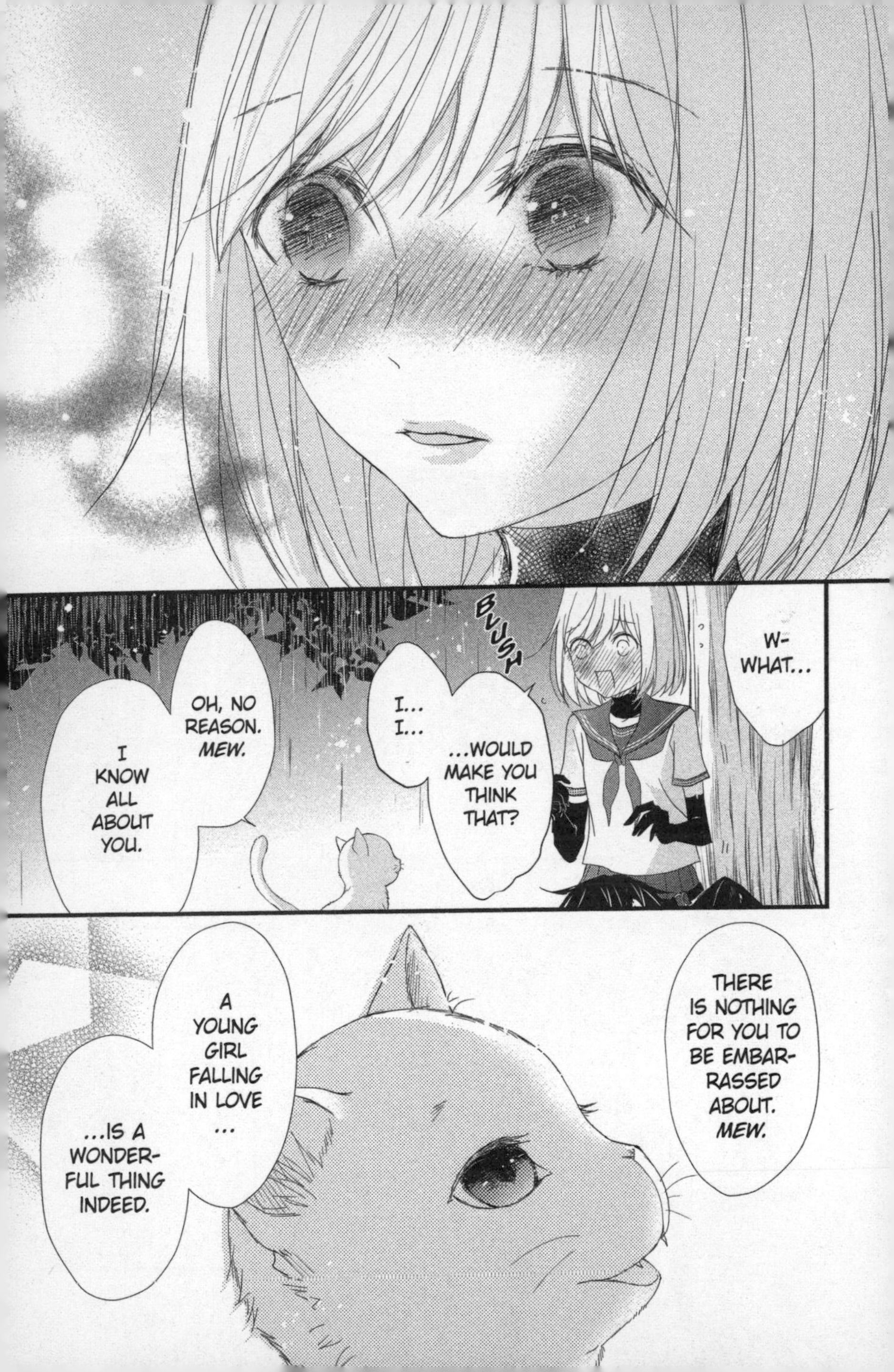
W- WHAT...
BLUSH
I... I...
...WOULD MAKE YOU THINK THAT?
OH, NO REASON. MEW.
I KNOW ALL ABOUT YOU.
THERE IS NOTHING FOR YOU TO BE EMBAR- RASSED ABOUT. MEW.
A YOUNG GIRL FALLING IN LOVE ...
...IS A WONDER- FUL THING INDEED.

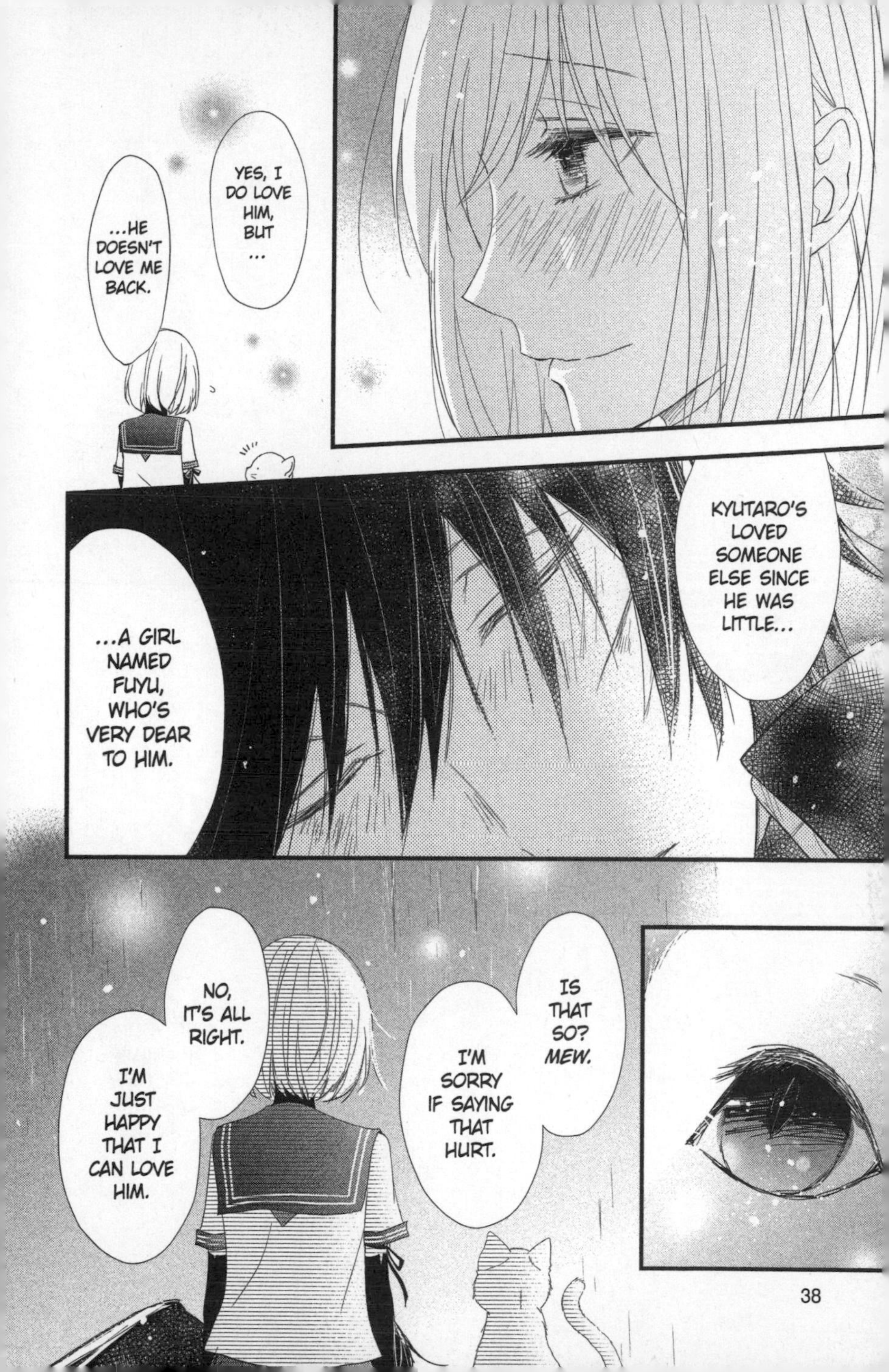
YES, I DO LOVE HIM, BUT ...
...HE DOESN'T LOVE ME BACK.
KYUTARO'S LOVED SOMEONE ELSE SINCE HE WAS LITTLE...
...A GIRL NAMED FUYU, WHO'S VERY DEAR TO HIM.
IS THAT SO? *MEW.*
I'M SORRY IF SAYING THAT HURT.
NO, IT'S ALL RIGHT.
I'M JUST HAPPY THAT I CAN LOVE HIM.

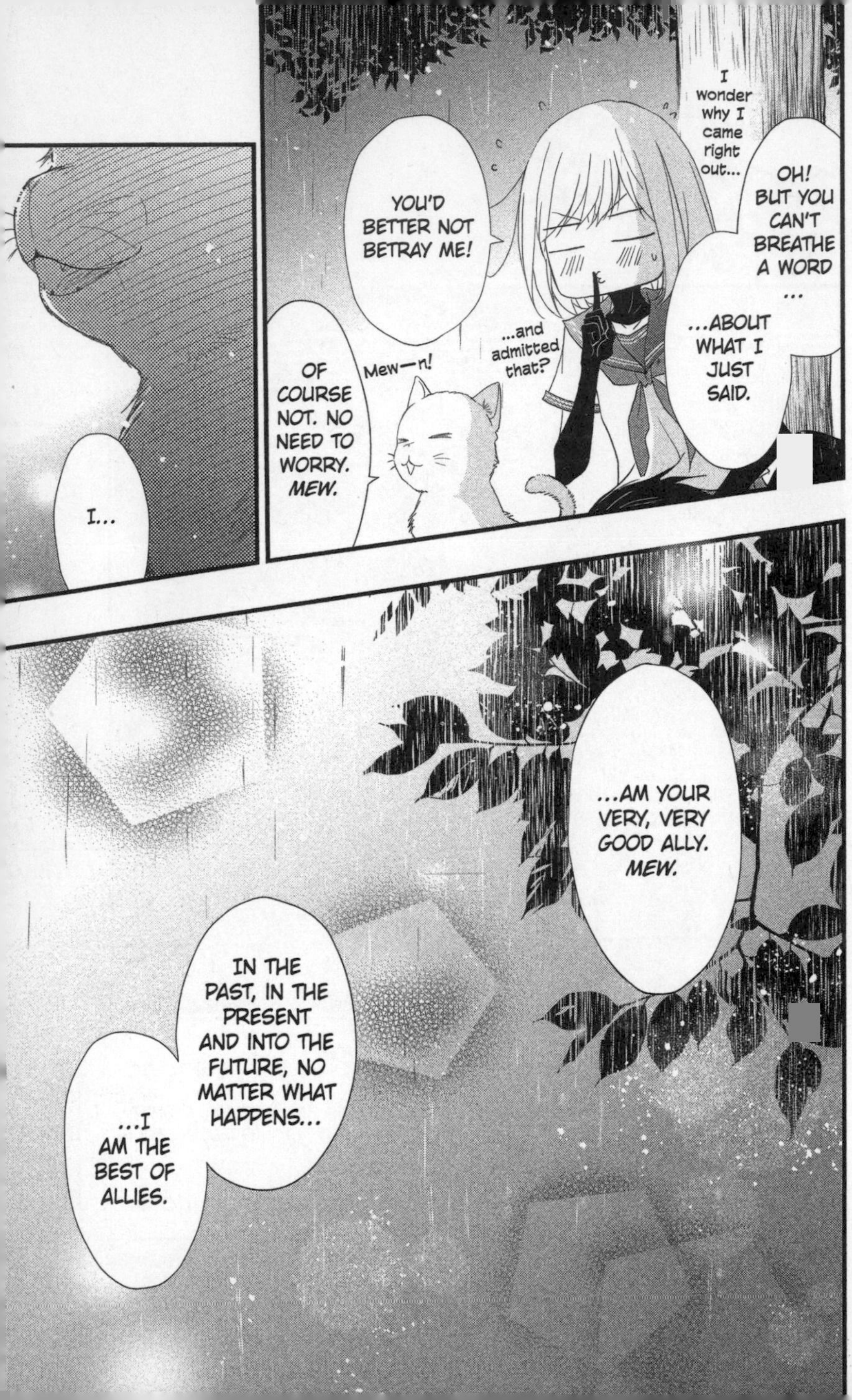
I wonder why I came right out...
OH! BUT YOU CAN'T BREATHE A WORD ...
...ABOUT WHAT I JUST SAID.
...and admitted that?
YOU'D BETTER NOT BETRAY ME!
Mew—n!
OF COURSE NOT. NO NEED TO WORRY. *MEW.*
I...
...AM YOUR VERY, VERY GOOD ALLY. *MEW.*
IN THE PAST, IN THE PRESENT AND INTO THE FUTURE, NO MATTER WHAT HAPPENS...
...I AM THE BEST OF ALLIES.

MONTHLY BETSUCOMI SALE DATE NOTICE ON TWITTER

CHAPTER 32

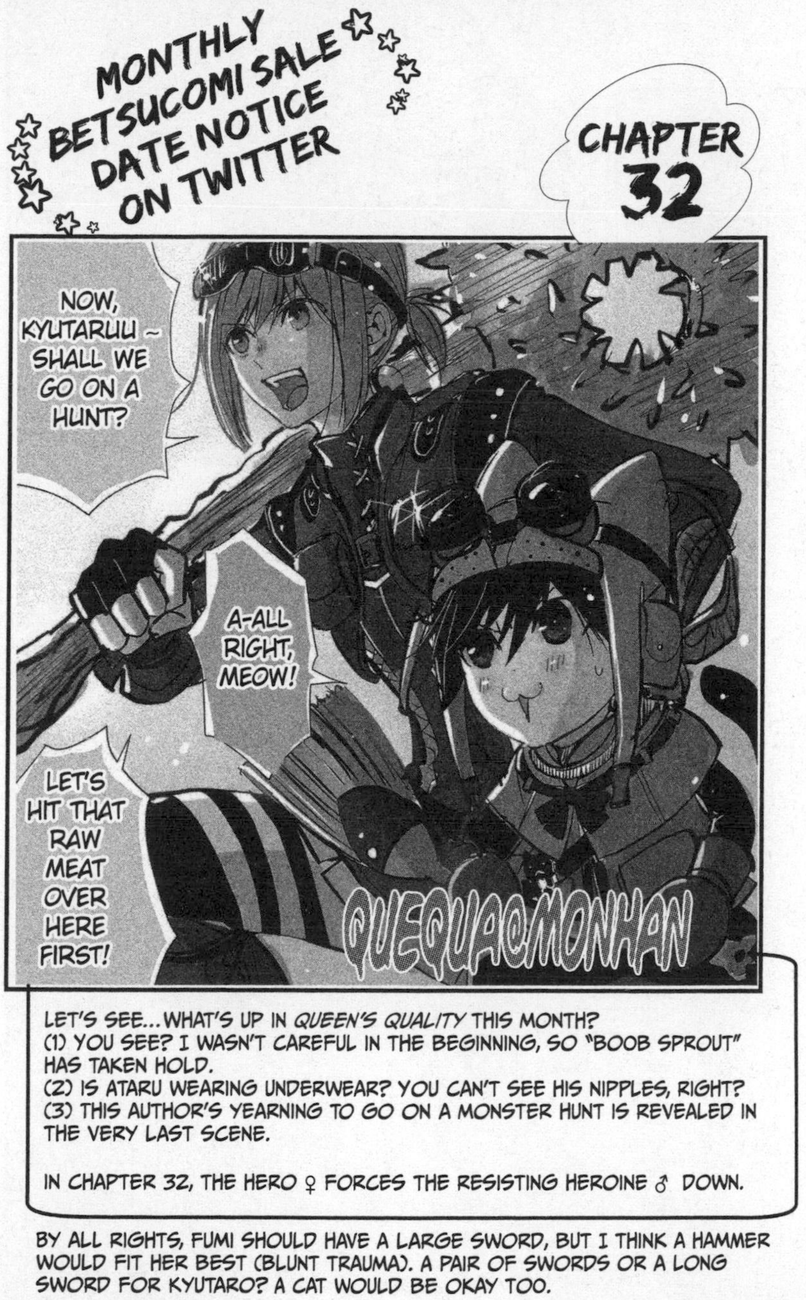
NOW, KYUTARUU~ SHALL WE GO ON A HUNT?
A-ALL RIGHT, MEOW!
LET'S HIT THAT RAW MEAT OVER HERE FIRST!
QUEQUA@MONHAN

LET'S SEE...WHAT'S UP IN *QUEEN'S QUALITY* THIS MONTH?
(1) YOU SEE? I WASN'T CAREFUL IN THE BEGINNING, SO "BOOB SPROUT" HAS TAKEN HOLD.
(2) IS ATARU WEARING UNDERWEAR? YOU CAN'T SEE HIS NIPPLES, RIGHT?
(3) THIS AUTHOR'S YEARNING TO GO ON A MONSTER HUNT IS REVEALED IN THE VERY LAST SCENE.

IN CHAPTER 32, THE HERO ♀ FORCES THE RESISTING HEROINE ♂ DOWN.

BY ALL RIGHTS, FUMI SHOULD HAVE A LARGE SWORD, BUT I THINK A HAMMER WOULD FIT HER BEST (BLUNT TRAUMA). A PAIR OF SWORDS OR A LONG SWORD FOR KYUTARO? A CAT WOULD BE OKAY TOO.

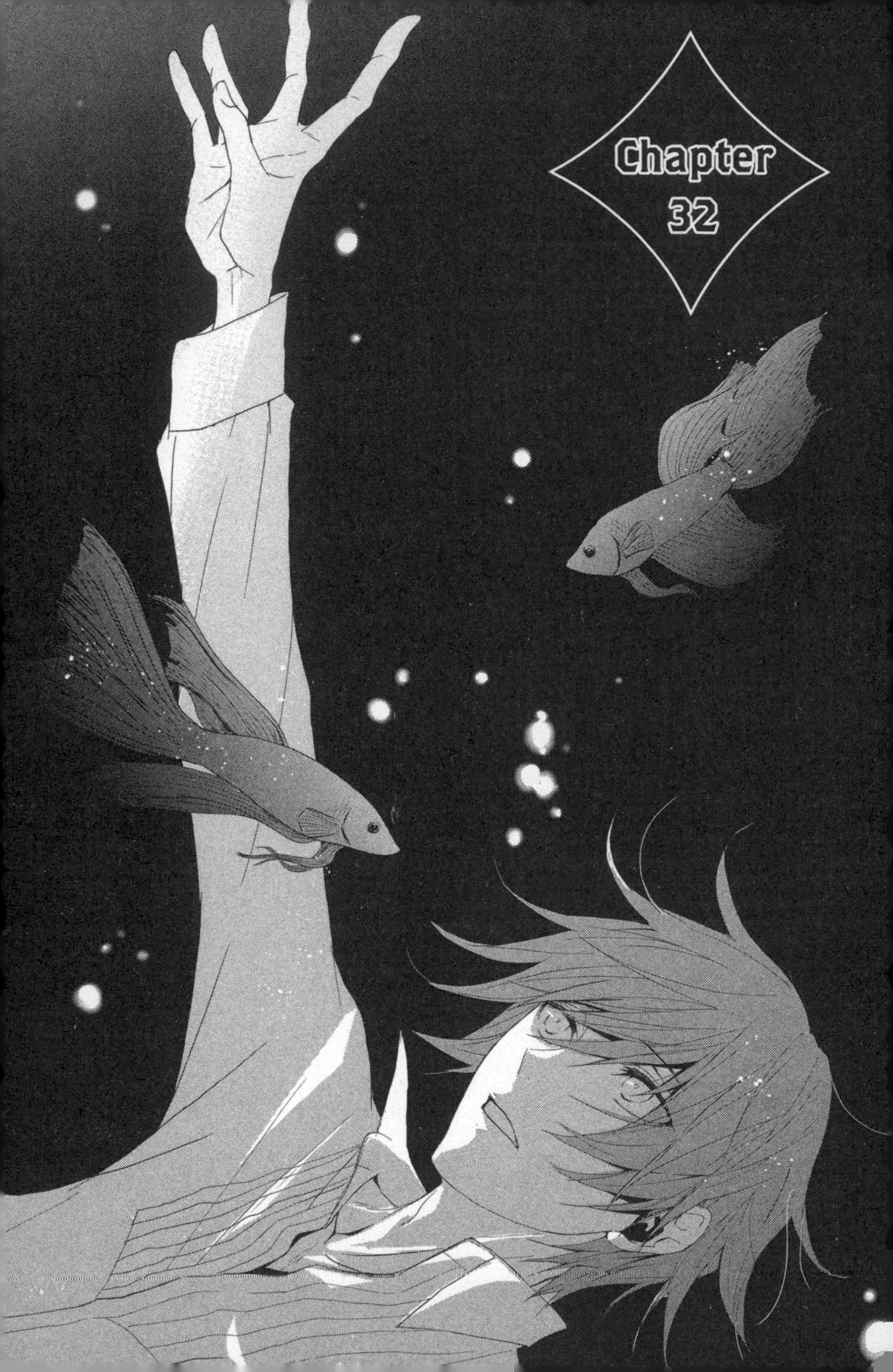
Chapter
32

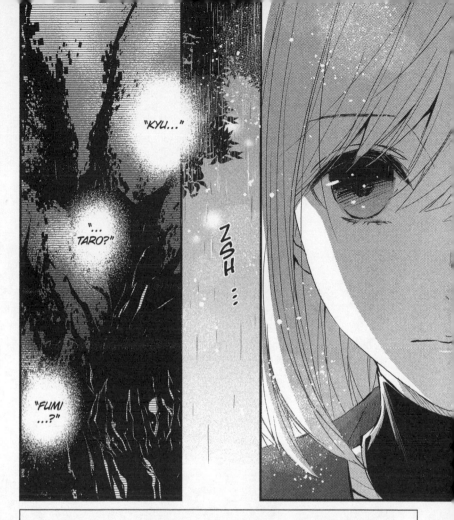

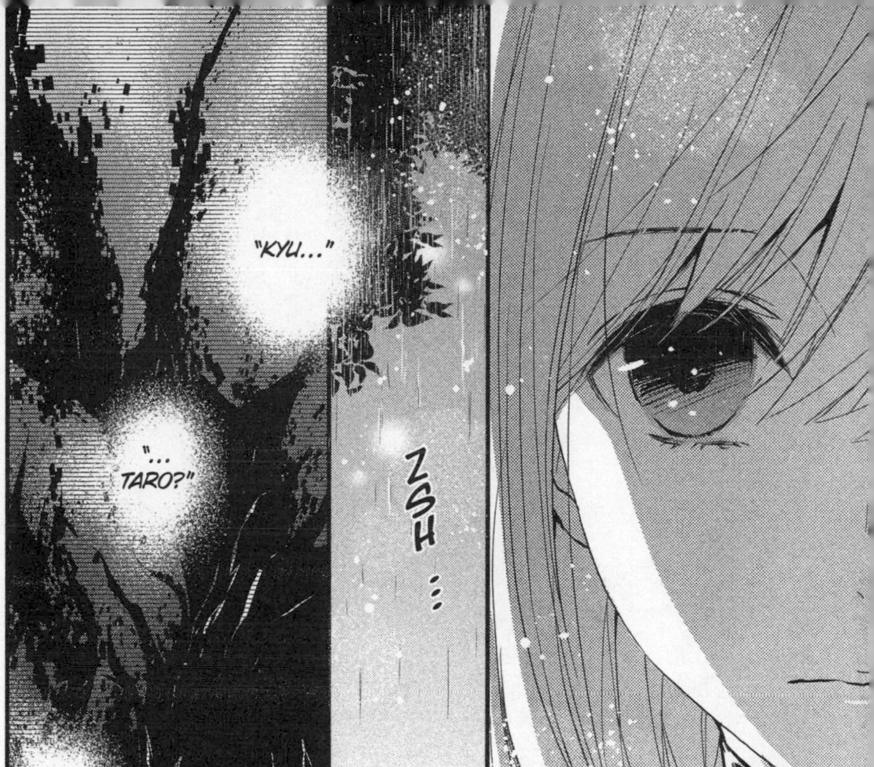
ZSH...
"KYU..."
"... TARO?"
"FUMI ...?"

I'm a dog lover who lived with dogs for many years, but in the course of drawing this cat, I've found that cats are very cute too. I suppose I'd come to love them more if I kept one.

However, I've been living with a Java sparrow lately and find myself raving about how cute birds are. I guess all living things are cute. They're all doing the best they can...even humans.

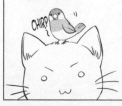

The Java sparrow always poops on my head, but he's cute, so I forgive him. *Mew.*

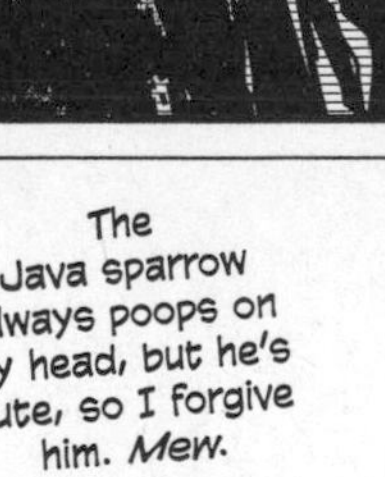
CHIRP

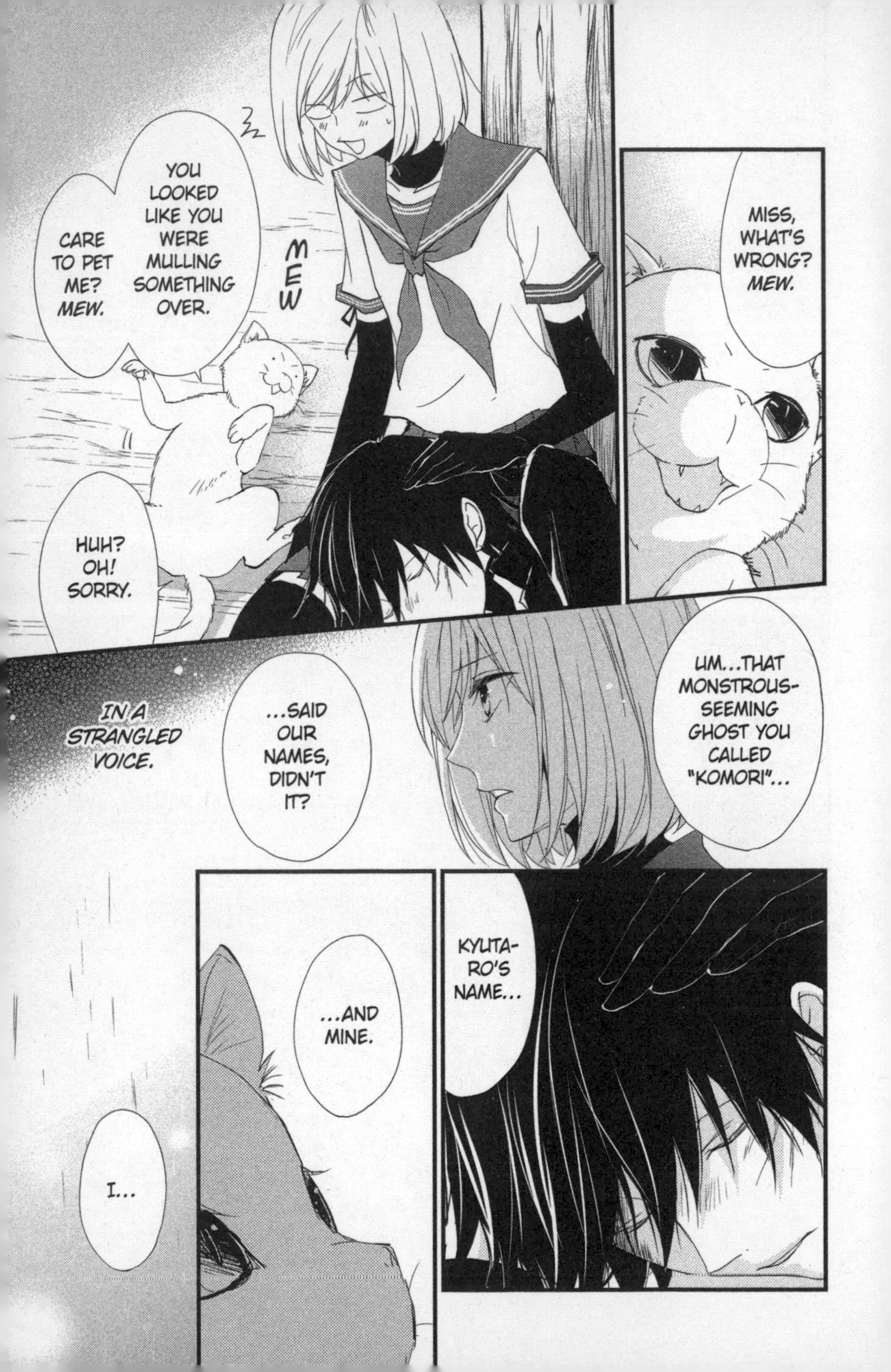
MISS, WHAT'S WRONG? MEW.
YOU LOOKED LIKE YOU WERE MULLING SOMETHING OVER.
MEW
CARE TO PET ME? MEW.
HUH? OH! SORRY.
UM...THAT MONSTROUS-SEEMING GHOST YOU CALLED "KOMORI"...
...SAID OUR NAMES, DIDN'T IT?
IN A STRANGLED VOICE.
KYUTA-RO'S NAME...
...AND MINE.
I...

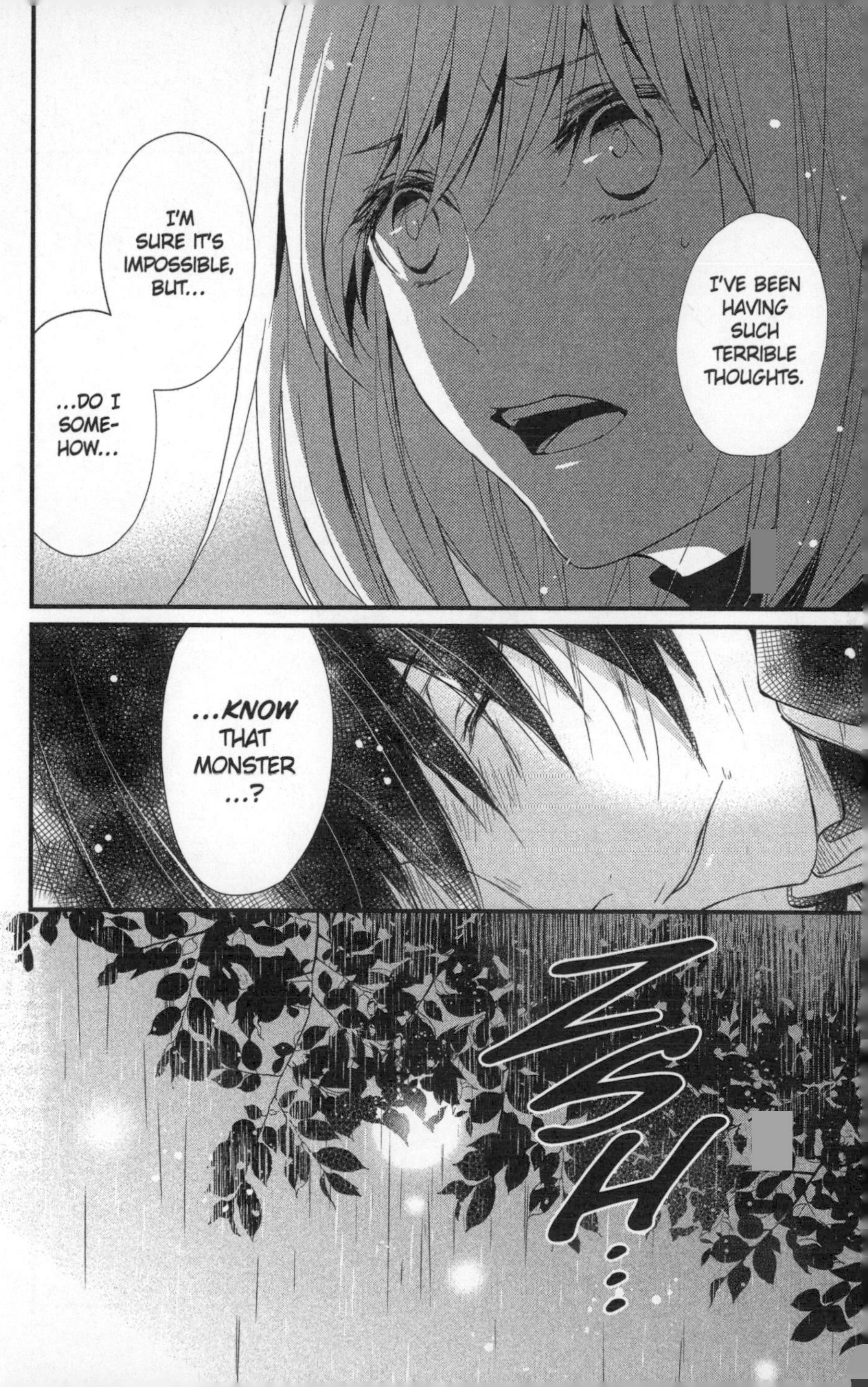
I'VE BEEN HAVING SUCH TERRIBLE THOUGHTS.
I'M SURE IT'S IMPOSSIBLE, BUT...
...DO I SOME-HOW...
...*KNOW* THAT MONSTER ...?
WSSH...

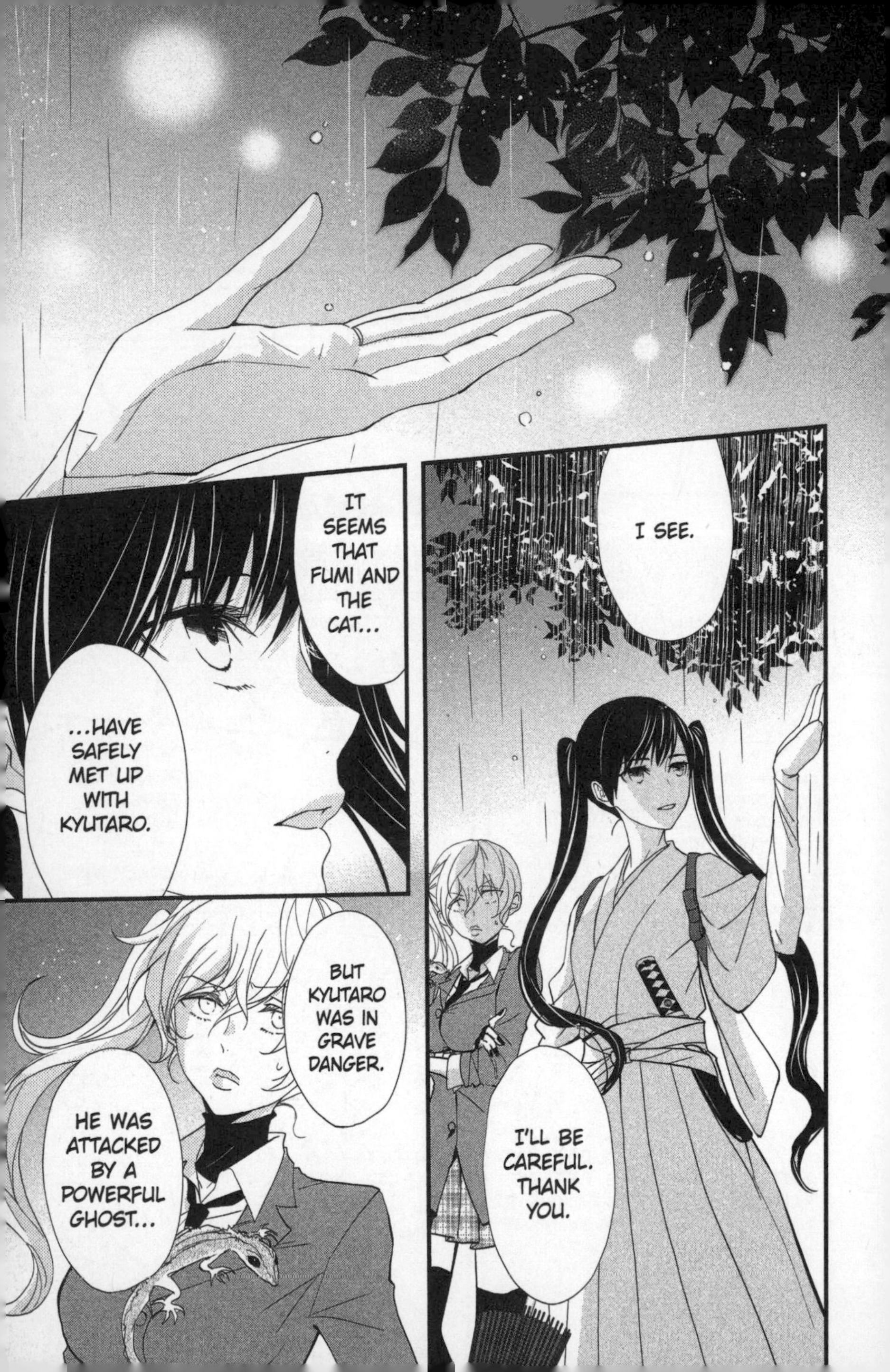
I SEE.
I'LL BE CAREFUL. THANK YOU.
IT SEEMS THAT FUMI AND THE CAT...
...HAVE SAFELY MET UP WITH KYUTARO.
BUT KYUTARO WAS IN GRAVE DANGER.
HE WAS ATTACKED BY A POWERFUL GHOST...

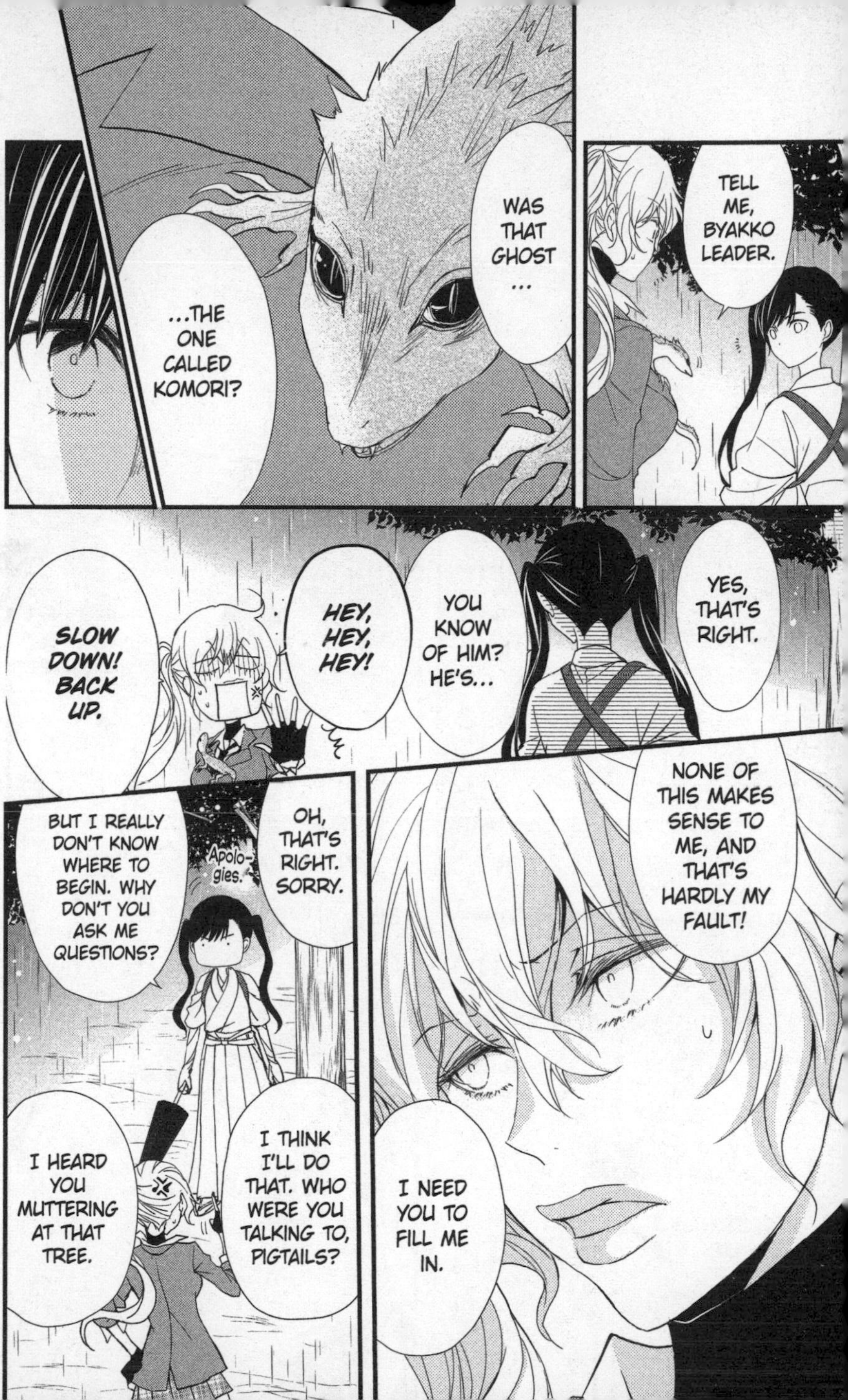
TELL ME, BYAKKO LEADER.
WAS THAT GHOST ...
...THE ONE CALLED KOMORI?
YES, THAT'S RIGHT.
YOU KNOW OF HIM? HE'S...
HEY, HEY, HEY!
SLOW DOWN! BACK UP.
NONE OF THIS MAKES SENSE TO ME, AND THAT'S HARDLY MY FAULT!
I NEED YOU TO FILL ME IN.
OH, THAT'S RIGHT. SORRY.
Apologies.
BUT I REALLY DON'T KNOW WHERE TO BEGIN. WHY DON'T YOU ASK ME QUESTIONS?
I THINK I'LL DO THAT. WHO WERE YOU TALKING TO, PIGTAILS?
I HEARD YOU MUTTERING AT THAT TREE.

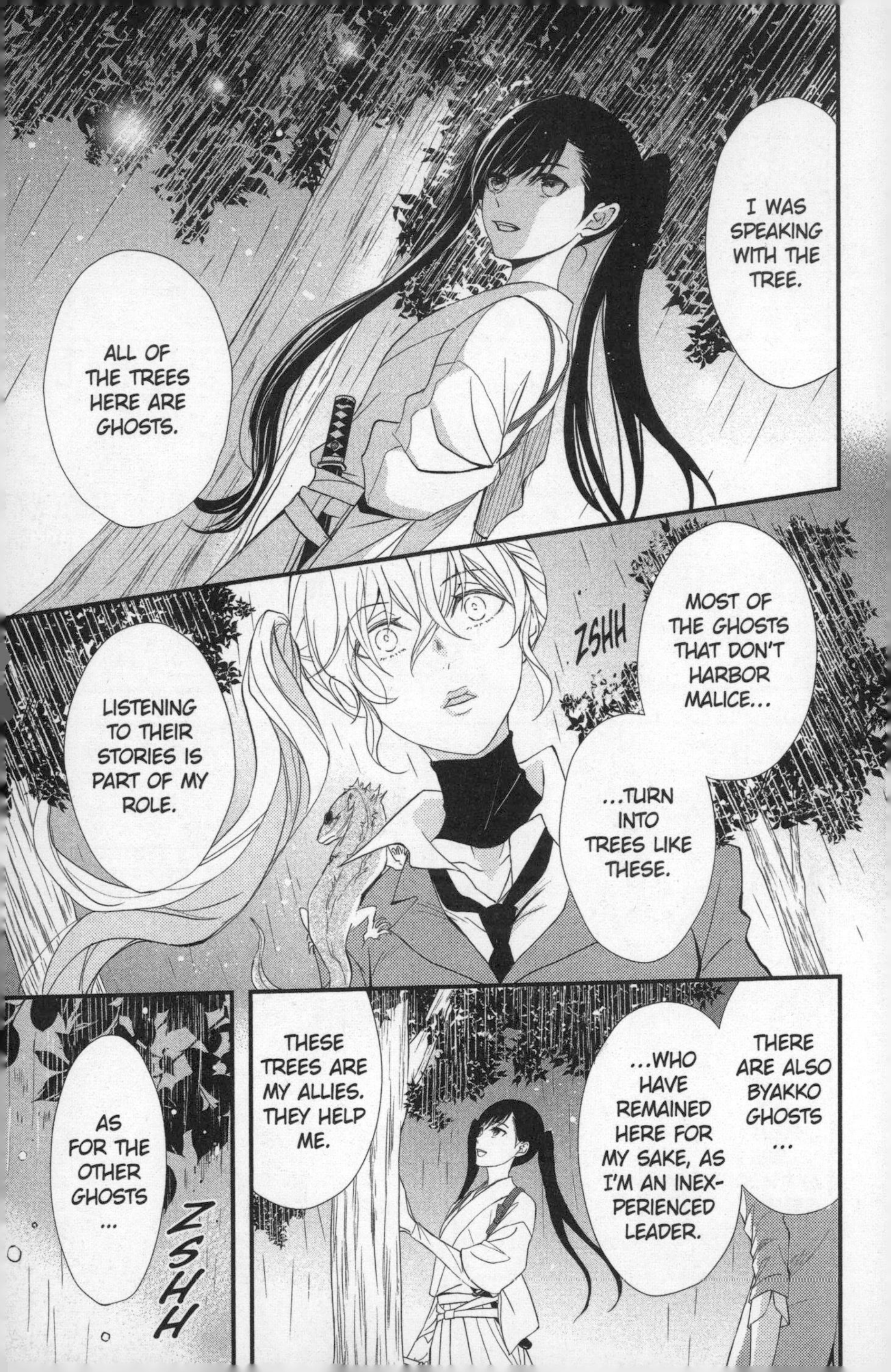
I WAS SPEAKING WITH THE TREE.
ALL OF THE TREES HERE ARE GHOSTS.
ZSHH
MOST OF THE GHOSTS THAT DON'T HARBOR MALICE...
...TURN INTO TREES LIKE THESE.
LISTENING TO THEIR STORIES IS PART OF MY ROLE.
THERE ARE ALSO BYAKKO GHOSTS ...
...WHO HAVE REMAINED HERE FOR MY SAKE, AS I'M AN INEXPERIENCED LEADER.
THESE TREES ARE MY ALLIES. THEY HELP ME.
AS FOR THE OTHER GHOSTS ...
ZSHH

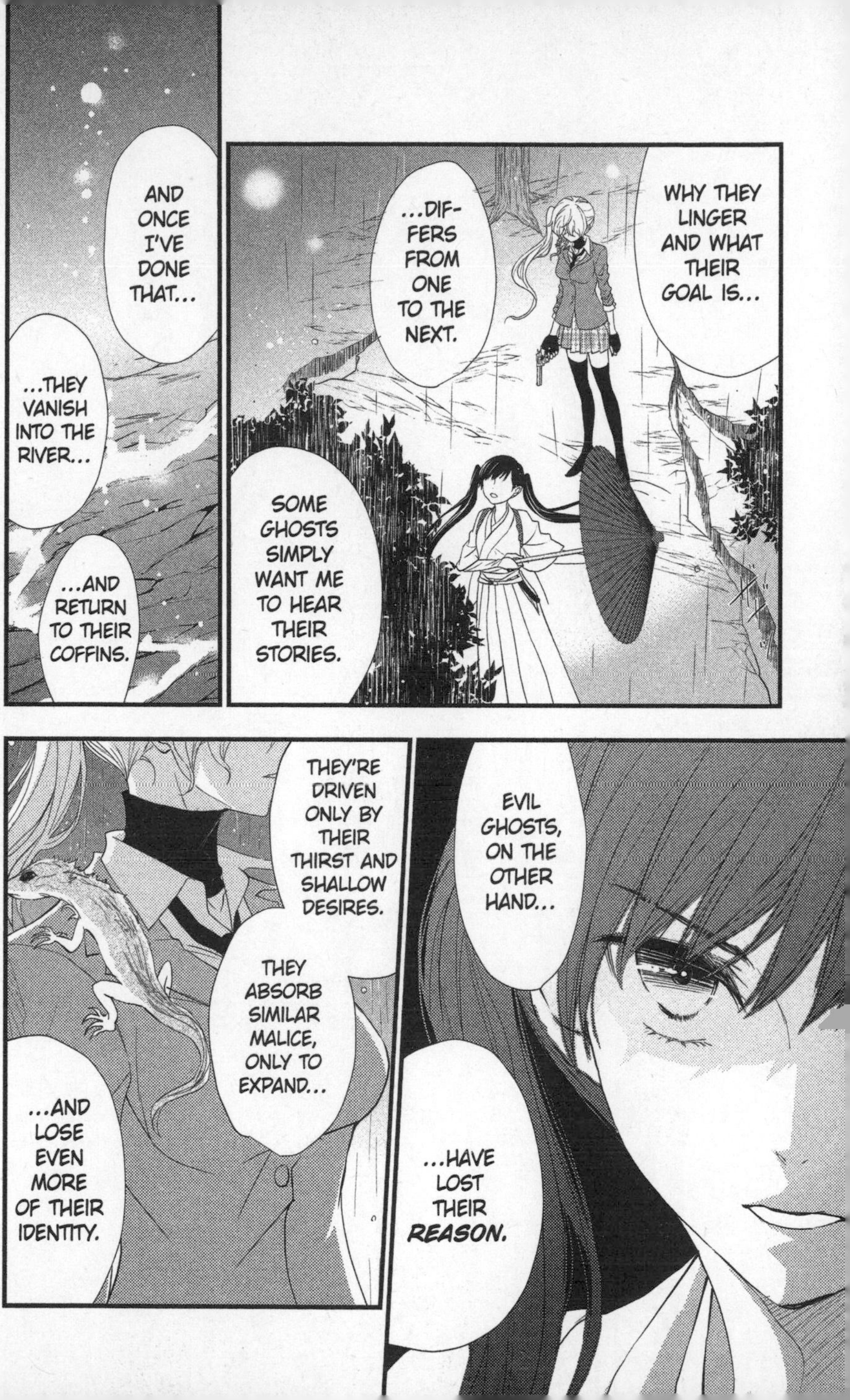
WHY THEY LINGER AND WHAT THEIR GOAL IS...
...DIFFERS FROM ONE TO THE NEXT.
SOME GHOSTS SIMPLY WANT ME TO HEAR THEIR STORIES.
AND ONCE I'VE DONE THAT...
...THEY VANISH INTO THE RIVER...
...AND RETURN TO THEIR COFFINS.
EVIL GHOSTS, ON THE OTHER HAND...
...HAVE LOST THEIR ***REASON.***
THEY'RE DRIVEN ONLY BY THEIR THIRST AND SHALLOW DESIRES.
THEY ABSORB SIMILAR MALICE, ONLY TO EXPAND...
...AND LOSE EVEN MORE OF THEIR IDENTITY.

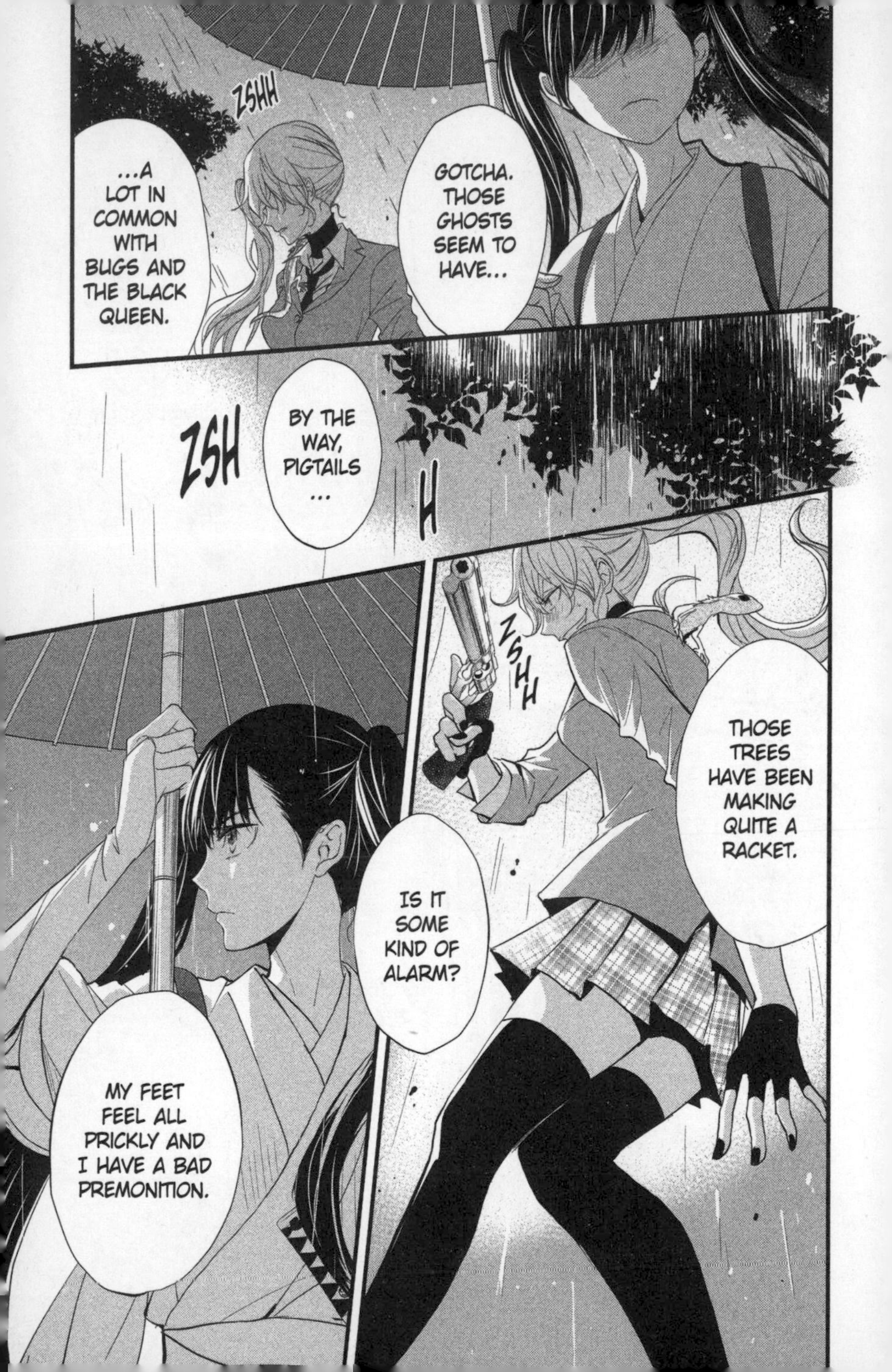
ZSHH
GOTCHA. THOSE GHOSTS SEEM TO HAVE...
...A LOT IN COMMON WITH BUGS AND THE BLACK QUEEN.
ZSH
H
BY THE WAY, PIGTAILS...
ZSHH
THOSE TREES HAVE BEEN MAKING QUITE A RACKET.
IS IT SOME KIND OF ALARM?
MY FEET FEEL ALL PRICKLY AND I HAVE A BAD PREMONITION.

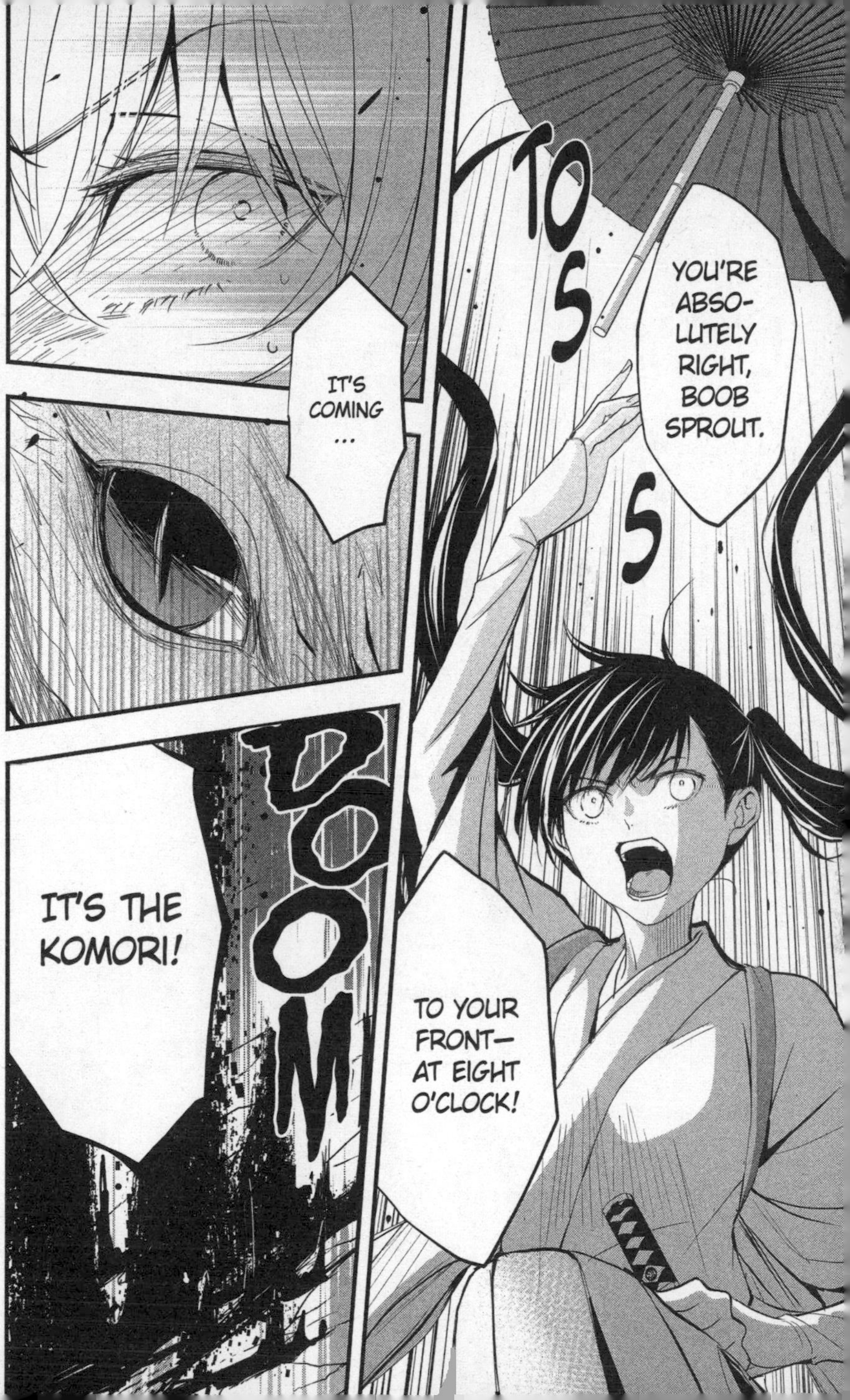
TOSS
YOU'RE ABSO-LUTELY RIGHT, BOOB SPROUT.
TO YOUR FRONT— AT EIGHT O'CLOCK!
IT'S COMING ...
DOOM
IT'S THE KOMORI!

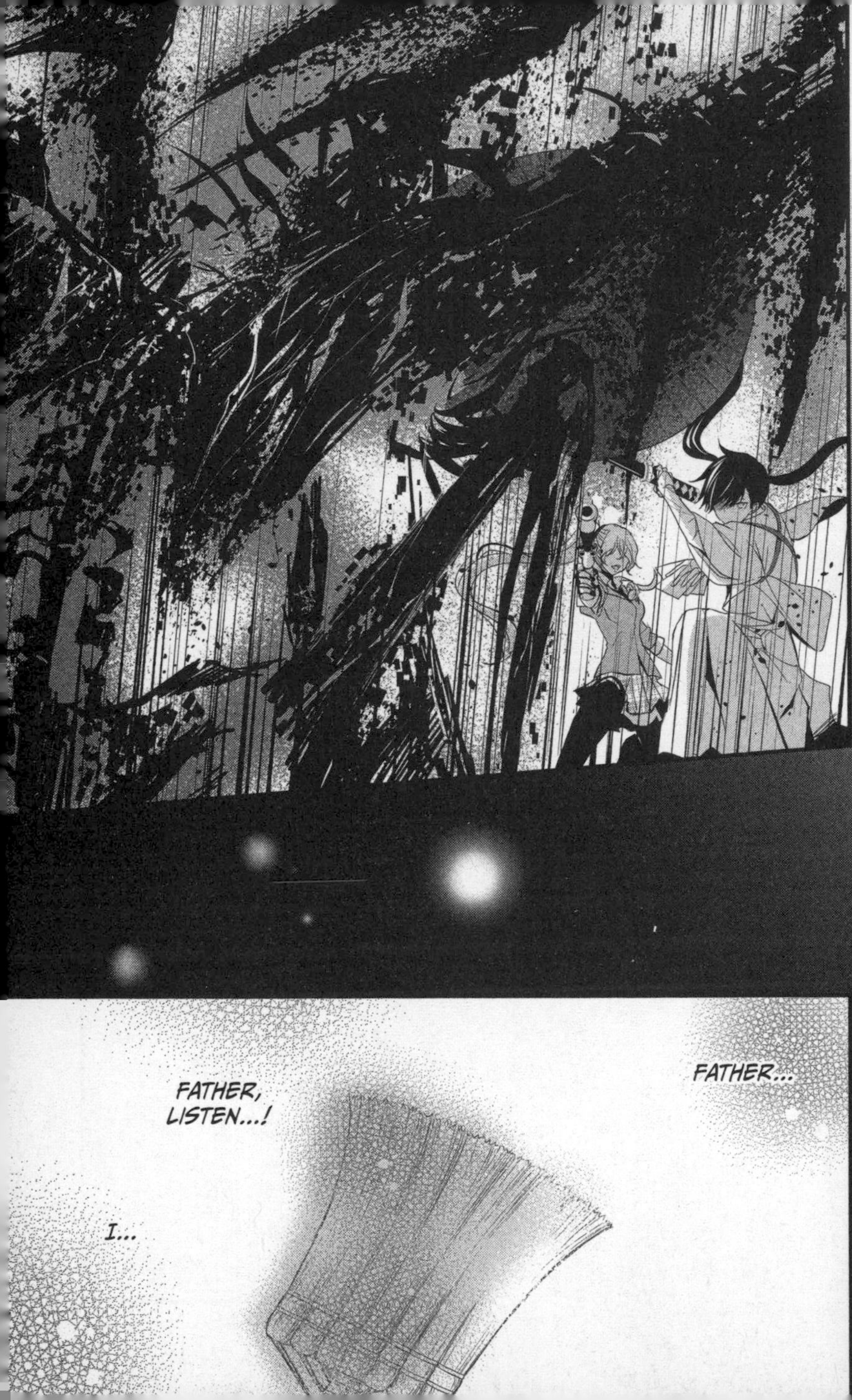
FATHER...
FATHER, LISTEN...!
I...

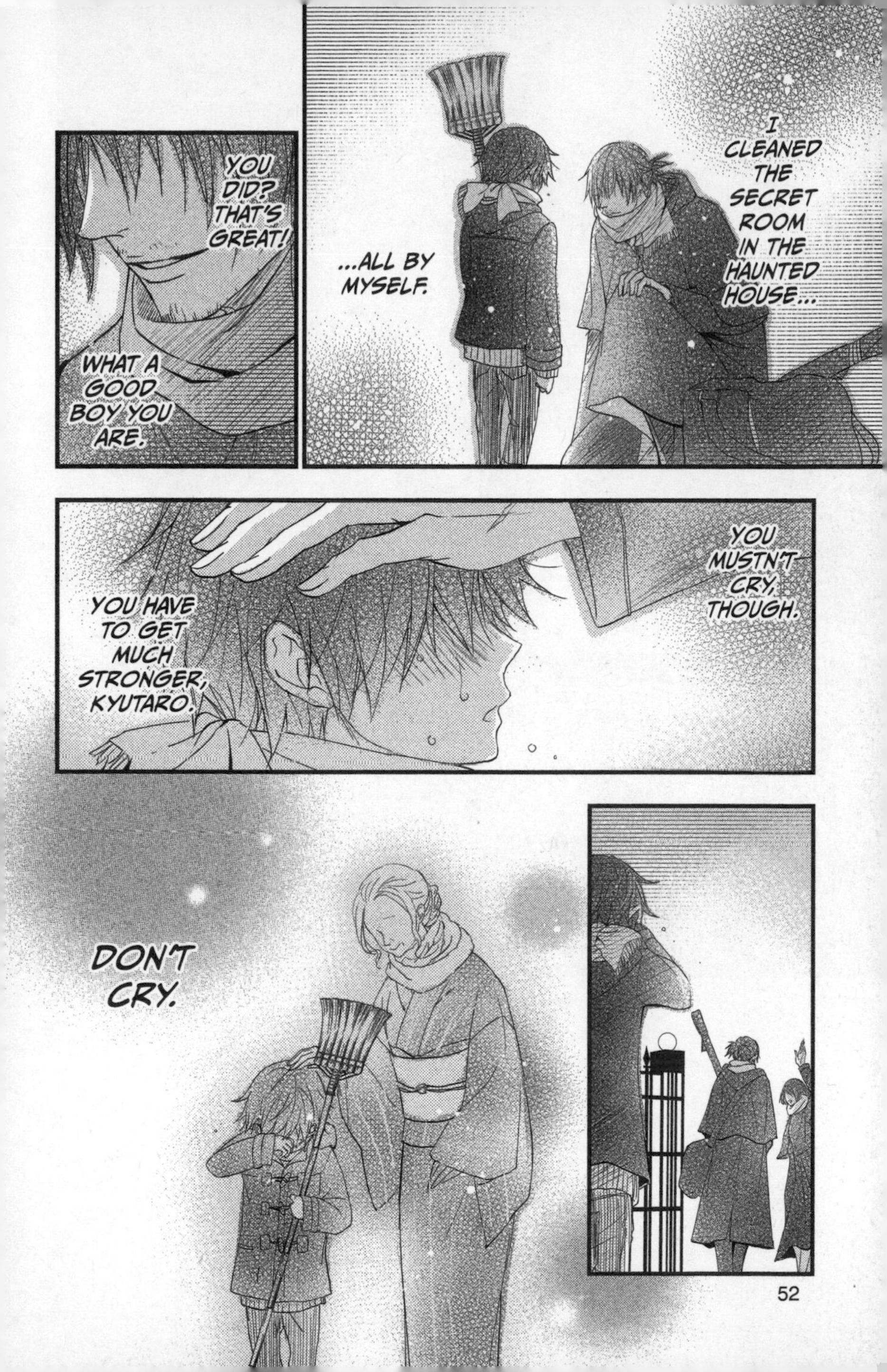
I CLEANED THE SECRET ROOM IN THE HAUNTED HOUSE...
...ALL BY MYSELF.
YOU DID? THAT'S GREAT!
WHAT A GOOD BOY YOU ARE.
YOU MUSTN'T CRY, THOUGH.
YOU HAVE TO GET MUCH STRONGER, KYUTARO.
DON'T CRY.

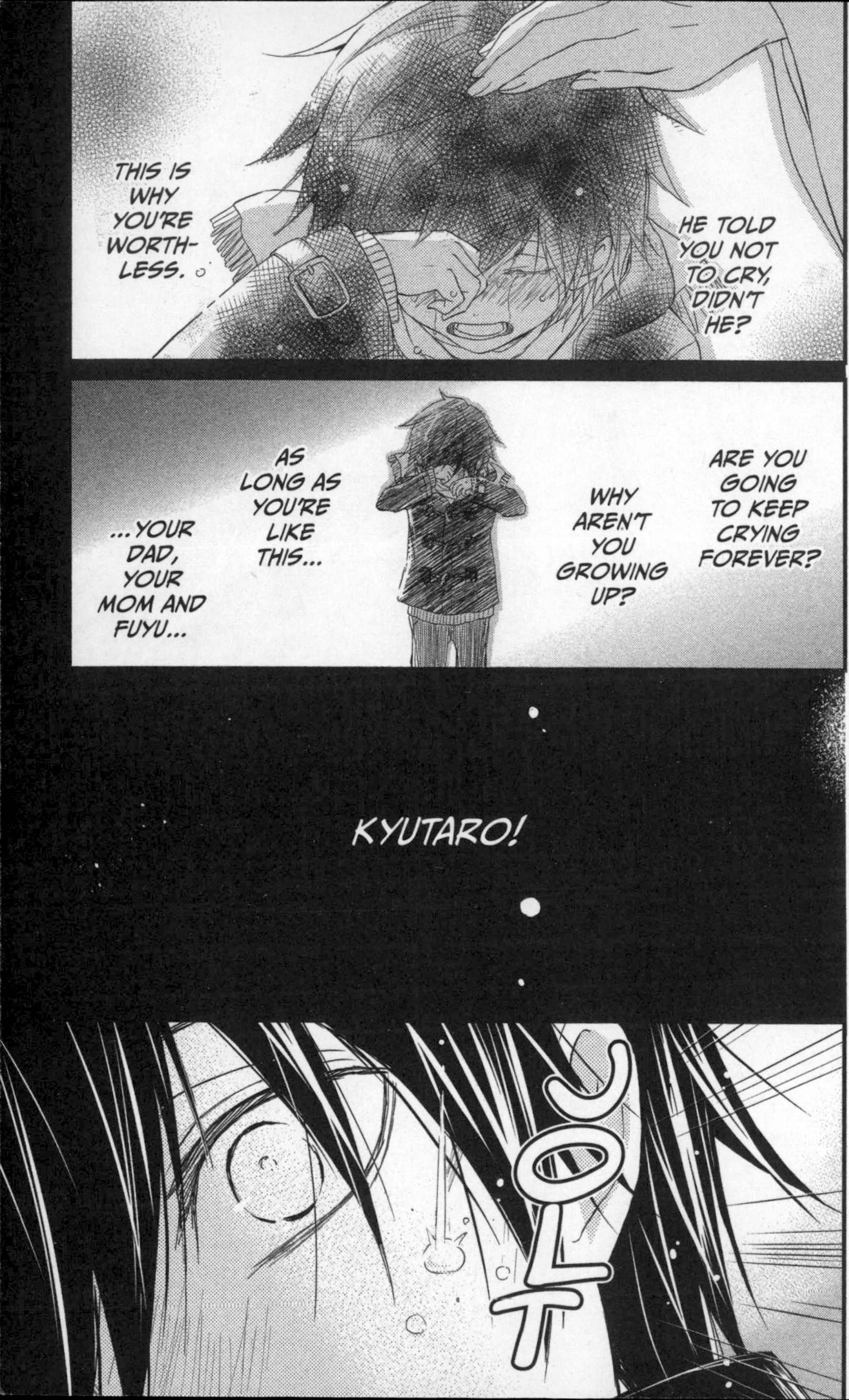
HE TOLD YOU NOT TO CRY, DIDN'T HE?
THIS IS WHY YOU'RE WORTH-LESS.
ARE YOU GOING TO KEEP CRYING FOREVER?
WHY AREN'T YOU GROWING UP?
AS LONG AS YOU'RE LIKE THIS...
...YOUR DAD, YOUR MOM AND FUYU...
KYUTARO!
JOLT

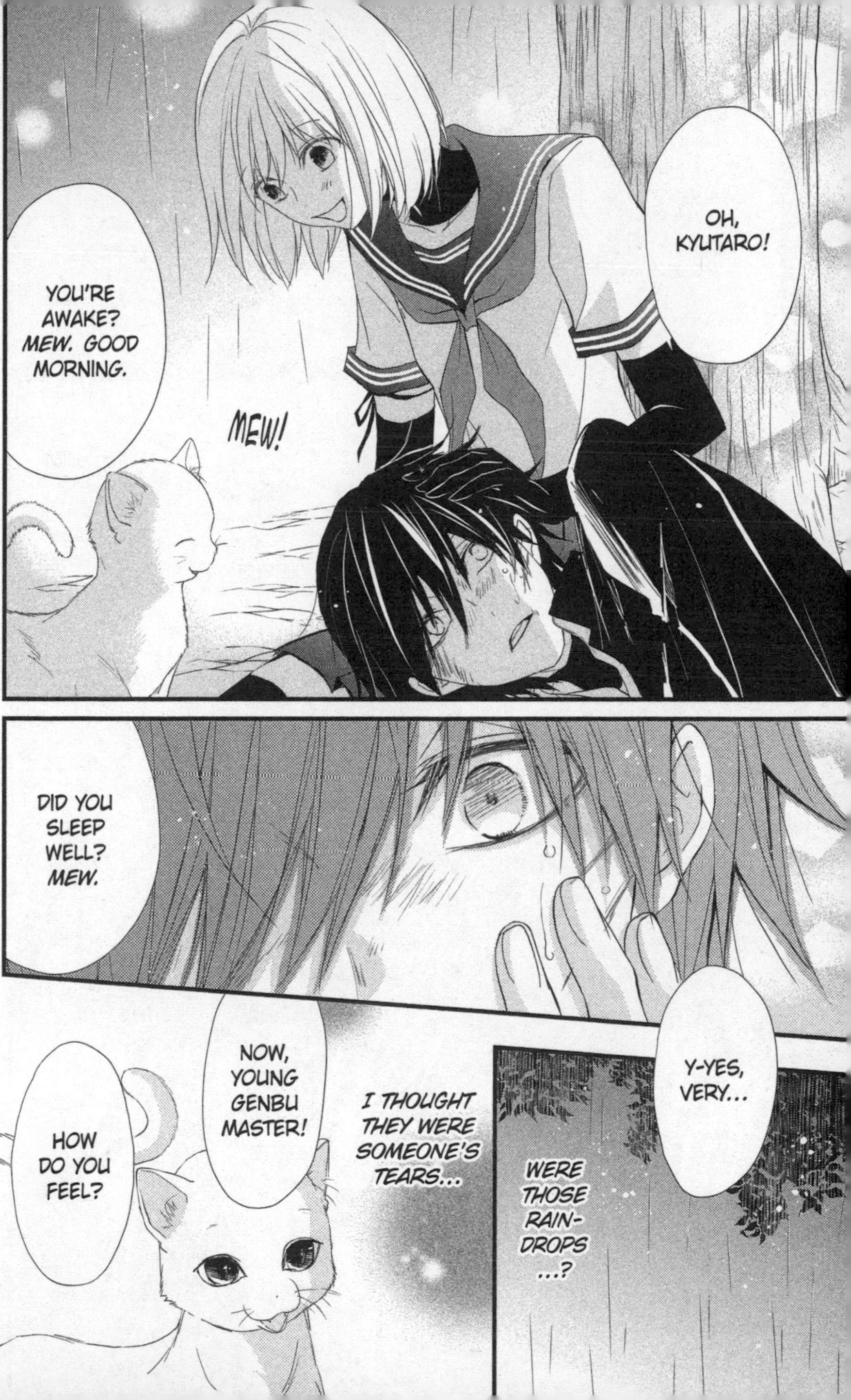
OH, KYUTARO!
MEW!
YOU'RE AWAKE? MEW. GOOD MORNING.
DID YOU SLEEP WELL? MEW.
Y-YES, VERY...
WERE THOSE RAIN-DROPS ...?
I THOUGHT THEY WERE SOMEONE'S TEARS...
NOW, YOUNG GENBU MASTER!
HOW DO YOU FEEL?

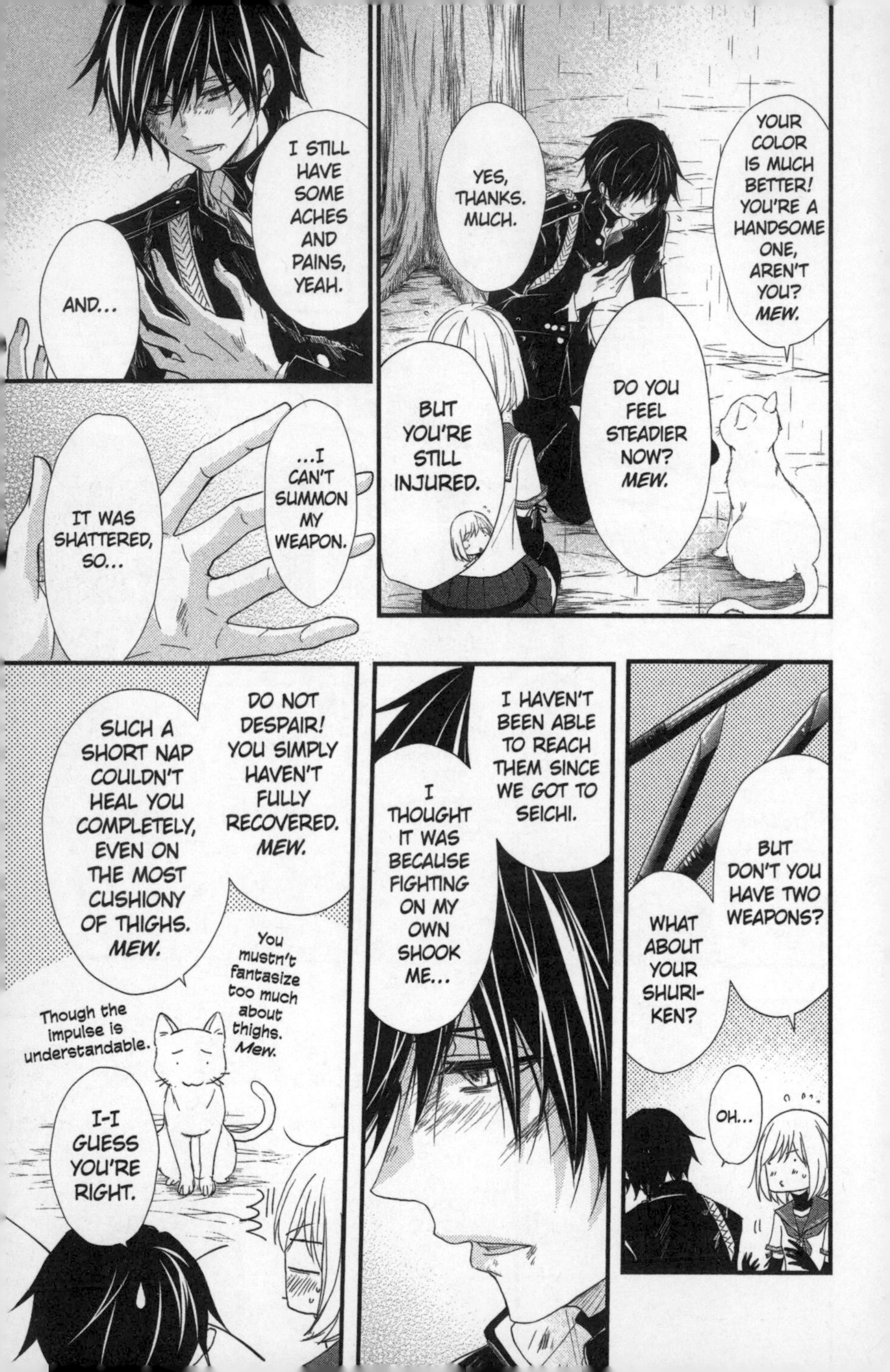
YOUR COLOR IS MUCH BETTER! YOU'RE A HANDSOME ONE, AREN'T YOU? MEW.
YES, THANKS. MUCH.
DO YOU FEEL STEADIER NOW? MEW.
BUT YOU'RE STILL INJURED.
I STILL HAVE SOME ACHES AND PAINS, YEAH.
AND...
...I CAN'T SUMMON MY WEAPON.
IT WAS SHATTERED, SO...
BUT DON'T YOU HAVE TWO WEAPONS?
WHAT ABOUT YOUR SHURIKEN?
OH...
I HAVEN'T BEEN ABLE TO REACH THEM SINCE WE GOT TO SEICHI.
I THOUGHT IT WAS BECAUSE FIGHTING ON MY OWN SHOOK ME...
DO NOT DESPAIR! YOU SIMPLY HAVEN'T FULLY RECOVERED. MEW.
SUCH A SHORT NAP COULDN'T HEAL YOU COMPLETELY, EVEN ON THE MOST CUSHIONY OF THIGHS. MEW.
You mustn't fantasize too much about thighs. Mew.
Though the impulse is understandable.
I-I GUESS YOU'RE RIGHT.

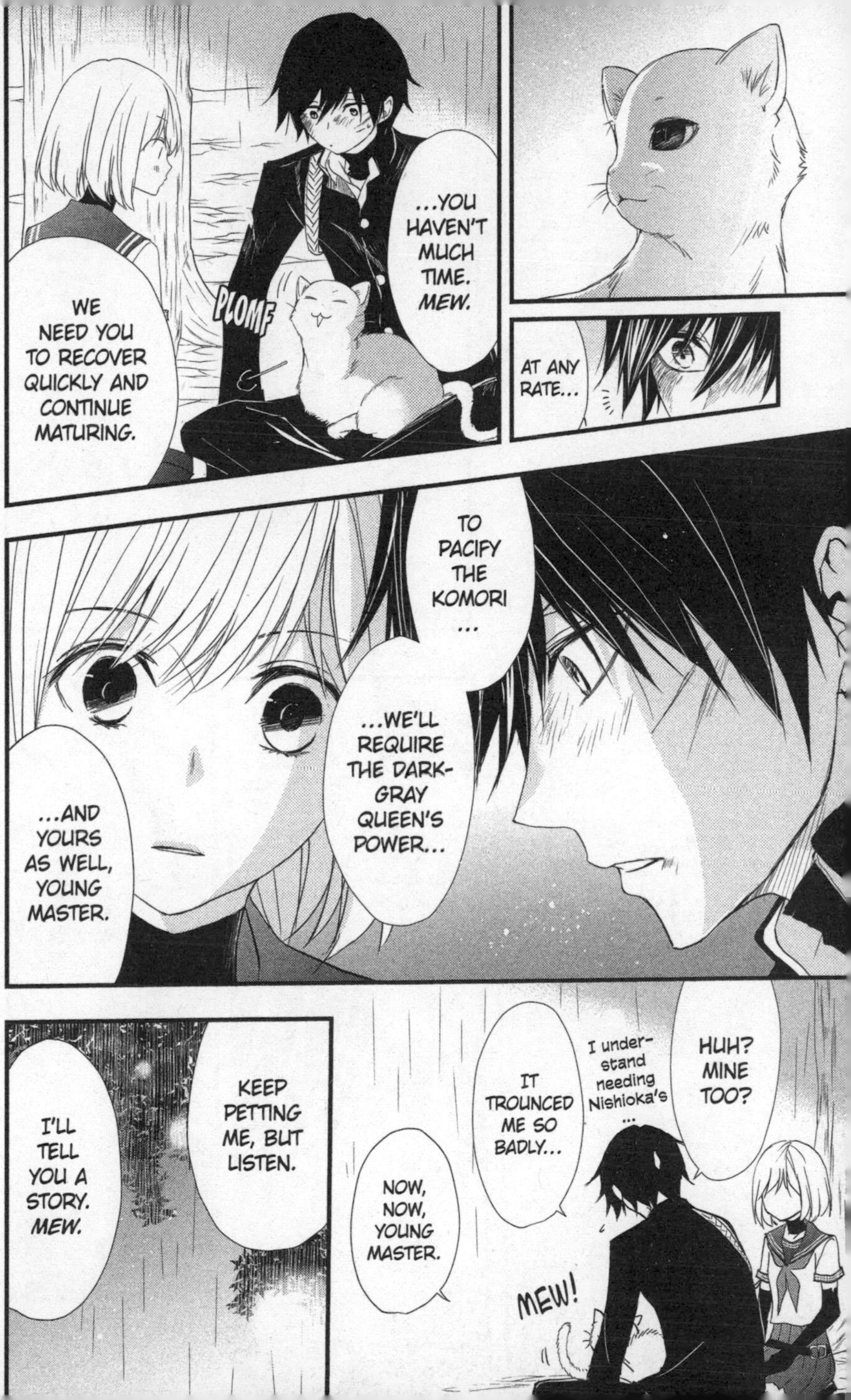
AT ANY RATE...
...YOU HAVEN'T MUCH TIME. *MEW.*
PLOMF
WE NEED YOU TO RECOVER QUICKLY AND CONTINUE MATURING.
TO PACIFY THE KOMORI ...
...WE'LL REQUIRE THE DARK-GRAY QUEEN'S POWER...
...AND YOURS AS WELL, YOUNG MASTER.
HUH? MINE TOO?
I understand needing Nishioka's ...
IT TROUNCED ME SO BADLY...
NOW, NOW, YOUNG MASTER.
MEW!
KEEP PETTING ME, BUT LISTEN.
I'LL TELL YOU A STORY. *MEW.*

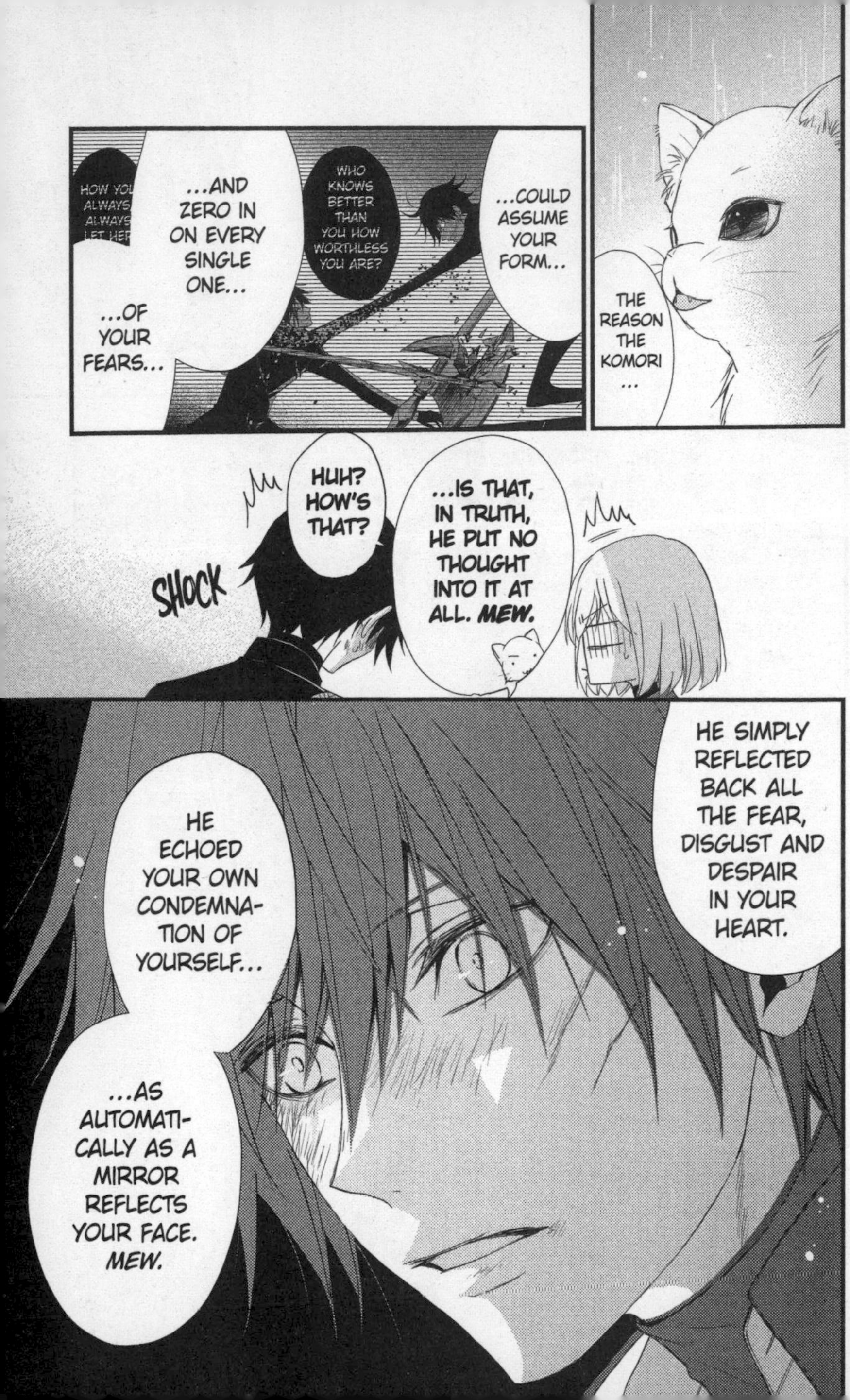
THE REASON THE KOMORI ...
...COULD ASSUME YOUR FORM...
WHO KNOWS BETTER THAN YOU HOW WORTHLESS YOU ARE?
...AND ZERO IN ON EVERY SINGLE ONE...
...OF YOUR FEARS...
HOW YOU ALWAYS ALWAYS LET HER
...IS THAT, IN TRUTH, HE PUT NO THOUGHT INTO IT AT ALL. MEW.
HUH? HOW'S THAT?
SHOCK
HE SIMPLY REFLECTED BACK ALL THE FEAR, DISGUST AND DESPAIR IN YOUR HEART.
HE ECHOED YOUR OWN CONDEMNATION OF YOURSELF...
...AS AUTOMATICALLY AS A MIRROR REFLECTS YOUR FACE. MEW.

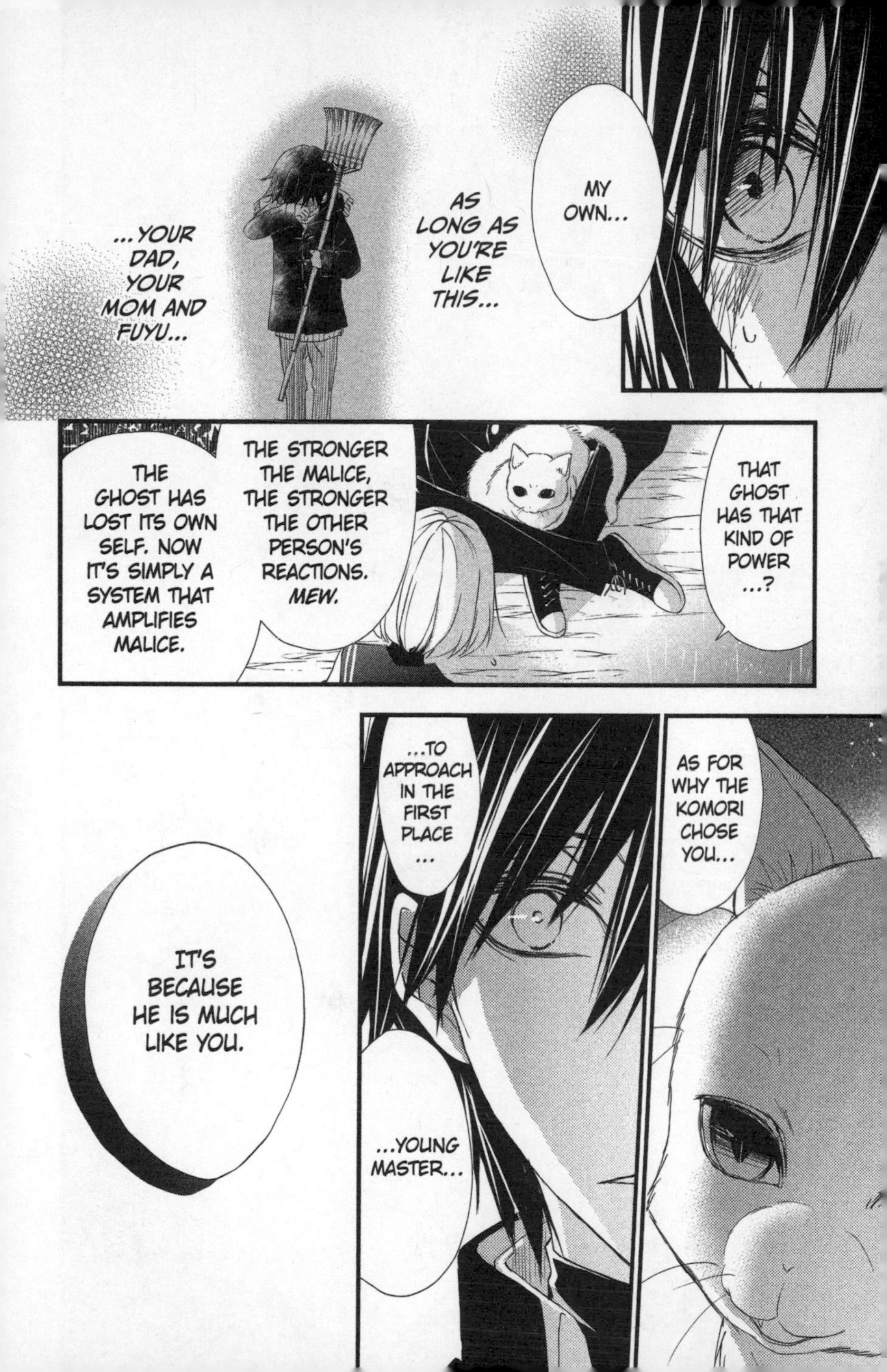
MY OWN...
AS LONG AS YOU'RE LIKE THIS...
...YOUR DAD, YOUR MOM AND FUYU...
THAT GHOST HAS THAT KIND OF POWER ...?
THE STRONGER THE MALICE, THE STRONGER THE OTHER PERSON'S REACTIONS. MEW.
THE GHOST HAS LOST ITS OWN SELF. NOW IT'S SIMPLY A SYSTEM THAT AMPLIFIES MALICE.
AS FOR WHY THE KOMORI CHOSE YOU...
...TO APPROACH IN THE FIRST PLACE ...
...YOUNG MASTER...
IT'S BECAUSE HE IS MUCH LIKE YOU.

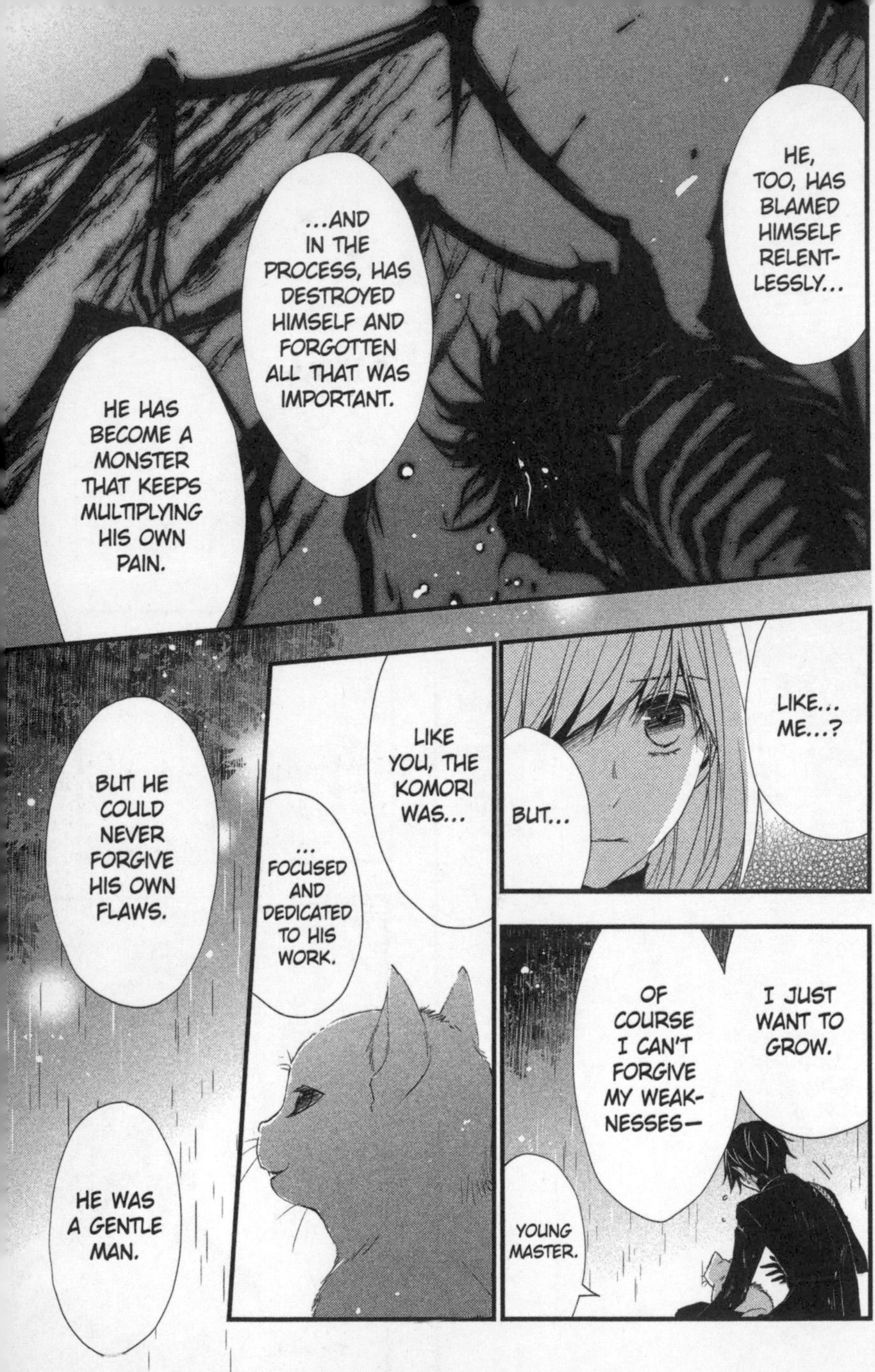
HE, TOO, HAS BLAMED HIMSELF RELENT-LESSLY...
...AND IN THE PROCESS, HAS DESTROYED HIMSELF AND FORGOTTEN ALL THAT WAS IMPORTANT.
HE HAS BECOME A MONSTER THAT KEEPS MULTIPLYING HIS OWN PAIN.
LIKE... ME...?
BUT...
I JUST WANT TO GROW.
OF COURSE I CAN'T FORGIVE MY WEAK-NESSES—
YOUNG MASTER.
LIKE YOU, THE KOMORI WAS...
...FOCUSED AND DEDICATED TO HIS WORK.
BUT HE COULD NEVER FORGIVE HIS OWN FLAWS.
HE WAS A GENTLE MAN.

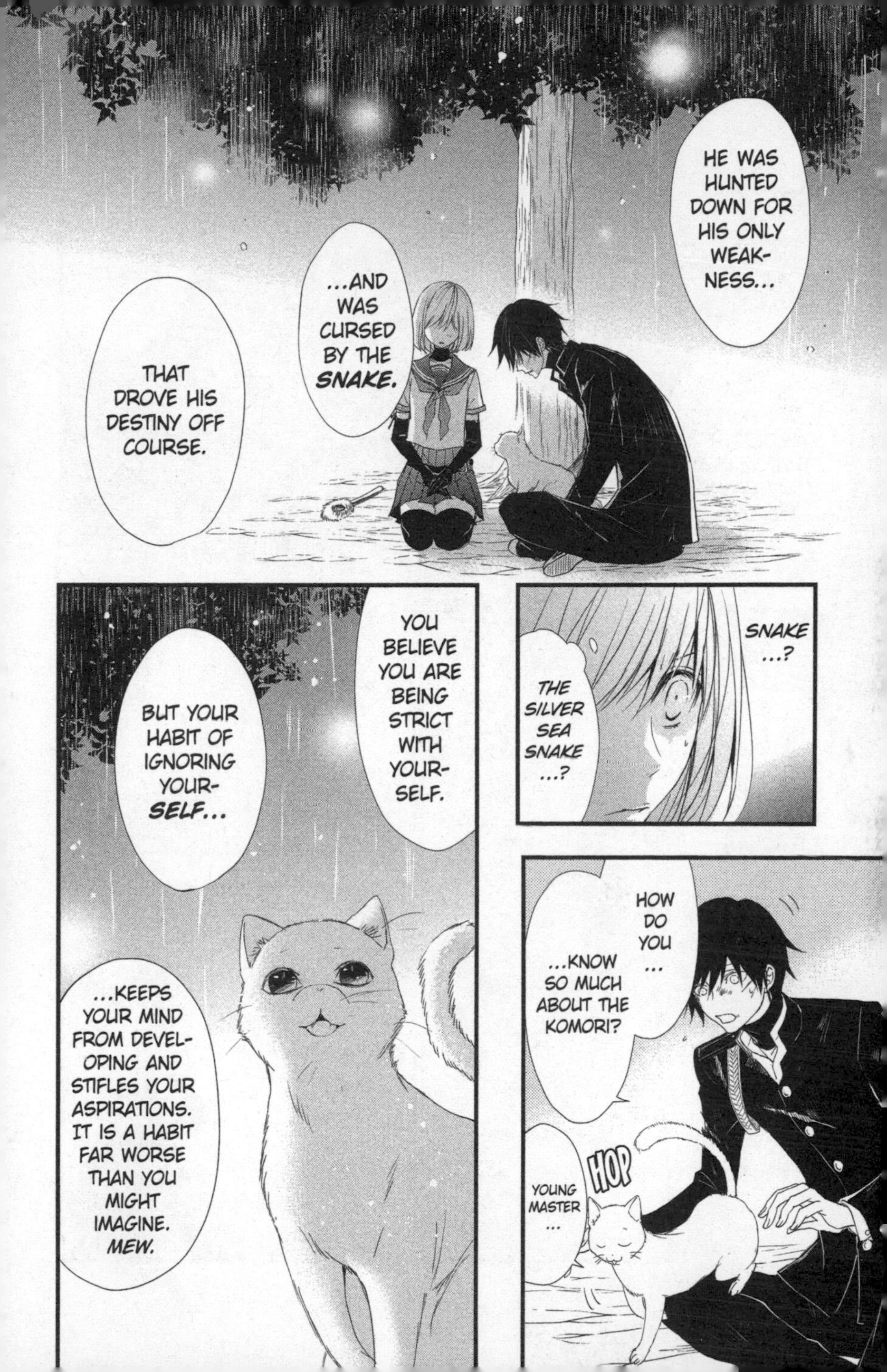
HE WAS HUNTED DOWN FOR HIS ONLY WEAKNESS...
...AND WAS CURSED BY THE *SNAKE.*
THAT DROVE HIS DESTINY OFF COURSE.
SNAKE ...?
THE SILVER SEA SNAKE ...?
HOW DO YOU ...
...KNOW SO MUCH ABOUT THE KOMORI?
HOP
YOUNG MASTER ...
YOU BELIEVE YOU ARE BEING STRICT WITH YOURSELF.
BUT YOUR HABIT OF IGNORING YOUR*SELF...*
...KEEPS YOUR MIND FROM DEVELOPING AND STIFLES YOUR ASPIRATIONS. IT IS A HABIT FAR WORSE THAN YOU MIGHT IMAGINE. *MEW.*

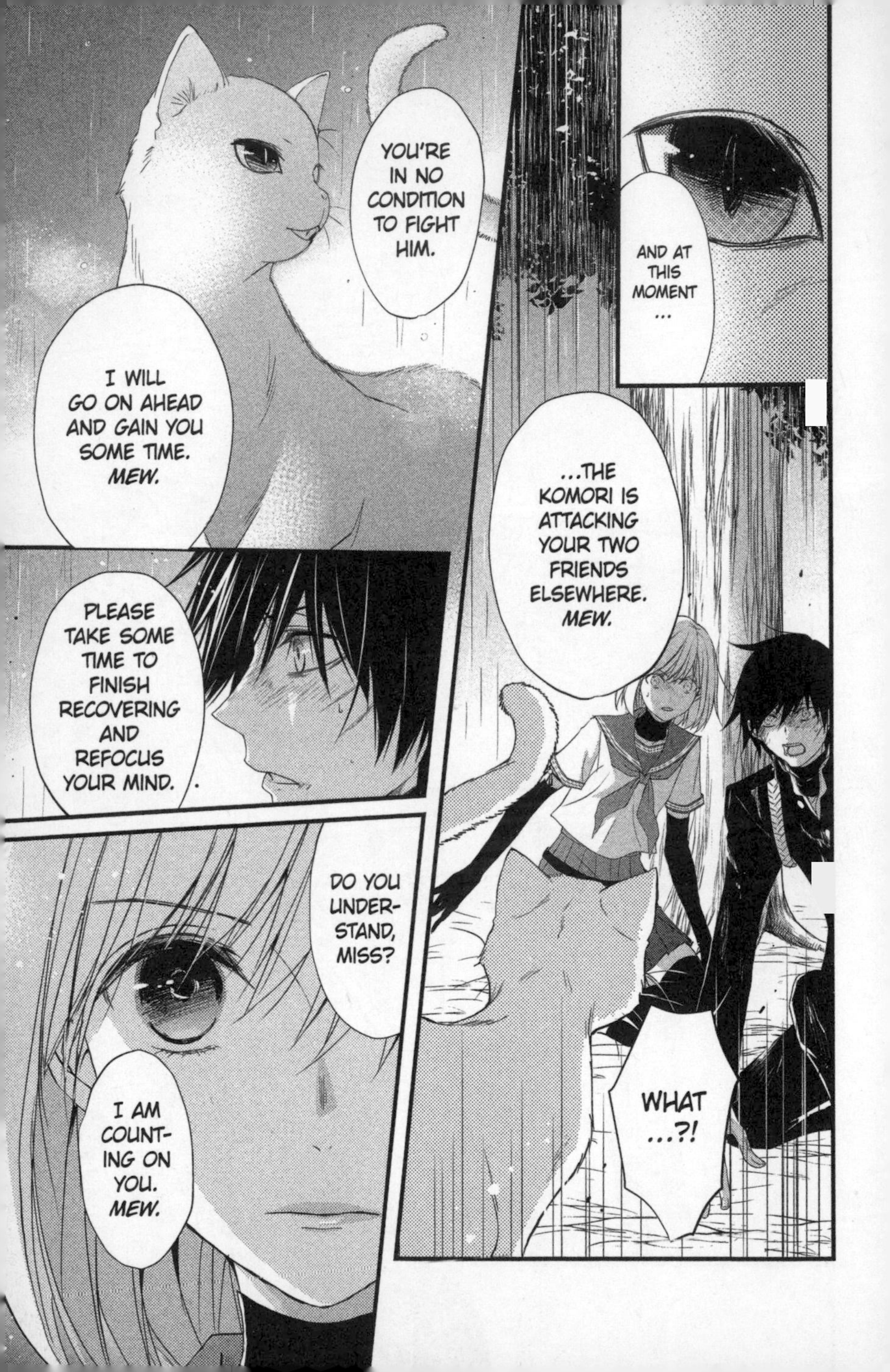
AND AT THIS MOMENT...
...THE KOMORI IS ATTACKING YOUR TWO FRIENDS ELSEWHERE. MEW.
WHAT...?!
YOU'RE IN NO CONDITION TO FIGHT HIM.
I WILL GO ON AHEAD AND GAIN YOU SOME TIME. MEW.
PLEASE TAKE SOME TIME TO FINISH RECOVERING AND REFOCUS YOUR MIND.
DO YOU UNDER-STAND, MISS?
I AM COUNT-ING ON YOU. MEW.

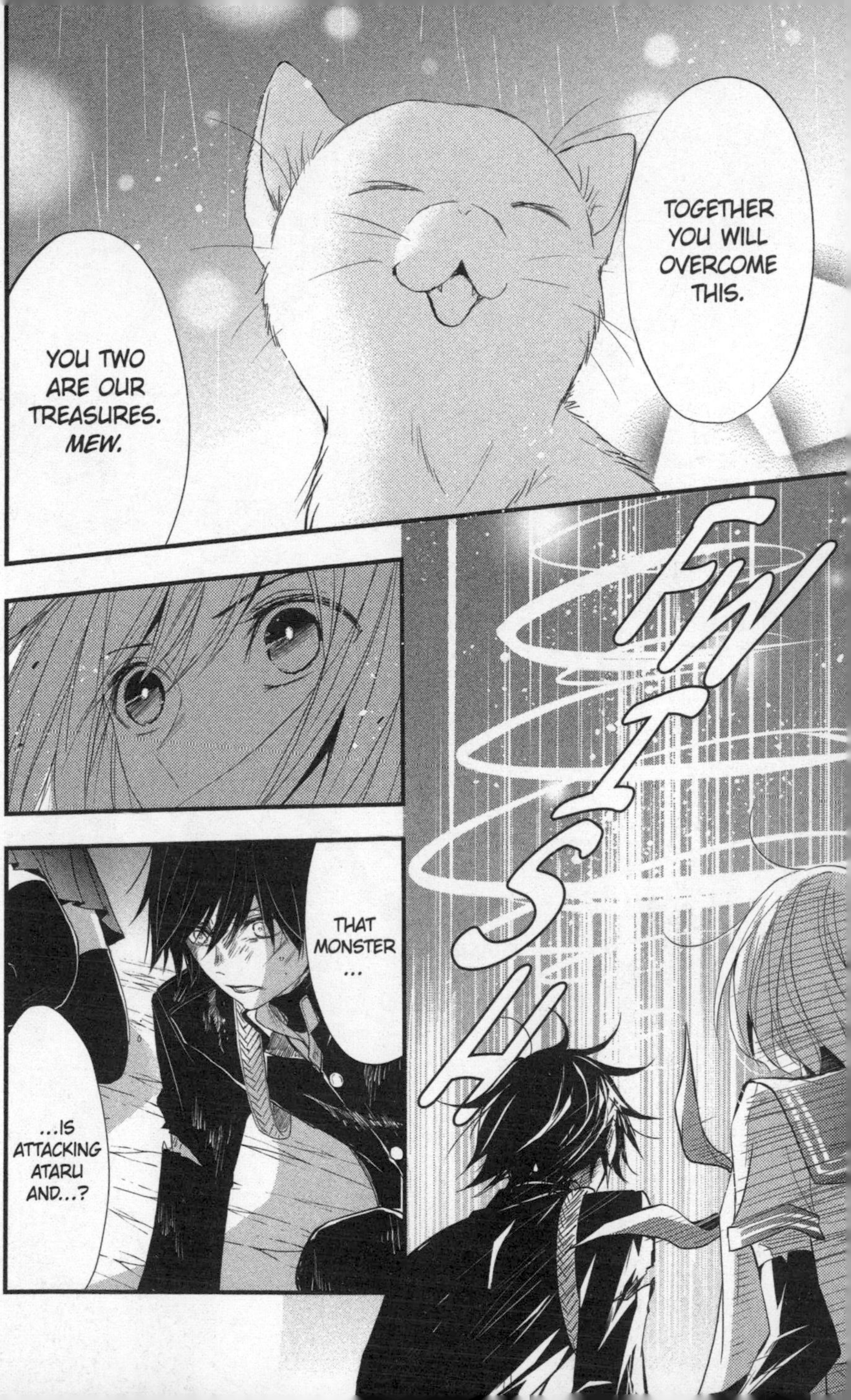
TOGETHER YOU WILL OVERCOME THIS.
YOU TWO ARE OUR TREASURES. *MEW.*
FWISH
THAT MONSTER...
...IS ATTACKING ATARU AND...?

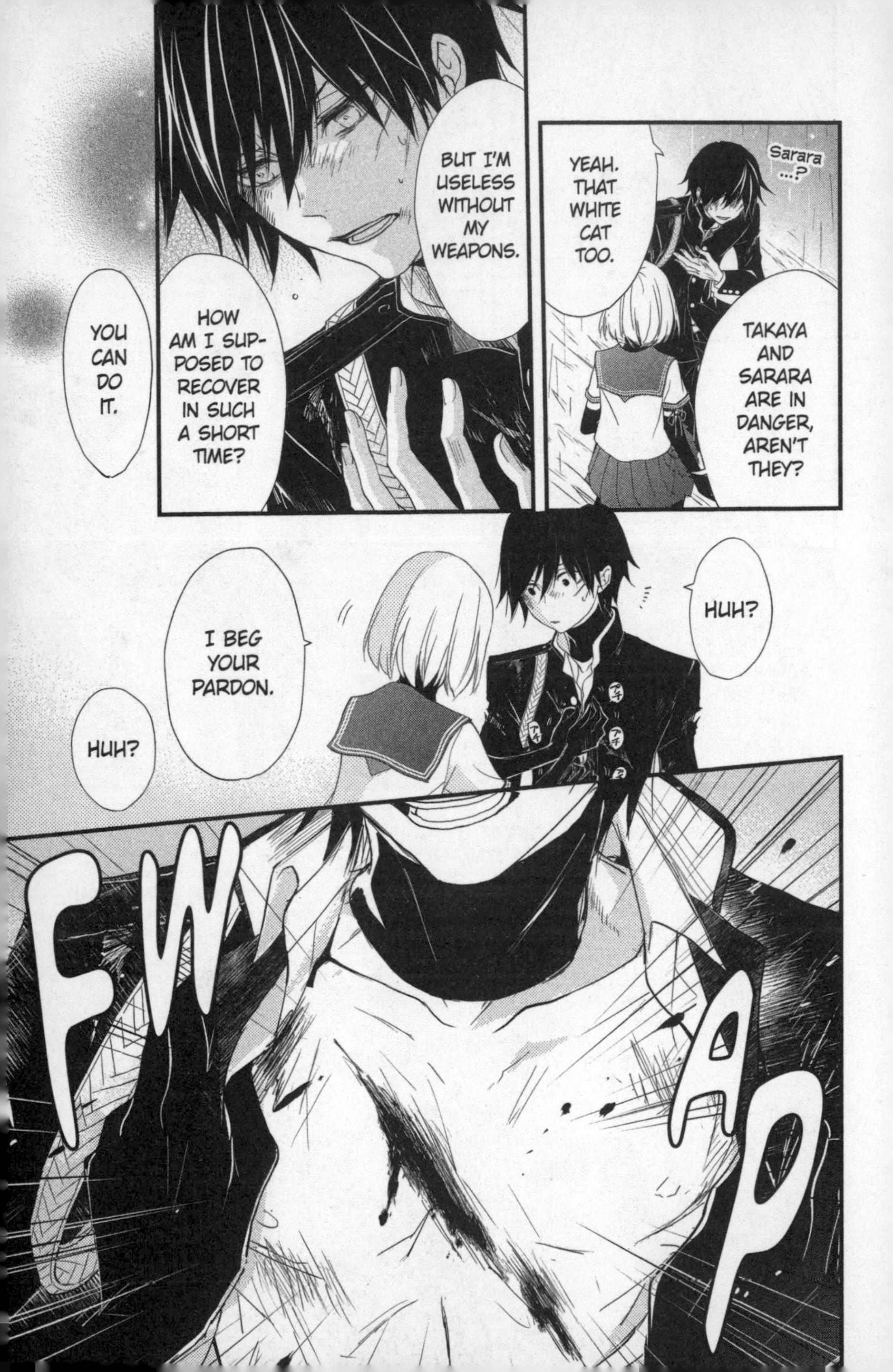

Sarara ...?
TAKAYA AND SARARA ARE IN DANGER, AREN'T THEY?
YEAH. THAT WHITE CAT TOO.
BUT I'M USELESS WITHOUT MY WEAPONS.
HOW AM I SUP-POSED TO RECOVER IN SUCH A SHORT TIME?
YOU CAN DO IT.
HUH?
I BEG YOUR PARDON.
HUH?
FWAP

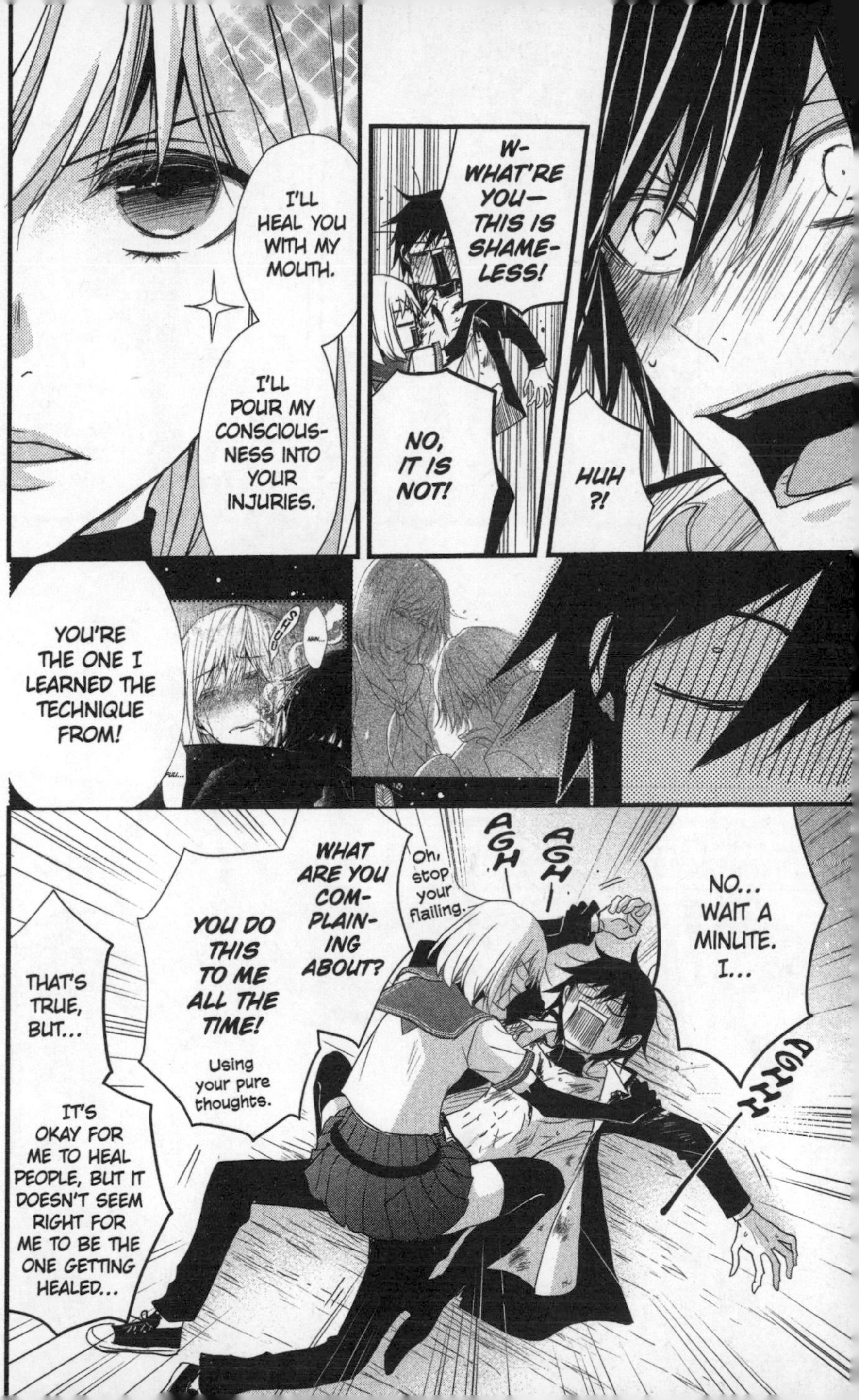
HUH?!
W-WHAT'RE YOU—THIS IS SHAMELESS!
NO, IT IS NOT!
I'LL HEAL YOU WITH MY MOUTH.
I'LL POUR MY CONSCIOUSNESS INTO YOUR INJURIES.
SHUU
NNN...
YOU'RE THE ONE I LEARNED THE TECHNIQUE FROM!
AGH AGH—
NO... WAIT A MINUTE. I...
AGHHH
Oh, stop your flailing.
WHAT ARE YOU COMPLAINING ABOUT?
YOU DO THIS TO ME ALL THE TIME!
Using your pure thoughts.
THAT'S TRUE, BUT...
IT'S OKAY FOR ME TO HEAL PEOPLE, BUT IT DOESN'T SEEM RIGHT FOR ME TO BE THE ONE GETTING HEALED...

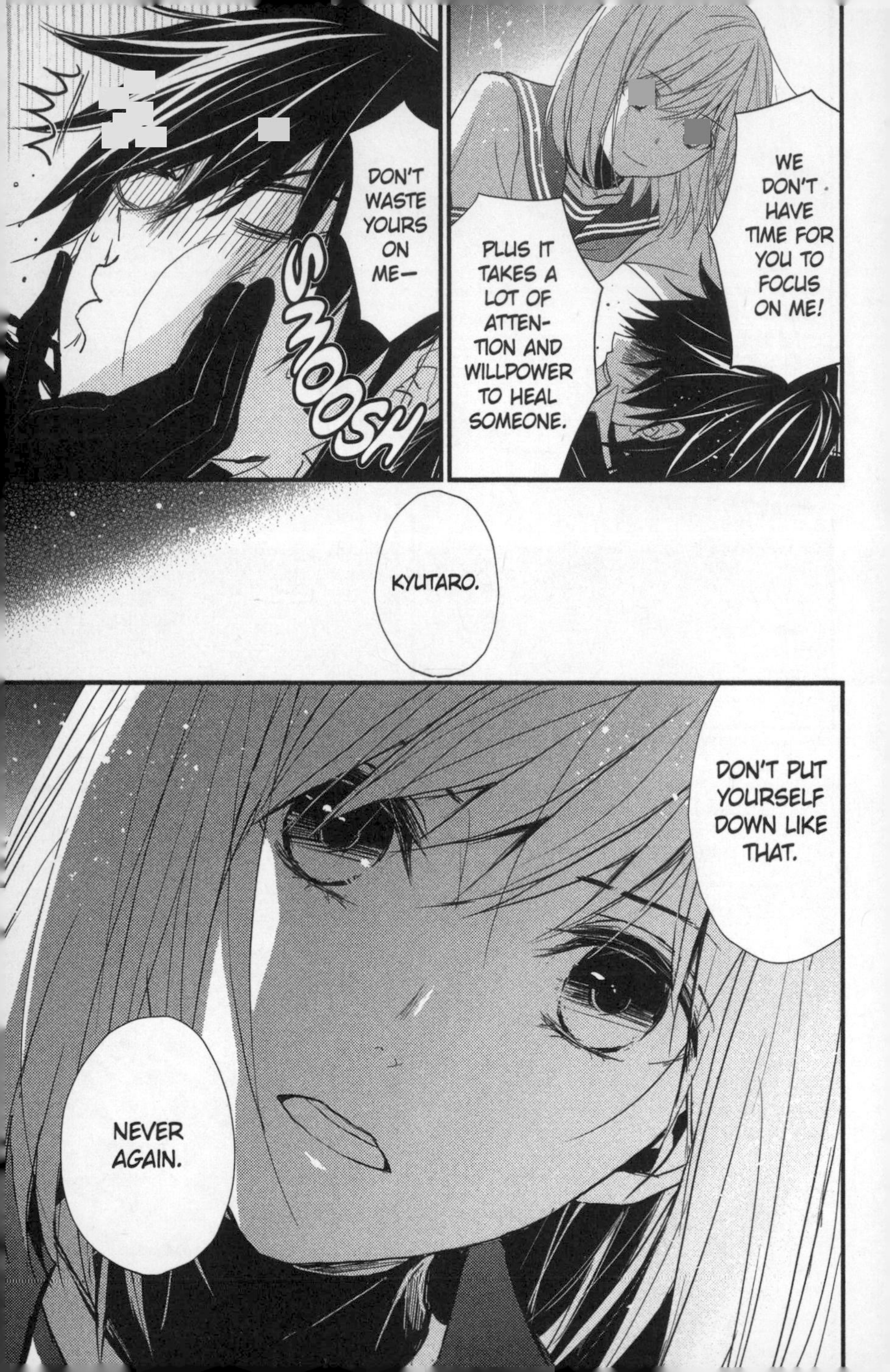
WE DON'T HAVE TIME FOR YOU TO FOCUS ON ME!
PLUS IT TAKES A LOT OF ATTEN-TION AND WILLPOWER TO HEAL SOMEONE.
DON'T WASTE YOURS ON ME—
SMOOSH
KYUTARO.
DON'T PUT YOURSELF DOWN LIKE THAT.
NEVER AGAIN.

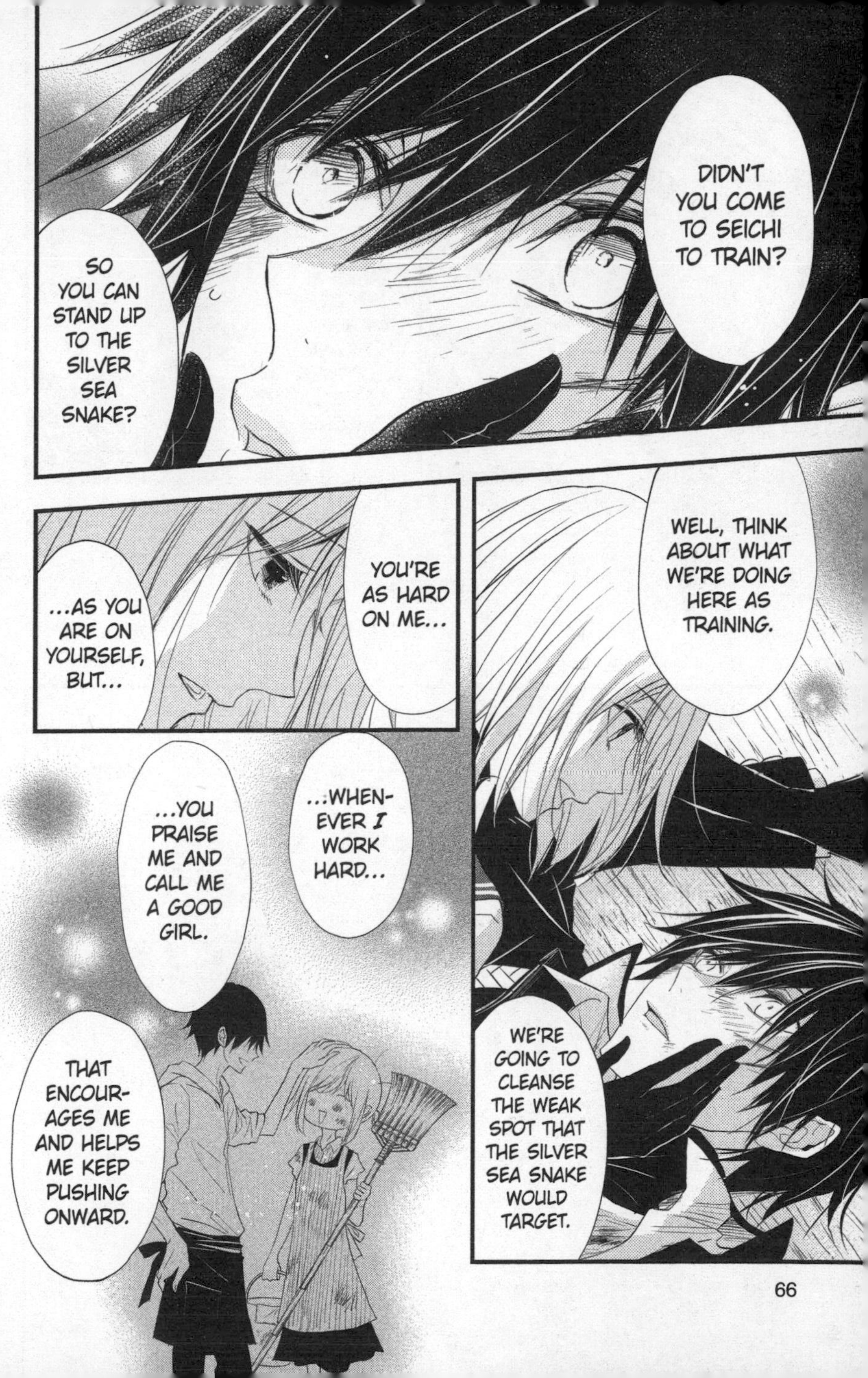
DIDN'T YOU COME TO SEICHI TO TRAIN?
SO YOU CAN STAND UP TO THE SILVER SEA SNAKE?
WELL, THINK ABOUT WHAT WE'RE DOING HERE AS TRAINING.
WE'RE GOING TO CLEANSE THE WEAK SPOT THAT THE SILVER SEA SNAKE WOULD TARGET.
YOU'RE AS HARD ON ME...
...AS YOU ARE ON YOURSELF, BUT...
...WHEN-EVER *I* WORK HARD...
...YOU PRAISE ME AND CALL ME A GOOD GIRL.
THAT ENCOUR-AGES ME AND HELPS ME KEEP PUSHING ONWARD.

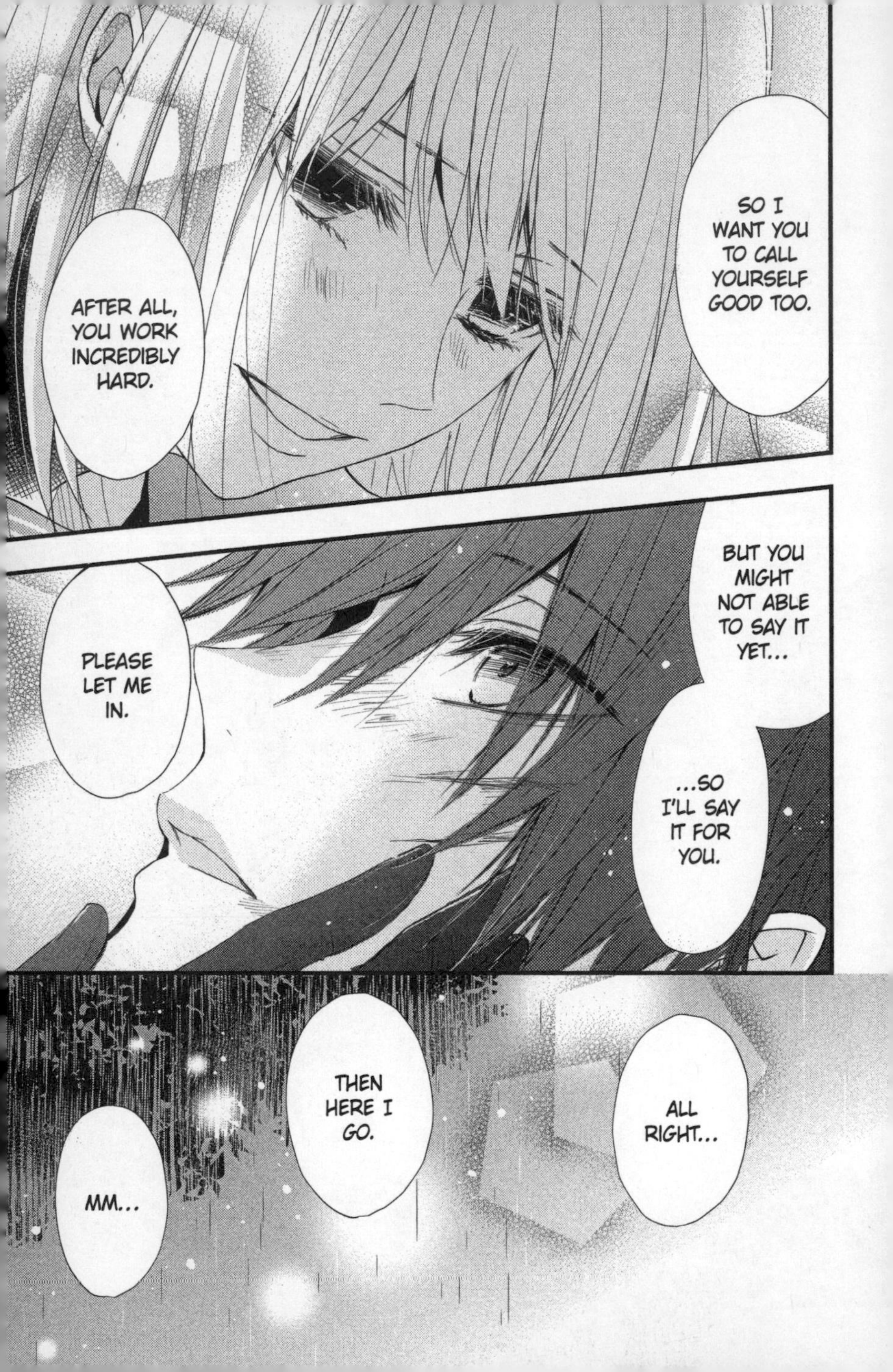
SO I WANT YOU TO CALL YOURSELF GOOD TOO.
AFTER ALL, YOU WORK INCREDIBLY HARD.
BUT YOU MIGHT NOT ABLE TO SAY IT YET...
...SO I'LL SAY IT FOR YOU.
PLEASE LET ME IN.
ALL RIGHT...
THEN HERE I GO.
MM...

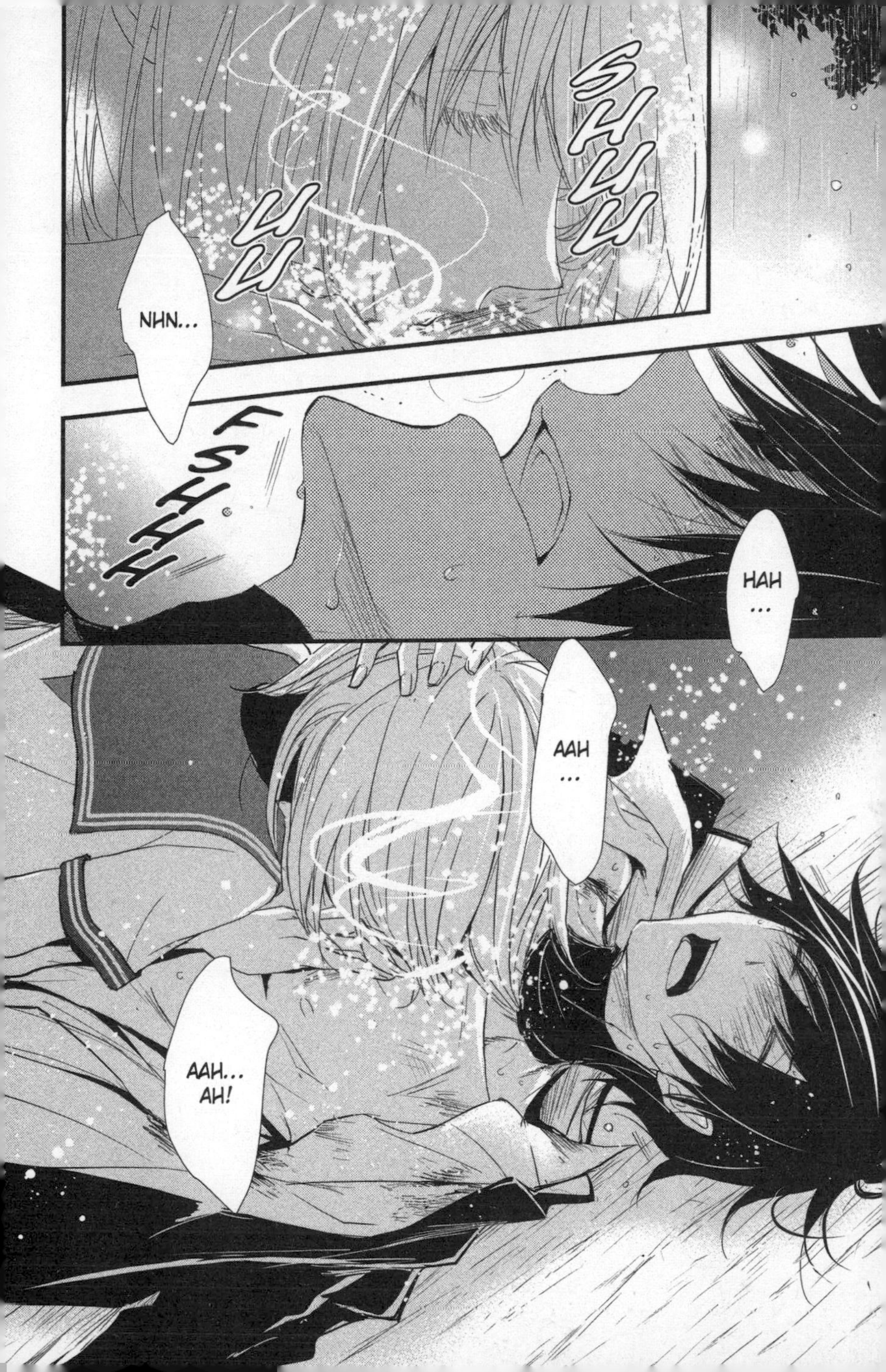
SHUUU
UUU
NHN...
HAH...
FSHHHH
AAH...
AAH... AH!

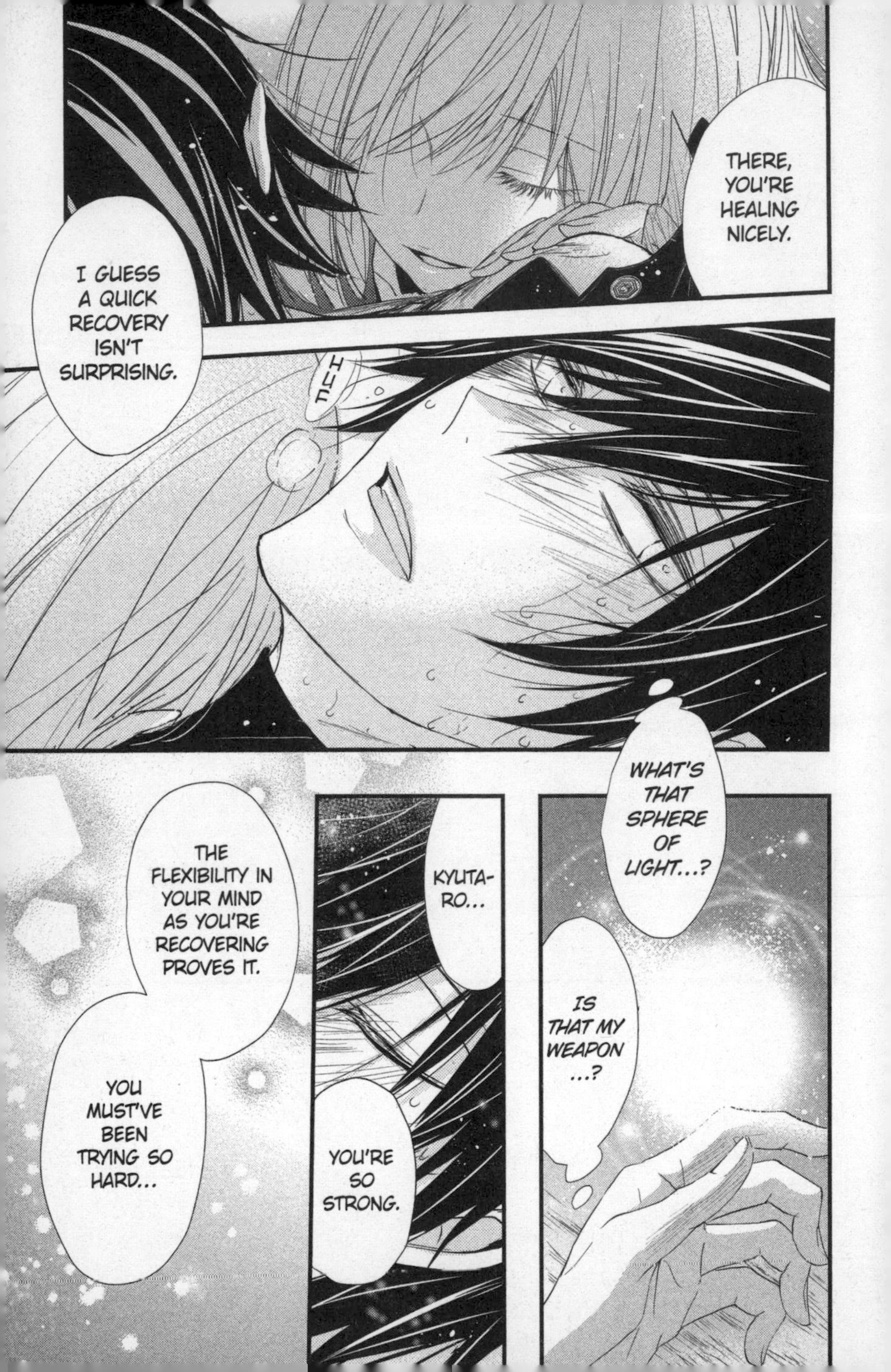
THERE, YOU'RE HEALING NICELY.
I GUESS A QUICK RECOVERY ISN'T SURPRISING.
HUF
WHAT'S THAT SPHERE OF LIGHT...?
IS THAT MY WEAPON ...?
KYUTA-RO...
YOU'RE SO STRONG.
THE FLEXIBILITY IN YOUR MIND AS YOU'RE RECOVERING PROVES IT.
YOU MUST'VE BEEN TRYING SO HARD...

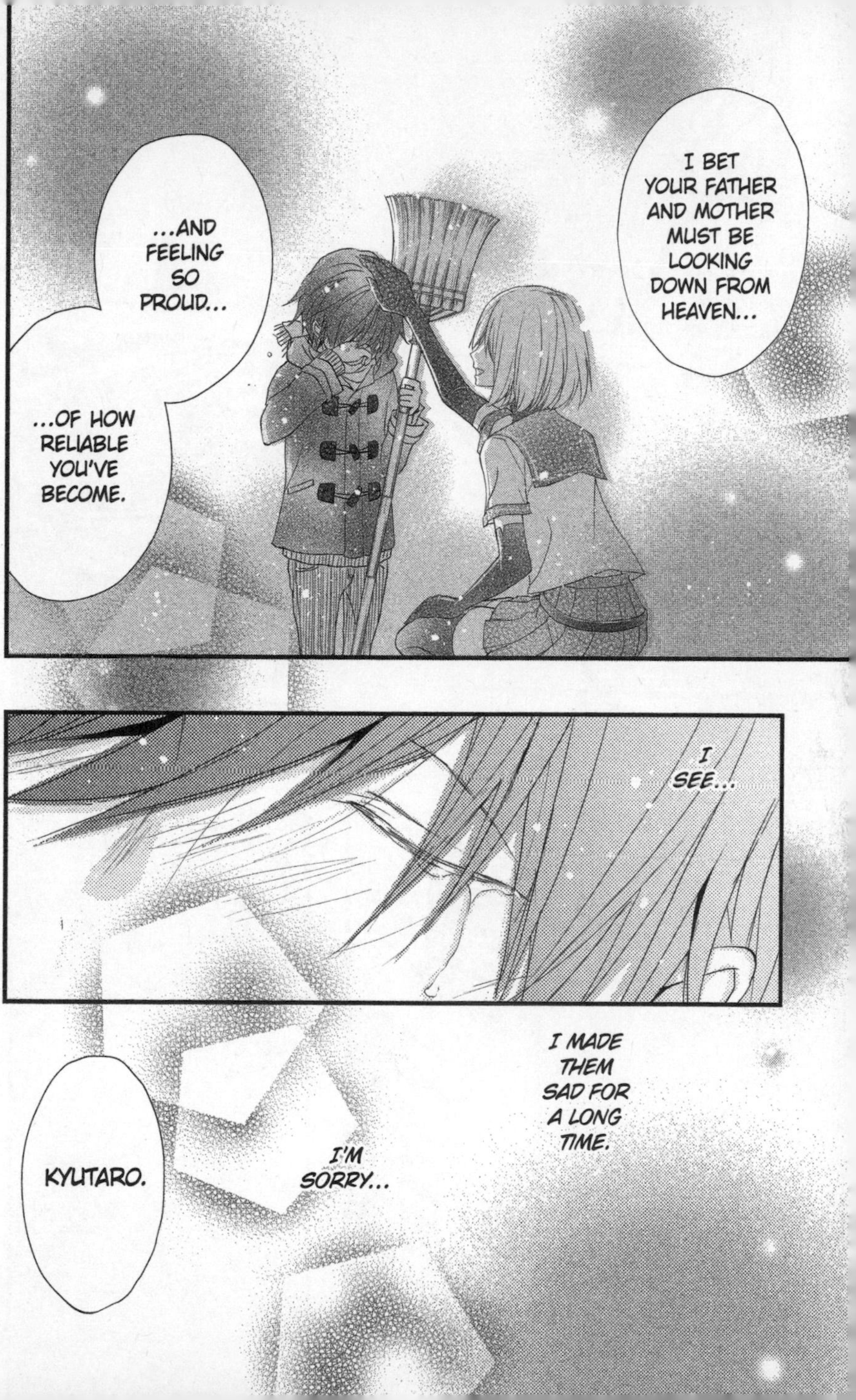
I BET YOUR FATHER AND MOTHER MUST BE LOOKING DOWN FROM HEAVEN...
...AND FEELING SO PROUD...
...OF HOW RELIABLE YOU'VE BECOME.
I SEE...
I MADE THEM SAD FOR A LONG TIME.
I'M SORRY...
KYUTARO.

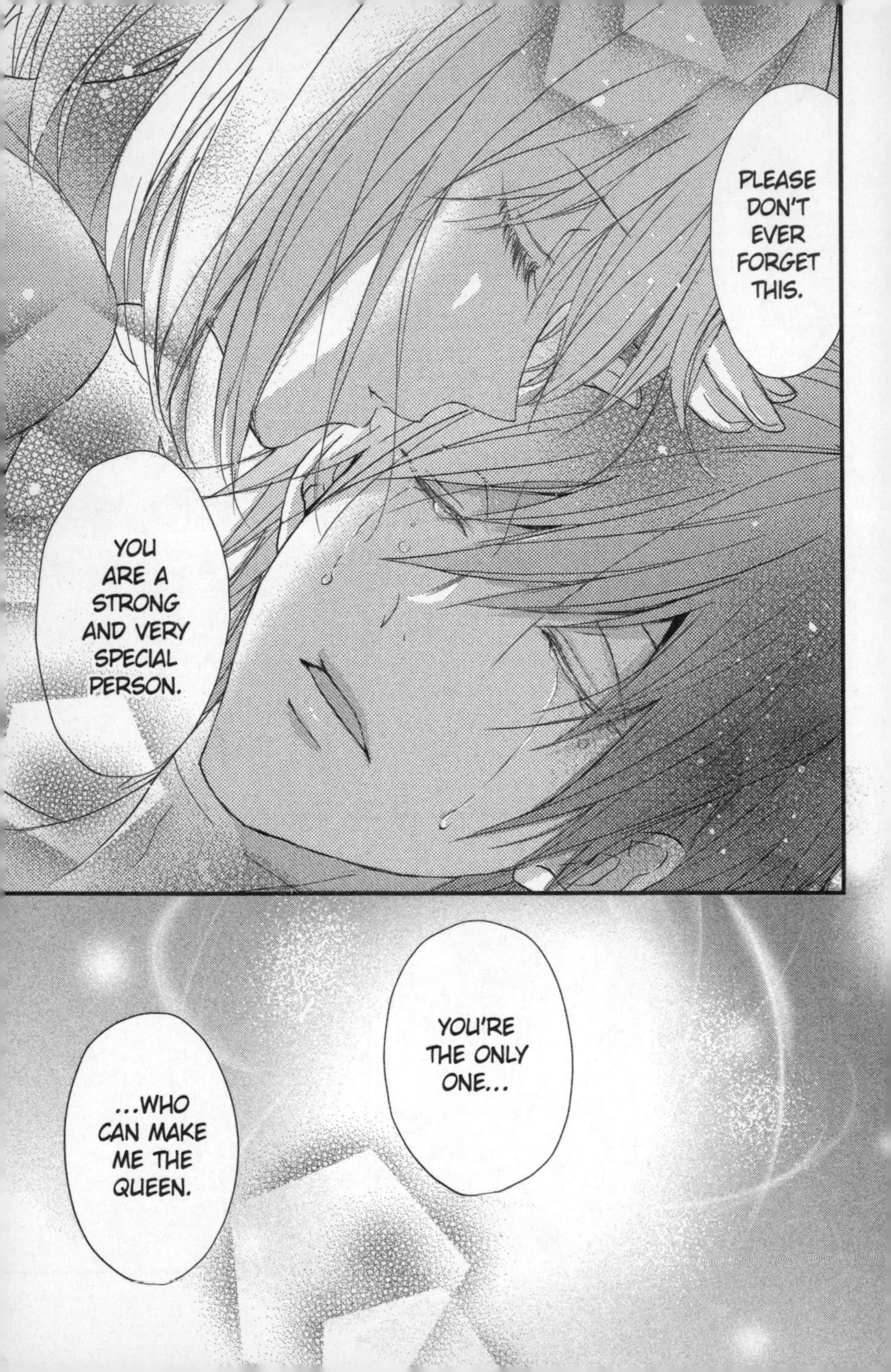
PLEASE DON'T EVER FORGET THIS.
YOU ARE A STRONG AND VERY SPECIAL PERSON.
YOU'RE THE ONLY ONE...
...WHO CAN MAKE ME THE QUEEN.

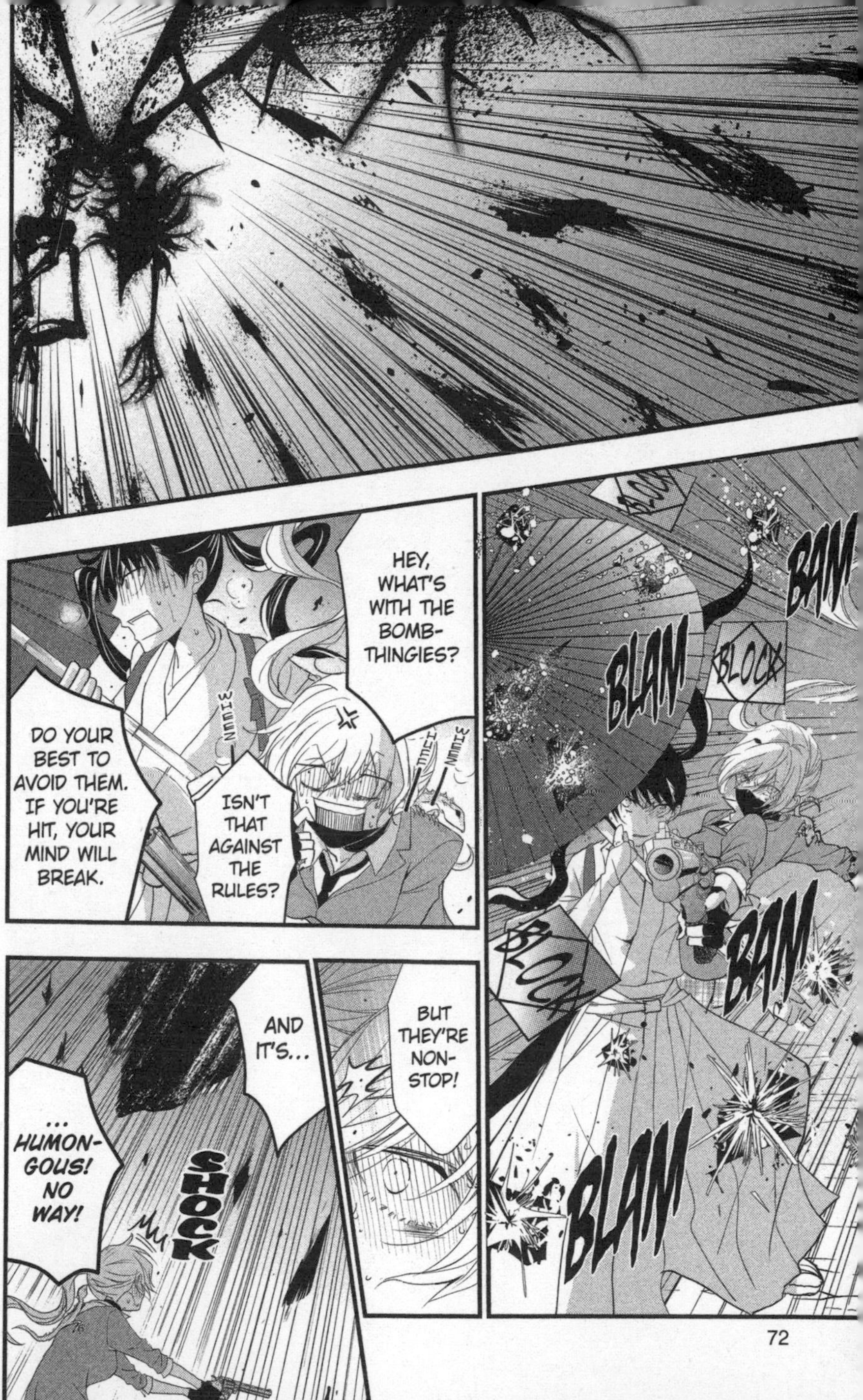
BLOCK
BAM
BLAM
BLOCK
BLOCK
BAM
BLAM
HEY, WHAT'S WITH THE BOMB-THINGIES?
WHEEN
WHEEN
ISN'T THAT AGAINST THE RULES?
DO YOUR BEST TO AVOID THEM. IF YOU'RE HIT, YOUR MIND WILL BREAK.
BUT THEY'RE NON-STOP!
AND IT'S...
...HUMON-GOUS! NO WAY!
SHOCK

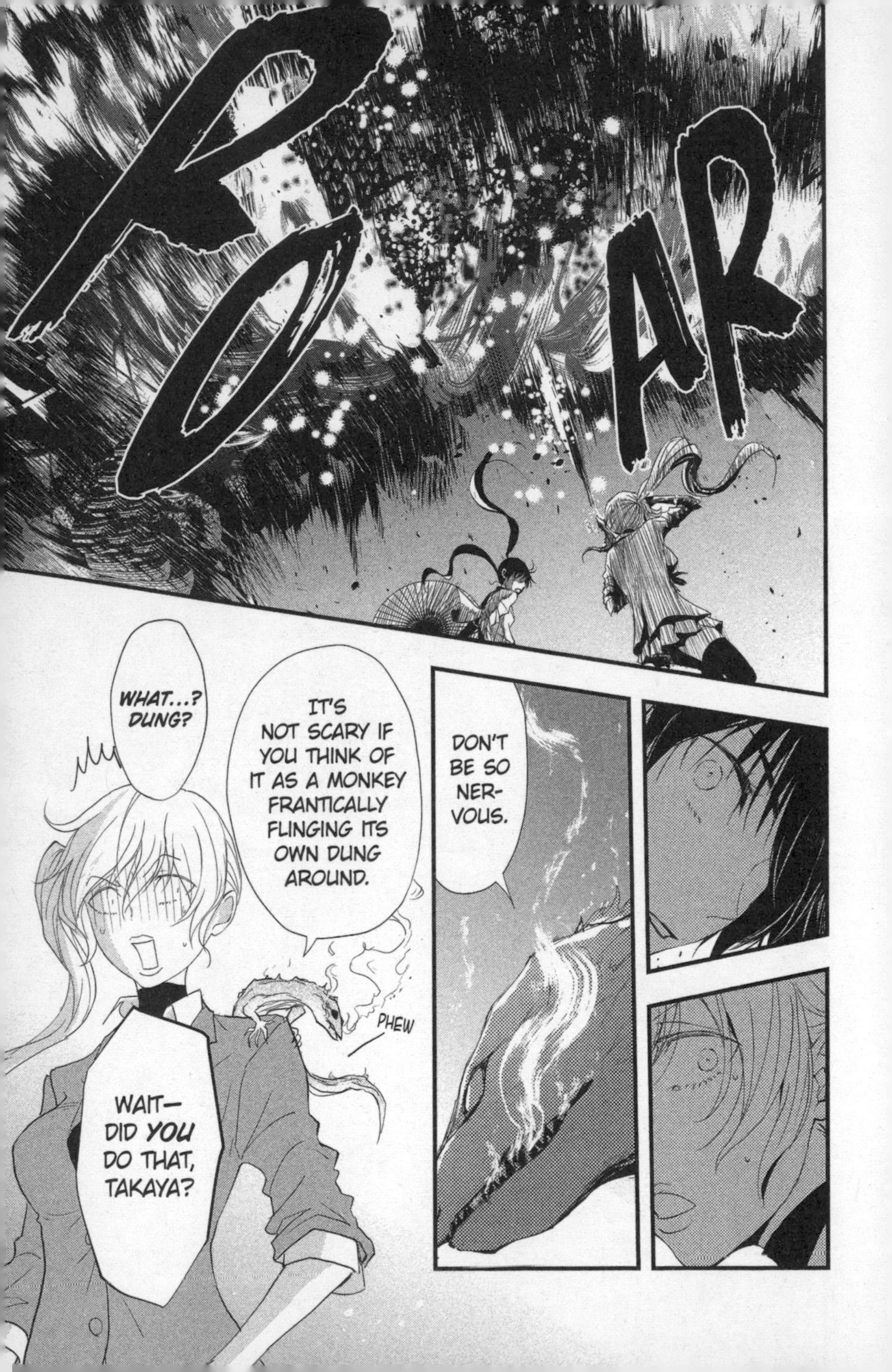
ROAR
DON'T BE SO NER-VOUS.
IT'S NOT SCARY IF YOU THINK OF IT AS A MONKEY FRANTICALLY FLINGING ITS OWN DUNG AROUND.
WHAT...? DUNG?
PHEW
WAIT— DID YOU DO THAT, TAKAYA?

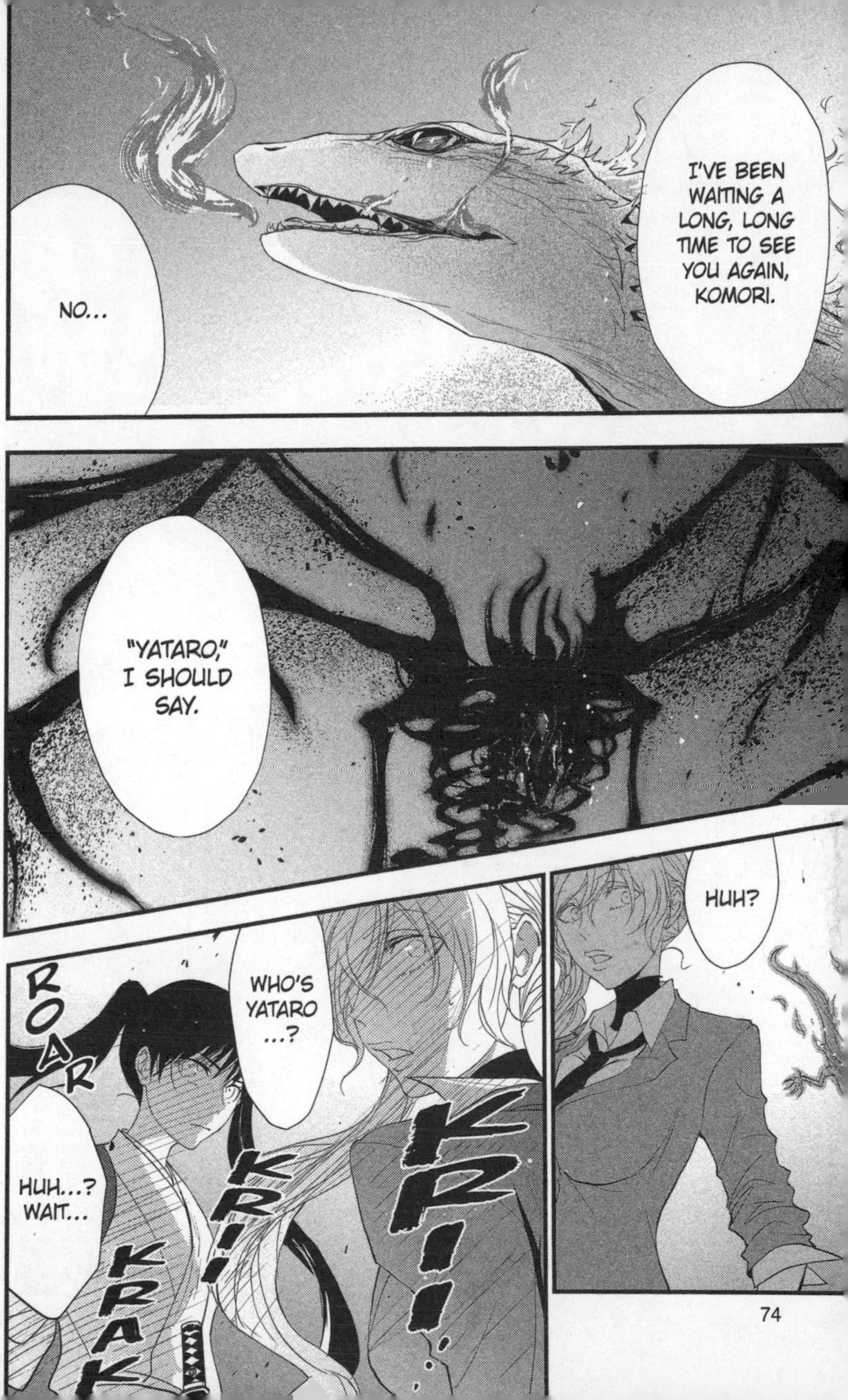
I'VE BEEN WAITING A LONG, LONG TIME TO SEE YOU AGAIN, KOMORI.
NO...
"YATARO," I SHOULD SAY.
HUH?
WHO'S YATARO ...?
ROAR
KRI...
KRI...
HUH...? WAIT...
KRAK
KRAK

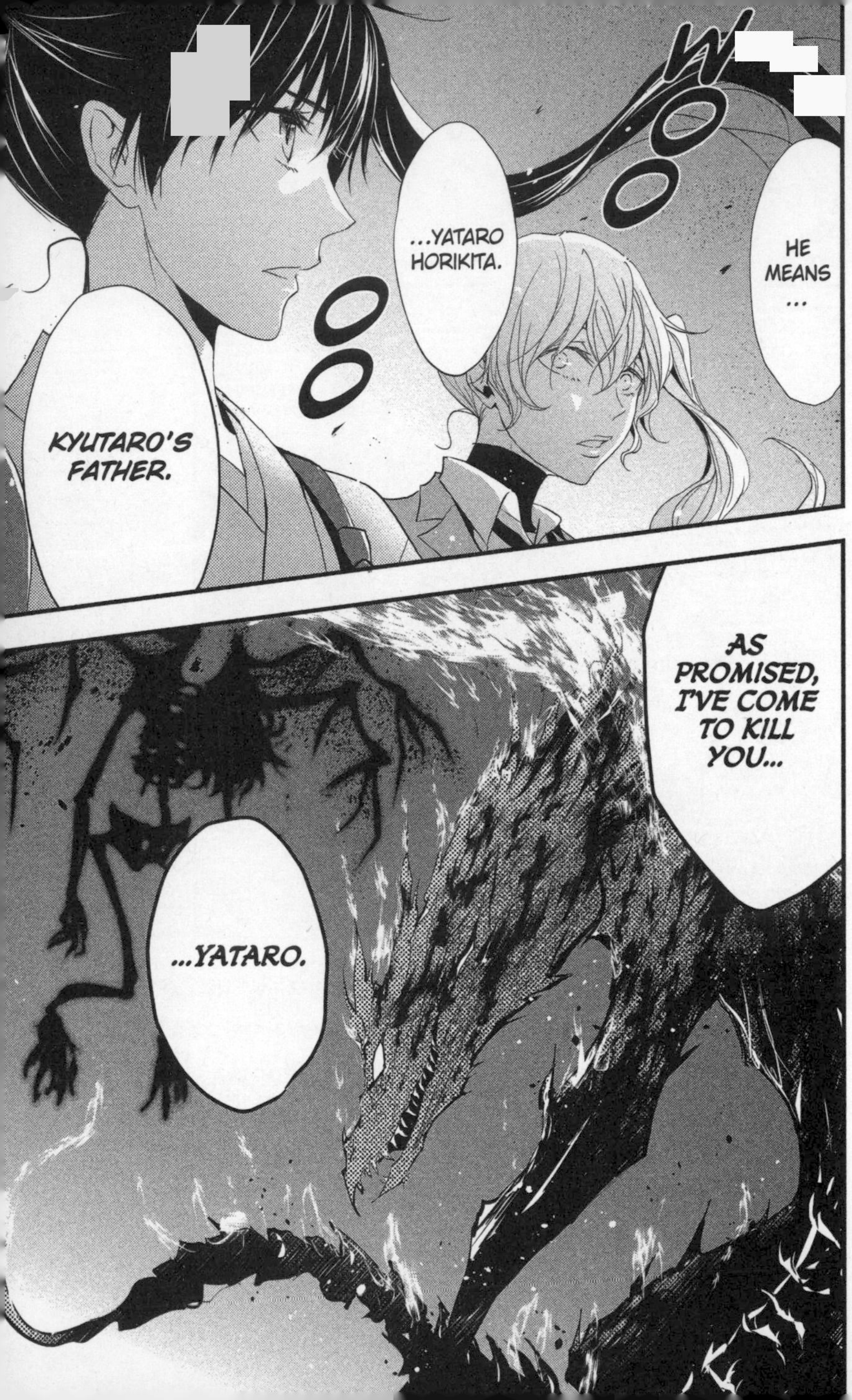
WOOOO
HE MEANS ...
...YATARO HORIKITA.
KYUTARO'S FATHER.
AS PROMISED, I'VE COME TO KILL YOU...
...YATARO.

MONTHLY BETSUCOMI SALE DATE NOTICE ON TWITTER

CHAPTER 33

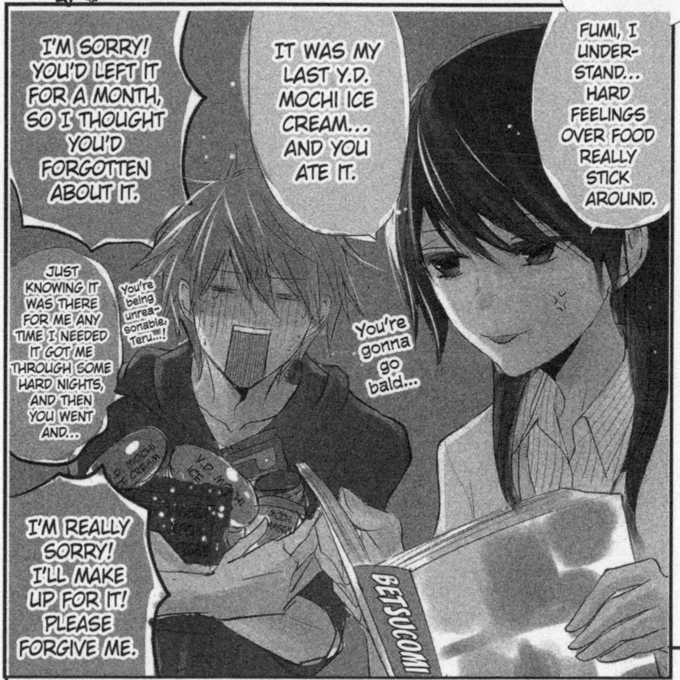
FUMI, I UNDER-STAND... HARD FEELINGS OVER FOOD REALLY STICK AROUND.
IT WAS MY LAST Y.D. MOCHI ICE CREAM... AND YOU ATE IT.
I'M SORRY! YOU'D LEFT IT FOR A MONTH, SO I THOUGHT YOU'D FORGOTTEN ABOUT IT.
You're gonna go bald...
You're being unrea-sonable, Teru...!
JUST KNOWING IT WAS THERE FOR ME ANY TIME I NEEDED IT GOT ME THROUGH SOME HARD NIGHTS, AND THEN YOU WENT AND...
I'M REALLY SORRY! I'LL MAKE UP FOR IT! PLEASE FORGIVE ME.
BETSUCOMI

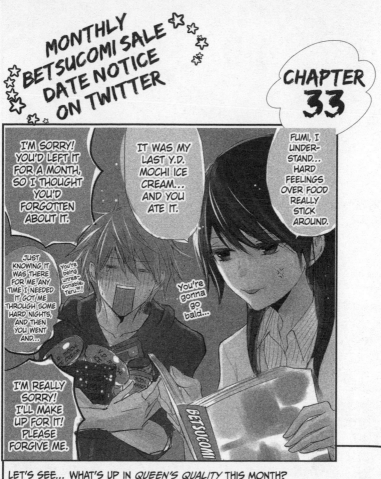

LET'S SEE... WHAT'S UP IN *QUEEN'S QUALITY* THIS MONTH?
(1) THE TWO OF THEM INSIST THAT SHE'S HEALING HIM AND THAT THEY ARE NOT KISSING.
(2) TAKAYA, YOU'RE TOO BIG, SO I CAN'T GET ALL OF YOU IN THE PICTURE! YOU'RE A PAIN TO DRAW.
(3) THIS FIXATION WITH THE BLACK EGG STARTED WITH A TEMPURA RICE BALL. CHAPTER 33 IS BUILT ON THE PREMISE THAT ANYONE CAN FLY THROUGH THE SKY IF THEY REALLY WANT TO.

ONCE AGAIN, WE HAVE KUROSAKI AND TERU FROM *DENGEKI DAISY*. WHEN I DRAW THINGS LIKE THIS ON TWITTER, I'M HAPPY TO SEE THAT THERE ARE STILL PEOPLE WHO ENJOY THEM! (MORE THAN *QUEEQUA* CHARACTERS.) THERE ARE LINE STAMPS AVAILABLE NOW FOR *DAISY* AND *QUEEQUA* CHARACTERS.

LIKE THIS ONE. →

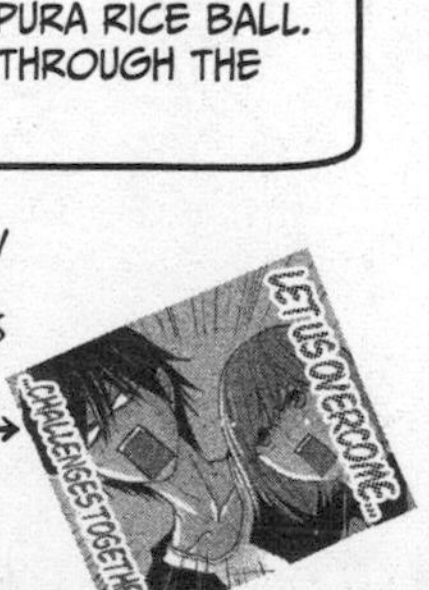
LET US OVERCOME...
...CHALLENGES TOGETHER!!

DO A SEARCH FOR "KYOUSUKE MOTOMI'S FRIENDS WITH EYES ROLLED BACK."

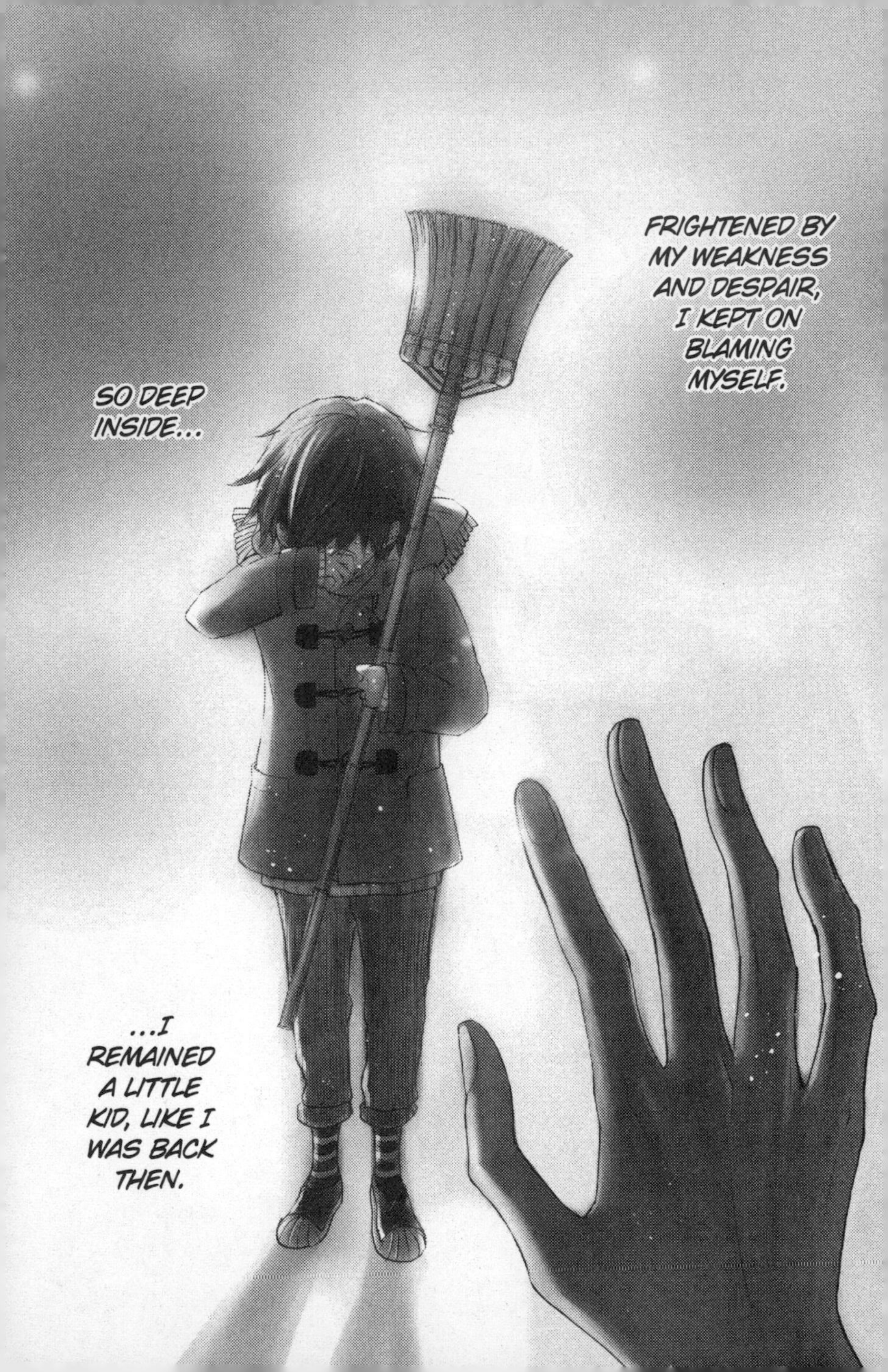
FRIGHTENED BY MY WEAKNESS AND DESPAIR, I KEPT ON BLAMING MYSELF.
SO DEEP INSIDE...
...I REMAINED A LITTLE KID, LIKE I WAS BACK THEN.

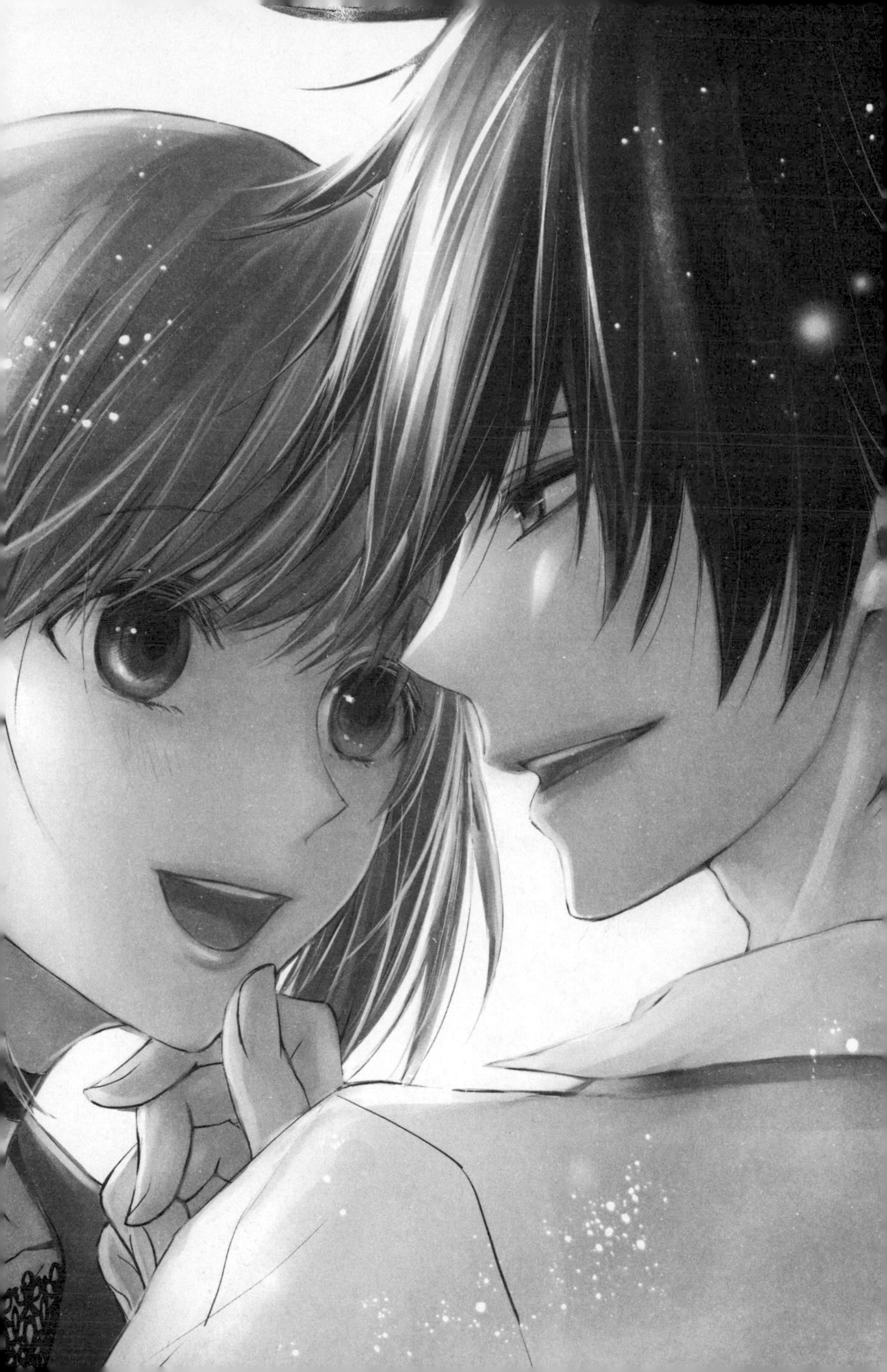

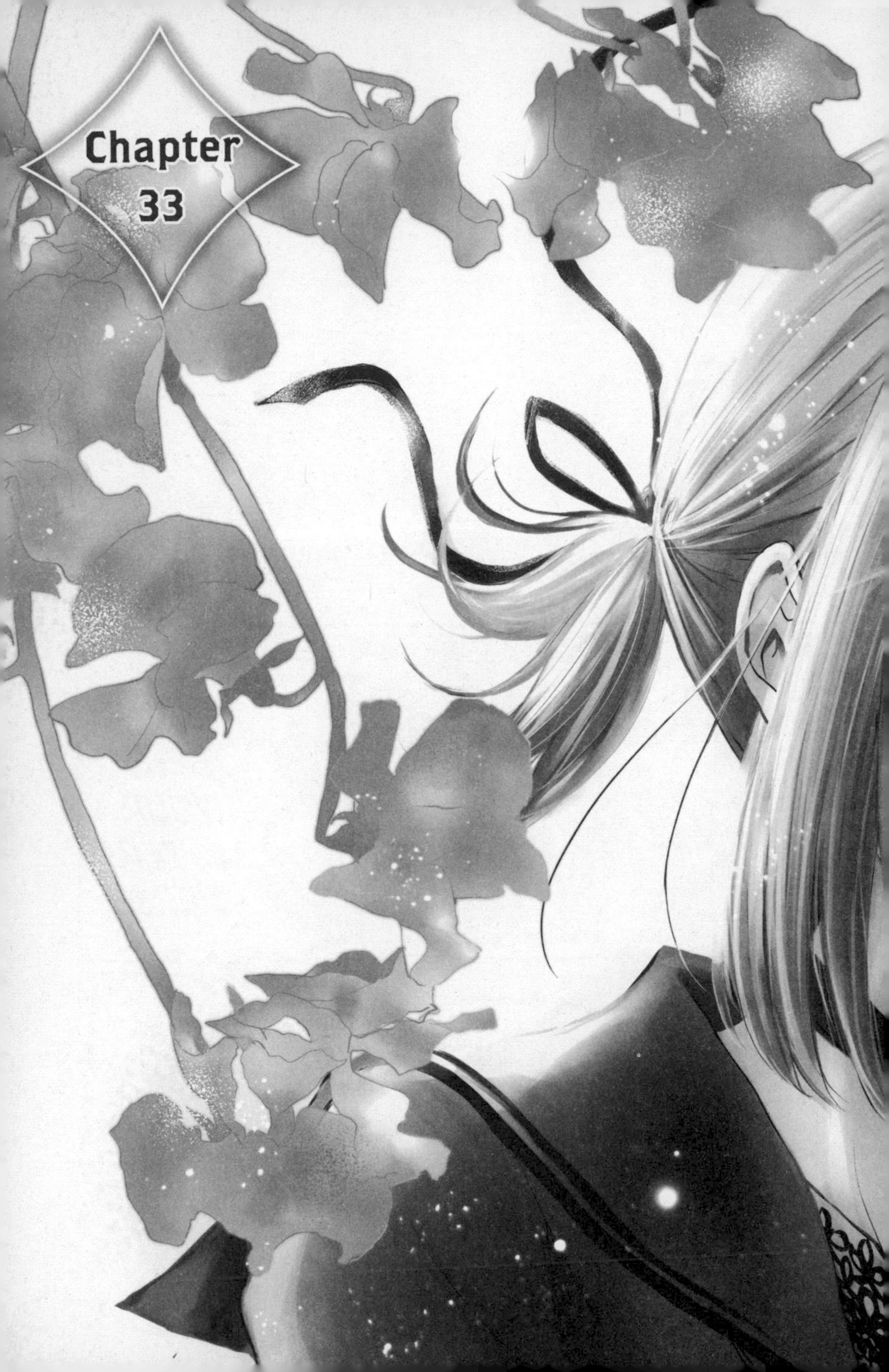
Chapter
33

IT'S EASY! SEND YOUR LETTERS HERE!

KYOUSUKE MOTOMI
C/O QUEEN'S QUALITY EDITOR
VIZ MEDIA
P.O. BOX 77010
SAN FRANCISCO, CA 94107

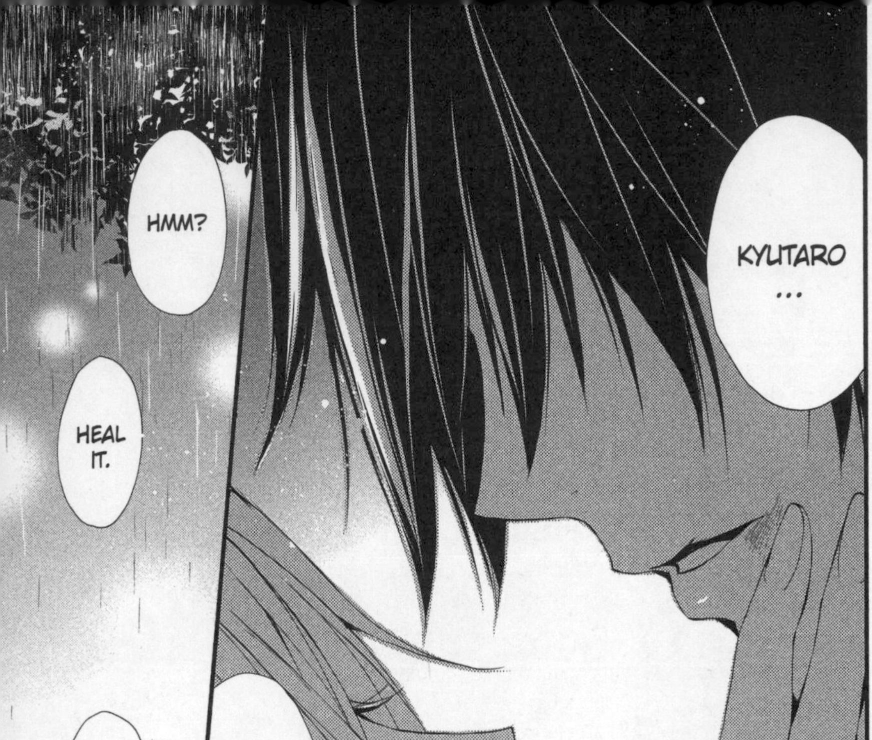
KYUTARO...
HMM?
HEAL IT.
THERE'S ANOTHER INJURY HERE.
OKAY.

During summer 2018, when I was preparing this volume, it was so hot that polishing up the scene where Takaya's covered in flames just made me feel even hotter and more uncomfortable.

I'd always planned for Takaya to turn into a giant lizard, but I think I should have turned him into a marlin or something. Maybe Fumi should have psyched herself up to become a mermaid. No, Kyutaro would have gotten mad.

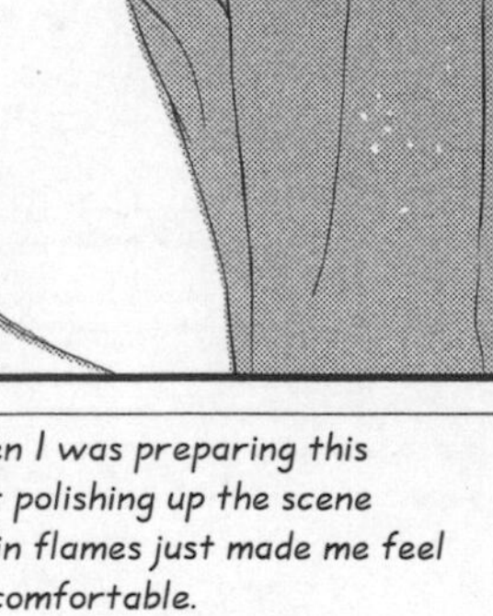
No way...
A fishy-smelling old man wouldn't be popular.

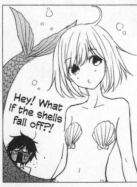

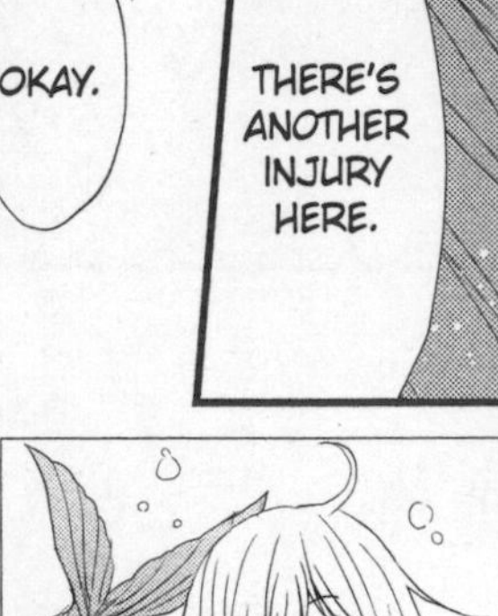
Hey! What if the shells fall off?!

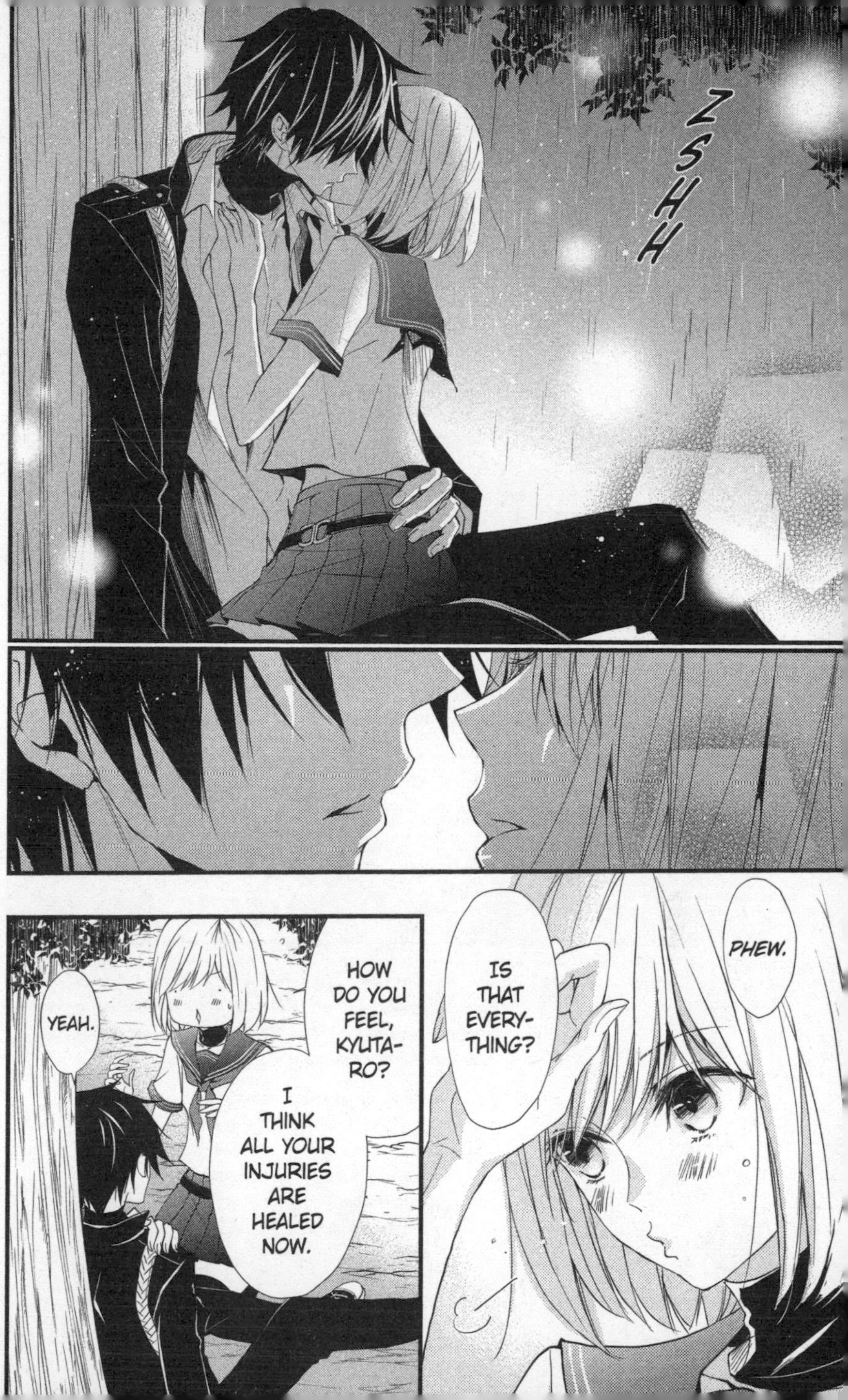
ZSHH
PHEW.
IS THAT EVERYTHING?
HOW DO YOU FEEL, KYUTARO?
I THINK ALL YOUR INJURIES ARE HEALED NOW.
YEAH.

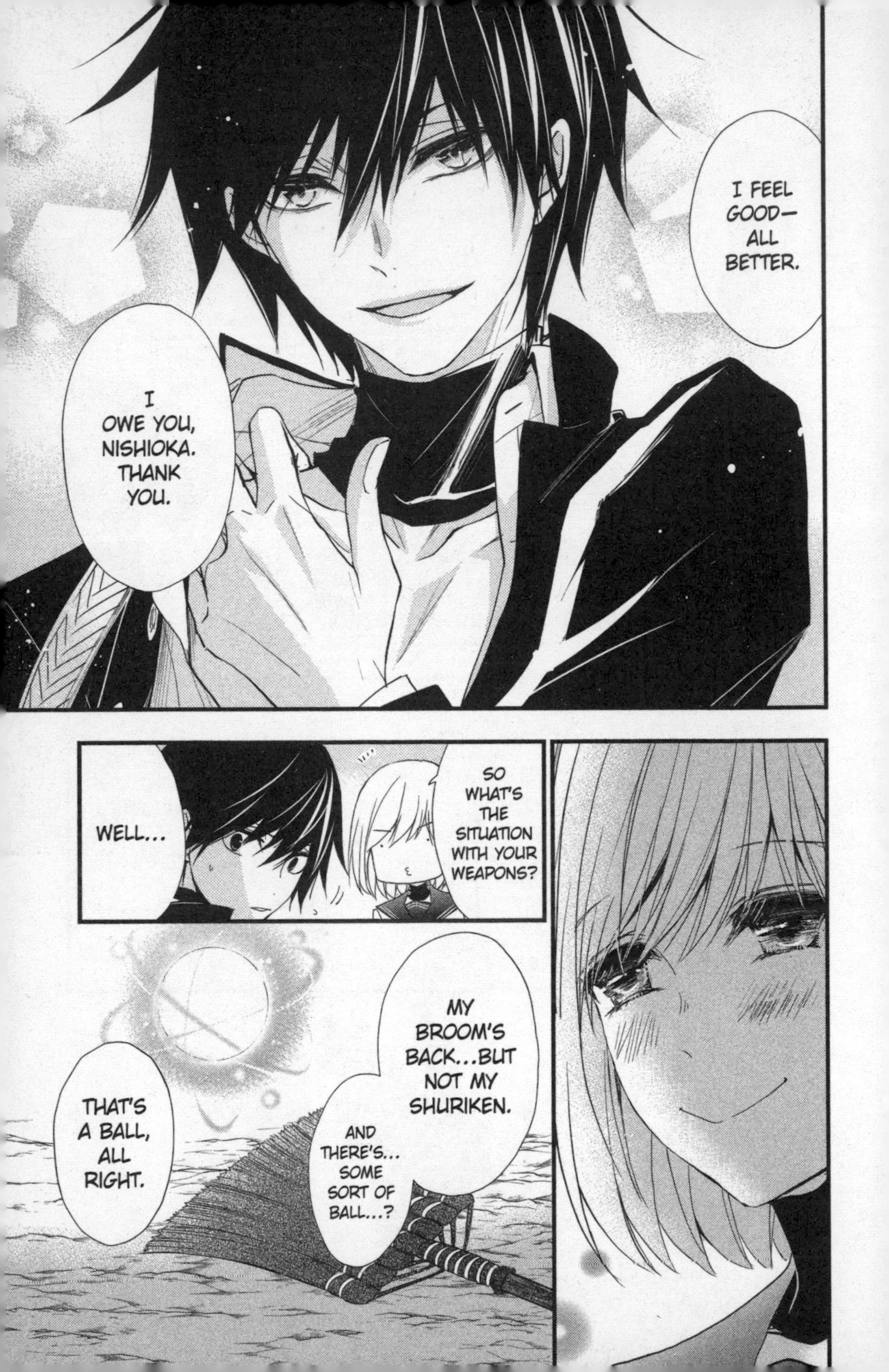
I FEEL GOOD— ALL BETTER.
I OWE YOU, NISHIOKA. THANK YOU.
SO WHAT'S THE SITUATION WITH YOUR WEAPONS?
WELL...
MY BROOM'S BACK...BUT NOT MY SHURIKEN.
AND THERE'S... SOME SORT OF BALL...?
THAT'S A BALL, ALL RIGHT.

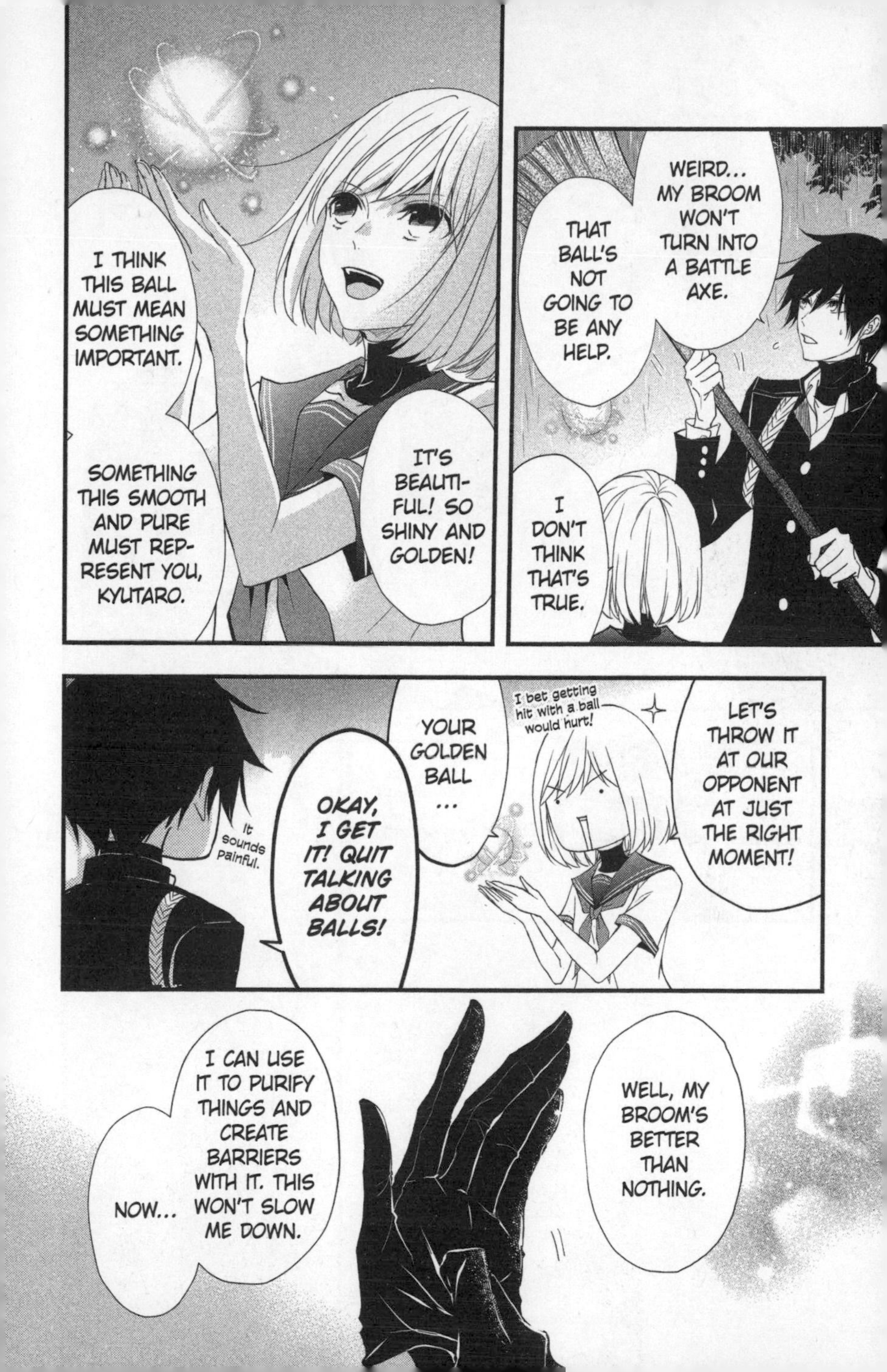
WEIRD... MY BROOM WON'T TURN INTO A BATTLE AXE.
THAT BALL'S NOT GOING TO BE ANY HELP.
I DON'T THINK THAT'S TRUE.
I THINK THIS BALL MUST MEAN SOMETHING IMPORTANT.
IT'S BEAUTI-FUL! SO SHINY AND GOLDEN!
SOMETHING THIS SMOOTH AND PURE MUST REP-RESENT YOU, KYUTARO.
LET'S THROW IT AT OUR OPPONENT AT JUST THE RIGHT MOMENT!
I bet getting hit with a ball would hurt!
YOUR GOLDEN BALL ...
OKAY, I GET IT! QUIT TALKING ABOUT BALLS!
It sounds painful.
WELL, MY BROOM'S BETTER THAN NOTHING.
I CAN USE IT TO PURIFY THINGS AND CREATE BARRIERS WITH IT. THIS WON'T SLOW ME DOWN.
NOW...

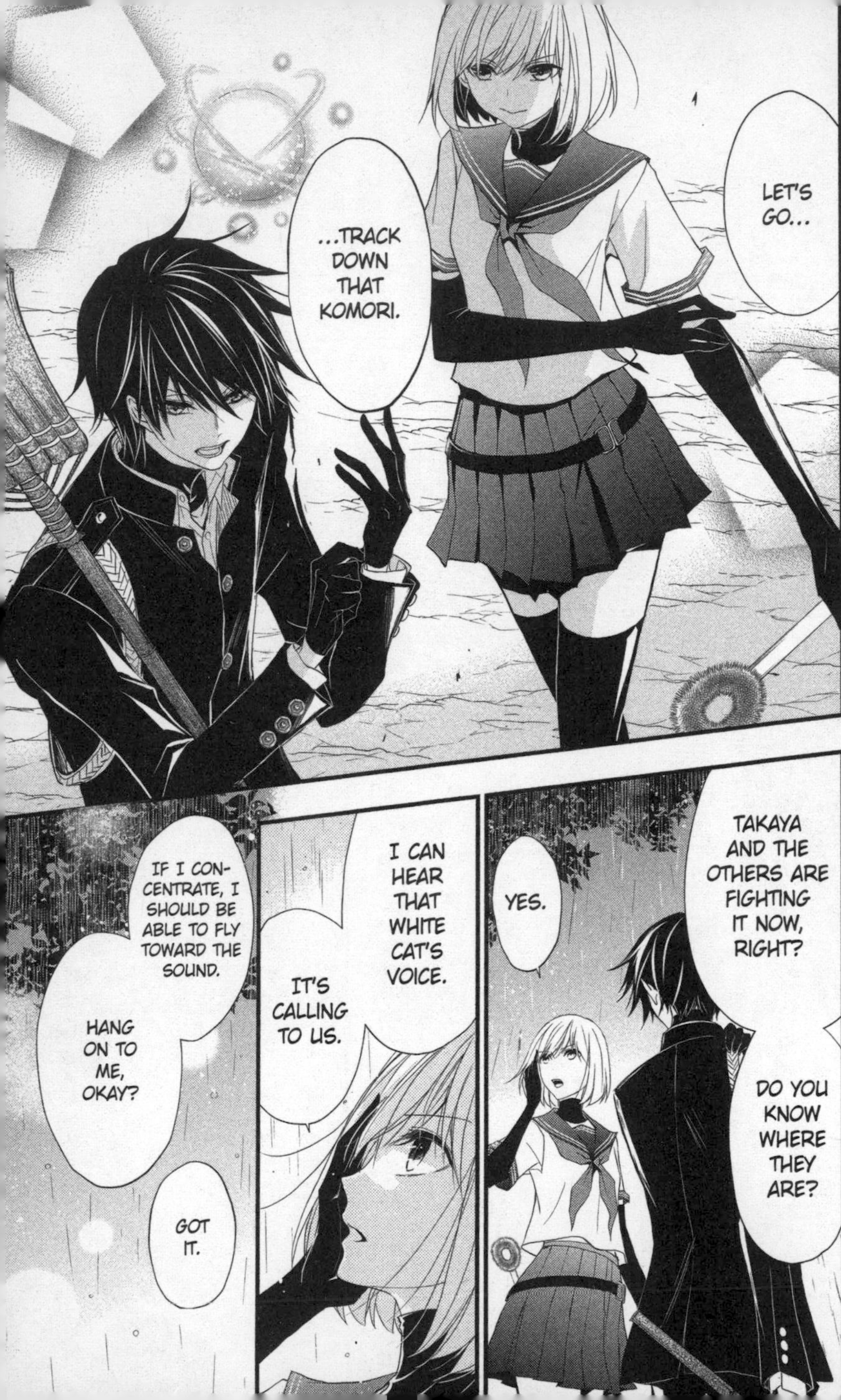
LET'S GO...
...TRACK DOWN THAT KOMORI.
TAKAYA AND THE OTHERS ARE FIGHTING IT NOW, RIGHT?
YES.
DO YOU KNOW WHERE THEY ARE?
I CAN HEAR THAT WHITE CAT'S VOICE.
IT'S CALLING TO US.
IF I CON-CENTRATE, I SHOULD BE ABLE TO FLY TOWARD THE SOUND.
HANG ON TO ME, OKAY?
GOT IT.

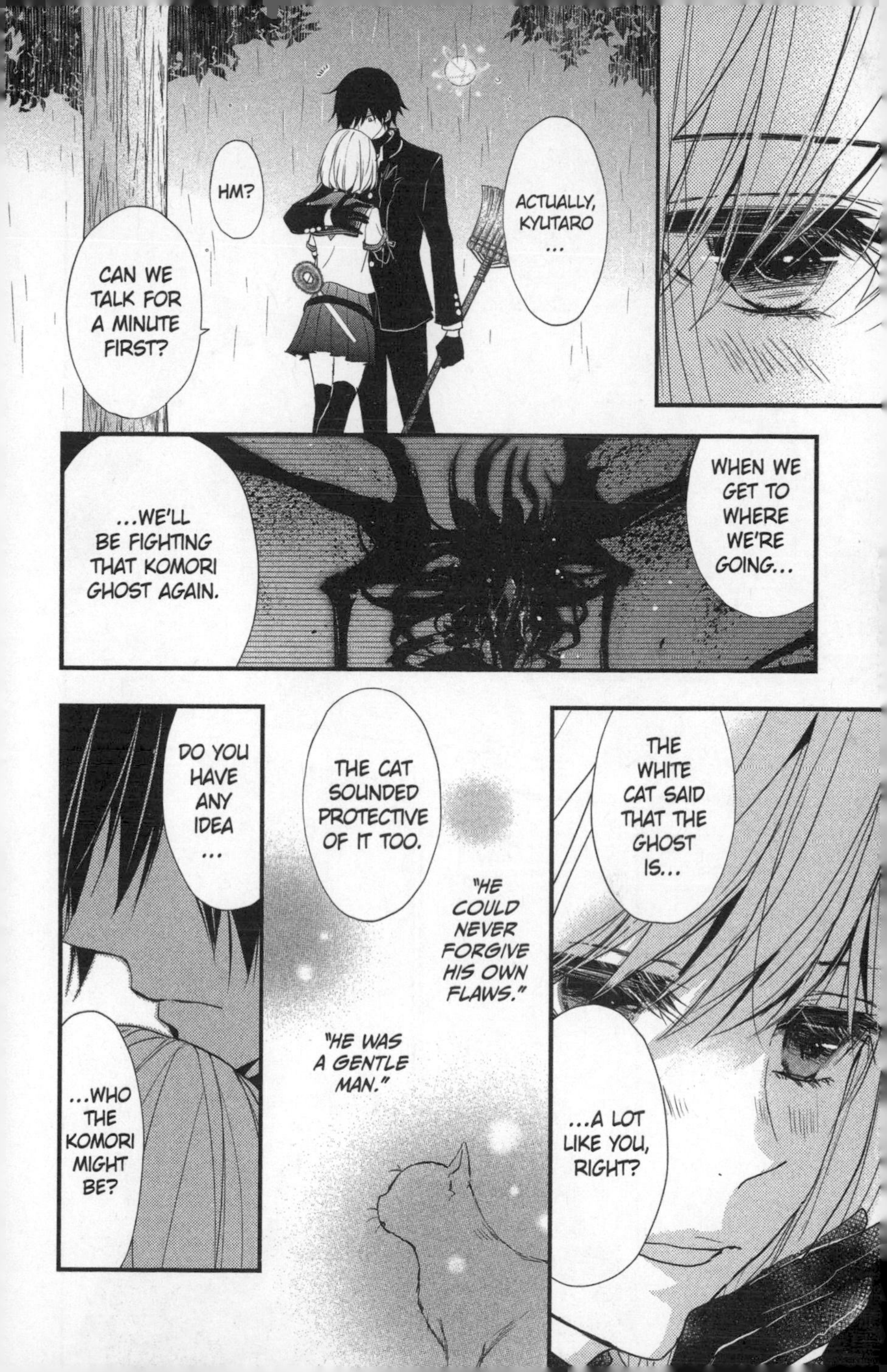
ACTUALLY, KYUTARO ...
HM?
CAN WE TALK FOR A MINUTE FIRST?
WHEN WE GET TO WHERE WE'RE GOING...
...WE'LL BE FIGHTING THAT KOMORI GHOST AGAIN.
THE WHITE CAT SAID THAT THE GHOST IS...
...A LOT LIKE YOU, RIGHT?
"HE COULD NEVER FORGIVE HIS OWN FLAWS."
"HE WAS A GENTLE MAN."
THE CAT SOUNDED PROTECTIVE OF IT TOO.
DO YOU HAVE ANY IDEA ...
...WHO THE KOMORI MIGHT BE?

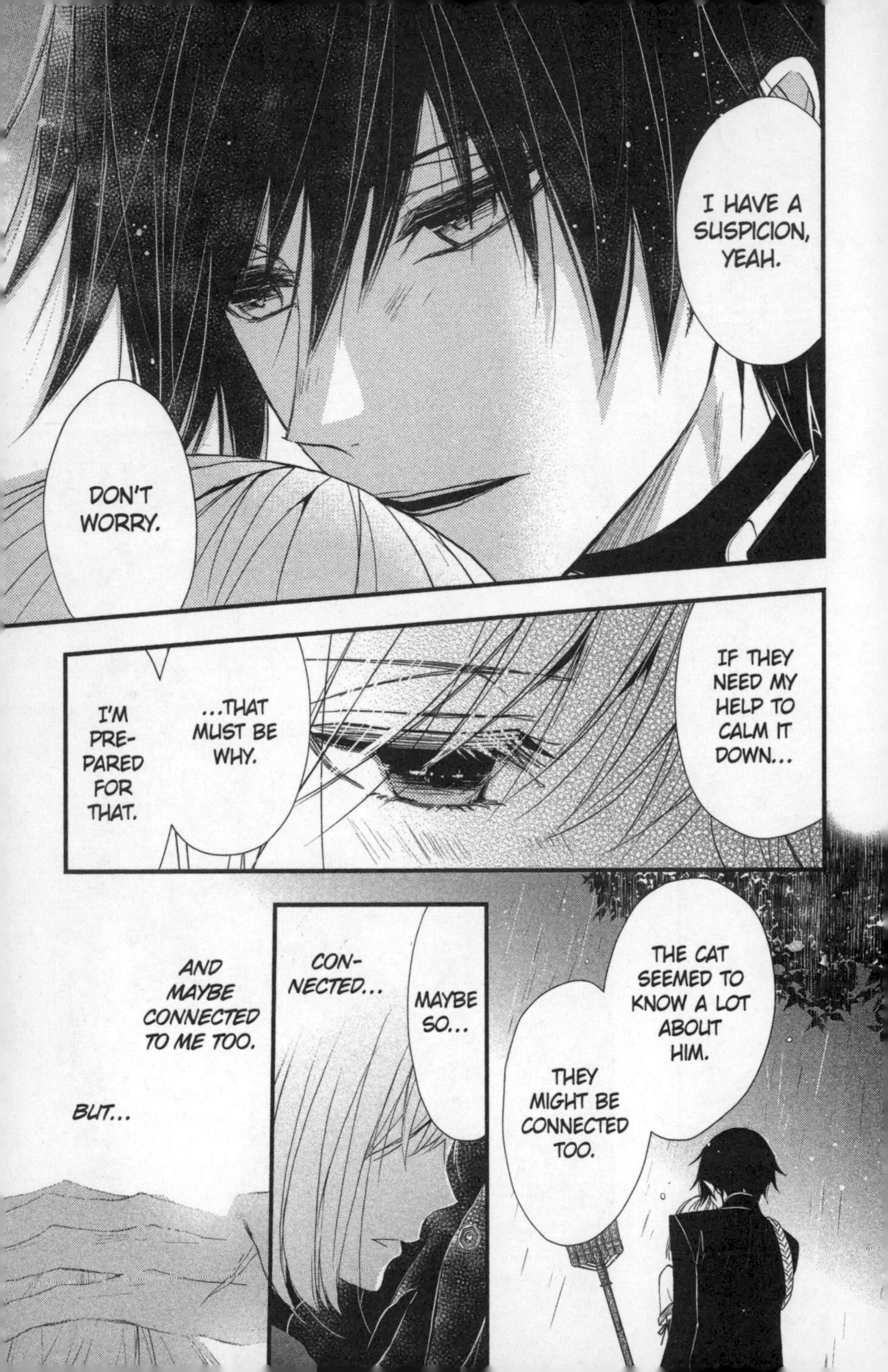
I HAVE A SUSPICION, YEAH.
DON'T WORRY.
IF THEY NEED MY HELP TO CALM IT DOWN...
...THAT MUST BE WHY.
I'M PRE-PARED FOR THAT.
THE CAT SEEMED TO KNOW A LOT ABOUT HIM.
THEY MIGHT BE CONNECTED TOO.
MAYBE SO...
CON-NECTED...
AND MAYBE CONNECTED TO ME TOO.
BUT...

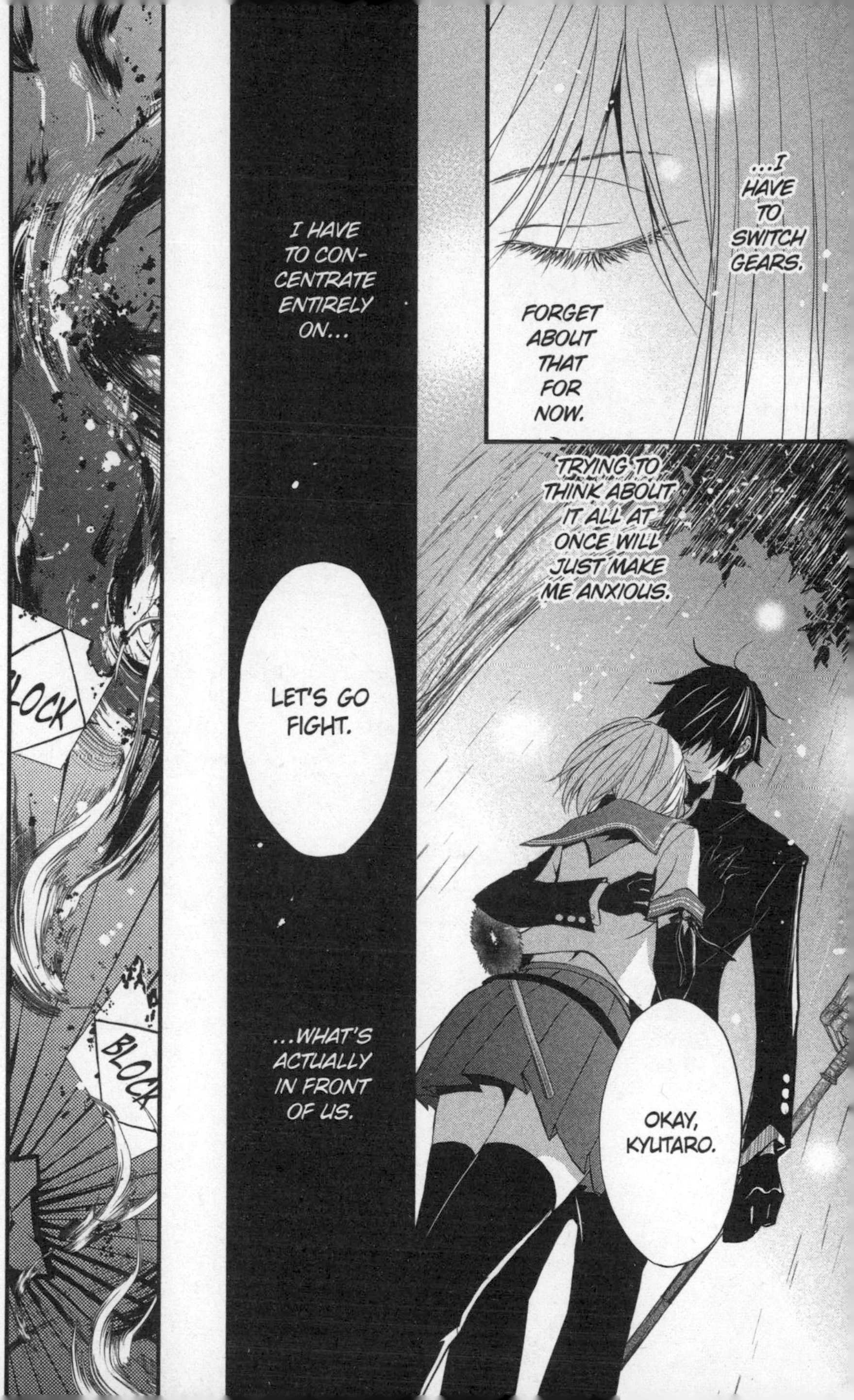
...I HAVE TO SWITCH GEARS.
FORGET ABOUT THAT FOR NOW.
TRYING TO THINK ABOUT IT ALL AT ONCE WILL JUST MAKE ME ANXIOUS.
OKAY, KYUTARO.
I HAVE TO CON-CENTRATE ENTIRELY ON...
LET'S GO FIGHT.
...WHAT'S ACTUALLY IN FRONT OF US.
BLOCK
BLOCK

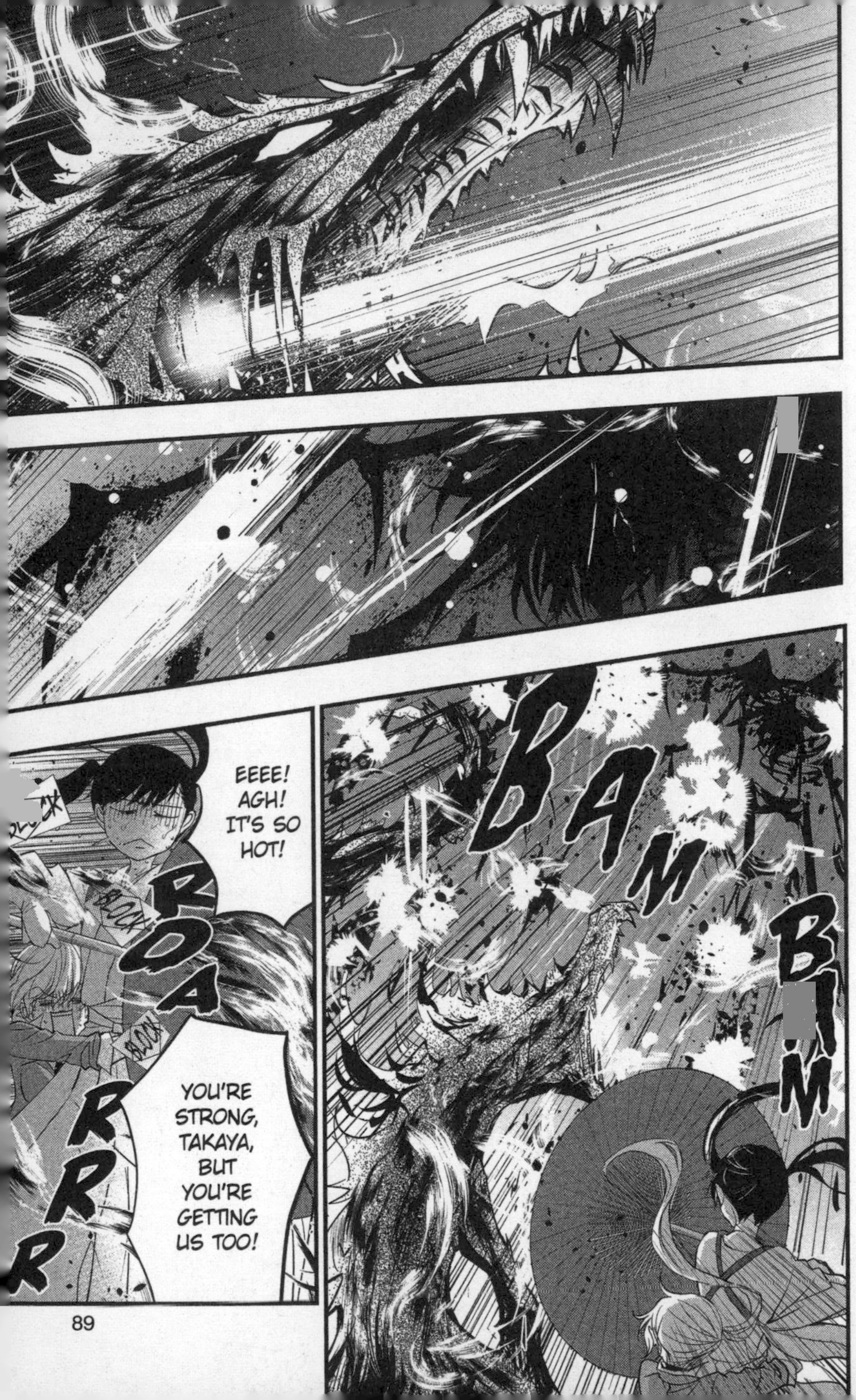
BAM
BIM
EEEE! AGH! IT'S SO HOT!
ROAR
RRR
BLOCK
BLOCK
YOU'RE STRONG, TAKAYA, BUT YOU'RE GETTING US TOO!

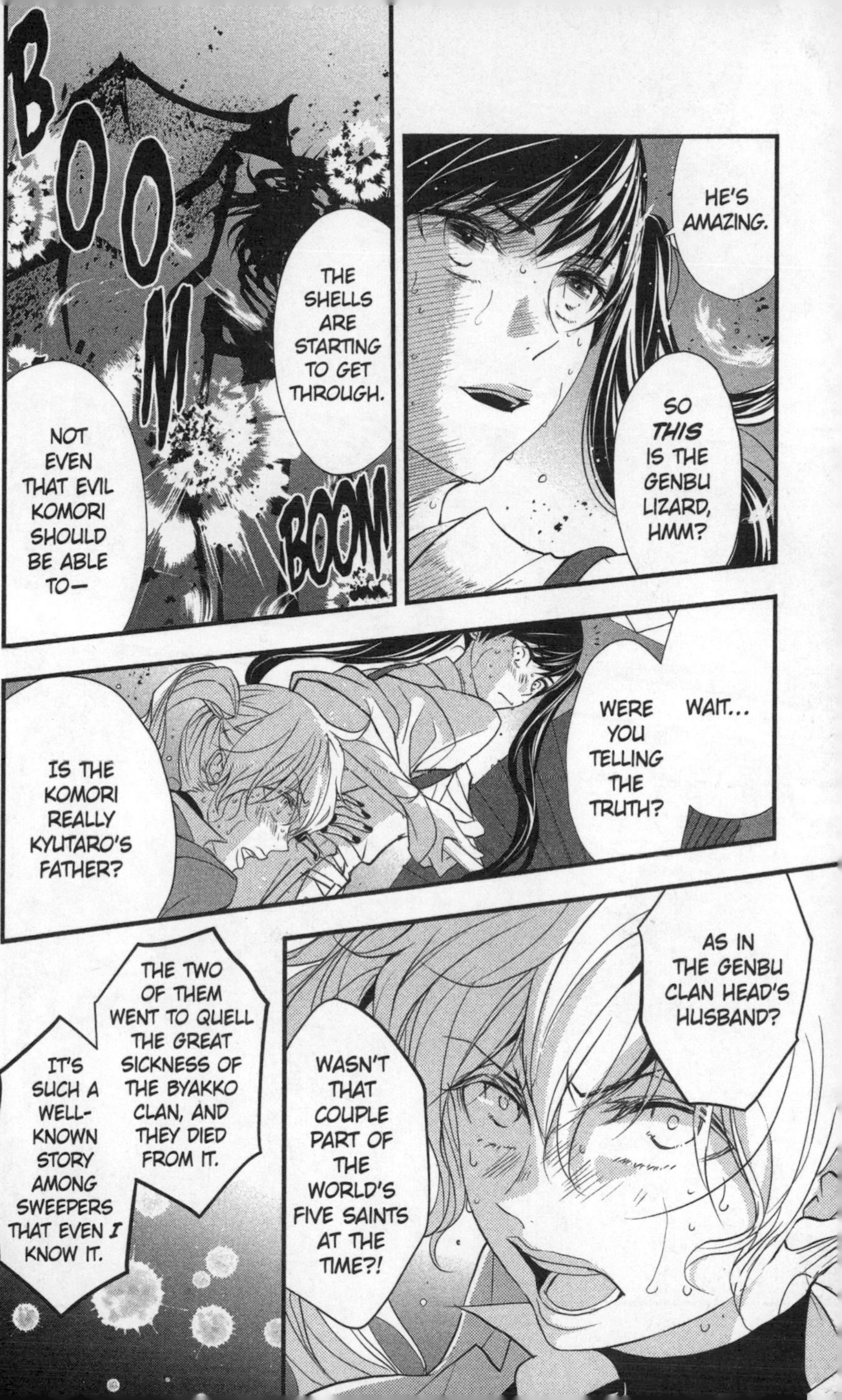
HE'S AMAZING.
SO *THIS* IS THE GENBU LIZARD, HMM?
BOOOM
THE SHELLS ARE STARTING TO GET THROUGH.
NOT EVEN THAT EVIL KOMORI SHOULD BE ABLE TO—
BOOM
WAIT...
WERE YOU TELLING THE TRUTH?
IS THE KOMORI REALLY KYUTARO'S FATHER?
AS IN THE GENBU CLAN HEAD'S HUSBAND?
WASN'T THAT COUPLE PART OF THE WORLD'S FIVE SAINTS AT THE TIME?!
THE TWO OF THEM WENT TO QUELL THE GREAT SICKNESS OF THE BYAKKO CLAN, AND THEY DIED FROM IT.
IT'S SUCH A WELL-KNOWN STORY AMONG SWEEPERS THAT EVEN *I* KNOW IT.

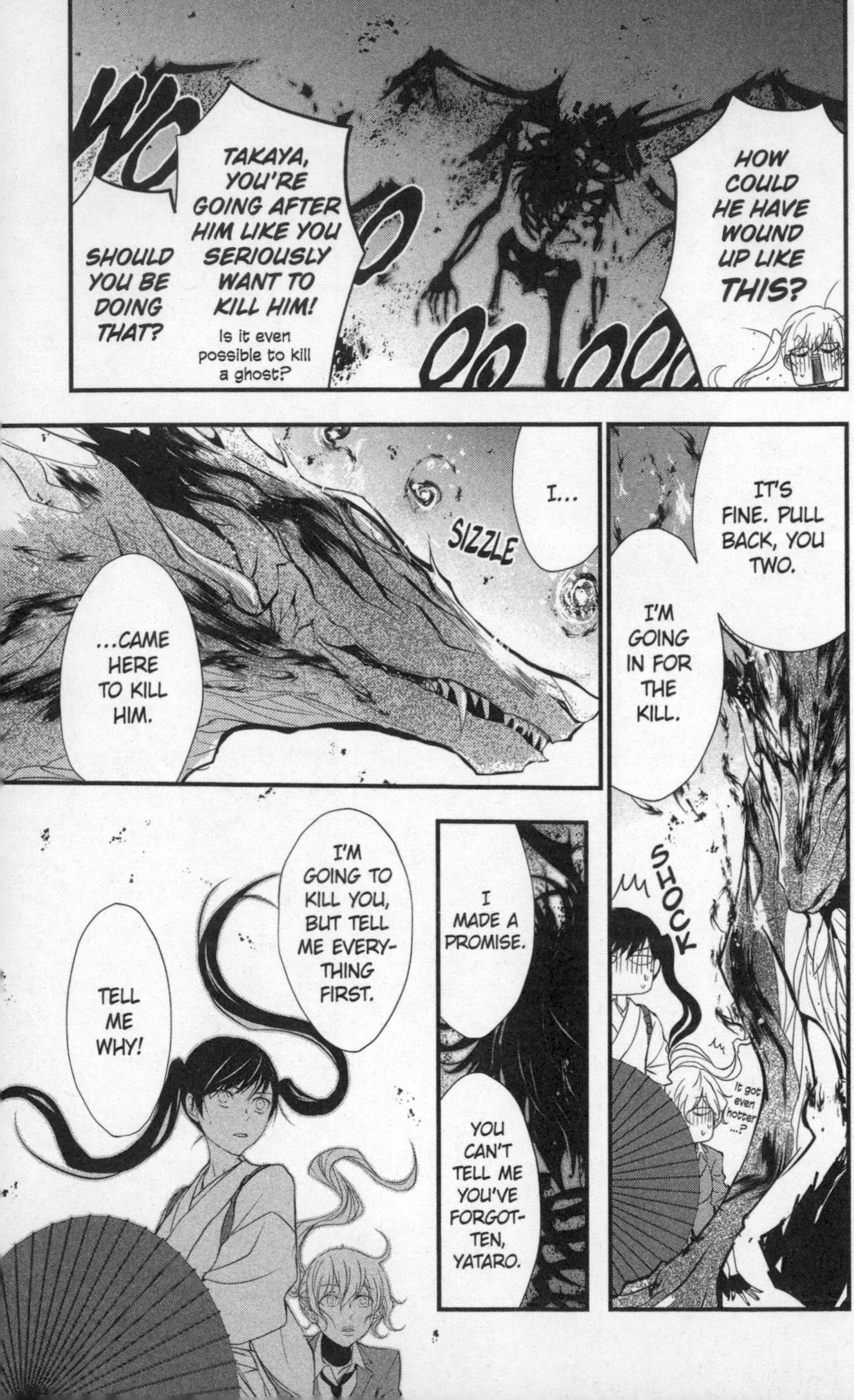
HOW COULD HE HAVE WOUND UP LIKE THIS?
TAKAYA, YOU'RE GOING AFTER HIM LIKE YOU SERIOUSLY WANT TO KILL HIM!
Is it even possible to kill a ghost?
SHOULD YOU BE DOING THAT?
IT'S FINE. PULL BACK, YOU TWO.
I'M GOING IN FOR THE KILL.
I...
SIZZLE
...CAME HERE TO KILL HIM.
SHOCK
It got even hotter ...?
I MADE A PROMISE.
YOU CAN'T TELL ME YOU'VE FORGOT-TEN, YATARO.
I'M GOING TO KILL YOU, BUT TELL ME EVERY-THING FIRST.
TELL ME WHY!

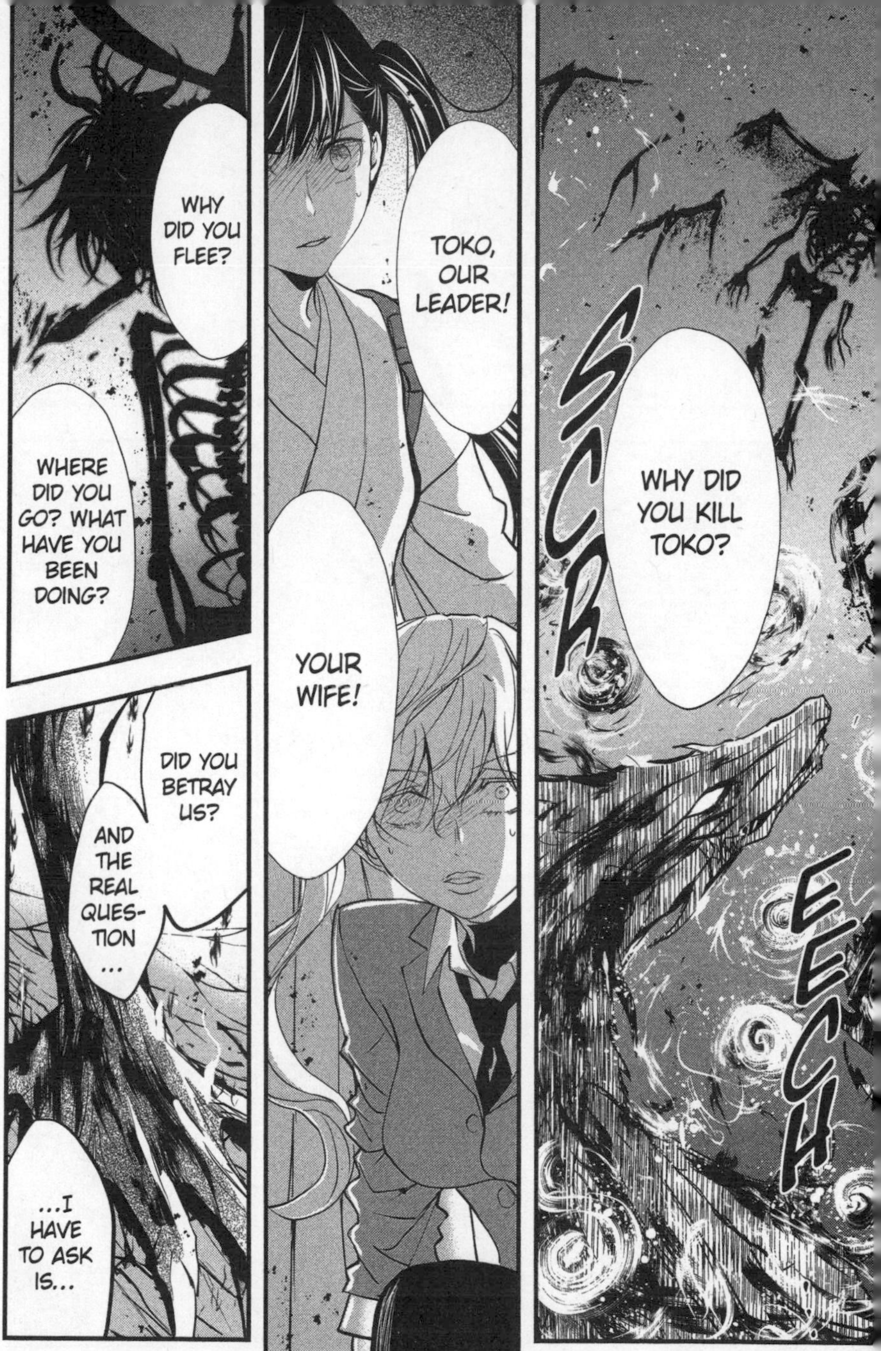
SCREECH
WHY DID YOU KILL TOKO?
TOKO, OUR LEADER!
YOUR WIFE!
WHY DID YOU FLEE?
WHERE DID YOU GO? WHAT HAVE YOU BEEN DOING?
DID YOU BETRAY US?
AND THE REAL QUES-TION ...
...I HAVE TO ASK IS...

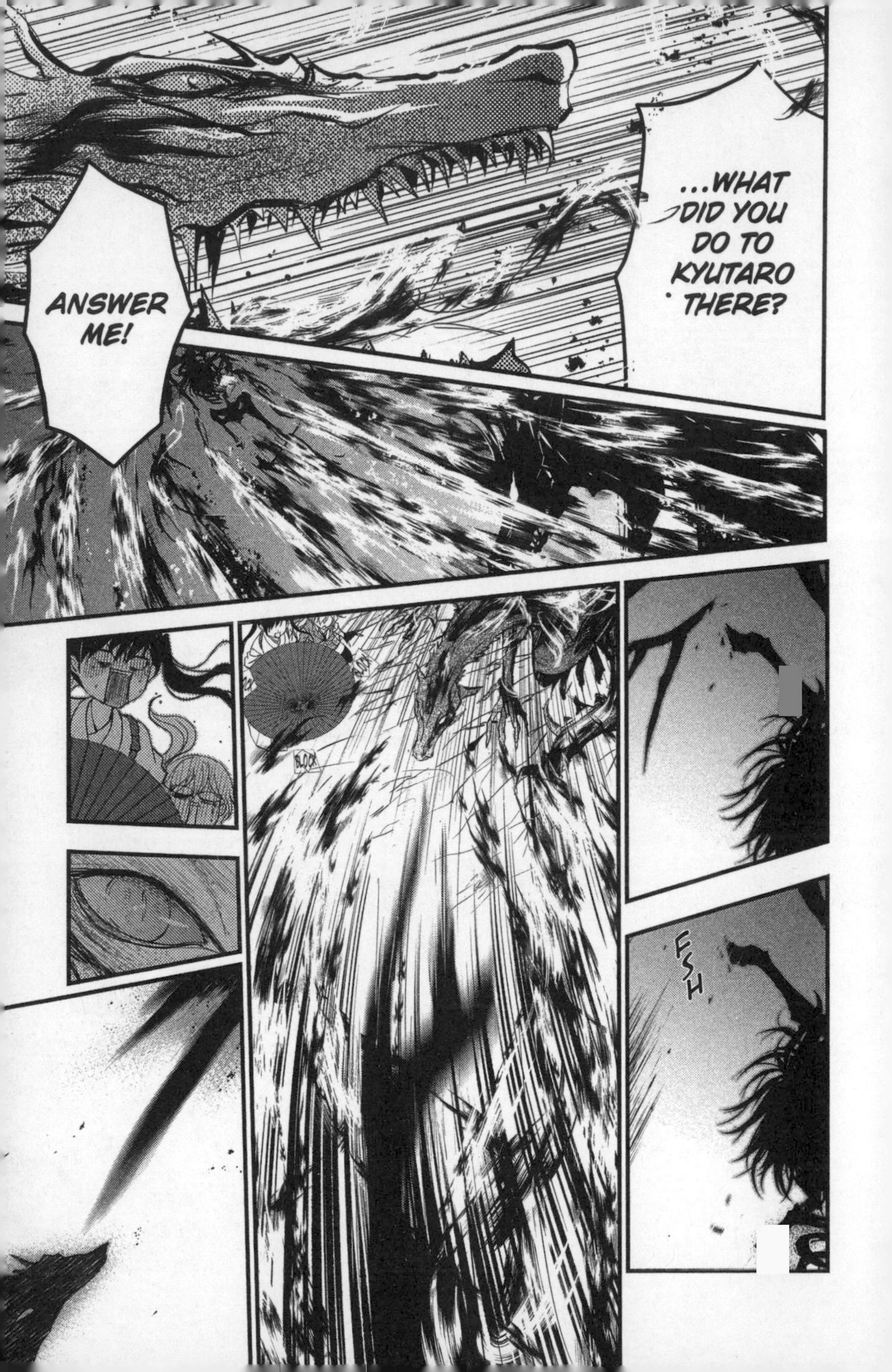
...WHAT DID YOU DO TO KYUTARO THERE?
ANSWER ME!
FSH
BLOCK

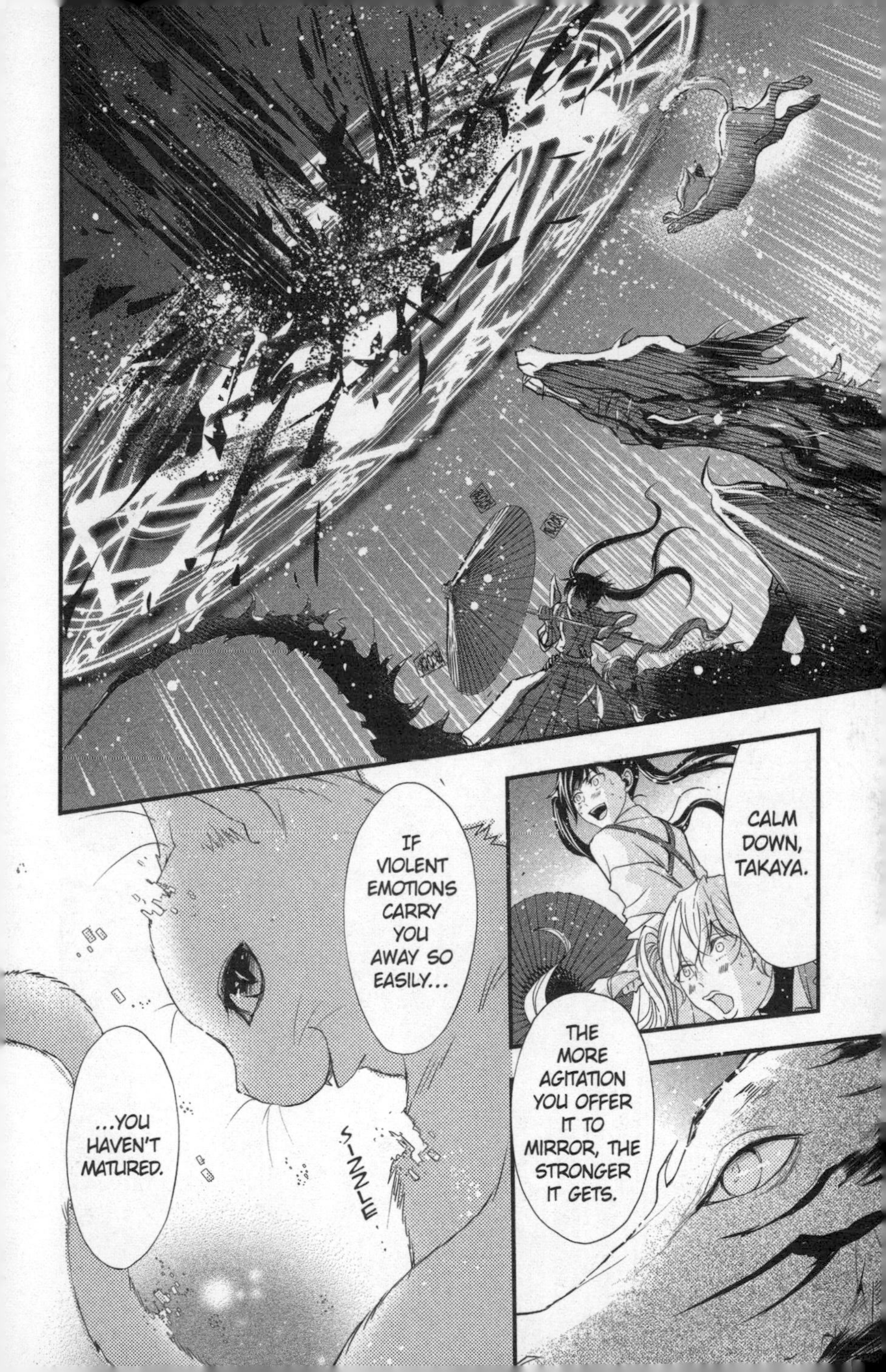
CALM DOWN, TAKAYA.
THE MORE AGITATION YOU OFFER IT TO MIRROR, THE STRONGER IT GETS.
IF VIOLENT EMOTIONS CARRY YOU AWAY SO EASILY...
SIZZLE
...YOU HAVEN'T MATURED.

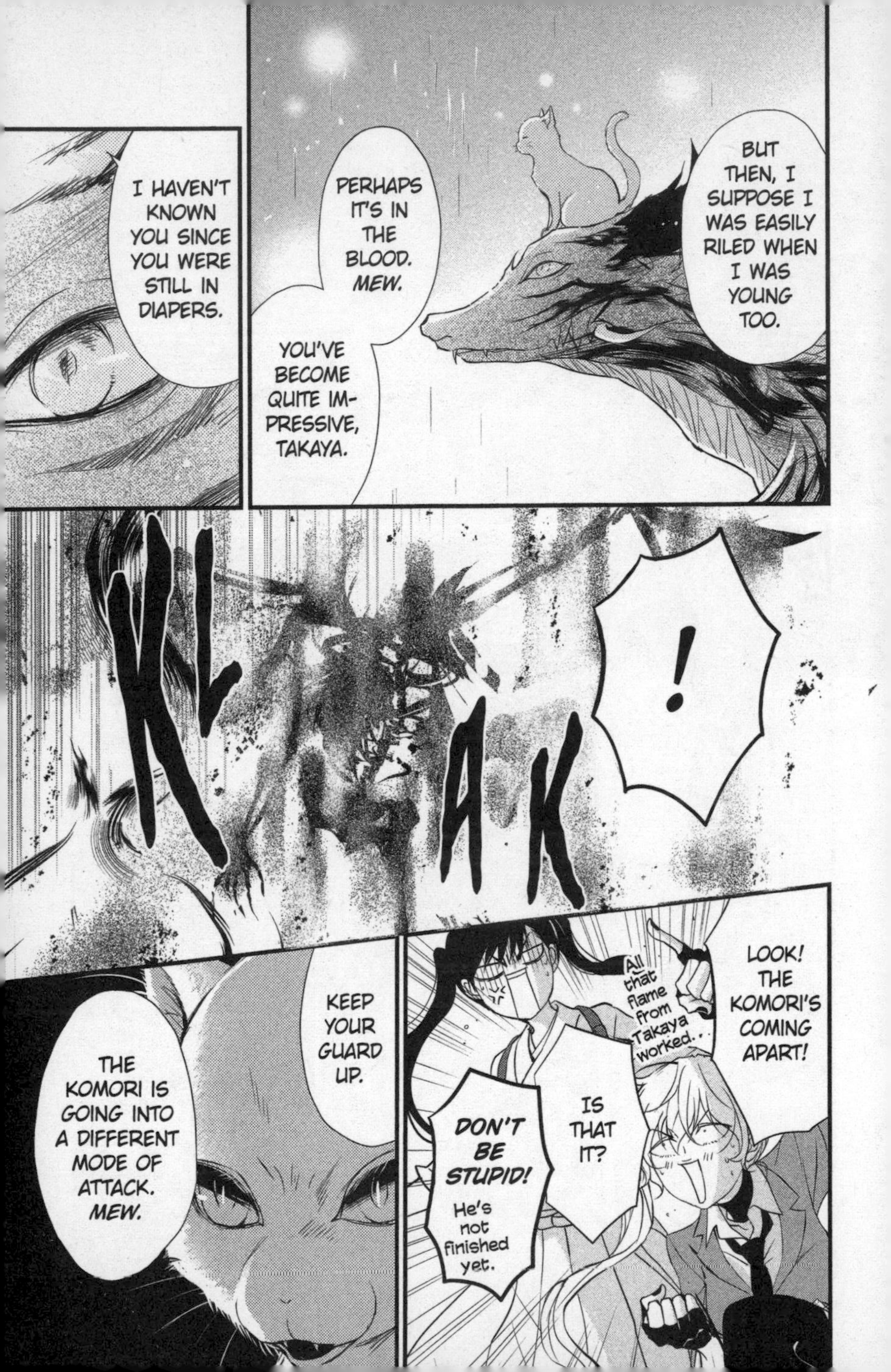
BUT THEN, I SUPPOSE I WAS EASILY RILED WHEN I WAS YOUNG TOO.
PERHAPS IT'S IN THE BLOOD. *MEW.*
YOU'VE BECOME QUITE IM-PRESSIVE, TAKAYA.
I HAVEN'T KNOWN YOU SINCE YOU WERE STILL IN DIAPERS.
!
KLAK
LOOK! THE KOMORI'S COMING APART!
All that flame from Takaya worked...
IS THAT IT?
DON'T BE STUPID!
He's not finished yet.
KEEP YOUR GUARD UP.
THE KOMORI IS GOING INTO A DIFFERENT MODE OF ATTACK. *MEW.*

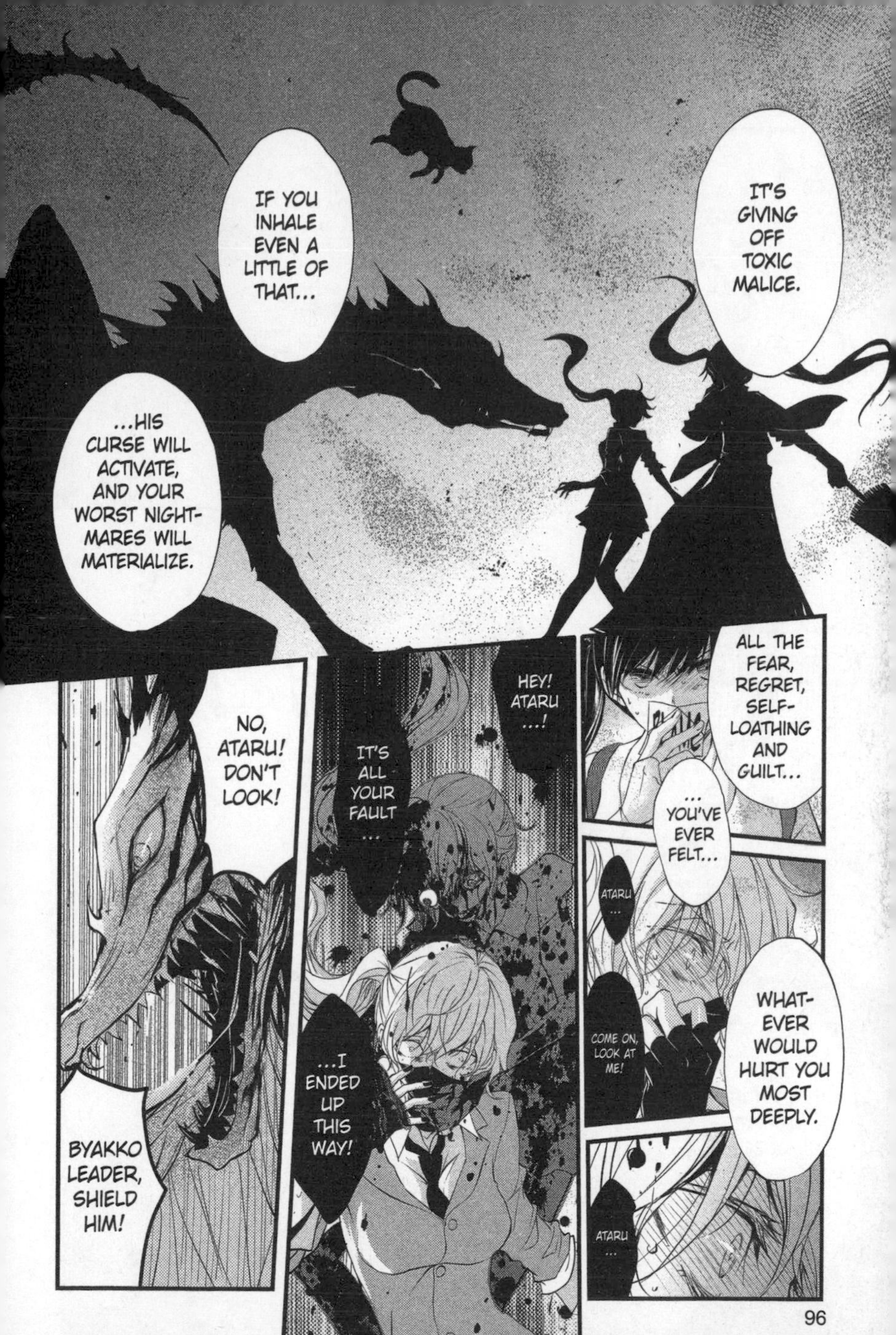
IT'S GIVING OFF TOXIC MALICE.
IF YOU INHALE EVEN A LITTLE OF THAT...
...HIS CURSE WILL ACTIVATE, AND YOUR WORST NIGHT-MARES WILL MATERIALIZE.
ALL THE FEAR, REGRET, SELF-LOATHING AND GUILT...
...YOU'VE EVER FELT...
WHAT-EVER WOULD HURT YOU MOST DEEPLY.
ATARU...
COME ON, LOOK AT ME!
ATARU...
HEY! ATARU...!
IT'S ALL YOUR FAULT...
...I ENDED UP THIS WAY!
NO, ATARU! DON'T LOOK!
BYAKKO LEADER, SHIELD HIM!

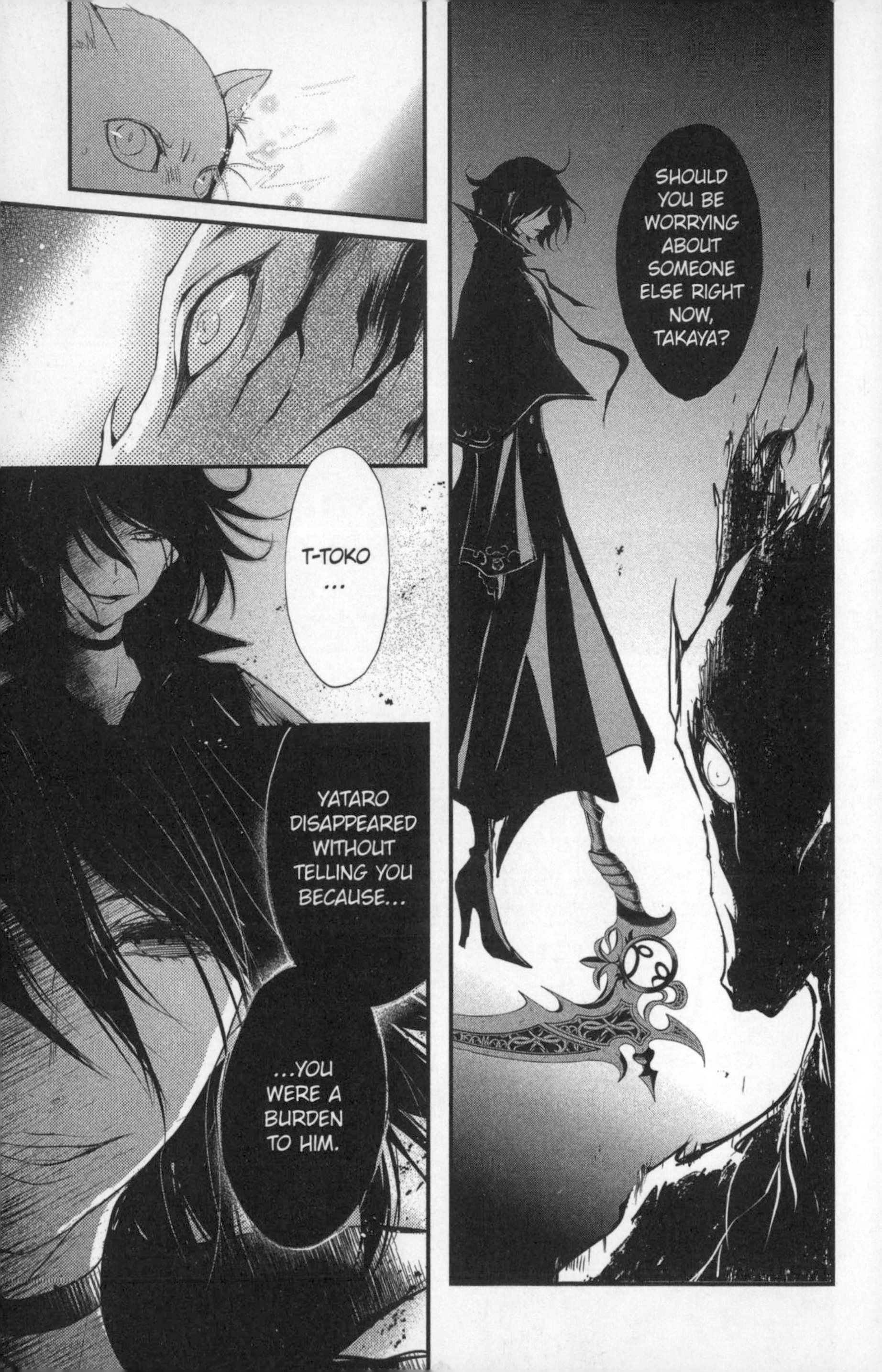
SHOULD YOU BE WORRYING ABOUT SOMEONE ELSE RIGHT NOW, TAKAYA?
T-TOKO ...
YATARO DISAPPEARED WITHOUT TELLING YOU BECAUSE...
...YOU WERE A BURDEN TO HIM.

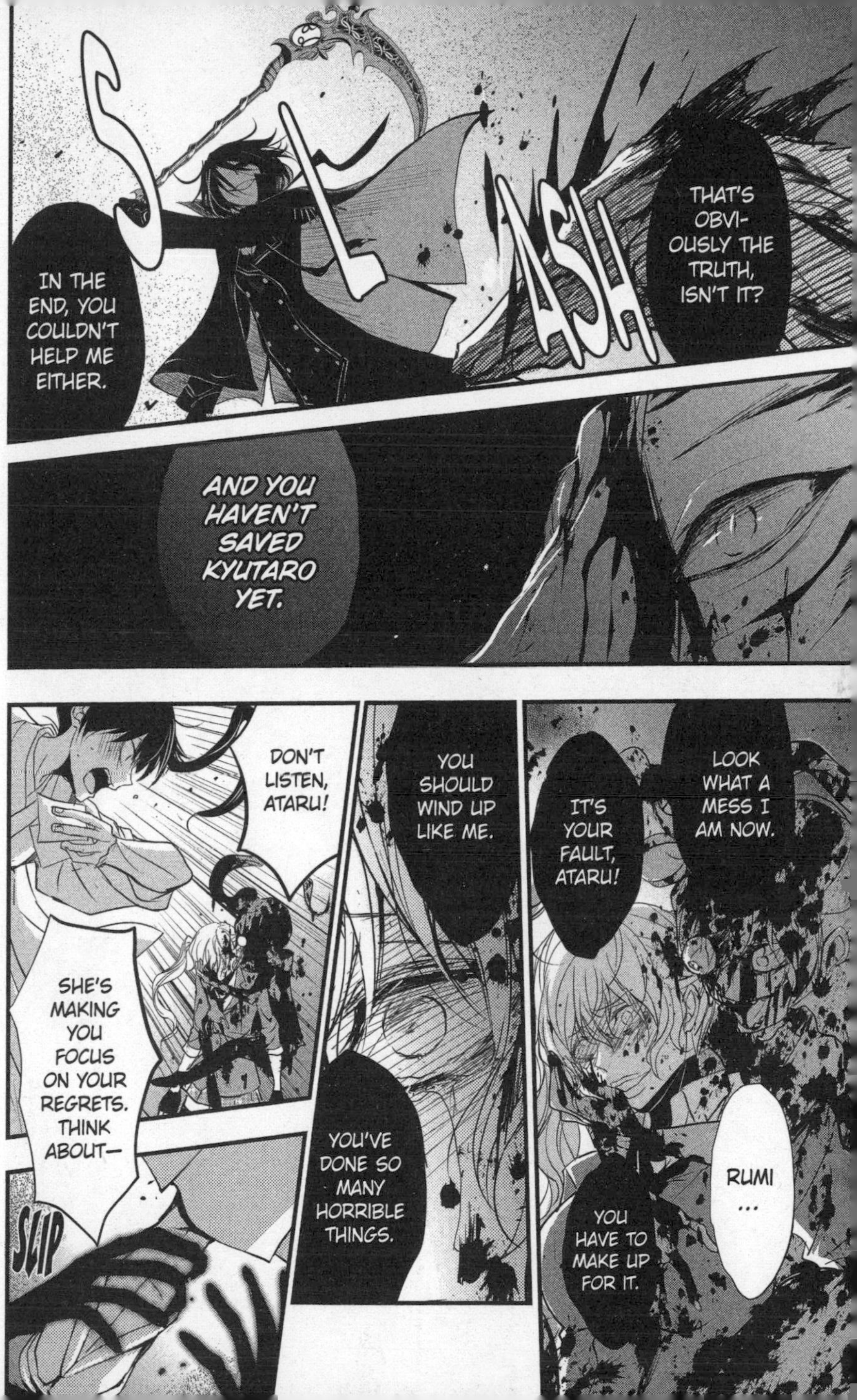
THAT'S OBVIOUSLY THE TRUTH, ISN'T IT?
SLASH
IN THE END, YOU COULDN'T HELP ME EITHER.
AND YOU HAVEN'T SAVED KYUTARO YET.
LOOK WHAT A MESS I AM NOW.
IT'S YOUR FAULT, ATARU!
RUMI...
YOU HAVE TO MAKE UP FOR IT.
YOU SHOULD WIND UP LIKE ME.
YOU'VE DONE SO MANY HORRIBLE THINGS.
DON'T LISTEN, ATARU!
SHE'S MAKING YOU FOCUS ON YOUR REGRETS. THINK ABOUT—
SLIP

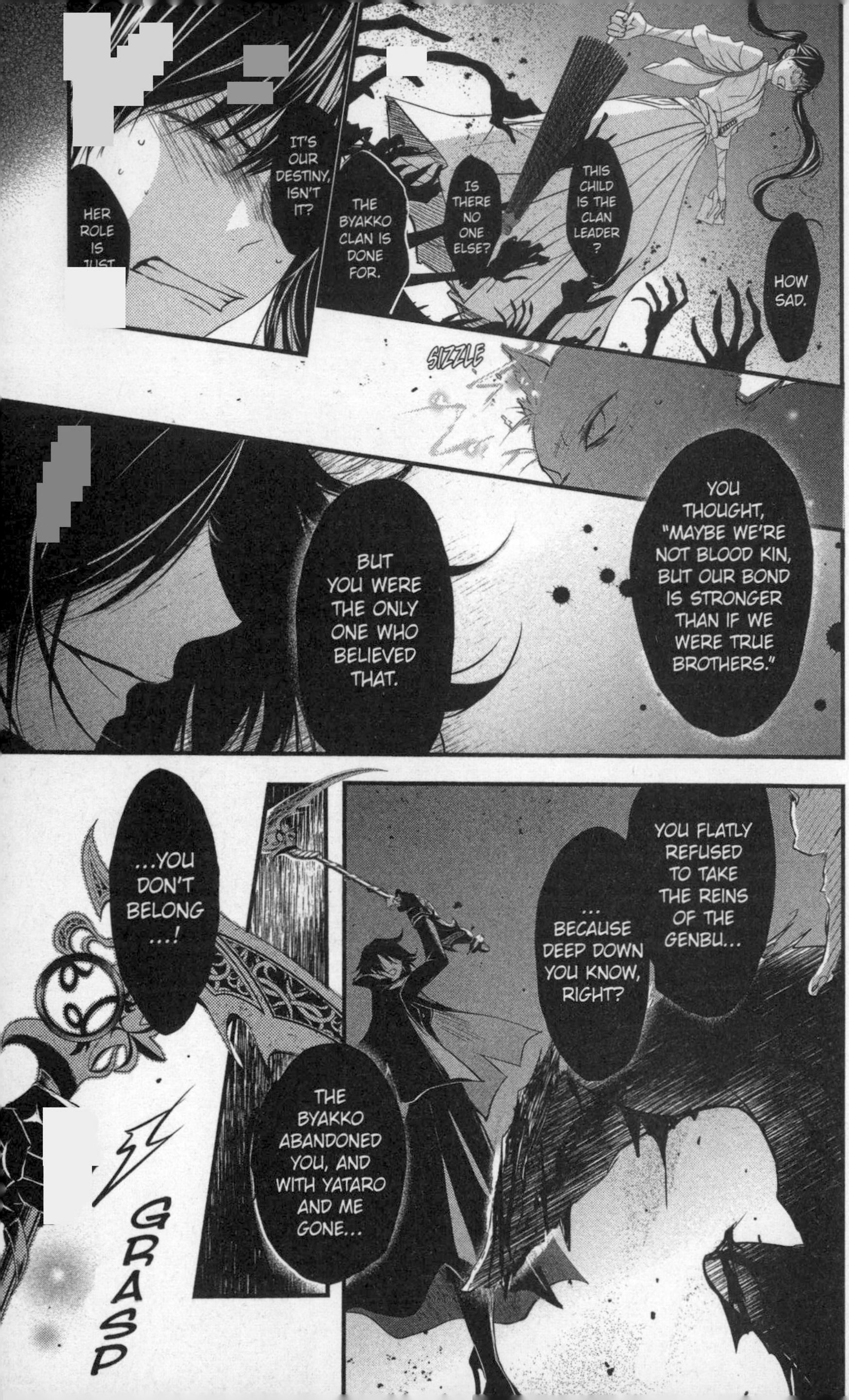
HOW SAD.
THIS CHILD IS THE CLAN LEADER?
IS THERE NO ONE ELSE?
THE BYAKKO CLAN IS DONE FOR.
IT'S OUR DESTINY, ISN'T IT?
HER ROLE IS JUST
SIZZLE
YOU THOUGHT, "MAYBE WE'RE NOT BLOOD KIN, BUT OUR BOND IS STRONGER THAN IF WE WERE TRUE BROTHERS."
BUT YOU WERE THE ONLY ONE WHO BELIEVED THAT.
YOU FLATLY REFUSED TO TAKE THE REINS OF THE GENBU...
...BECAUSE DEEP DOWN YOU KNOW, RIGHT?
THE BYAKKO ABANDONED YOU, AND WITH YATARO AND ME GONE...
...YOU DON'T BELONG...!
GRASP

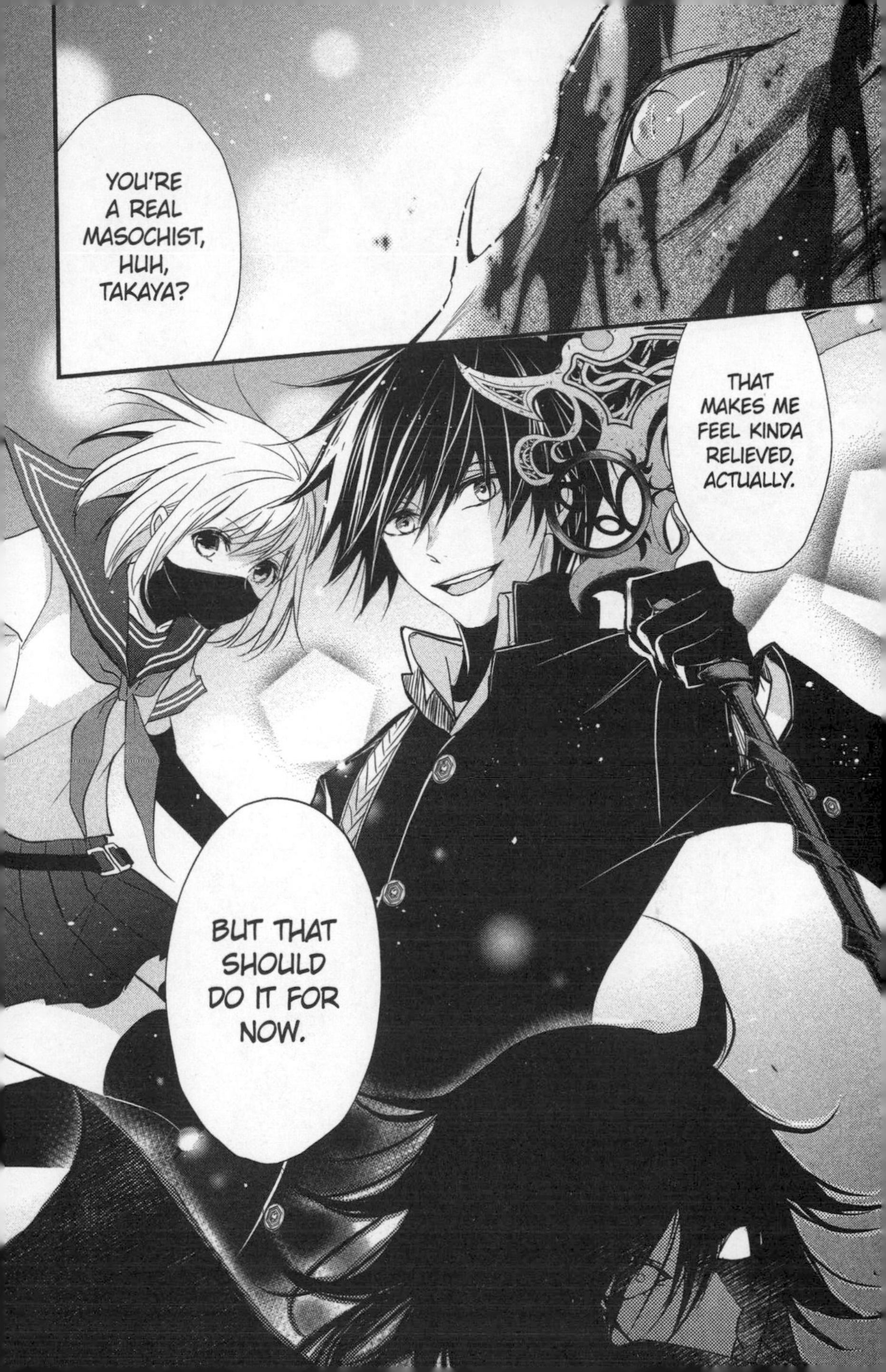
YOU'RE A REAL MASOCHIST, HUH, TAKAYA?
THAT MAKES ME FEEL KINDA RELIEVED, ACTUALLY.
BUT THAT SHOULD DO IT FOR NOW.

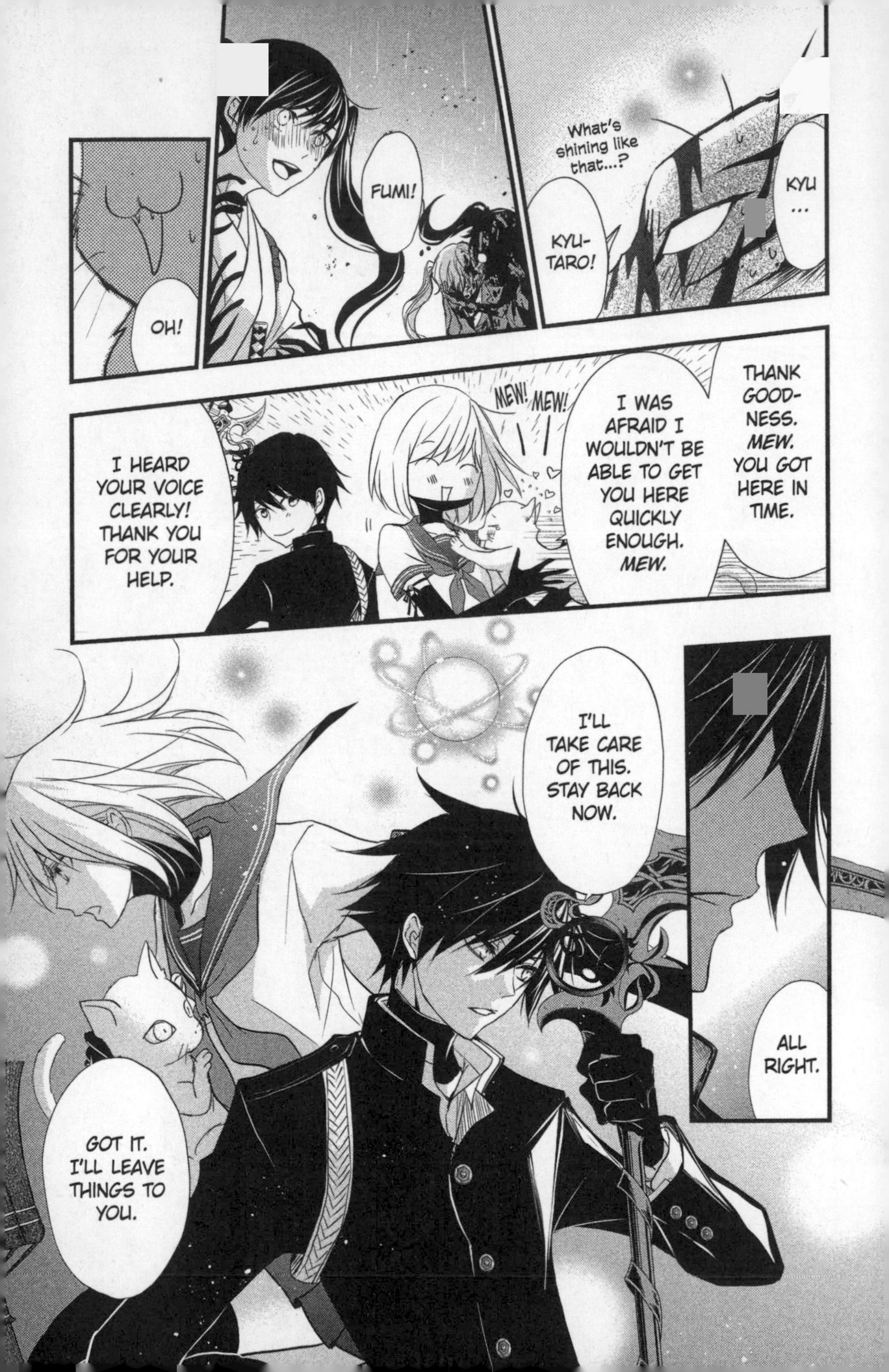
KYU ...
What's shining like that...?
KYU-TARO!
FUMI!
OH!
THANK GOODNESS. MEW. YOU GOT HERE IN TIME.
I WAS AFRAID I WOULDN'T BE ABLE TO GET YOU HERE QUICKLY ENOUGH. MEW.
MEW! MEW!
I HEARD YOUR VOICE CLEARLY! THANK YOU FOR YOUR HELP.
I'LL TAKE CARE OF THIS. STAY BACK NOW.
ALL RIGHT.
GOT IT. I'LL LEAVE THINGS TO YOU.

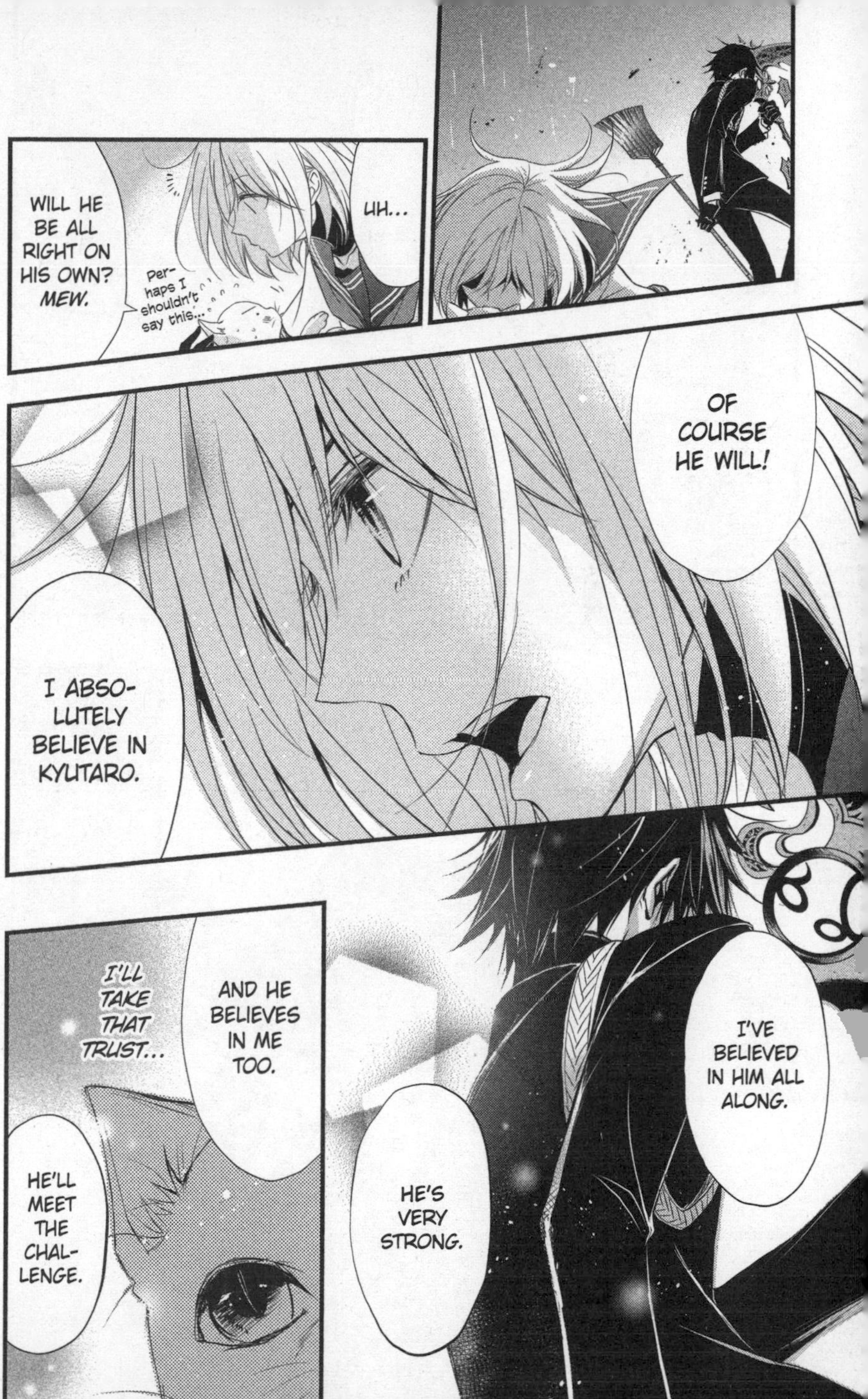
UH...
WILL HE BE ALL RIGHT ON HIS OWN? MEW.
Perhaps I shouldn't say this...
OF COURSE HE WILL!
I ABSOLUTELY BELIEVE IN KYUTARO.
I'VE BELIEVED IN HIM ALL ALONG.
HE'S VERY STRONG.
AND HE BELIEVES IN ME TOO.
I'LL TAKE THAT TRUST...
HE'LL MEET THE CHALLENGE.

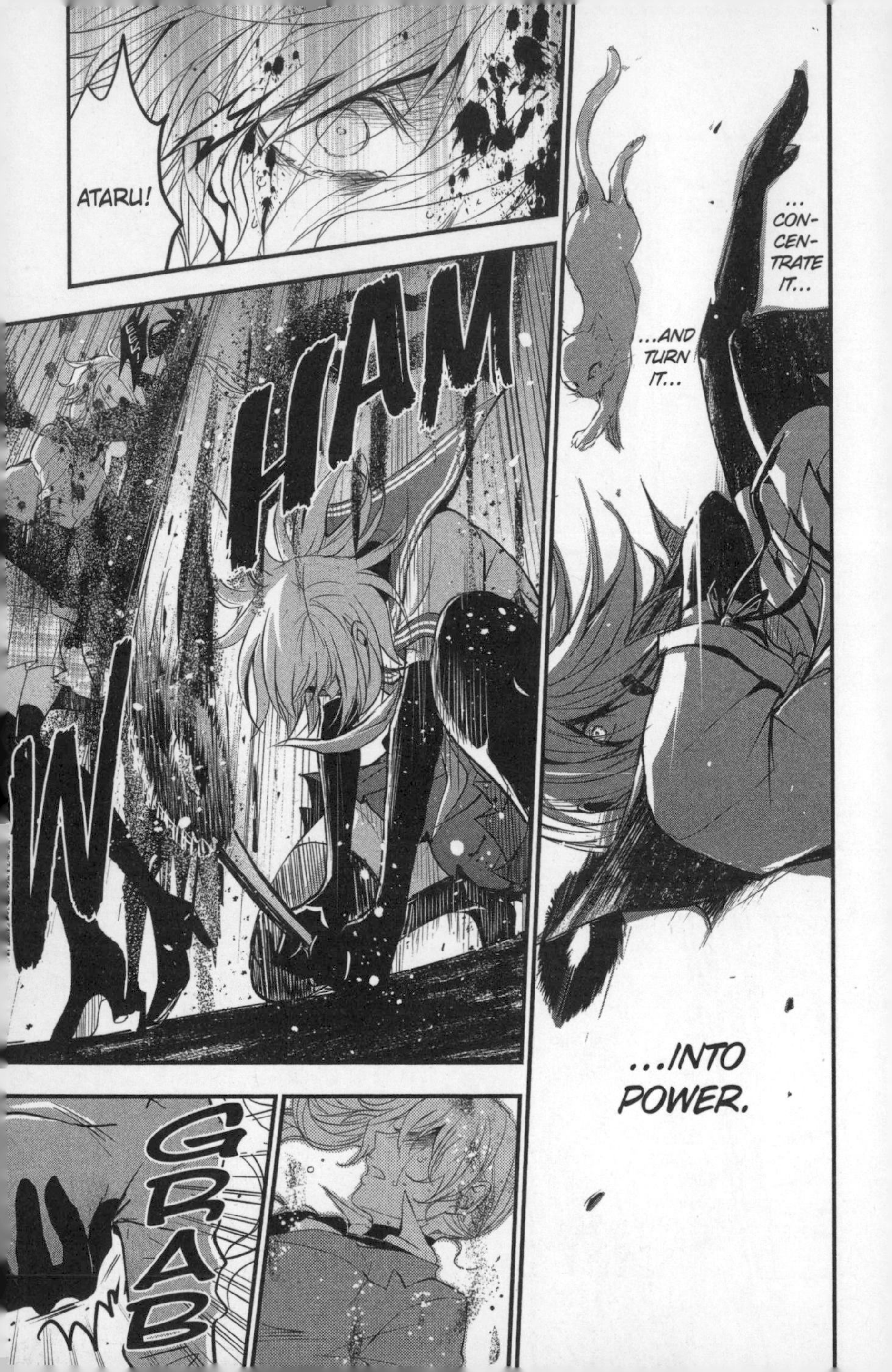
...CONCEN-TRATE IT...
...AND TURN IT...
...INTO POWER.
ATARU!
EEK!
WHAM
GRAB

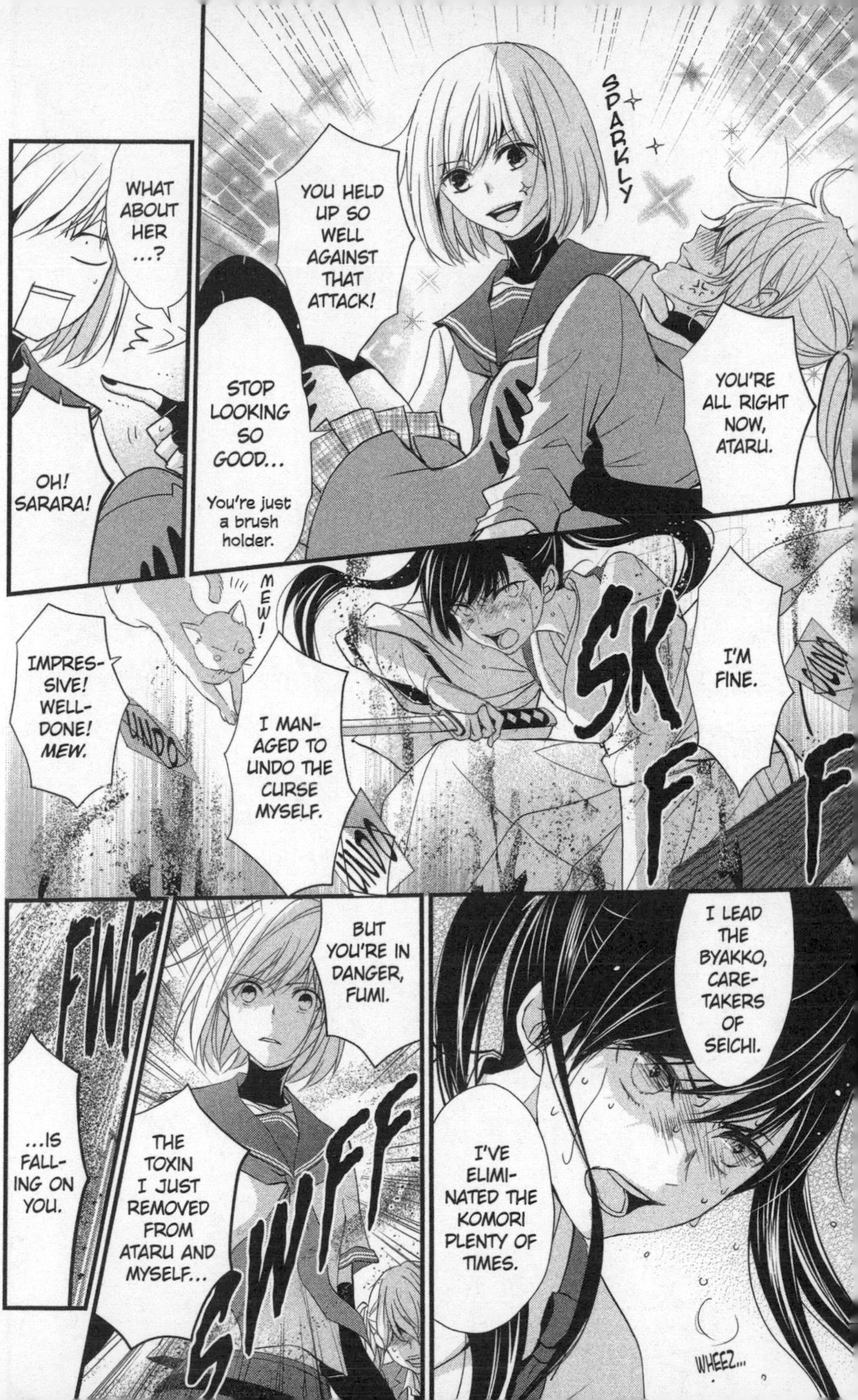
SPARKLY
YOU HELD UP SO WELL AGAINST THAT ATTACK!
YOU'RE ALL RIGHT NOW, ATARU.
STOP LOOKING SO GOOD...
You're just a brush holder.
WHAT ABOUT HER ...?
OH! SARARA!
SK F F
I'M FINE.
I MAN-AGED TO UNDO THE CURSE MYSELF.
UNDO
MEW!
IMPRES-SIVE! WELL-DONE! MEW.
UNDO
I LEAD THE BYAKKO, CARE-TAKERS OF SEICHI.
I'VE ELIMI-NATED THE KOMORI PLENTY OF TIMES.
WHEEZ...
BUT YOU'RE IN DANGER, FUMI.
SWFF
THE TOXIN I JUST REMOVED FROM ATARU AND MYSELF...
...IS FALL-ING ON YOU.
FWF

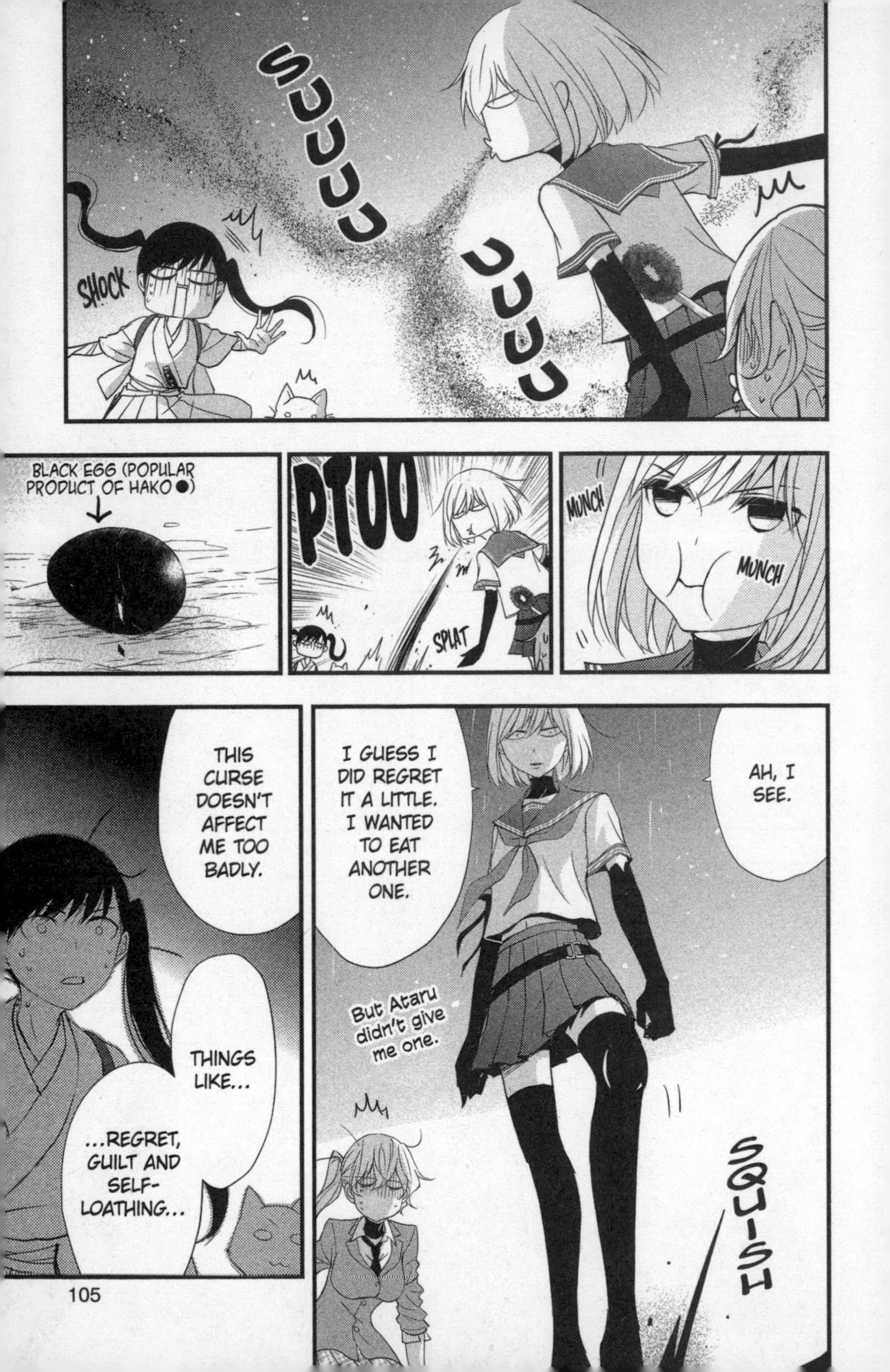
SUUUUUUUUUU
SHOCK
MUNCH
MUNCH
PTOO
SPLAT
BLACK EGG (POPULAR PRODUCT OF HAKO●)
AH, I SEE.
I GUESS I DID REGRET IT A LITTLE. I WANTED TO EAT ANOTHER ONE.
But Ataru didn't give me one.
SQUISH
THIS CURSE DOESN'T AFFECT ME TOO BADLY.
THINGS LIKE...
...REGRET, GUILT AND SELF-LOATHING...

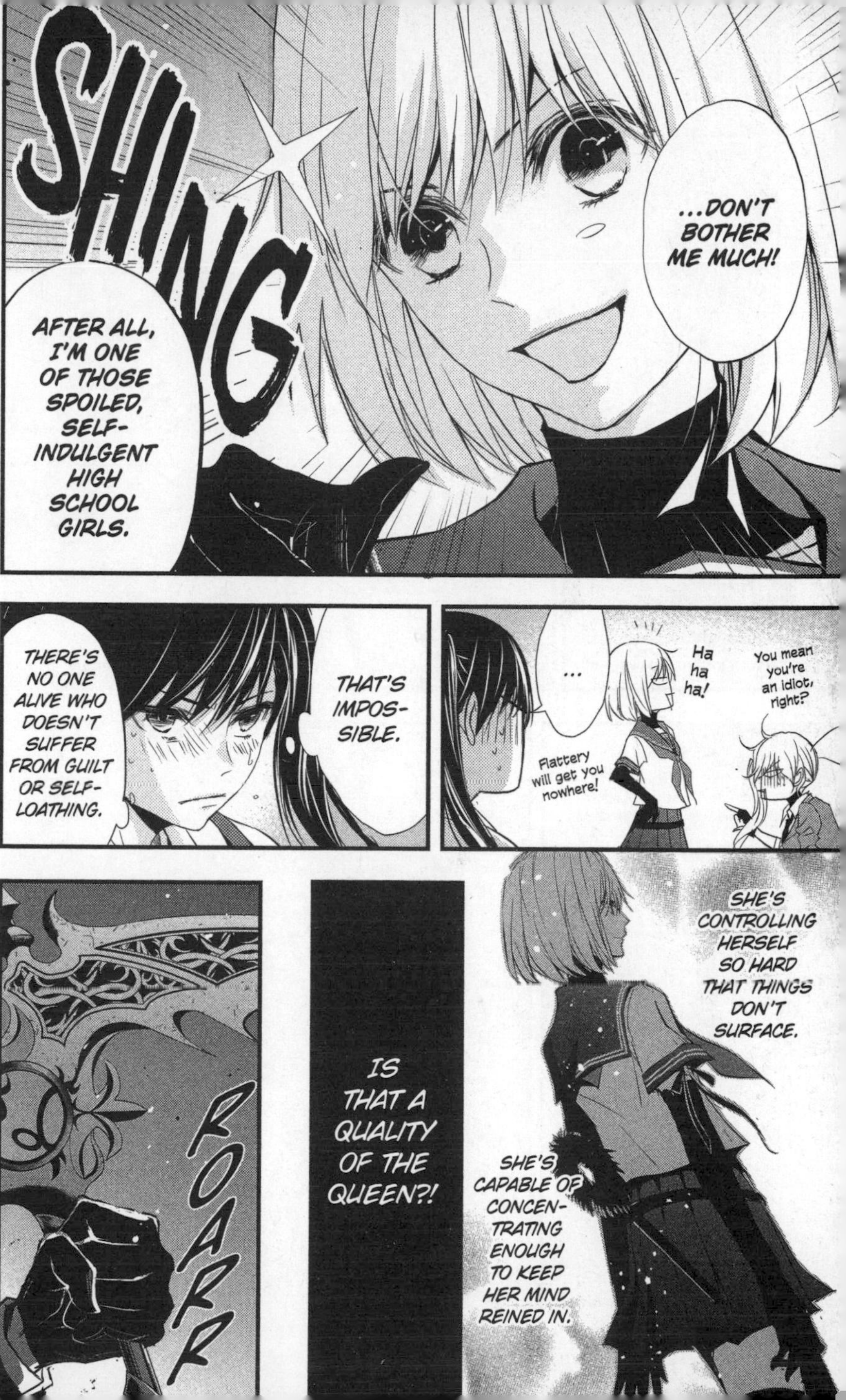
...DON'T BOTHER ME MUCH!
SHING
AFTER ALL, I'M ONE OF THOSE SPOILED, SELF-INDULGENT HIGH SCHOOL GIRLS.
You mean you're an idiot, right?
Ha ha ha!
...
Flattery will get you nowhere!
THAT'S IMPOSSIBLE.
THERE'S NO ONE ALIVE WHO DOESN'T SUFFER FROM GUILT OR SELF-LOATHING.
SHE'S CONTROLLING HERSELF SO HARD THAT THINGS DON'T SURFACE.
SHE'S CAPABLE OF CONCENTRATING ENOUGH TO KEEP HER MIND REINED IN.
IS THAT A QUALITY OF THE QUEEN?!
ROARR

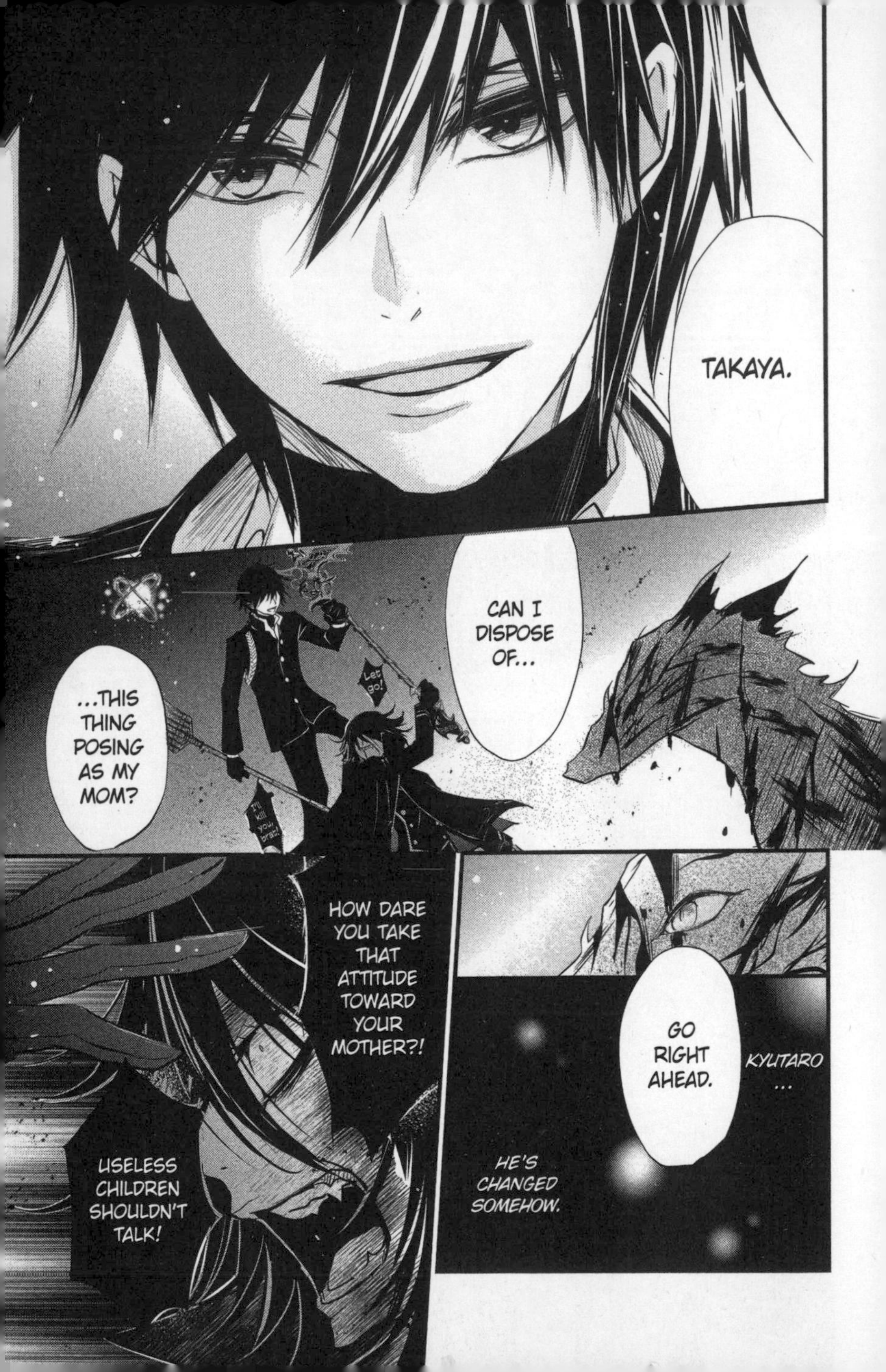
TAKAYA.
CAN I DISPOSE OF...
Let go!
...THIS THING POSING AS MY MOM?
I'll kill you, brat!
GO RIGHT AHEAD.
KYUTARO...
HE'S CHANGED SOMEHOW.
HOW DARE YOU TAKE THAT ATTITUDE TOWARD YOUR MOTHER?!
USELESS CHILDREN SHOULDN'T TALK!

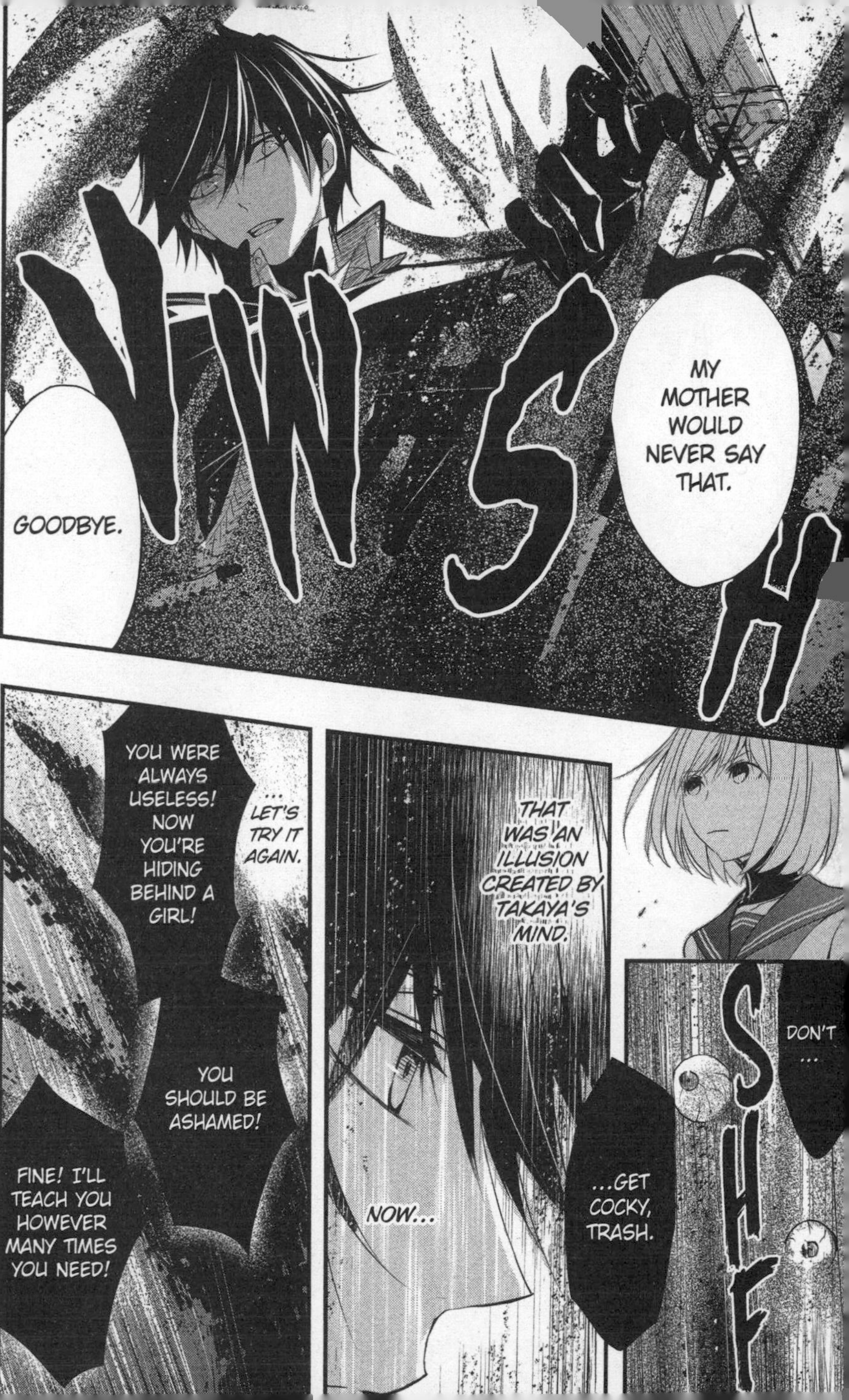
MY MOTHER WOULD NEVER SAY THAT.
VWSH
GOODBYE.
THAT WAS AN ILLUSION CREATED BY TAKAYA'S MIND.
DON'T ...
SHF
...GET COCKY, TRASH.
NOW...
... LET'S TRY IT AGAIN.
YOU WERE ALWAYS USELESS! NOW YOU'RE HIDING BEHIND A GIRL!
YOU SHOULD BE ASHAMED!
FINE! I'LL TEACH YOU HOWEVER MANY TIMES YOU NEED!

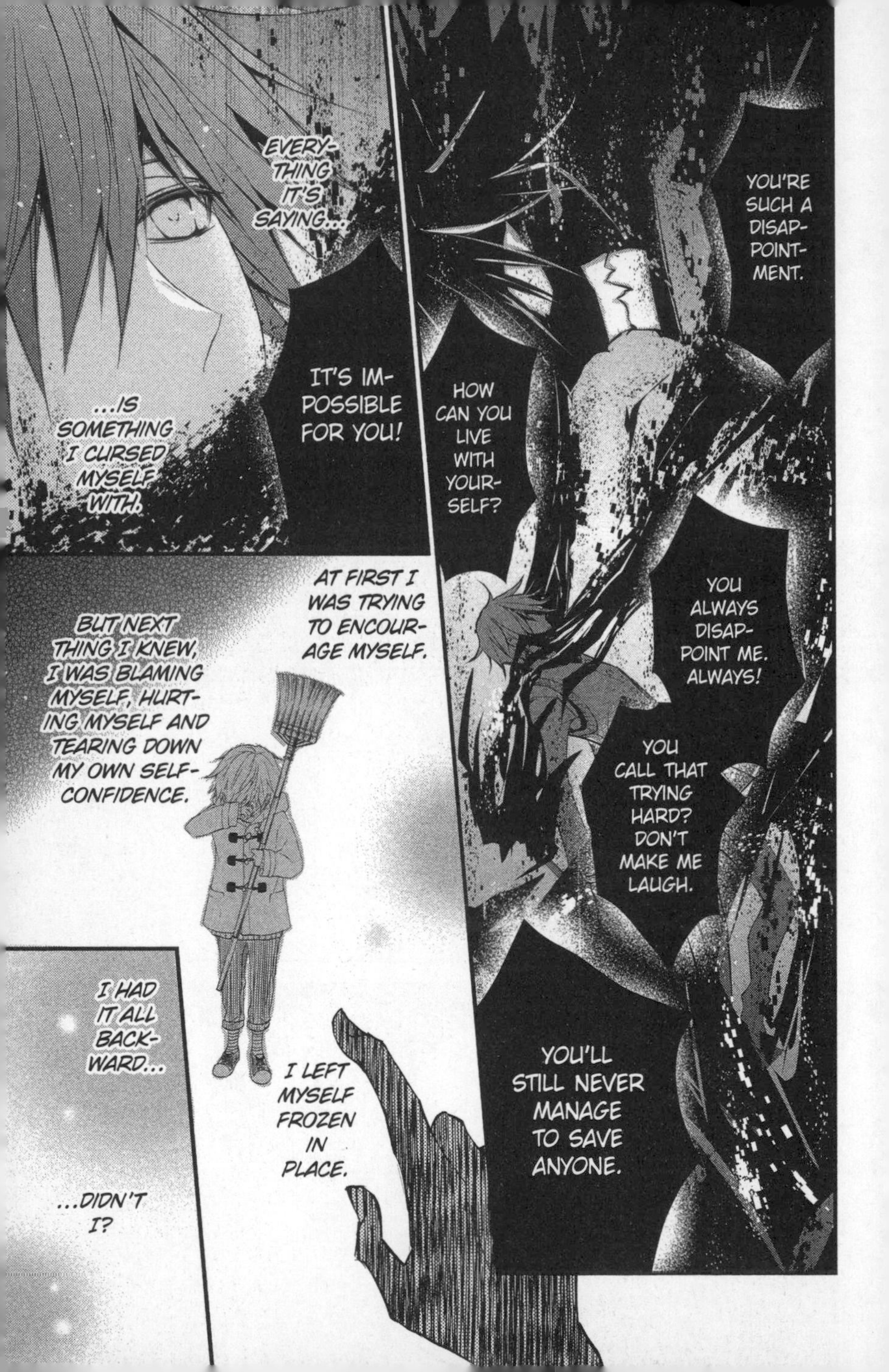

YOU'RE SUCH A DISAPPOINTMENT.
HOW CAN YOU LIVE WITH YOURSELF?
YOU ALWAYS DISAPPOINT ME. ALWAYS!
YOU CALL THAT TRYING HARD? DON'T MAKE ME LAUGH.
YOU'LL STILL NEVER MANAGE TO SAVE ANYONE.
IT'S IMPOSSIBLE FOR YOU!
EVERYTHING IT'S SAYING...
...IS SOMETHING I CURSED MYSELF WITH.
AT FIRST I WAS TRYING TO ENCOURAGE MYSELF.
BUT NEXT THING I KNEW, I WAS BLAMING MYSELF, HURTING MYSELF AND TEARING DOWN MY OWN SELF-CONFIDENCE.
I LEFT MYSELF FROZEN IN PLACE.
I HAD IT ALL BACKWARD...
...DIDN'T I?

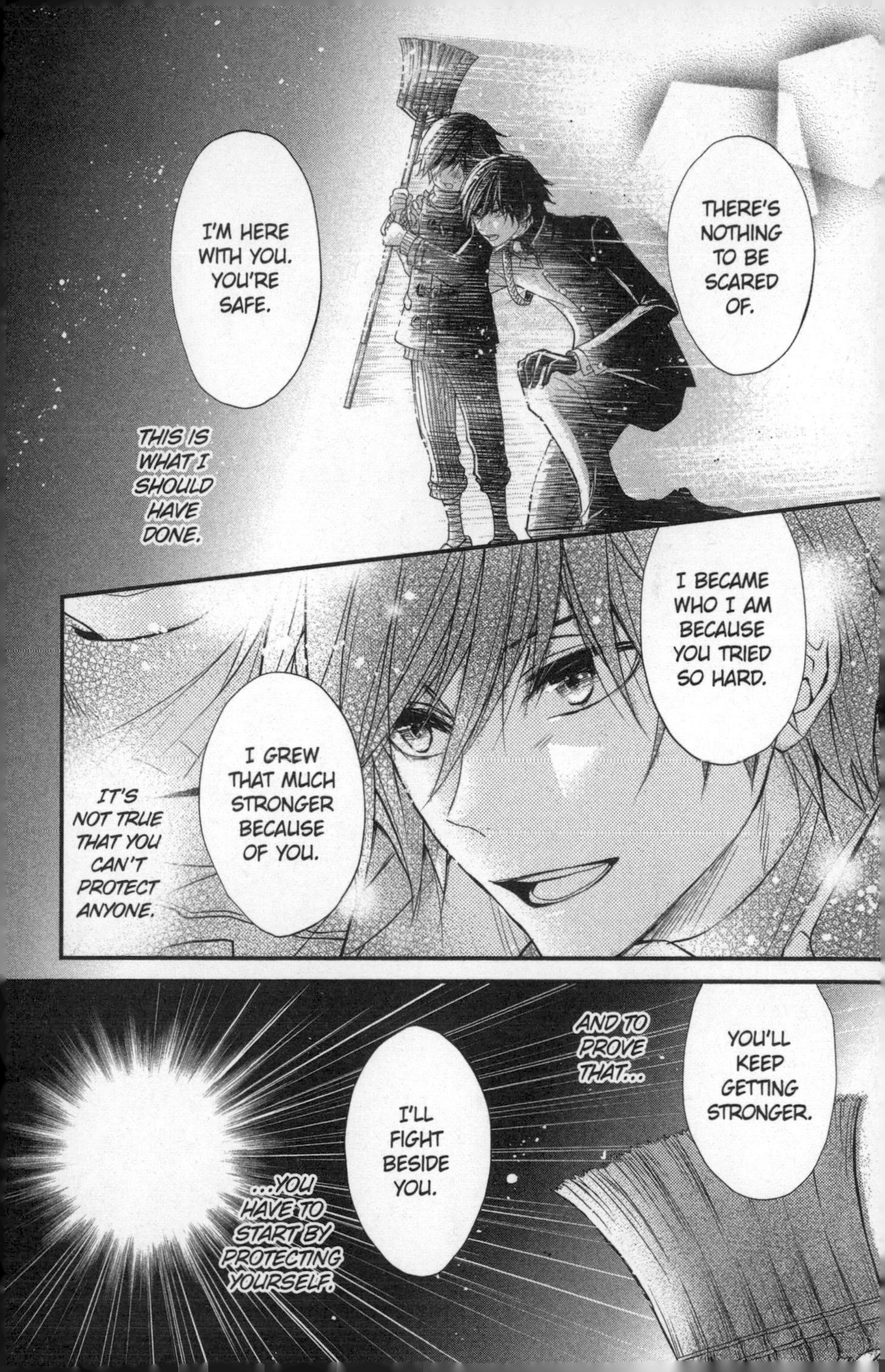
THERE'S NOTHING TO BE SCARED OF.
I'M HERE WITH YOU. YOU'RE SAFE.
THIS IS WHAT I SHOULD HAVE DONE.
I BECAME WHO I AM BECAUSE YOU TRIED SO HARD.
I GREW THAT MUCH STRONGER BECAUSE OF YOU.
IT'S NOT TRUE THAT YOU CAN'T PROTECT ANYONE.
YOU'LL KEEP GETTING STRONGER.
AND TO PROVE THAT...
I'LL FIGHT BESIDE YOU.
...YOU HAVE TO START BY PROTECTING YOURSELF.

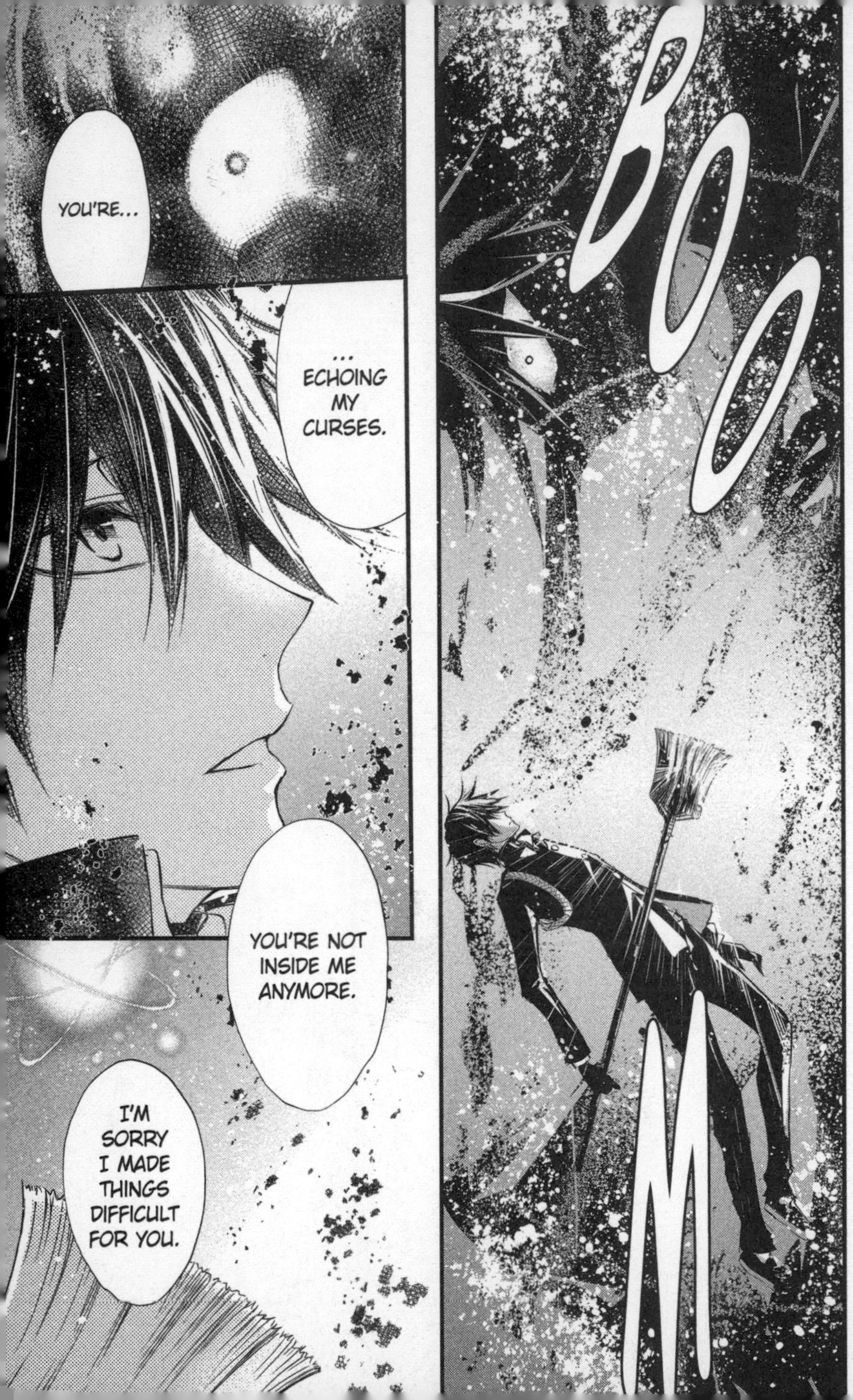
BOOOM
YOU'RE...
... ECHOING MY CURSES.
YOU'RE NOT INSIDE ME ANYMORE.
I'M SORRY I MADE THINGS DIFFICULT FOR YOU.

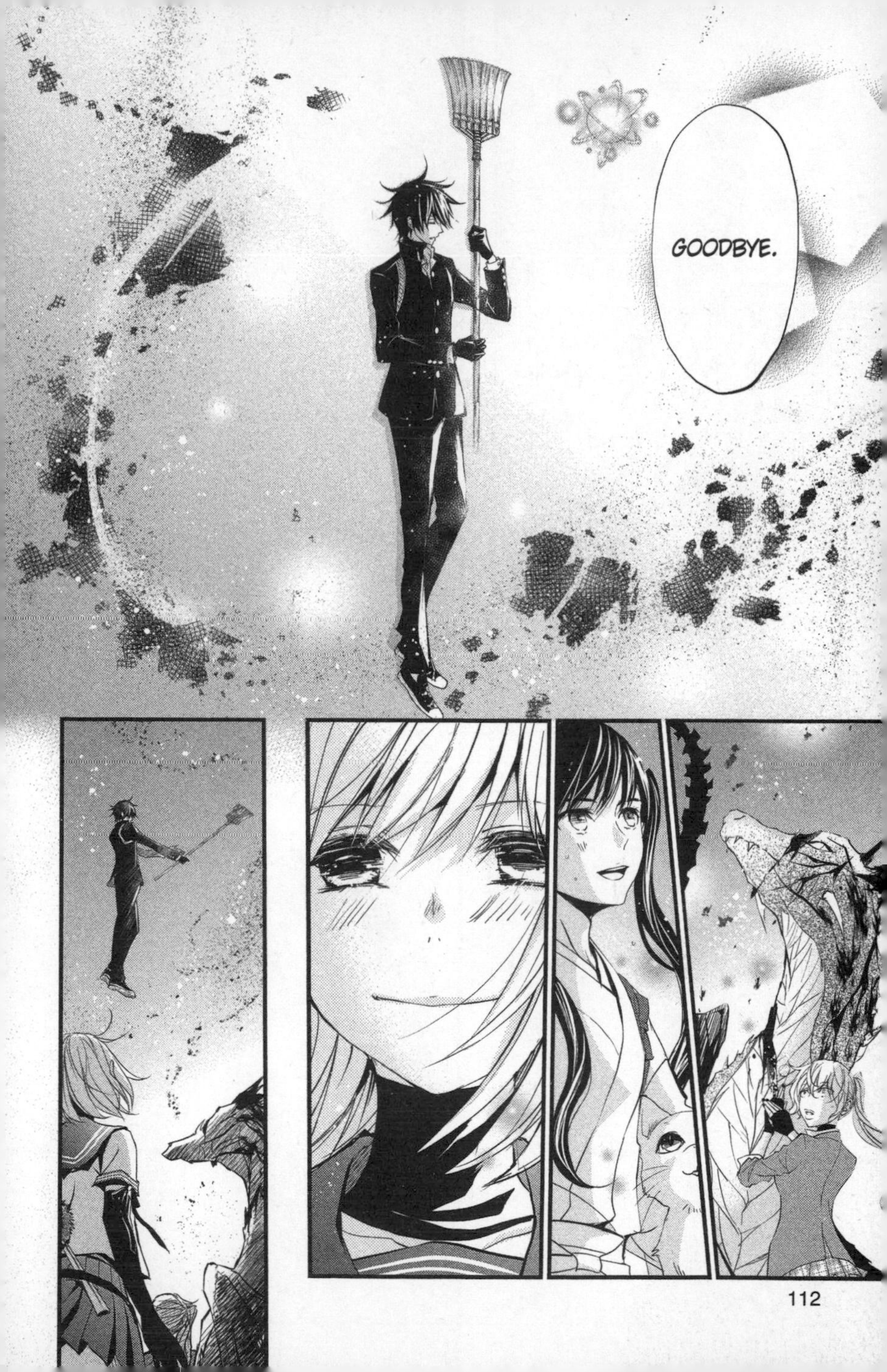
GOODBYE.

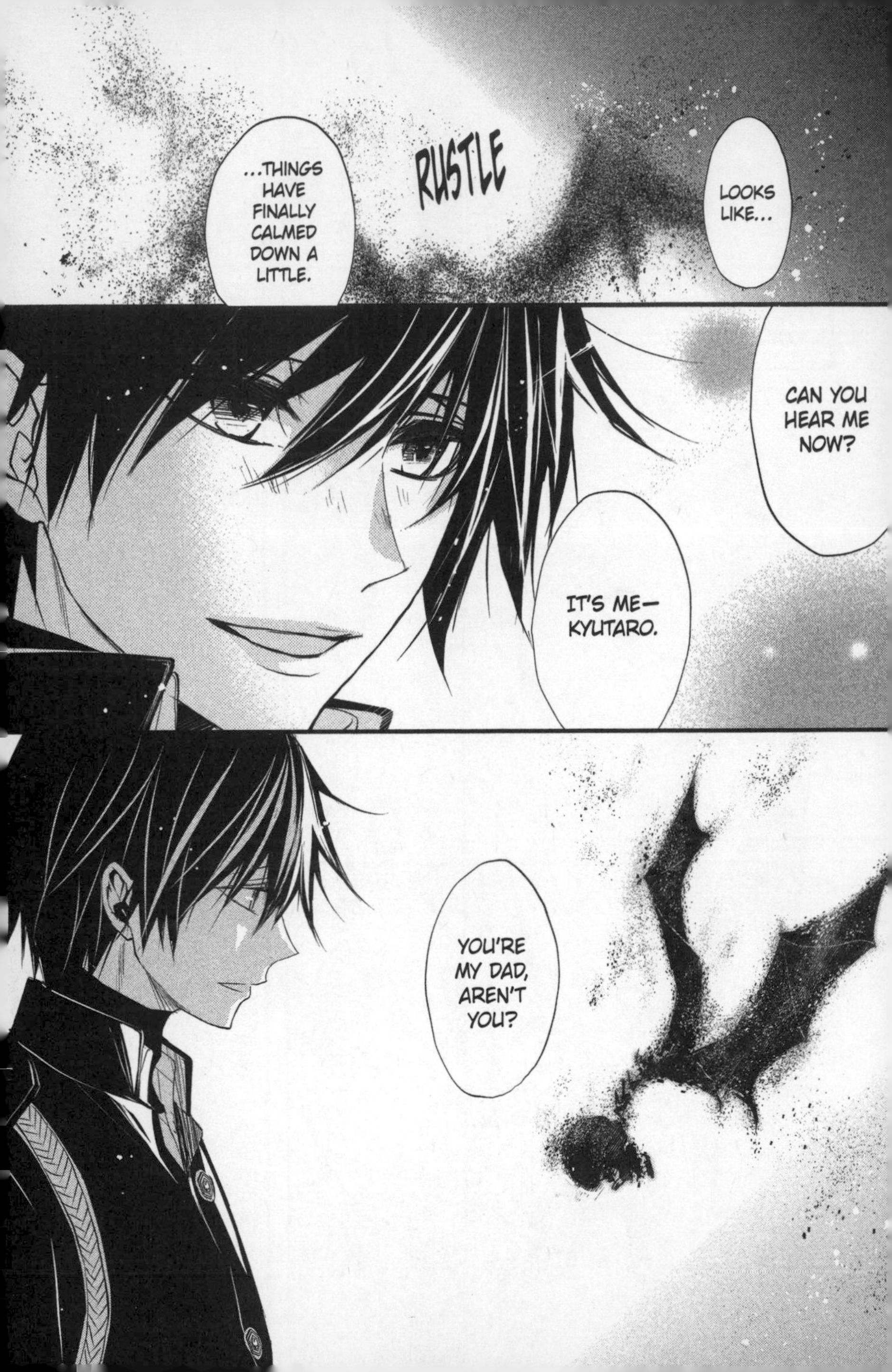
LOOKS LIKE...
RUSTLE
...THINGS HAVE FINALLY CALMED DOWN A LITTLE.
CAN YOU HEAR ME NOW?
IT'S ME—KYUTARO.
YOU'RE MY DAD, AREN'T YOU?

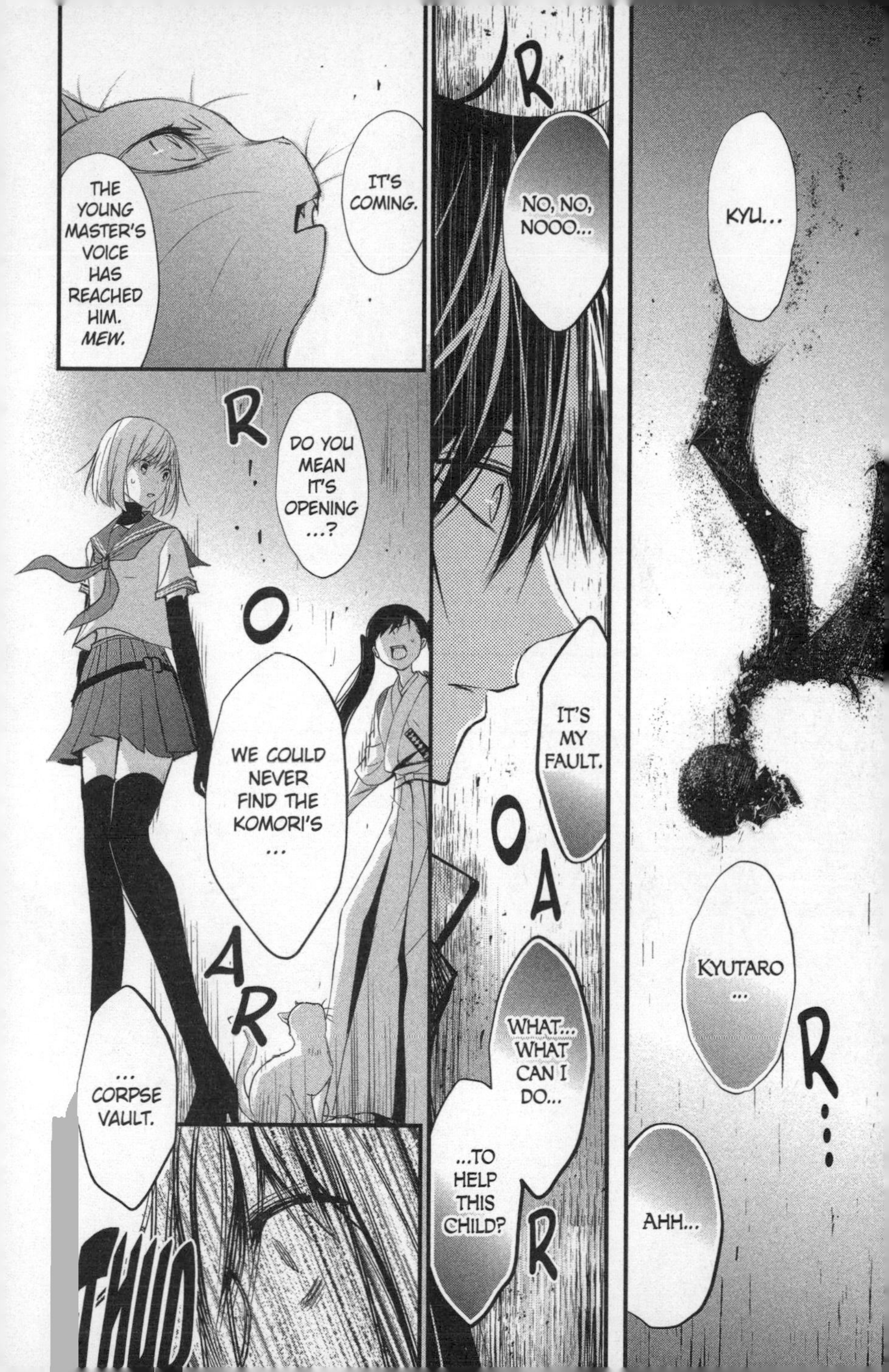
KYU...
KYUTARO ...
R...
AHH...
R
NO, NO, NOOO...
IT'S MY FAULT.
O
A
WHAT... WHAT CAN I DO...
...TO HELP THIS CHILD?
R
IT'S COMING.
THE YOUNG MASTER'S VOICE HAS REACHED HIM. MEW.
DO YOU MEAN IT'S OPENING ...?
R
O
WE COULD NEVER FIND THE KOMORI'S ...
AR
... CORPSE VAULT.
THUD

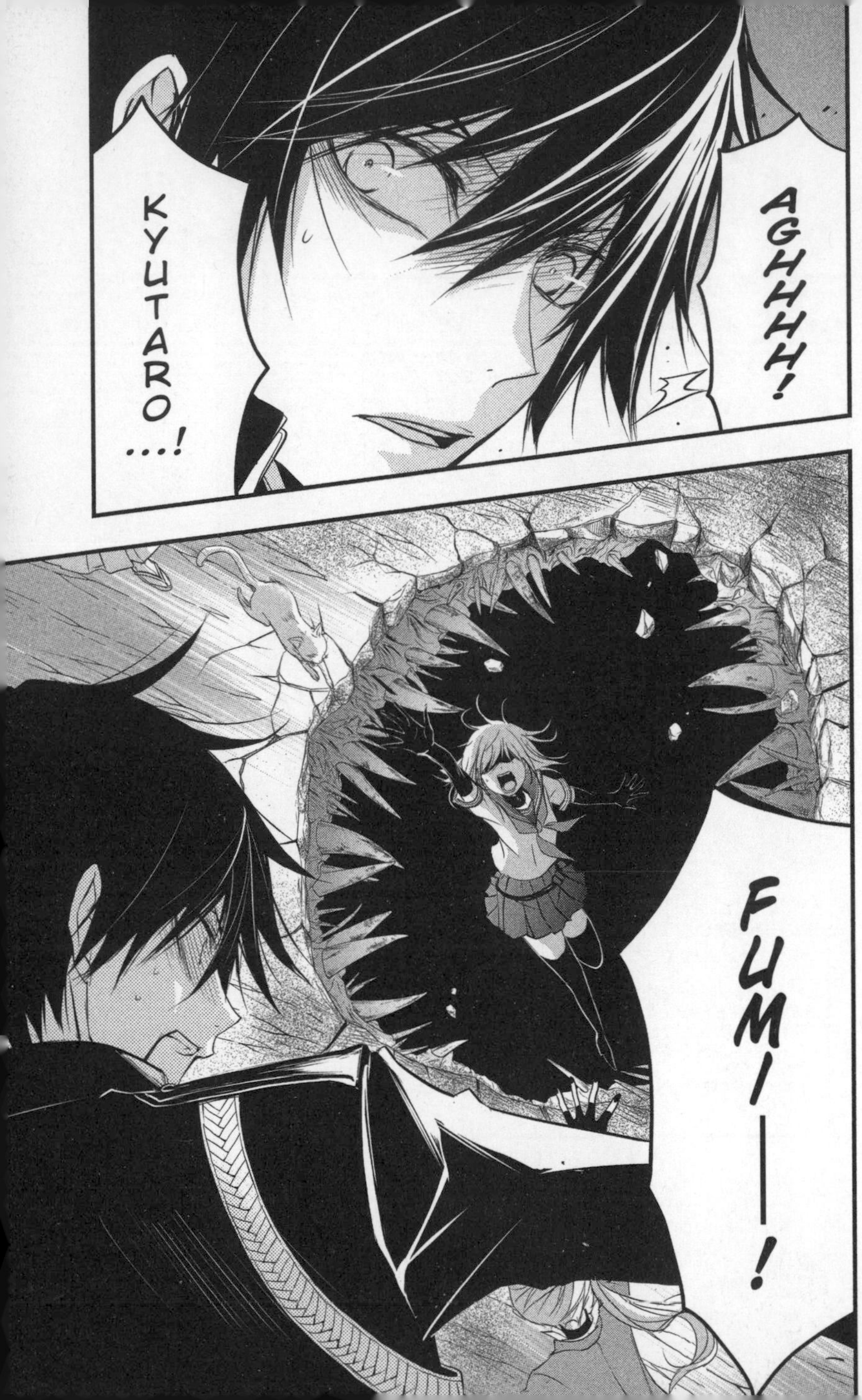
AGHHHH!
KYUTARO...!
FUMI——!

MONTHLY BETSUCOMI SALE DATE NOTICE ON TWITTER

CHAPTER 34

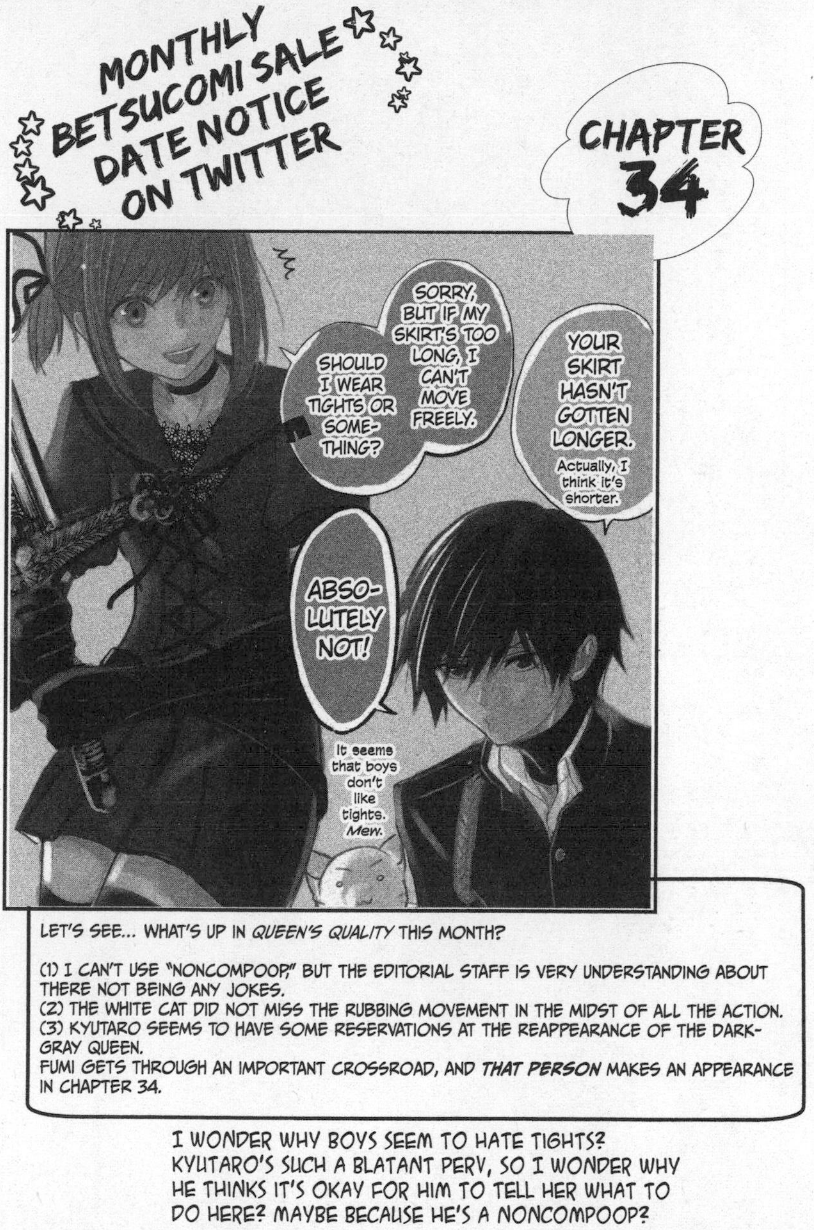
YOUR SKIRT HASN'T GOTTEN LONGER.
Actually, I think it's shorter.
SORRY, BUT IF MY SKIRT'S TOO LONG, I CAN'T MOVE FREELY.
SHOULD I WEAR TIGHTS OR SOME-THING?
ABSO-LUTELY NOT!
It seems that boys don't like tights. *Mew.*

LET'S SEE... WHAT'S UP IN *QUEEN'S QUALITY* THIS MONTH?

(1) I CAN'T USE "NONCOMPOOP," BUT THE EDITORIAL STAFF IS VERY UNDERSTANDING ABOUT THERE NOT BEING ANY JOKES.
(2) THE WHITE CAT DID NOT MISS THE RUBBING MOVEMENT IN THE MIDST OF ALL THE ACTION.
(3) KYUTARO SEEMS TO HAVE SOME RESERVATIONS AT THE REAPPEARANCE OF THE DARK-GRAY QUEEN.
FUMI GETS THROUGH AN IMPORTANT CROSSROAD, AND *THAT PERSON* MAKES AN APPEARANCE IN CHAPTER 34.

I WONDER WHY BOYS SEEM TO HATE TIGHTS? KYUTARO'S SUCH A BLATANT PERV, SO I WONDER WHY HE THINKS IT'S OKAY FOR HIM TO TELL HER WHAT TO DO HERE? MAYBE BECAUSE HE'S A NONCOMPOOP?

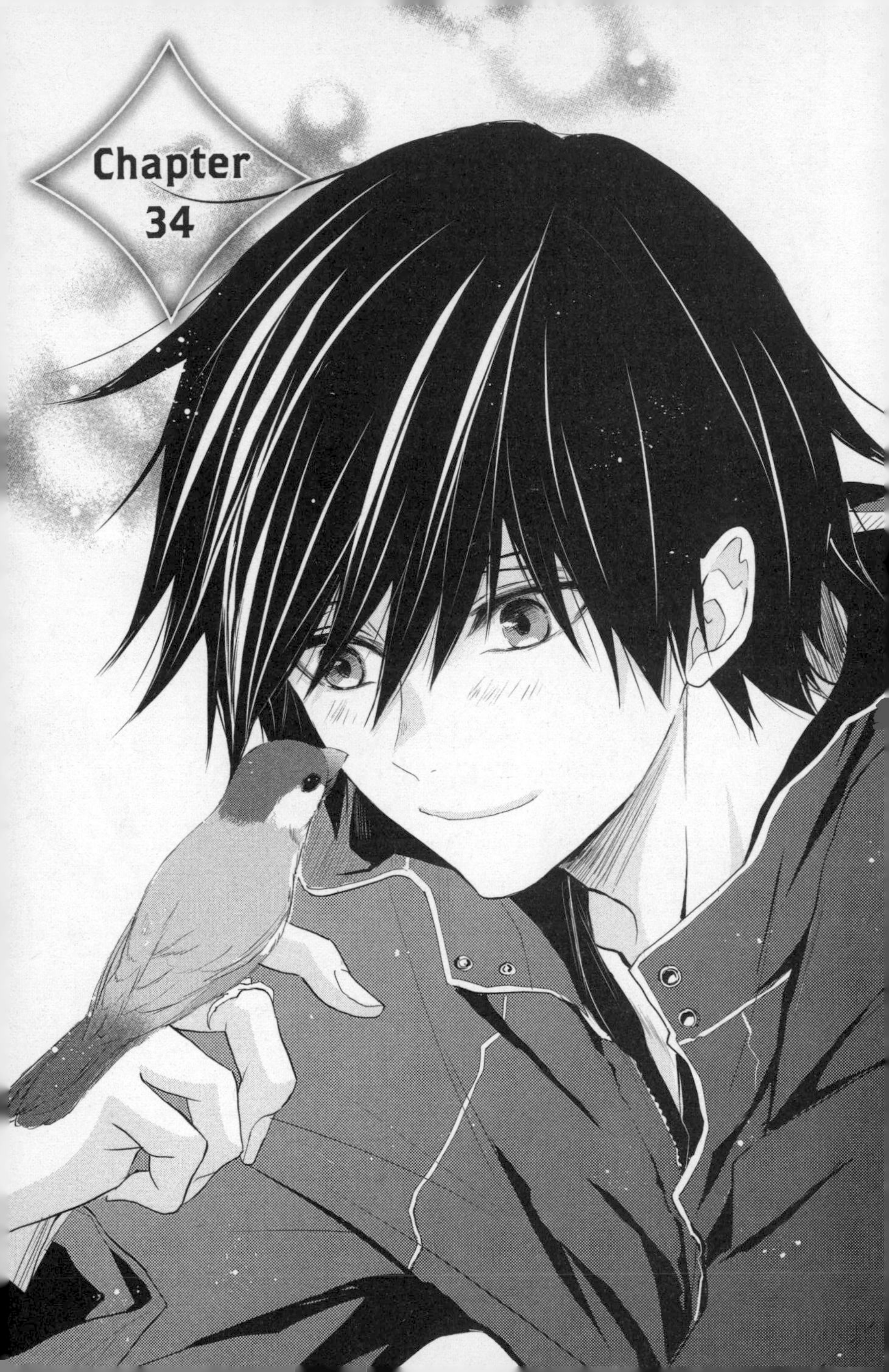
Chapter
34

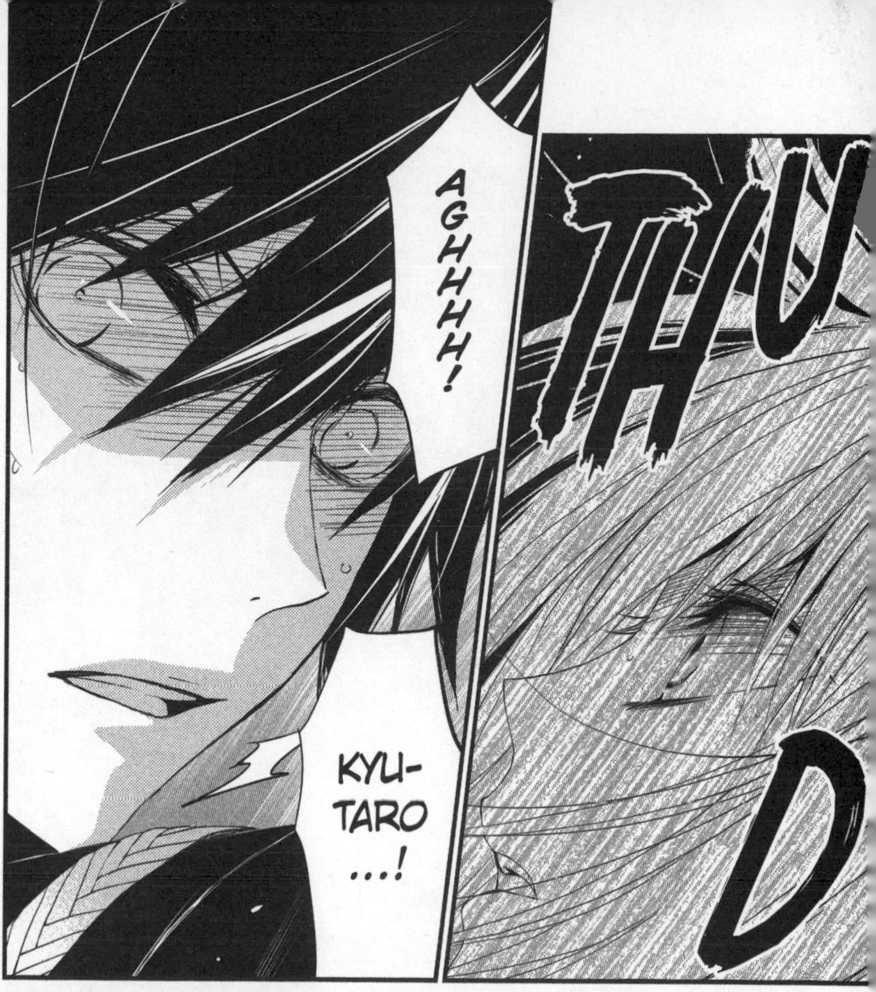
THUD
AGHHHH!
KYU-TARO ...!

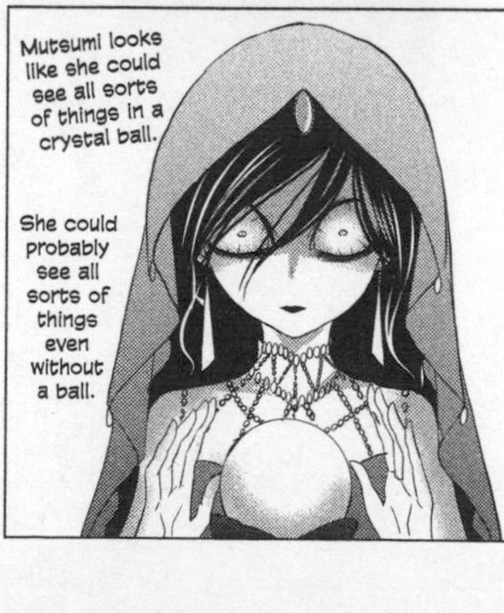
Mutsumi looks like she could see all sorts of things in a crystal ball.
She could probably see all sorts of things even without a ball.

Speaking of balls, I'd like to have a crystal ball. There's a sense of romance about them. If I bought one and practiced using it, maybe it'd show me how my story should go. That would be amazing!

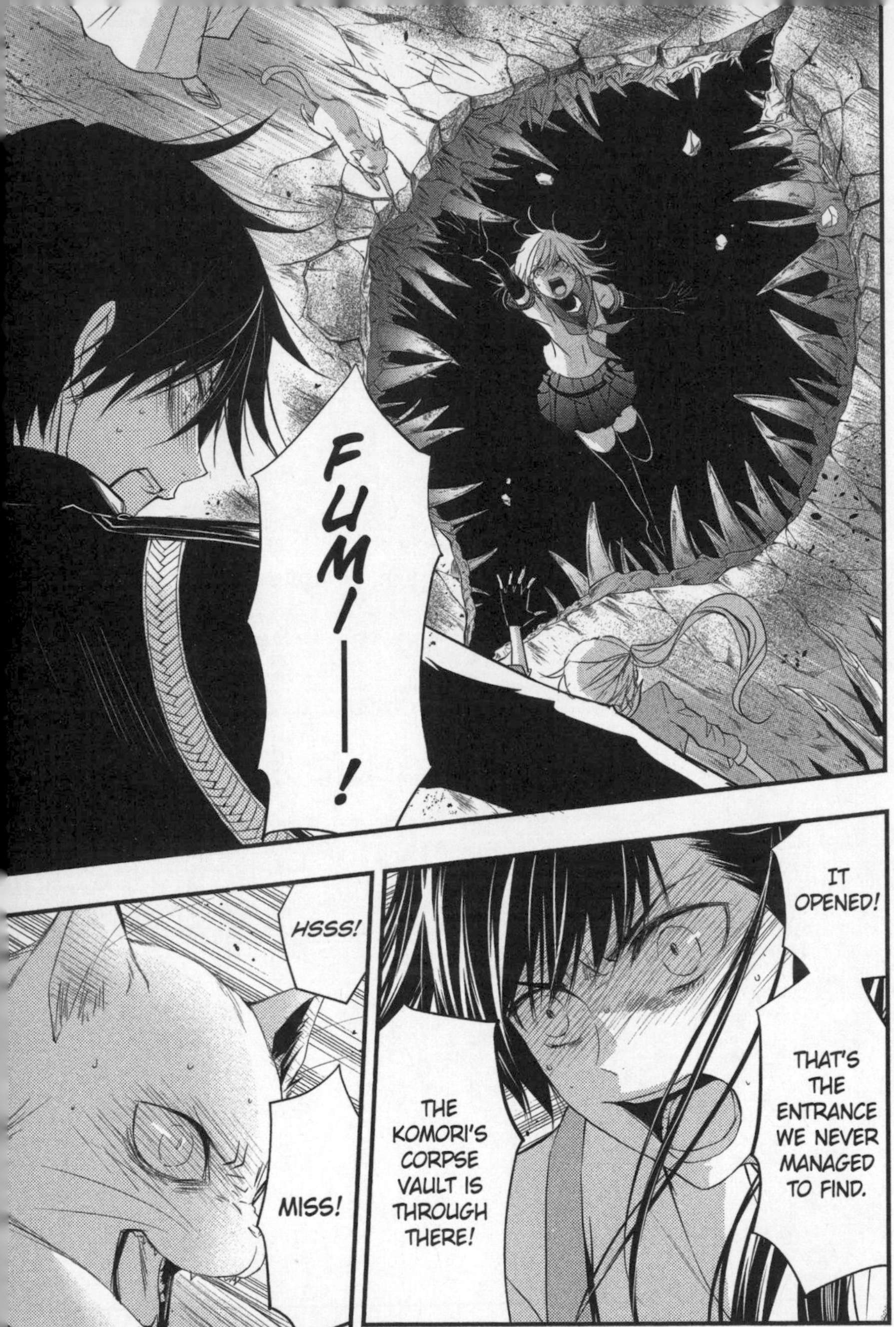
FUMI——!
IT OPENED!
THAT'S THE ENTRANCE WE NEVER MANAGED TO FIND.
THE KOMORI'S CORPSE VAULT IS THROUGH THERE!
HSSS!
MISS!

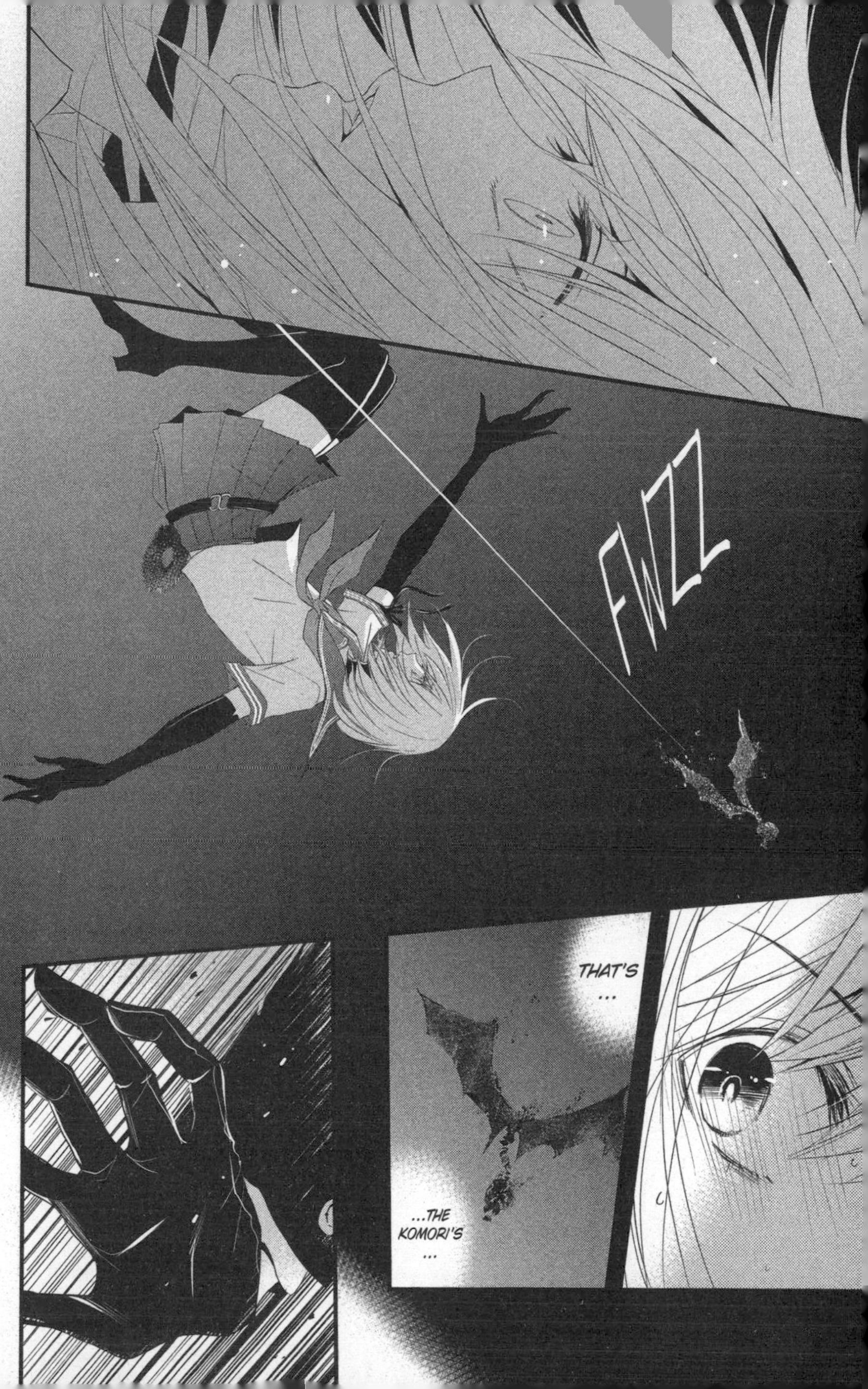
FWZZ
THAT'S ...
...THE KOMORI'S ...

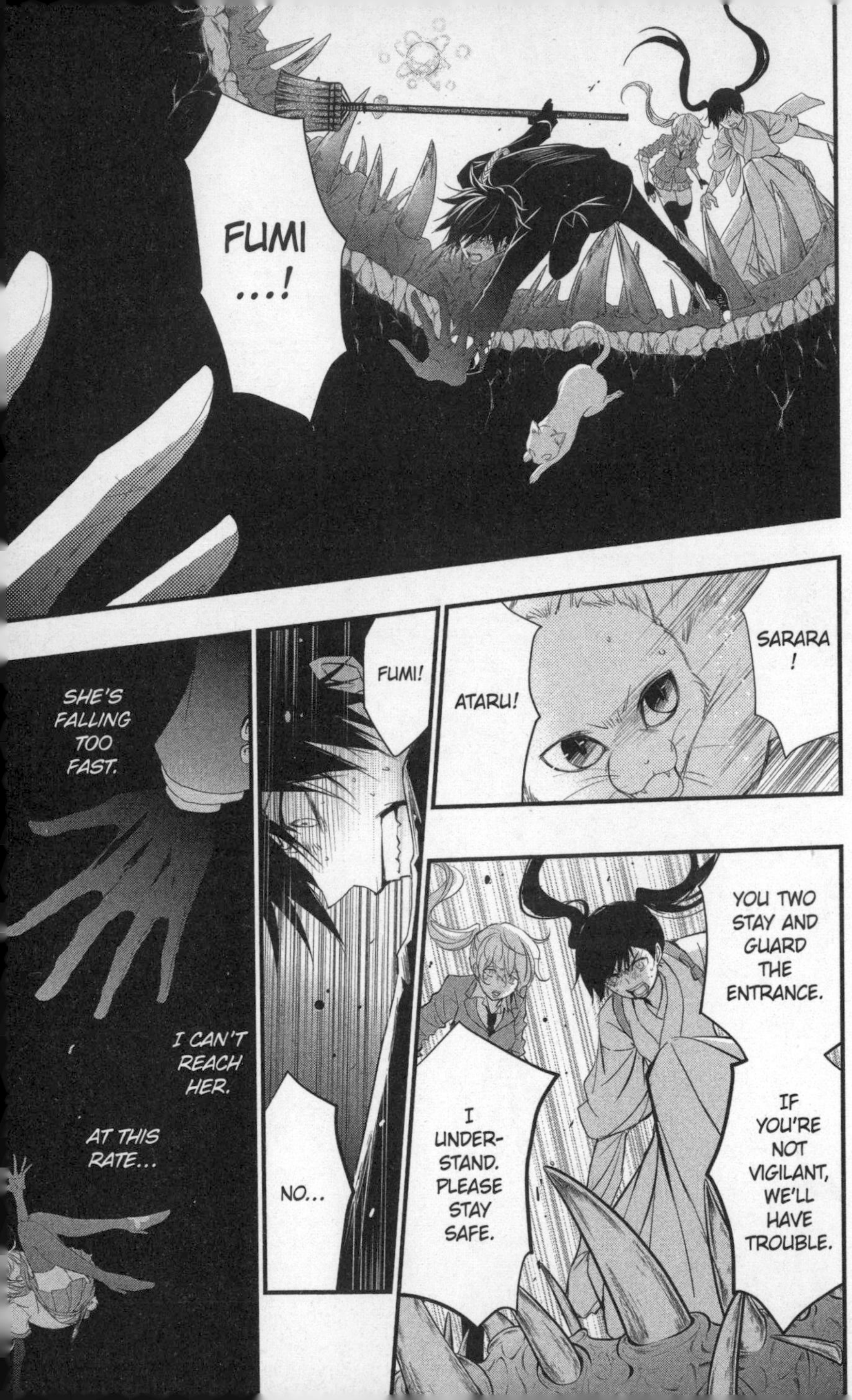
FUMI ...!
SARARA !
ATARU!
YOU TWO STAY AND GUARD THE ENTRANCE.
IF YOU'RE NOT VIGILANT, WE'LL HAVE TROUBLE.
I UNDER-STAND. PLEASE STAY SAFE.
FUMI!
NO...
SHE'S FALLING TOO FAST.
I CAN'T REACH HER.
AT THIS RATE...

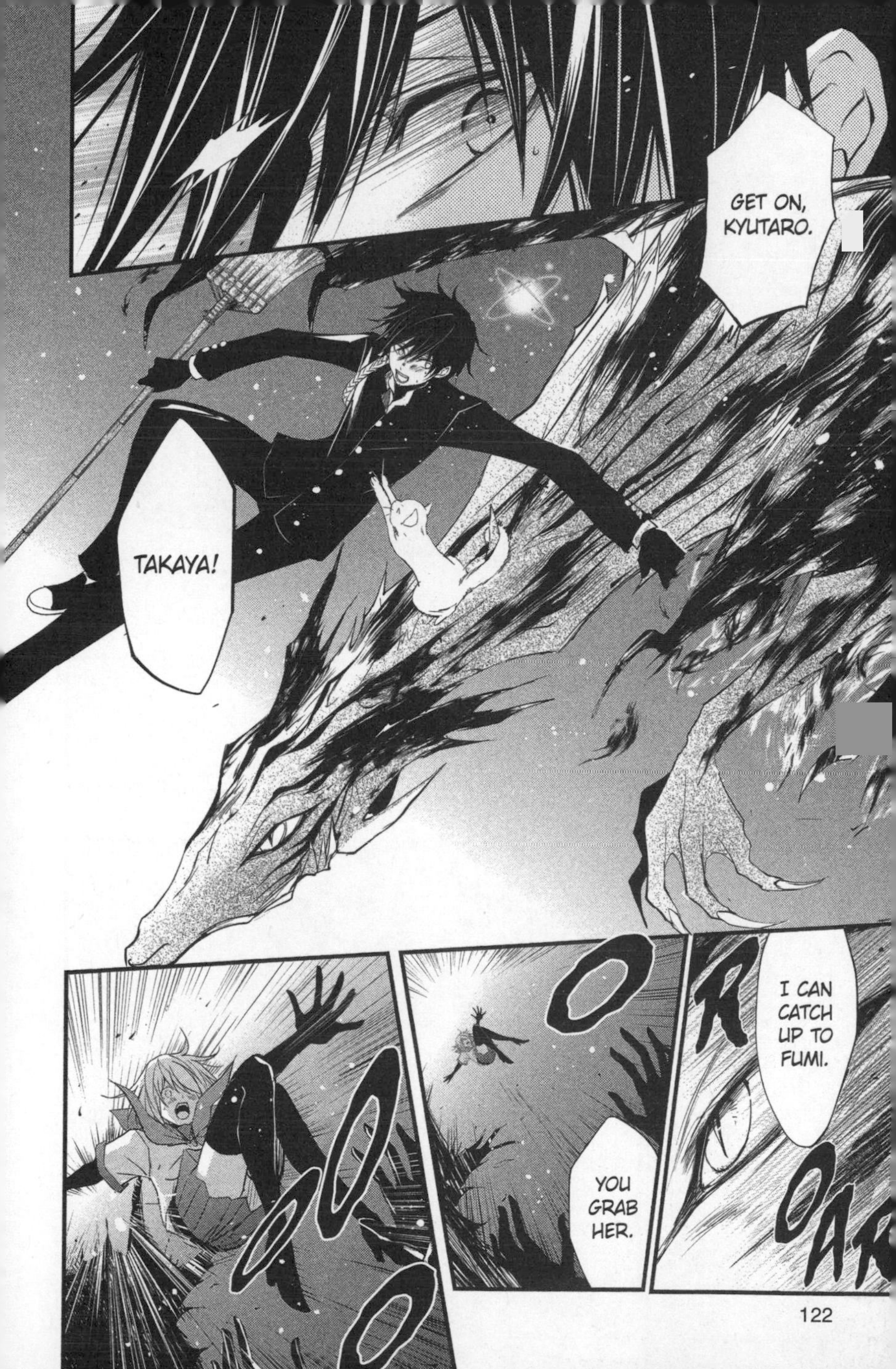
GET ON, KYUTARO.
TAKAYA!
I CAN CATCH UP TO FUMI.
YOU GRAB HER.

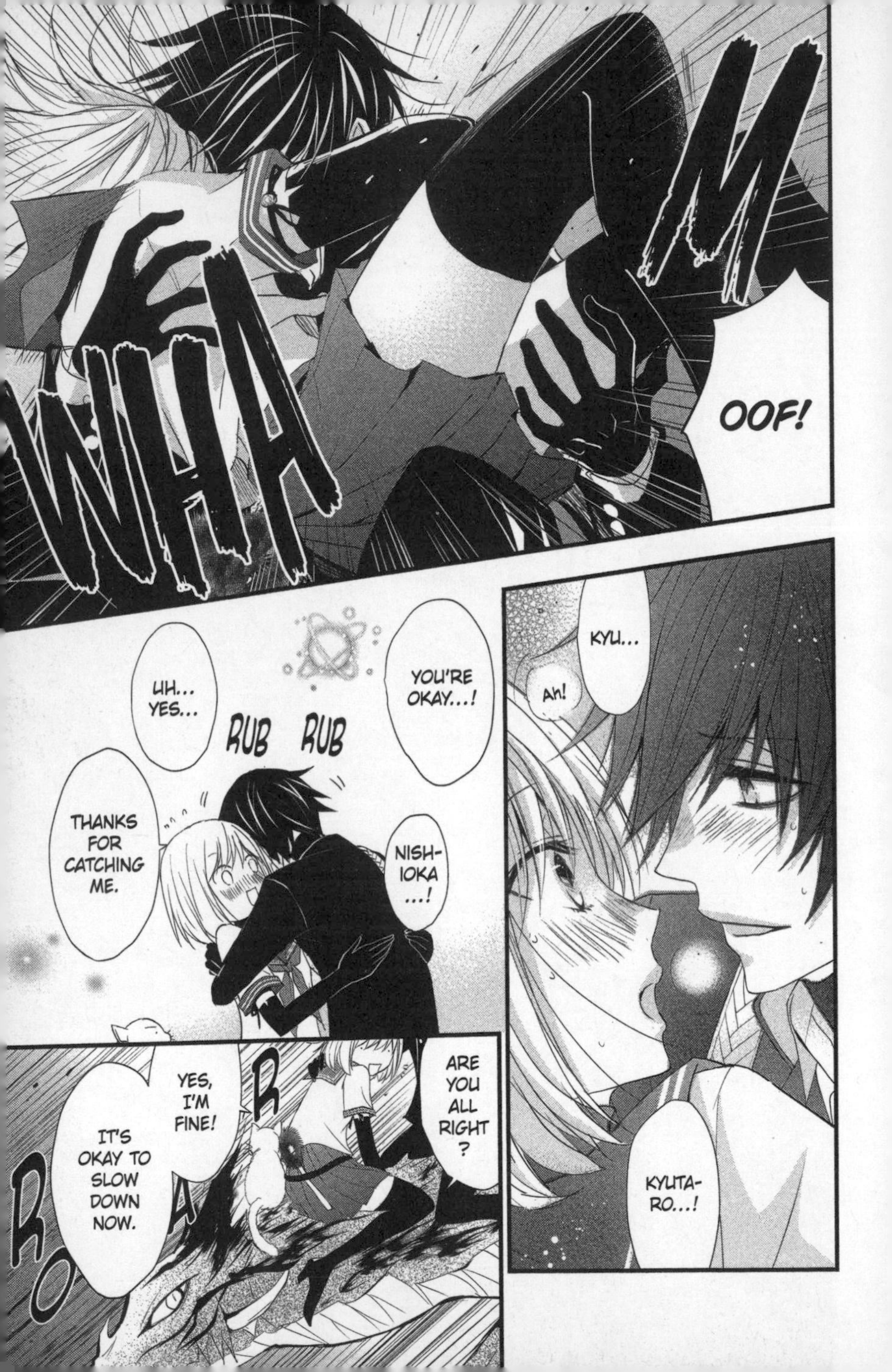
WHAM
OOF!
KYU...
Ah!
KYUTA-RO...!
YOU'RE OKAY...!
UH... YES...
RUB RUB
NISH-IOKA...!
THANKS FOR CATCHING ME.
ARE YOU ALL RIGHT?
YES, I'M FINE!
IT'S OKAY TO SLOW DOWN NOW.
ROAR

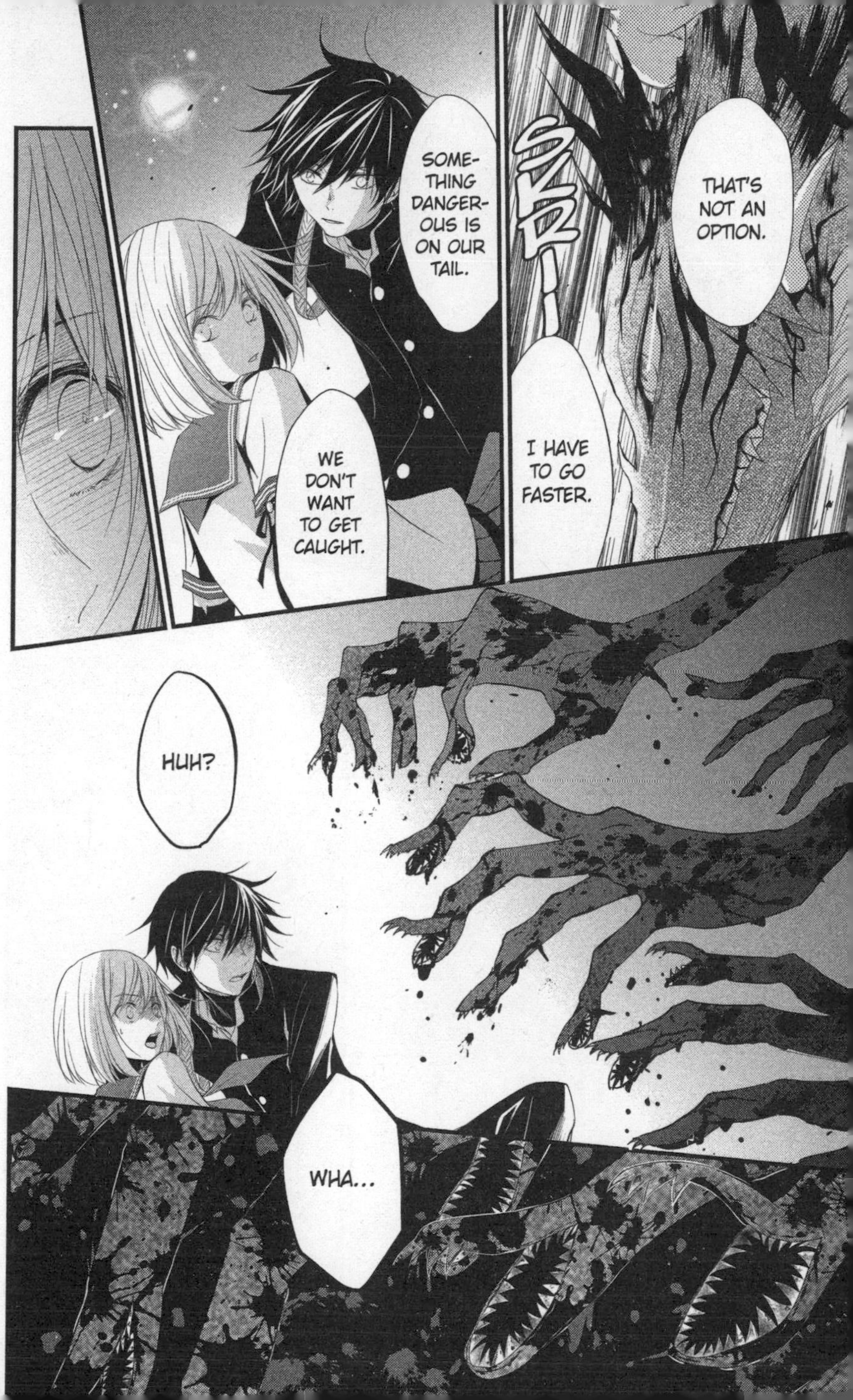
SKRI
THAT'S NOT AN OPTION.
I HAVE TO GO FASTER.
SOME-THING DANGER-OUS IS ON OUR TAIL.
WE DON'T WANT TO GET CAUGHT.
HUH?
WHA...

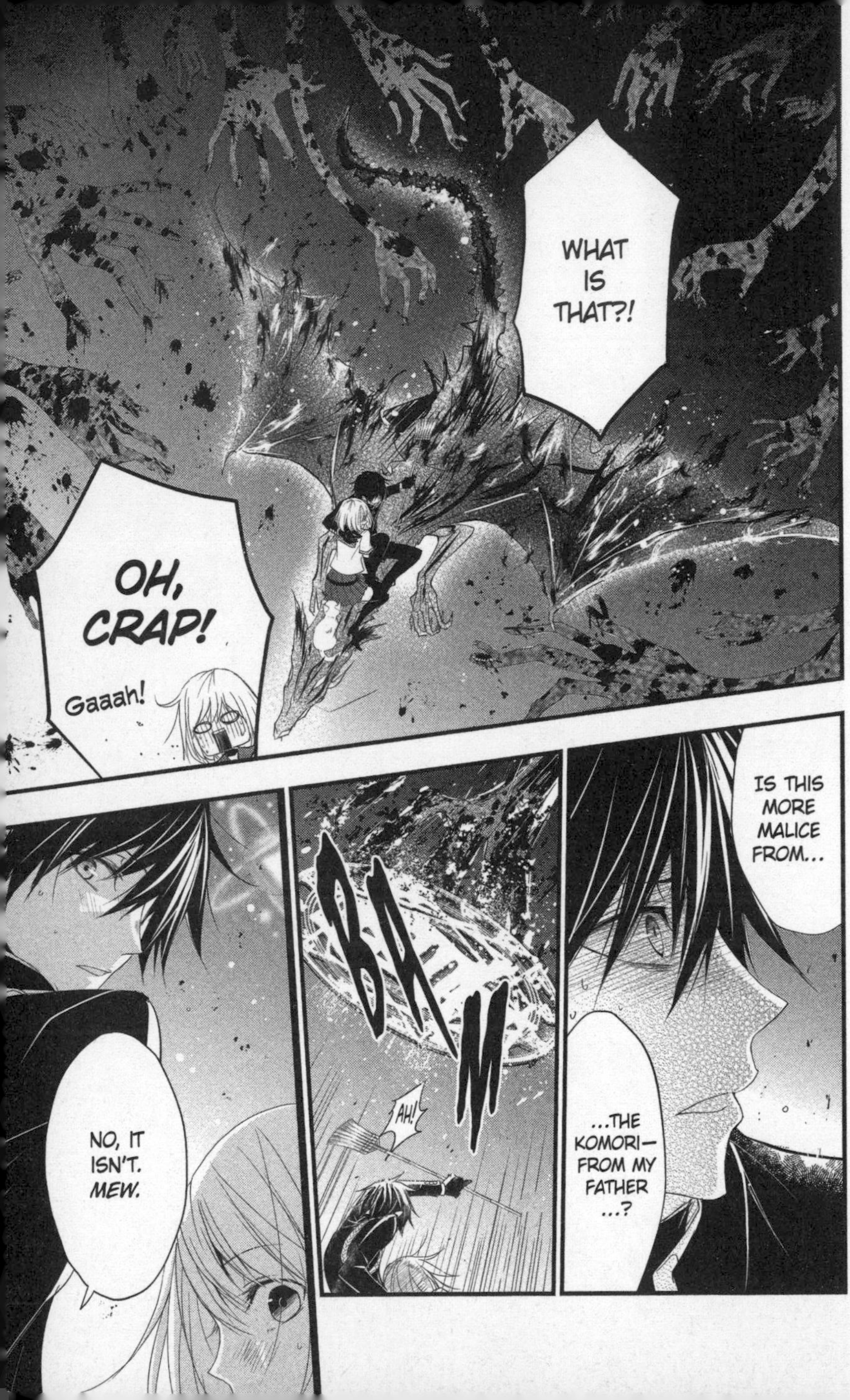
WHAT IS THAT?!
OH, CRAP!
Gaaah!
IS THIS MORE MALICE FROM...
...THE KOMORI— FROM MY FATHER ...?
BAM
AH!
NO, IT ISN'T. *MEW.*

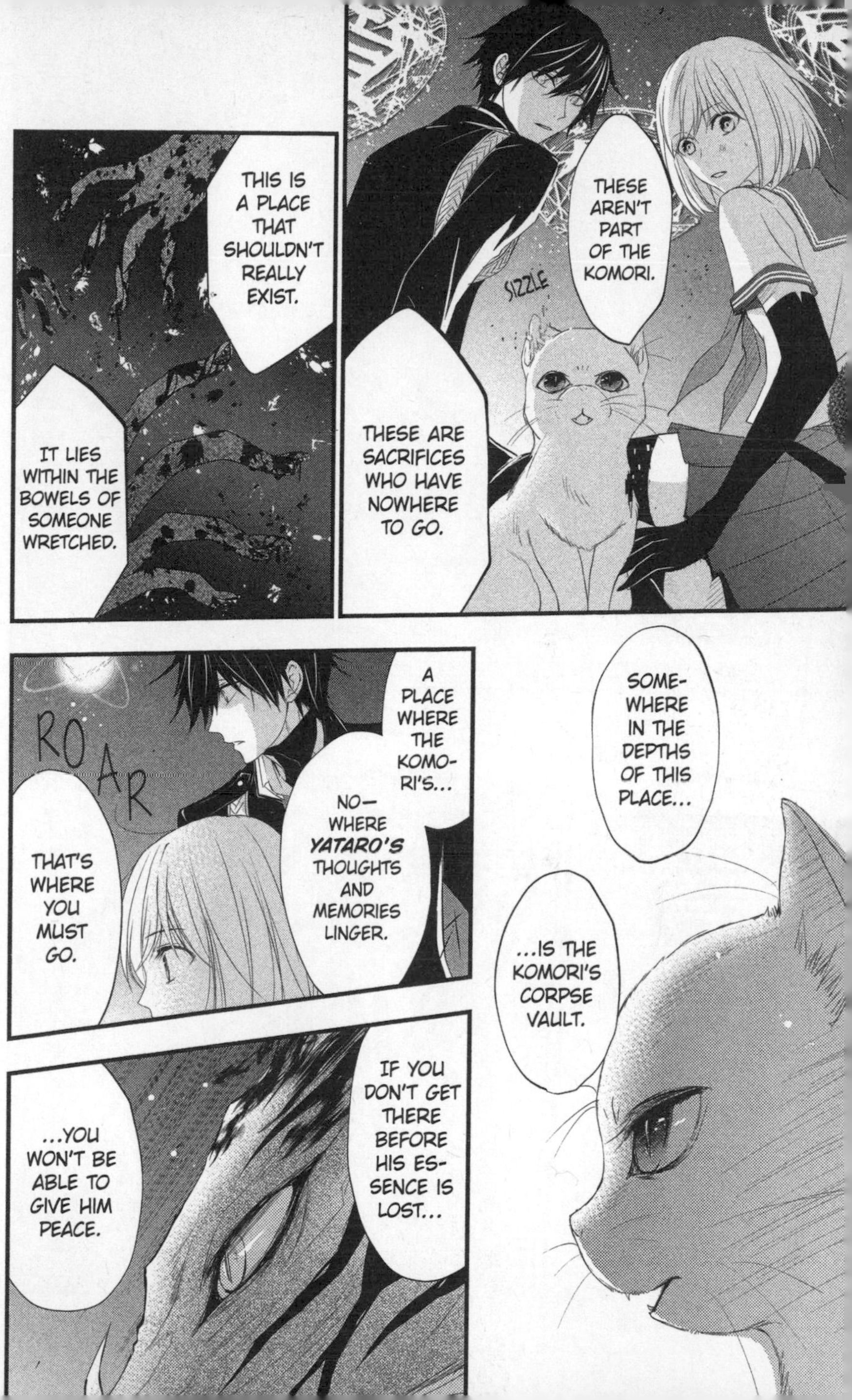
THESE AREN'T PART OF THE KOMORI.
SIZZLE
THESE ARE SACRIFICES WHO HAVE NOWHERE TO GO.
THIS IS A PLACE THAT SHOULDN'T REALLY EXIST.
IT LIES WITHIN THE BOWELS OF SOMEONE WRETCHED.
SOME-WHERE IN THE DEPTHS OF THIS PLACE...
...IS THE KOMORI'S CORPSE VAULT.
A PLACE WHERE THE KOMO-RI'S...
NO— WHERE *YATARO'S* THOUGHTS AND MEMORIES LINGER.
ROAR
THAT'S WHERE YOU MUST GO.
IF YOU DON'T GET THERE BEFORE HIS ES-SENCE IS LOST...
...YOU WON'T BE ABLE TO GIVE HIM PEACE.

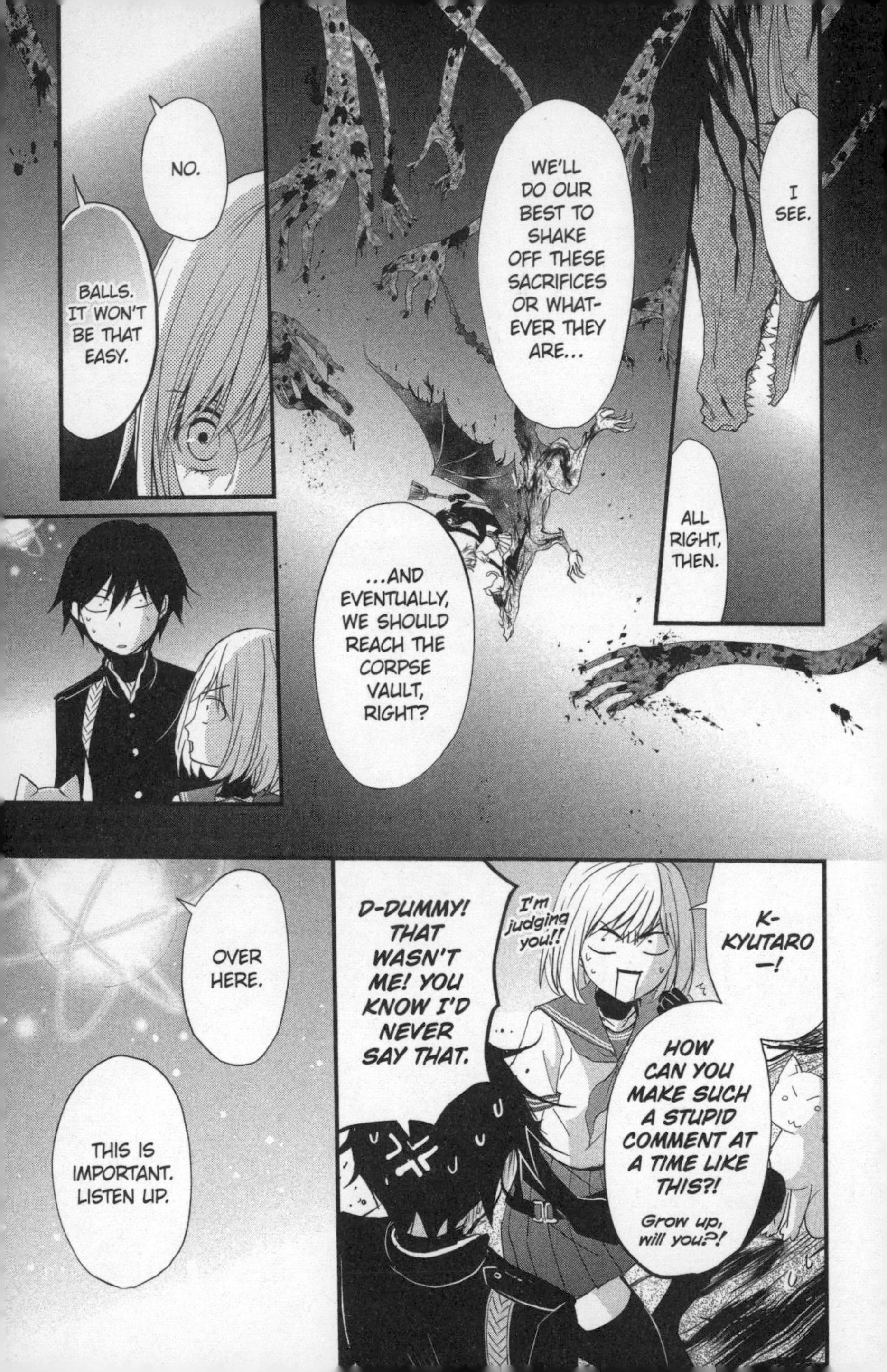
I SEE.
ALL RIGHT, THEN.
WE'LL DO OUR BEST TO SHAKE OFF THESE SACRIFICES OR WHAT-EVER THEY ARE...
...AND EVENTUALLY, WE SHOULD REACH THE CORPSE VAULT, RIGHT?
NO.
BALLS. IT WON'T BE THAT EASY.
K-KYUTARO—!
HOW CAN YOU MAKE SUCH A STUPID COMMENT AT A TIME LIKE THIS?!
Grow up, will you?!
I'm judging you!!
D-DUMMY! THAT WASN'T ME! YOU KNOW I'D NEVER SAY THAT.
...
OVER HERE.
THIS IS IMPORTANT. LISTEN UP.

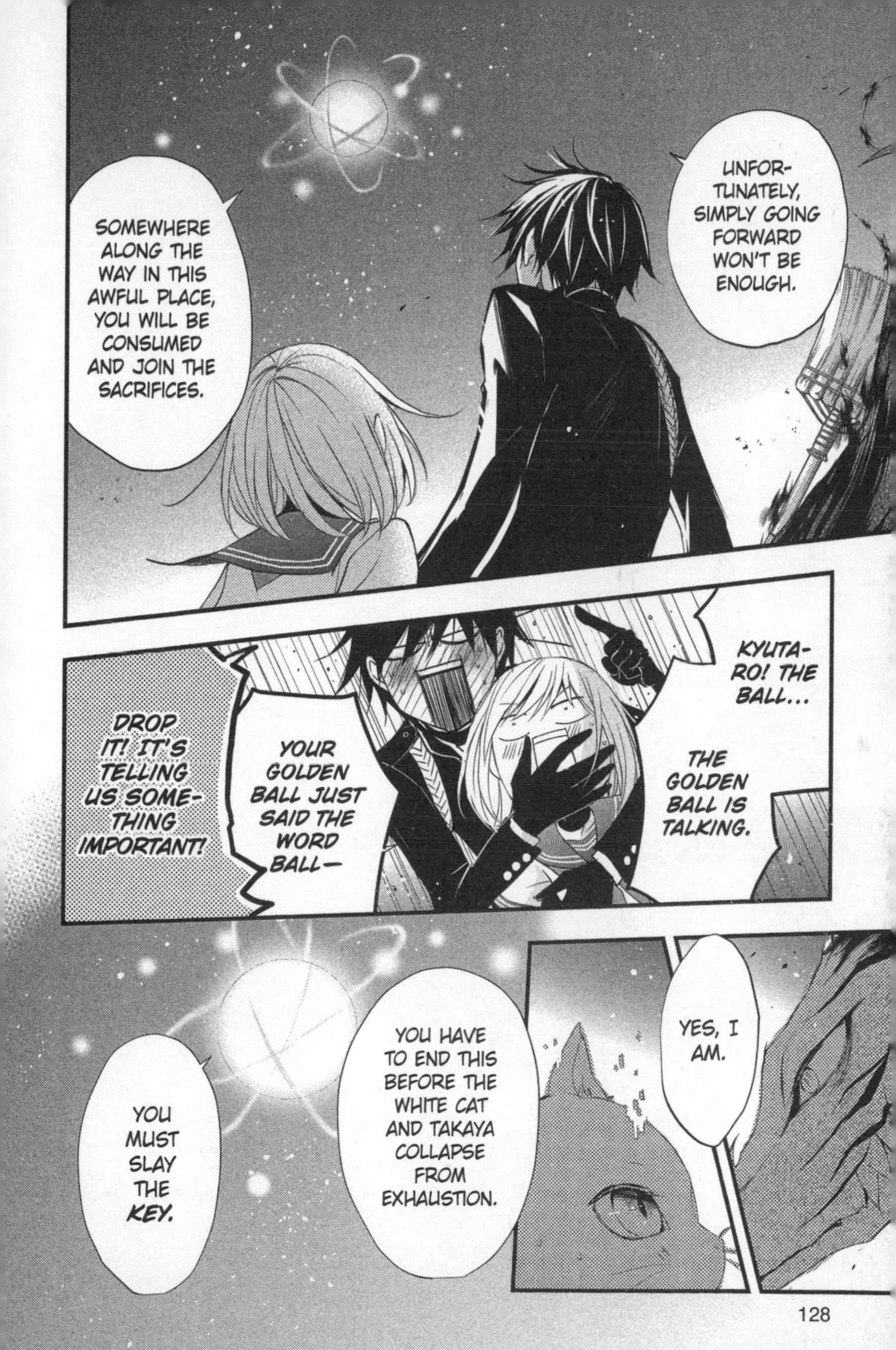

UNFOR-TUNATELY, SIMPLY GOING FORWARD WON'T BE ENOUGH.
SOMEWHERE ALONG THE WAY IN THIS AWFUL PLACE, YOU WILL BE CONSUMED AND JOIN THE SACRIFICES.
KYUTA-RO! THE BALL...
THE GOLDEN BALL IS TALKING.
YOUR GOLDEN BALL JUST SAID THE WORD BALL—
DROP IT! IT'S TELLING US SOME-THING IMPORTANT!
YES, I AM.
YOU HAVE TO END THIS BEFORE THE WHITE CAT AND TAKAYA COLLAPSE FROM EXHAUSTION.
YOU MUST SLAY THE KEY.

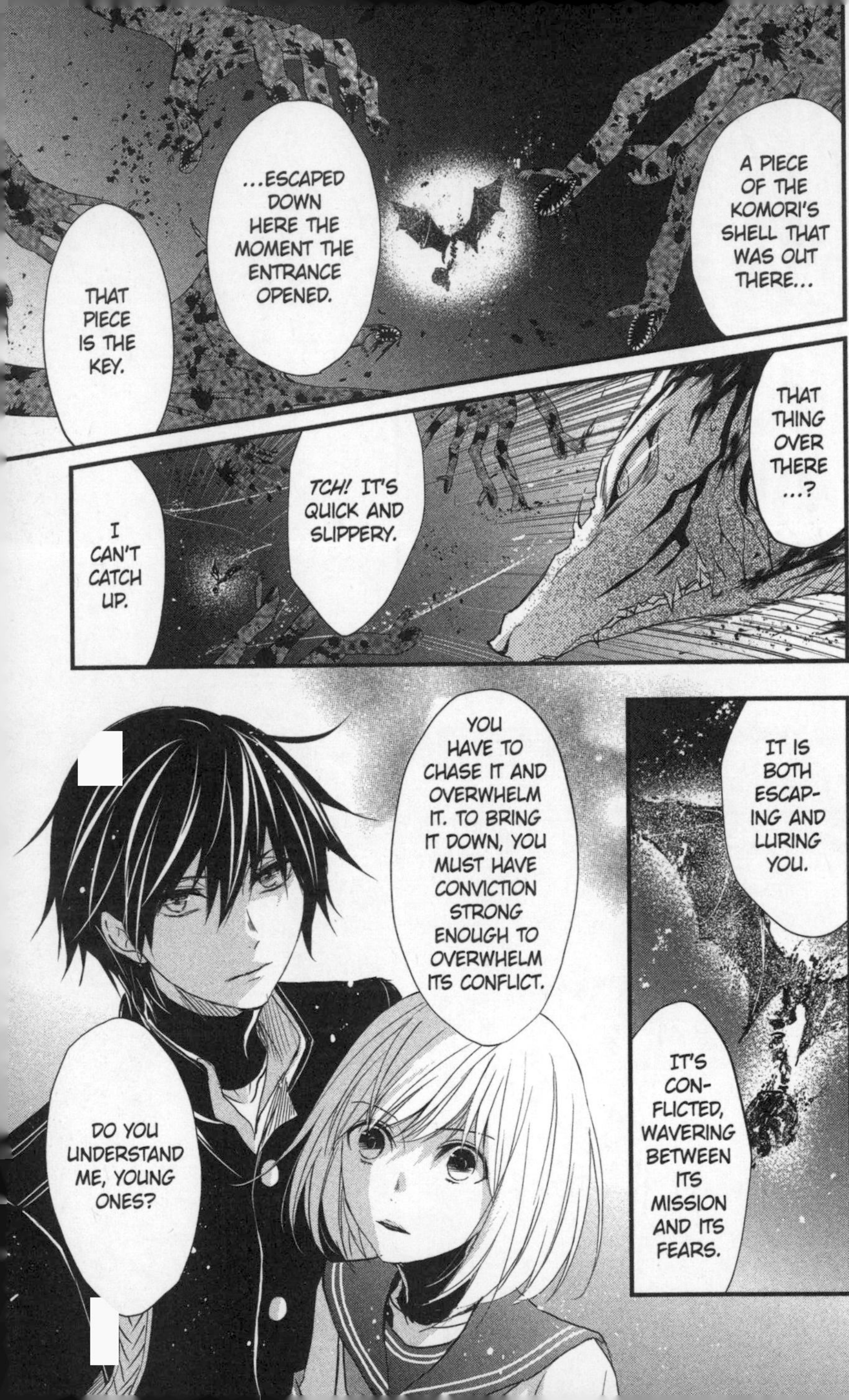
A PIECE OF THE KOMORI'S SHELL THAT WAS OUT THERE...
...ESCAPED DOWN HERE THE MOMENT THE ENTRANCE OPENED.
THAT PIECE IS THE KEY.
THAT THING OVER THERE ...?
TCH! IT'S QUICK AND SLIPPERY.
I CAN'T CATCH UP.
IT IS BOTH ESCAPING AND LURING YOU.
IT'S CONFLICTED, WAVERING BETWEEN ITS MISSION AND ITS FEARS.
YOU HAVE TO CHASE IT AND OVERWHELM IT. TO BRING IT DOWN, YOU MUST HAVE CONVICTION STRONG ENOUGH TO OVERWHELM ITS CONFLICT.
DO YOU UNDERSTAND ME, YOUNG ONES?

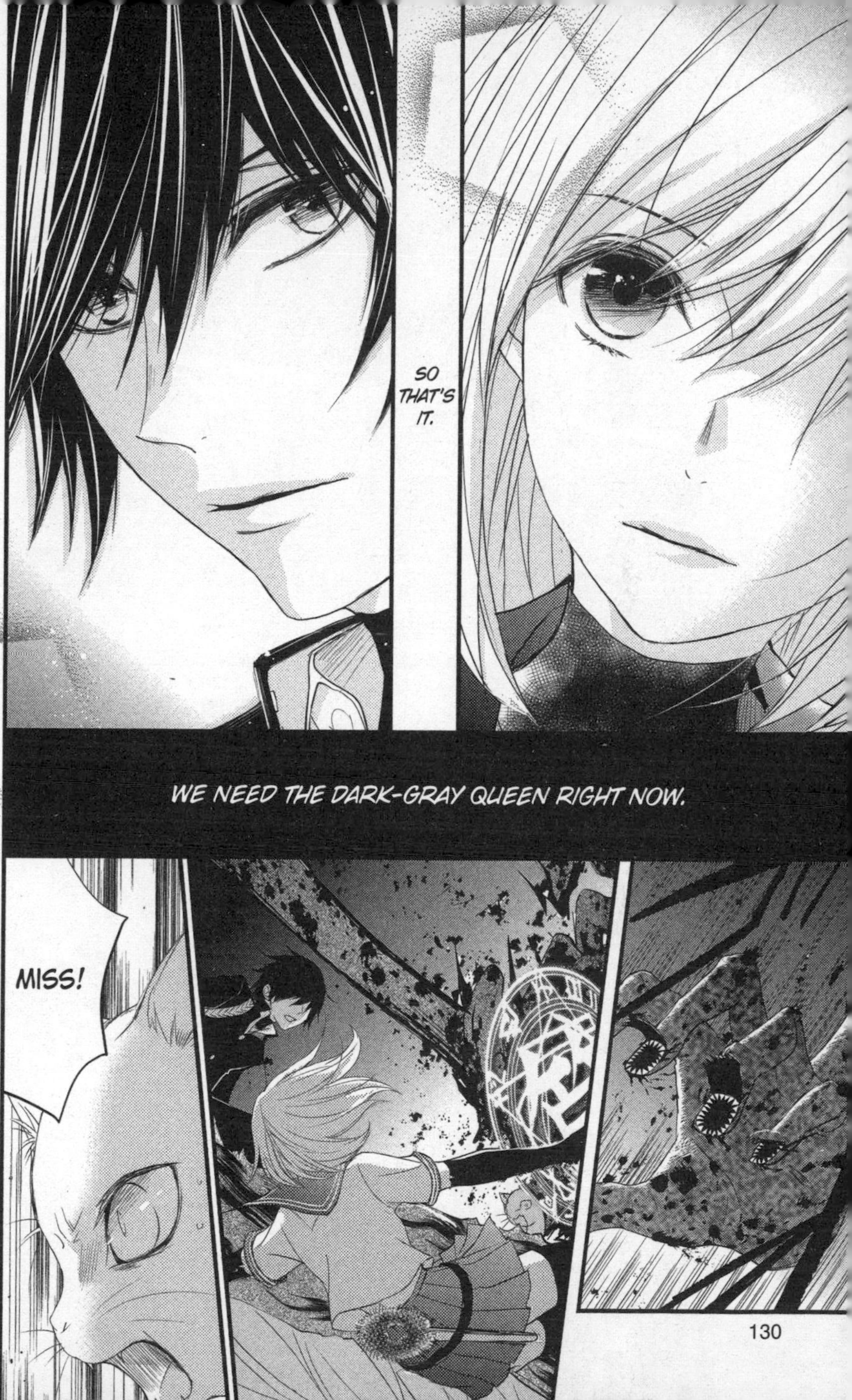
SO THAT'S IT.
WE NEED THE DARK-GRAY QUEEN RIGHT NOW.
MISS!

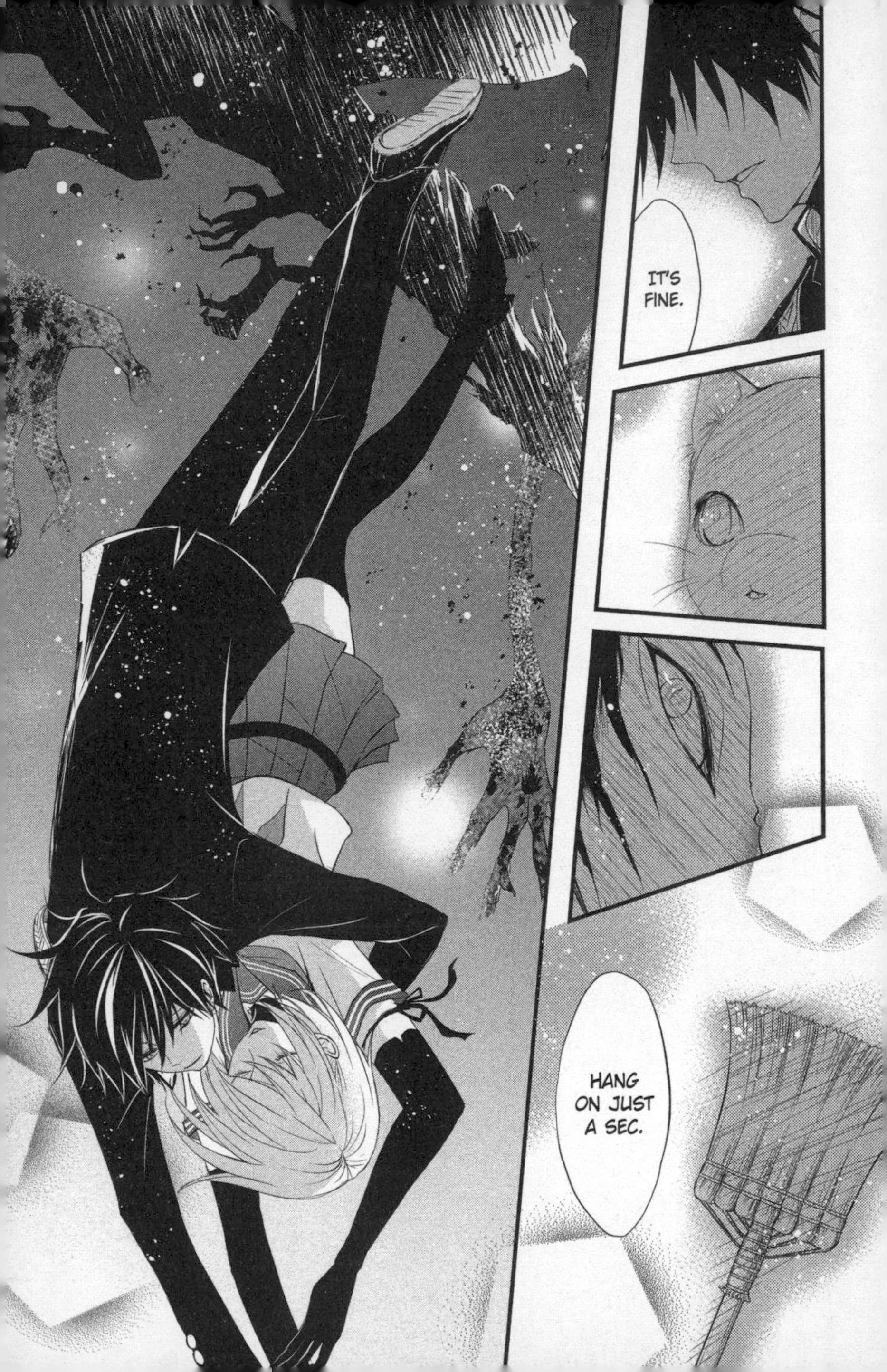
IT'S FINE.
HANG ON JUST A SEC.

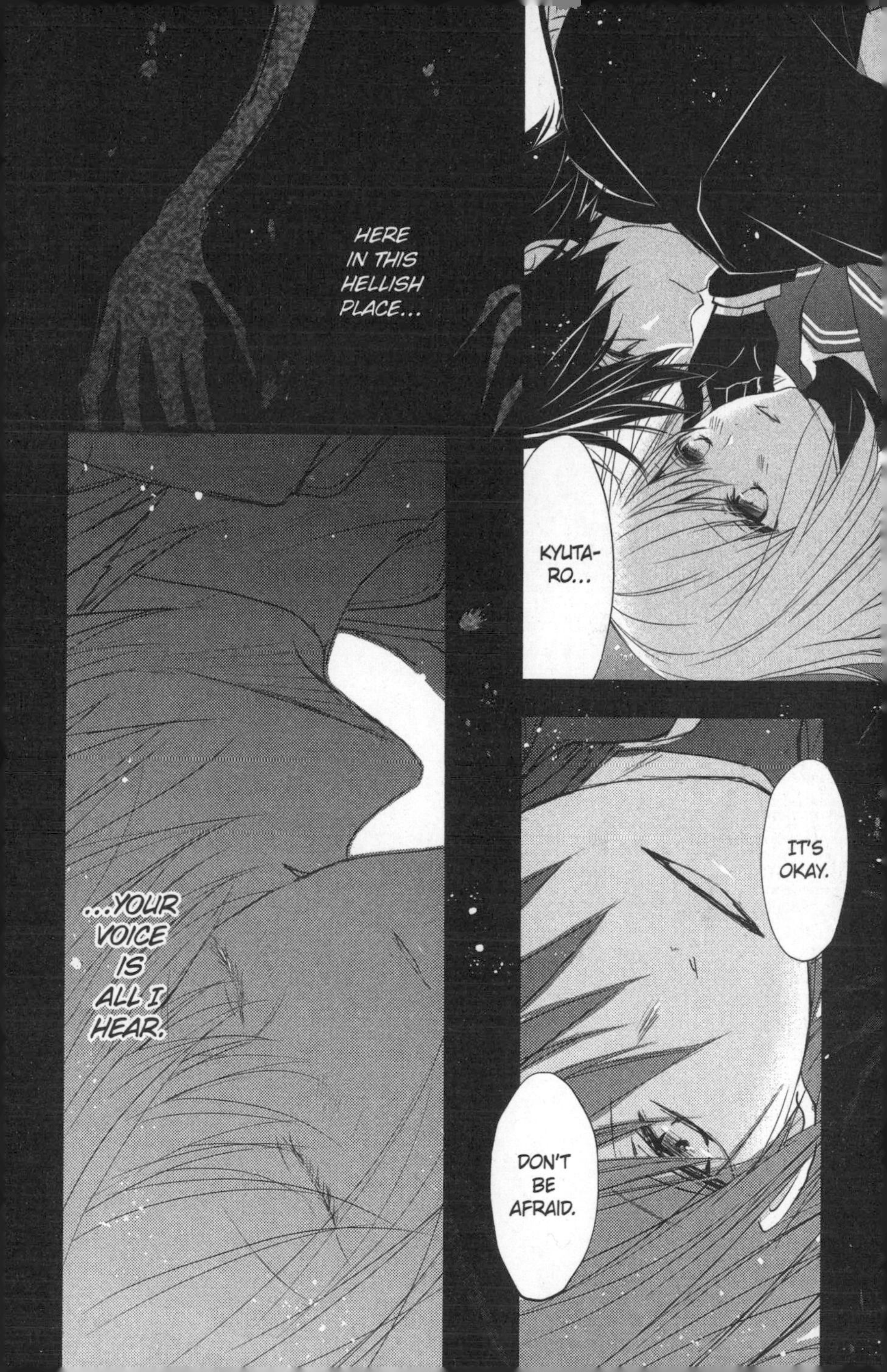
KYUTA-RO...
HERE IN THIS HELLISH PLACE...
IT'S OKAY.
DON'T BE AFRAID.
...YOUR VOICE IS ALL I HEAR.

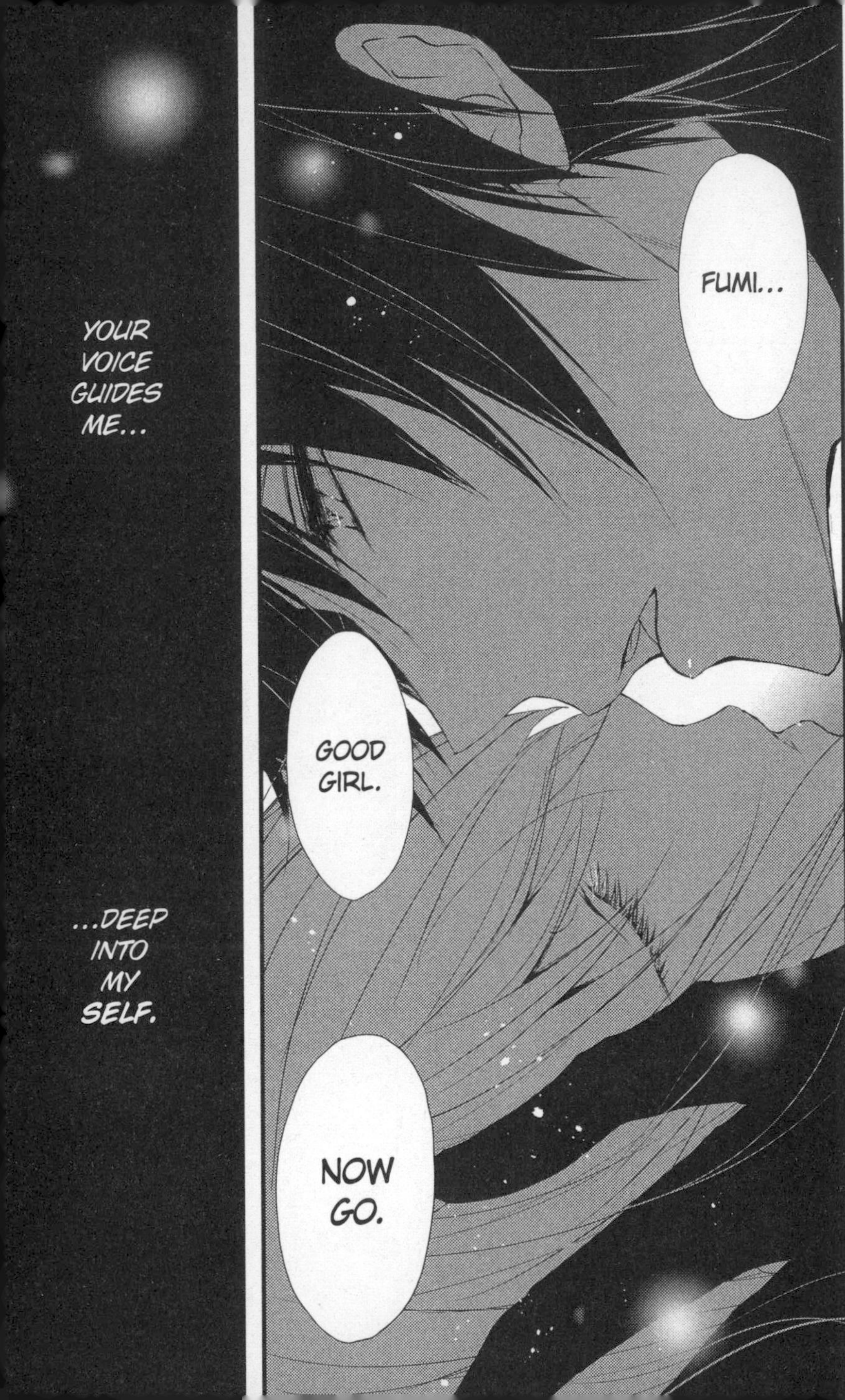
FUMI...
GOOD GIRL.
NOW GO.
YOUR VOICE GUIDES ME...
...DEEP INTO MY SELF.

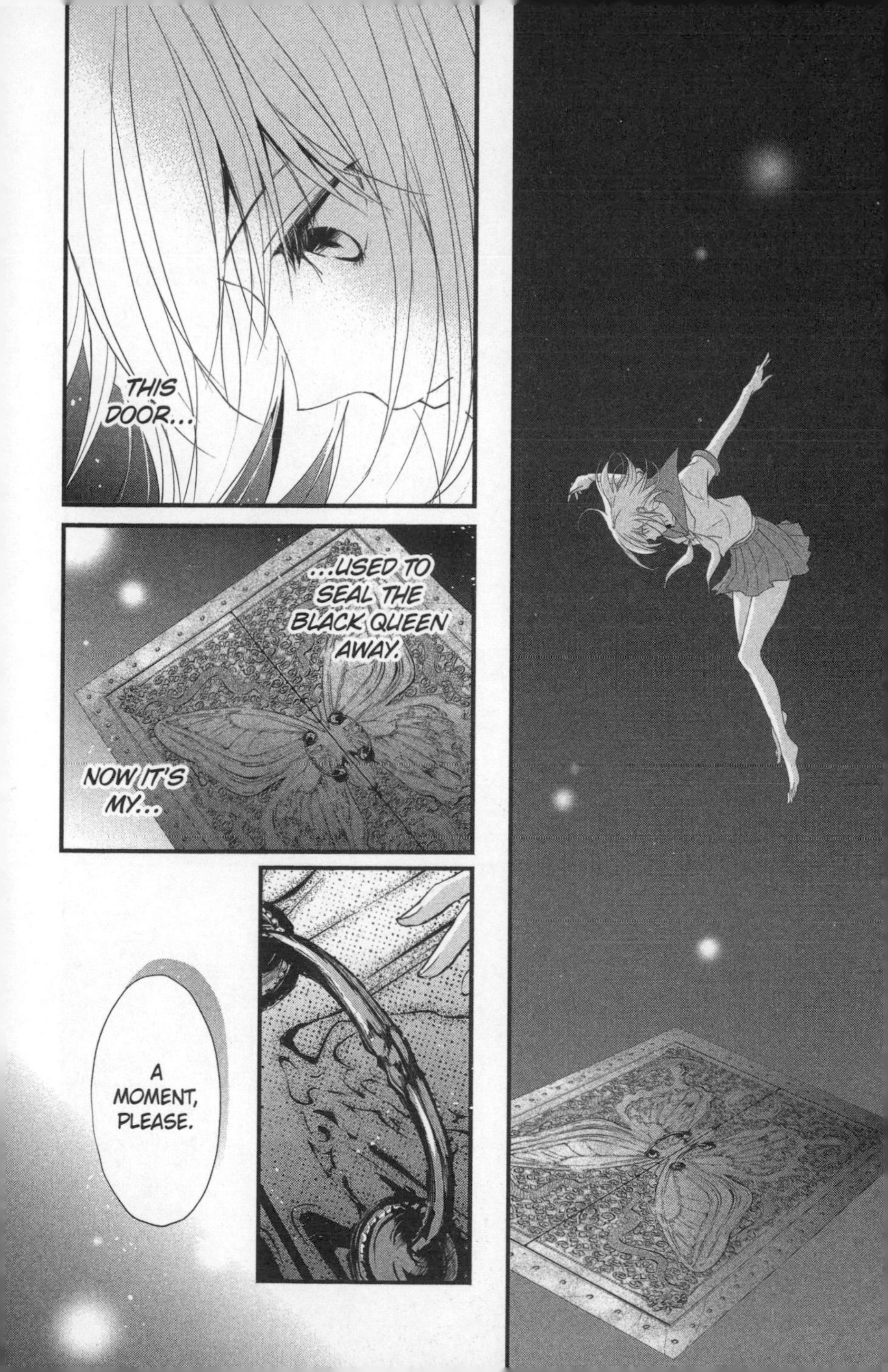
THIS DOOR...
...USED TO SEAL THE BLACK QUEEN AWAY.
NOW IT'S MY...
A MOMENT, PLEASE.

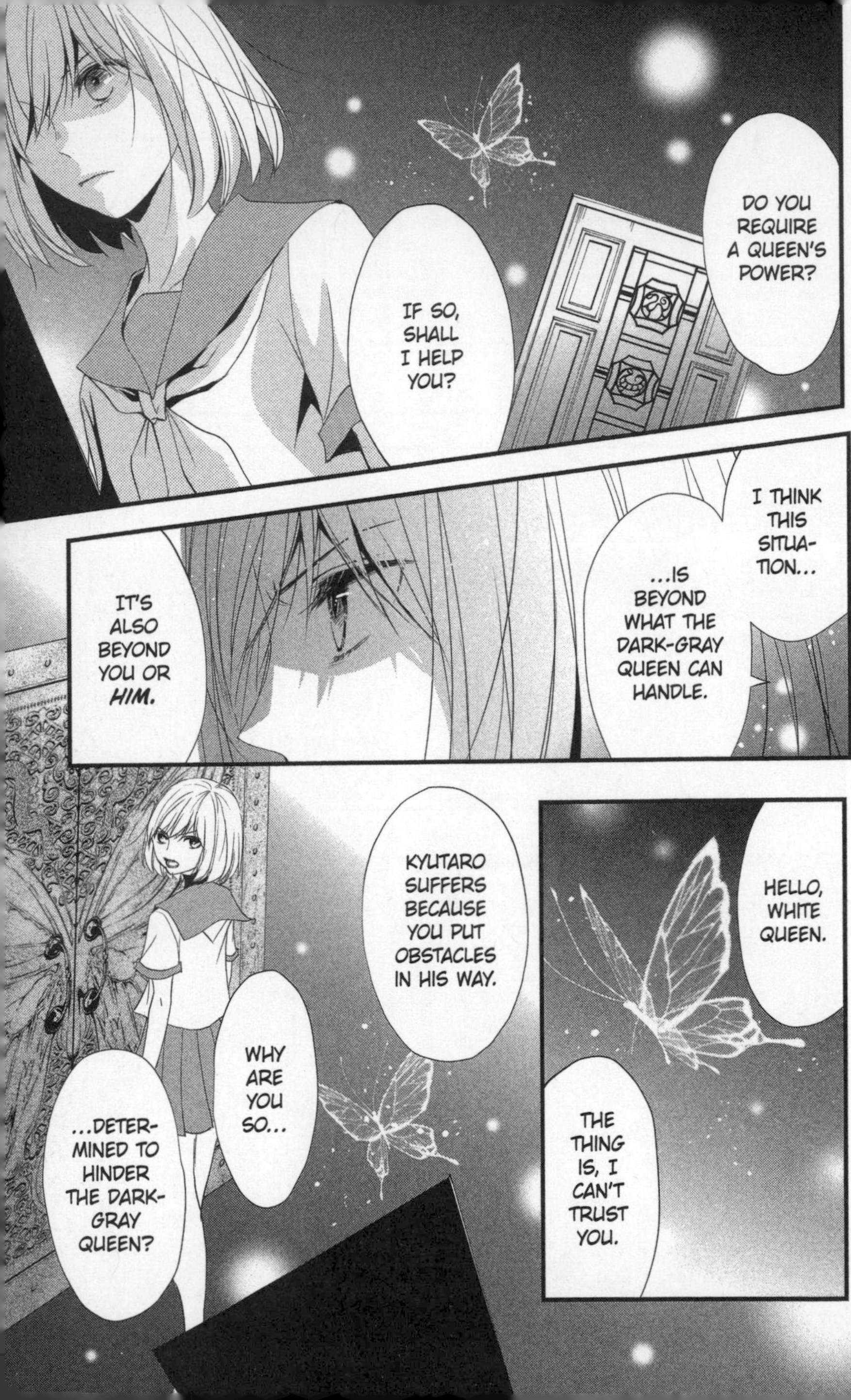
DO YOU REQUIRE A QUEEN'S POWER?
IF SO, SHALL I HELP YOU?
I THINK THIS SITUATION...
...IS BEYOND WHAT THE DARK-GRAY QUEEN CAN HANDLE.
IT'S ALSO BEYOND YOU OR *HIM.*
HELLO, WHITE QUEEN.
THE THING IS, I CAN'T TRUST YOU.
KYUTARO SUFFERS BECAUSE YOU PUT OBSTACLES IN HIS WAY.
WHY ARE YOU SO...
...DETERMINED TO HINDER THE DARK-GRAY QUEEN?

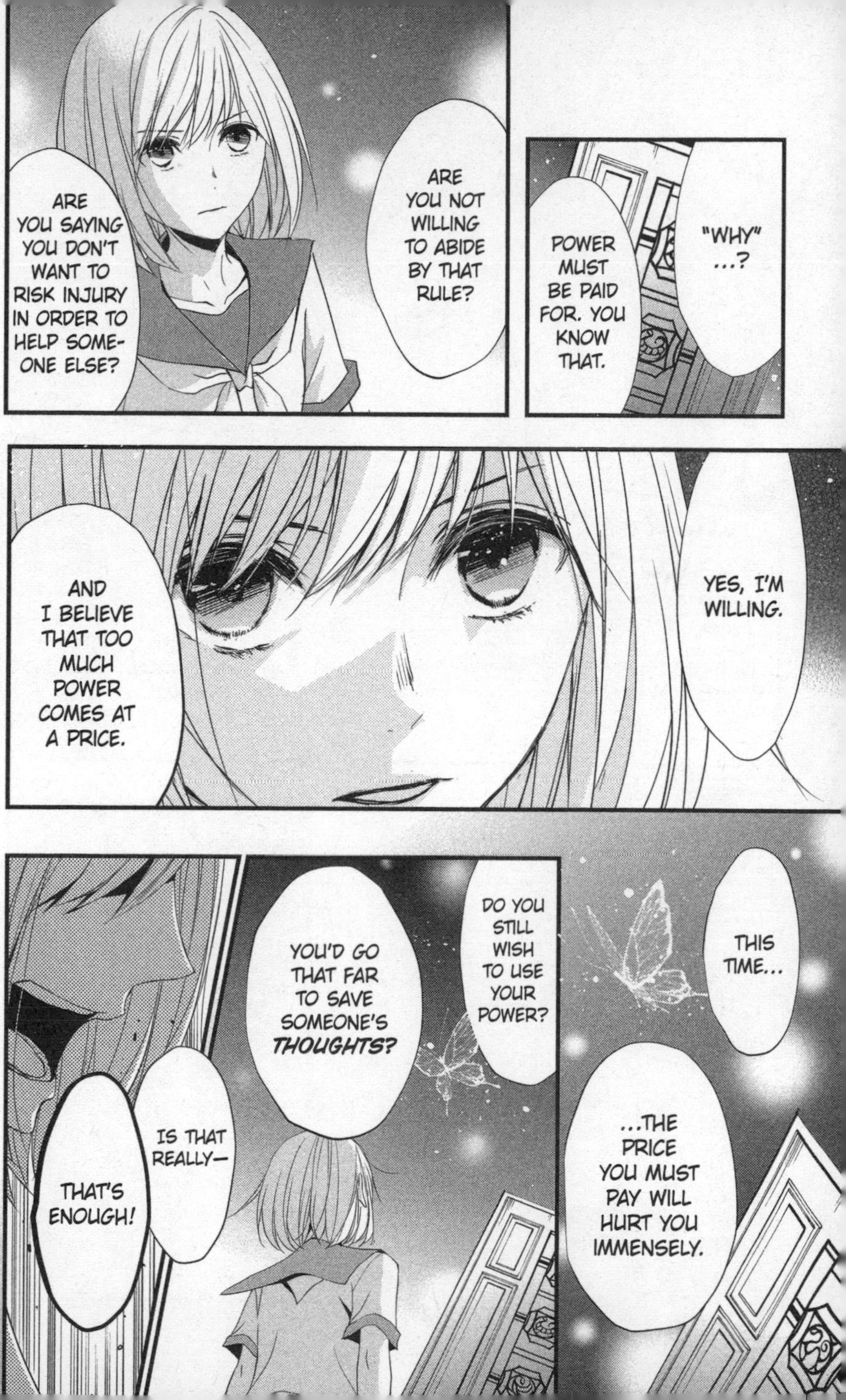
"WHY" ...?
POWER MUST BE PAID FOR. YOU KNOW THAT.
ARE YOU NOT WILLING TO ABIDE BY THAT RULE?
ARE YOU SAYING YOU DON'T WANT TO RISK INJURY IN ORDER TO HELP SOME-ONE ELSE?
YES, I'M WILLING.
AND I BELIEVE THAT TOO MUCH POWER COMES AT A PRICE.
THIS TIME...
...THE PRICE YOU MUST PAY WILL HURT YOU IMMENSELY.
DO YOU STILL WISH TO USE YOUR POWER?
YOU'D GO THAT FAR TO SAVE SOMEONE'S *THOUGHTS?*
IS THAT REALLY—
THAT'S ENOUGH!

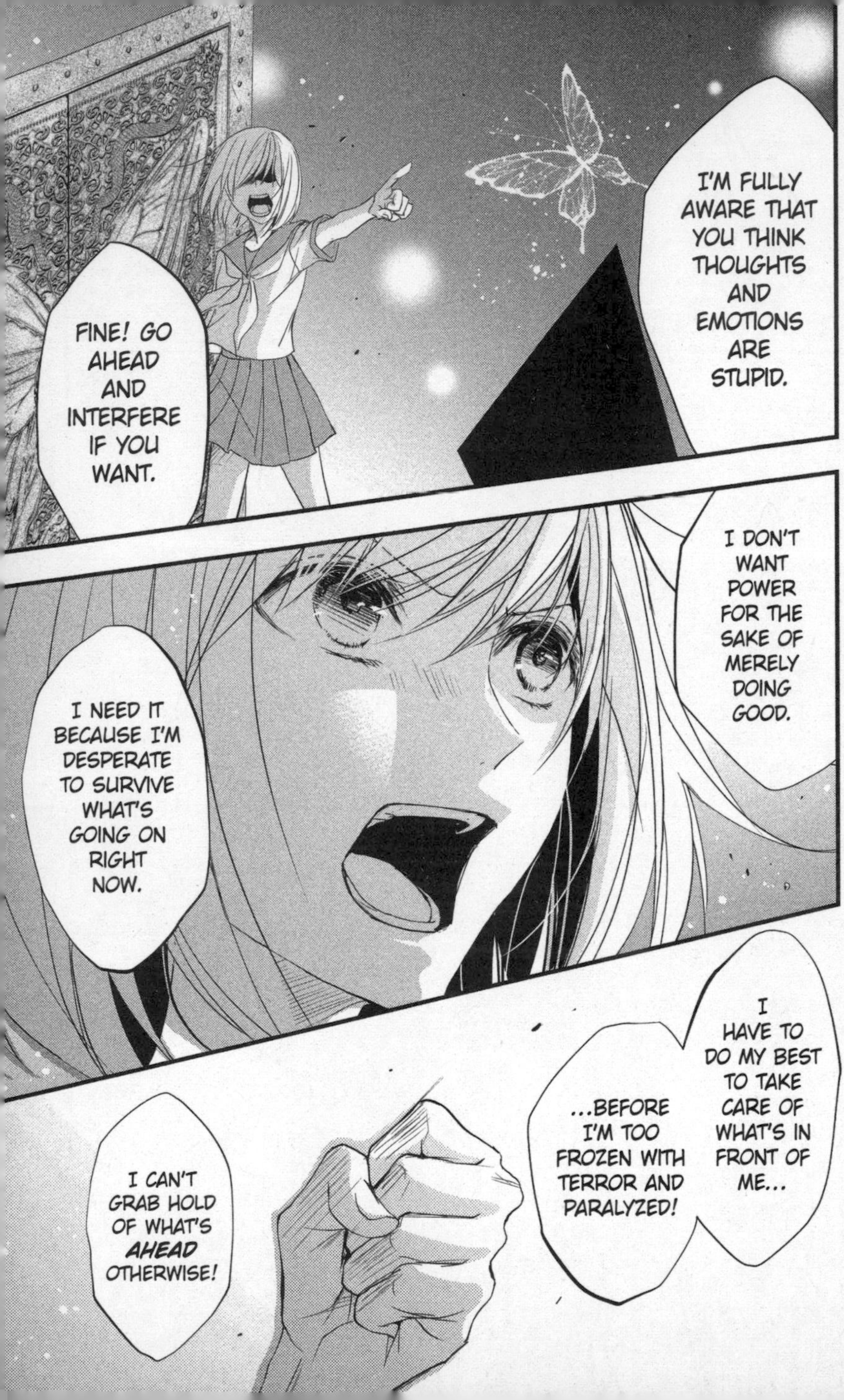
I'M FULLY AWARE THAT YOU THINK THOUGHTS AND EMOTIONS ARE STUPID.
FINE! GO AHEAD AND INTERFERE IF YOU WANT.
I DON'T WANT POWER FOR THE SAKE OF MERELY DOING GOOD.
I NEED IT BECAUSE I'M DESPERATE TO SURVIVE WHAT'S GOING ON RIGHT NOW.
I HAVE TO DO MY BEST TO TAKE CARE OF WHAT'S IN FRONT OF ME...
...BEFORE I'M TOO FROZEN WITH TERROR AND PARALYZED!
I CAN'T GRAB HOLD OF WHAT'S *AHEAD* OTHERWISE!

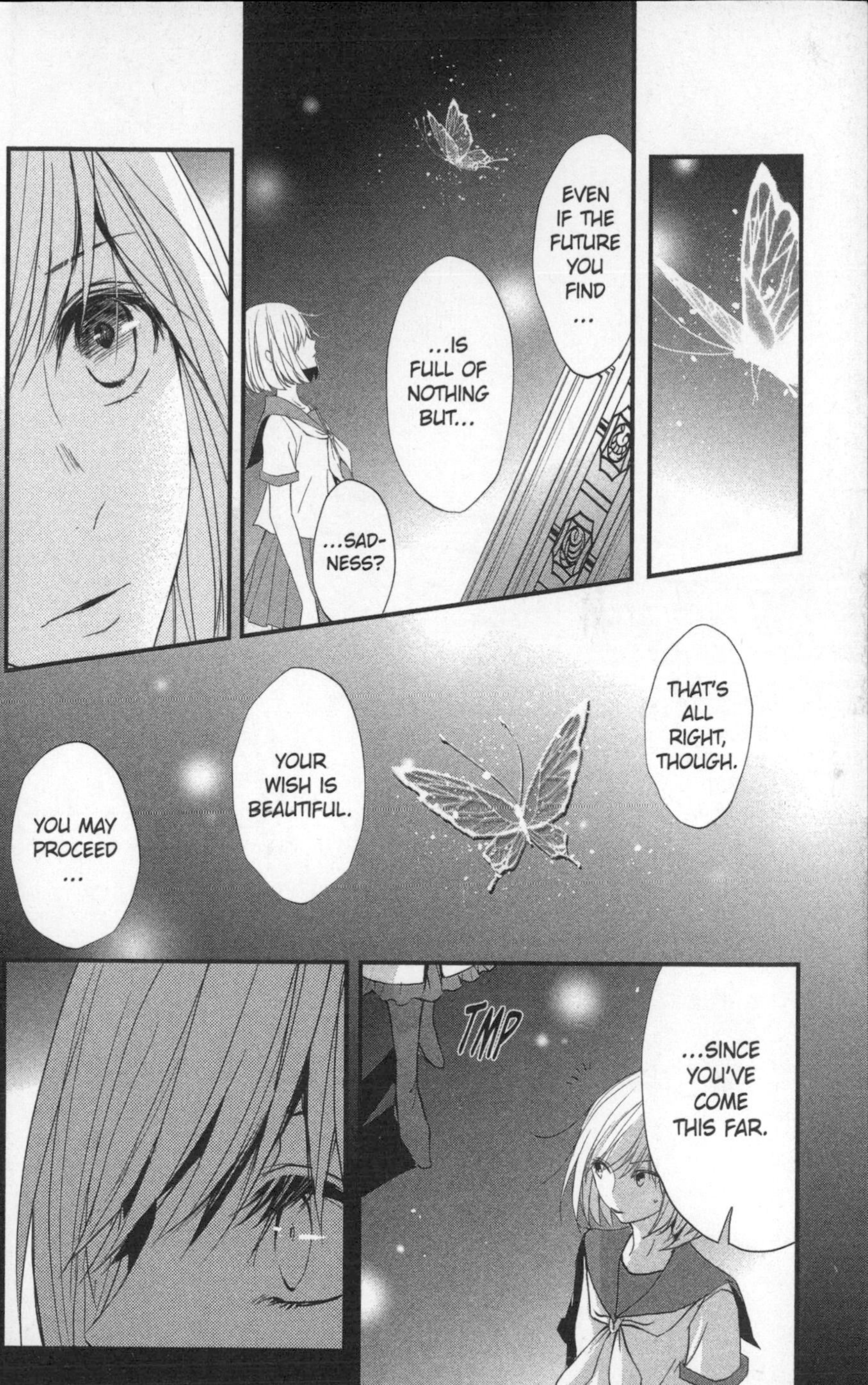
EVEN IF THE FUTURE YOU FIND ...
...IS FULL OF NOTHING BUT...
...SAD-NESS?
THAT'S ALL RIGHT, THOUGH.
YOUR WISH IS BEAUTIFUL.
YOU MAY PROCEED ...
...SINCE YOU'VE COME THIS FAR.
TMP

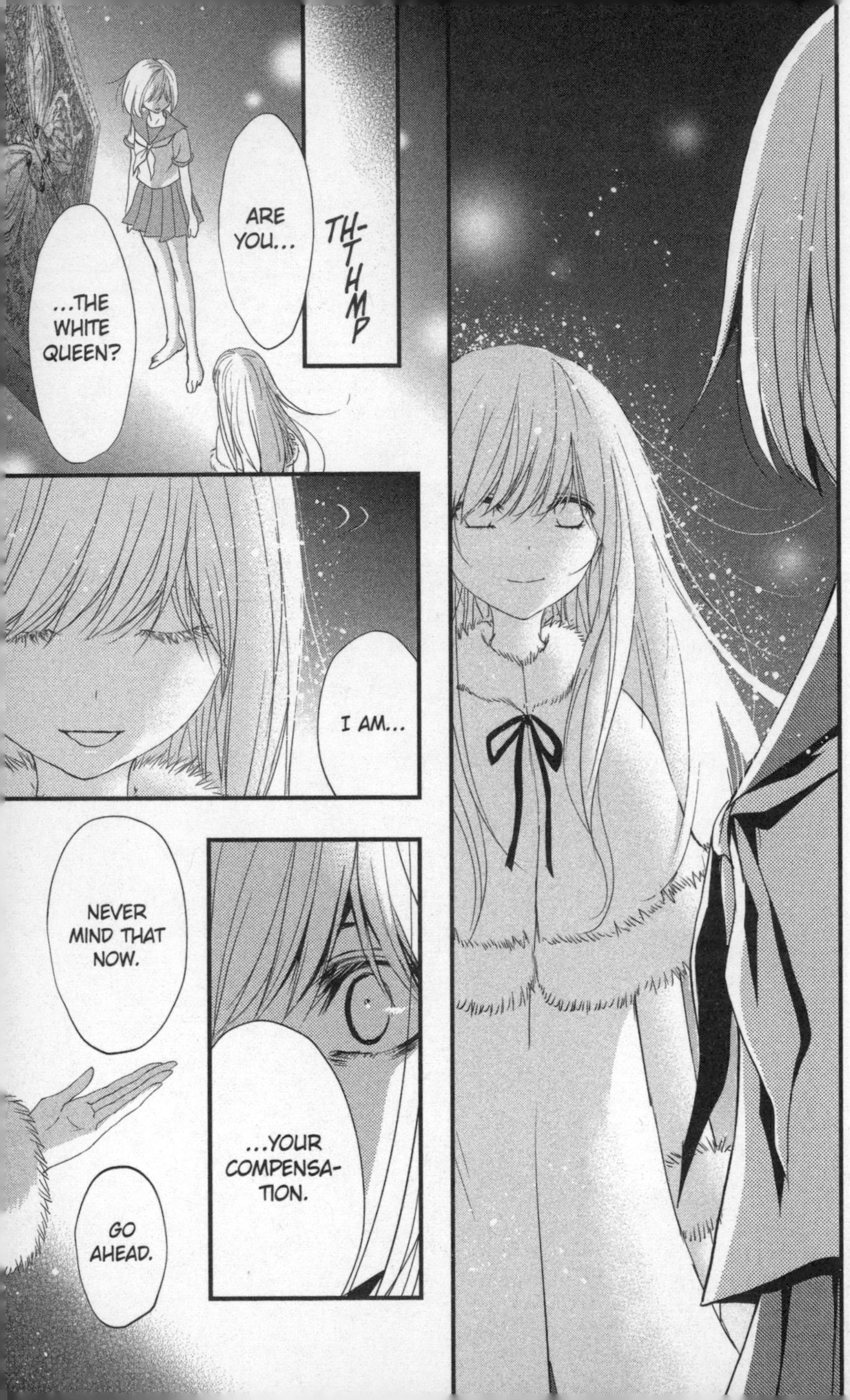
ARE YOU...
TH-THMP
...THE WHITE QUEEN?
I AM...
...YOUR COMPENSA-TION.
NEVER MIND THAT NOW.
GO AHEAD.

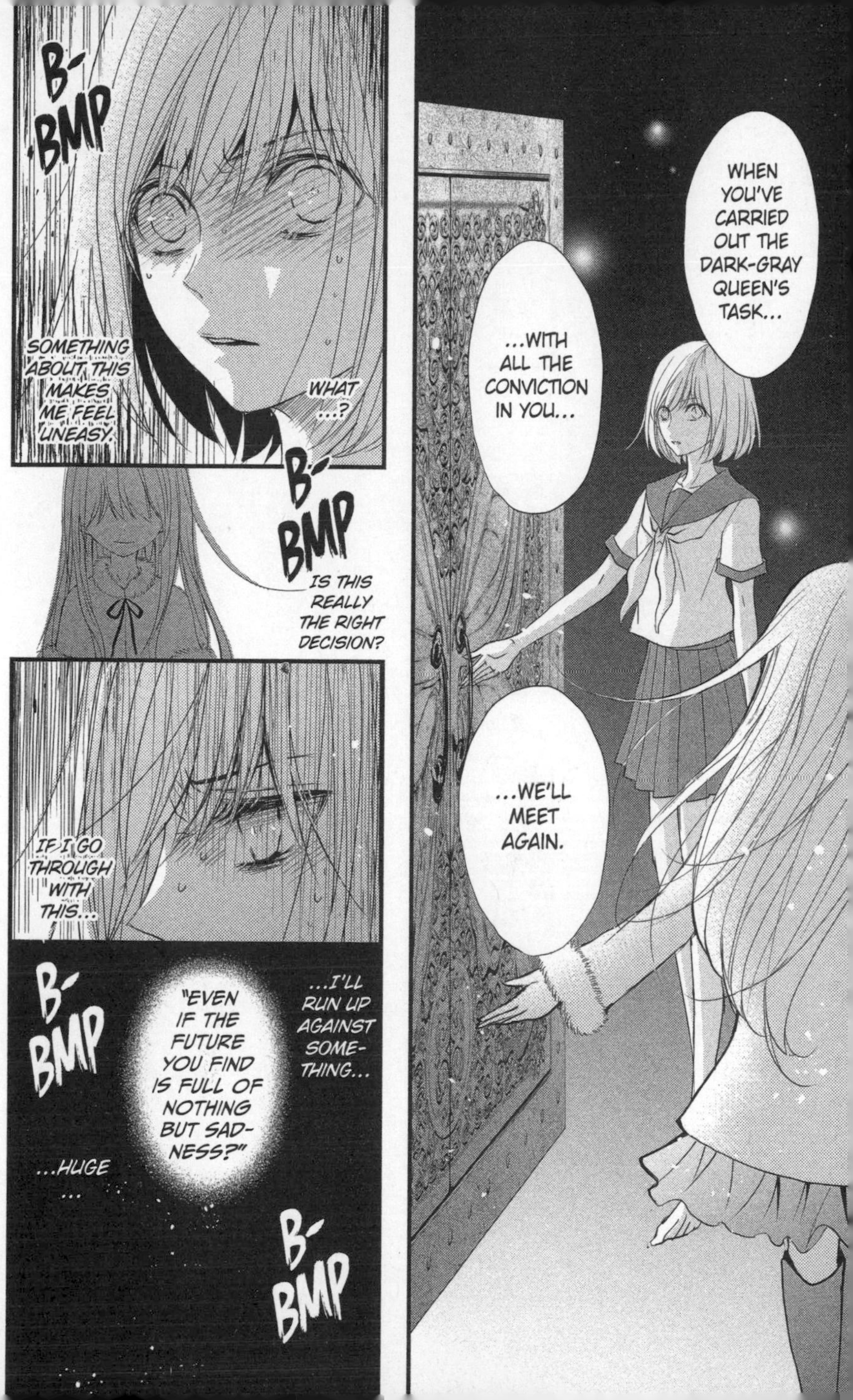
WHEN YOU'VE CARRIED OUT THE DARK-GRAY QUEEN'S TASK...
...WITH ALL THE CONVICTION IN YOU...
...WE'LL MEET AGAIN.
B-BMP
WHAT ...?
SOMETHING ABOUT THIS MAKES ME FEEL UNEASY.
B-BMP
IS THIS REALLY THE RIGHT DECISION?
IF I GO THROUGH WITH THIS...
...I'LL RUN UP AGAINST SOME-THING...
"EVEN IF THE FUTURE YOU FIND IS FULL OF NOTHING BUT SAD-NESS?"
B-BMP
...HUGE ...
B-BMP

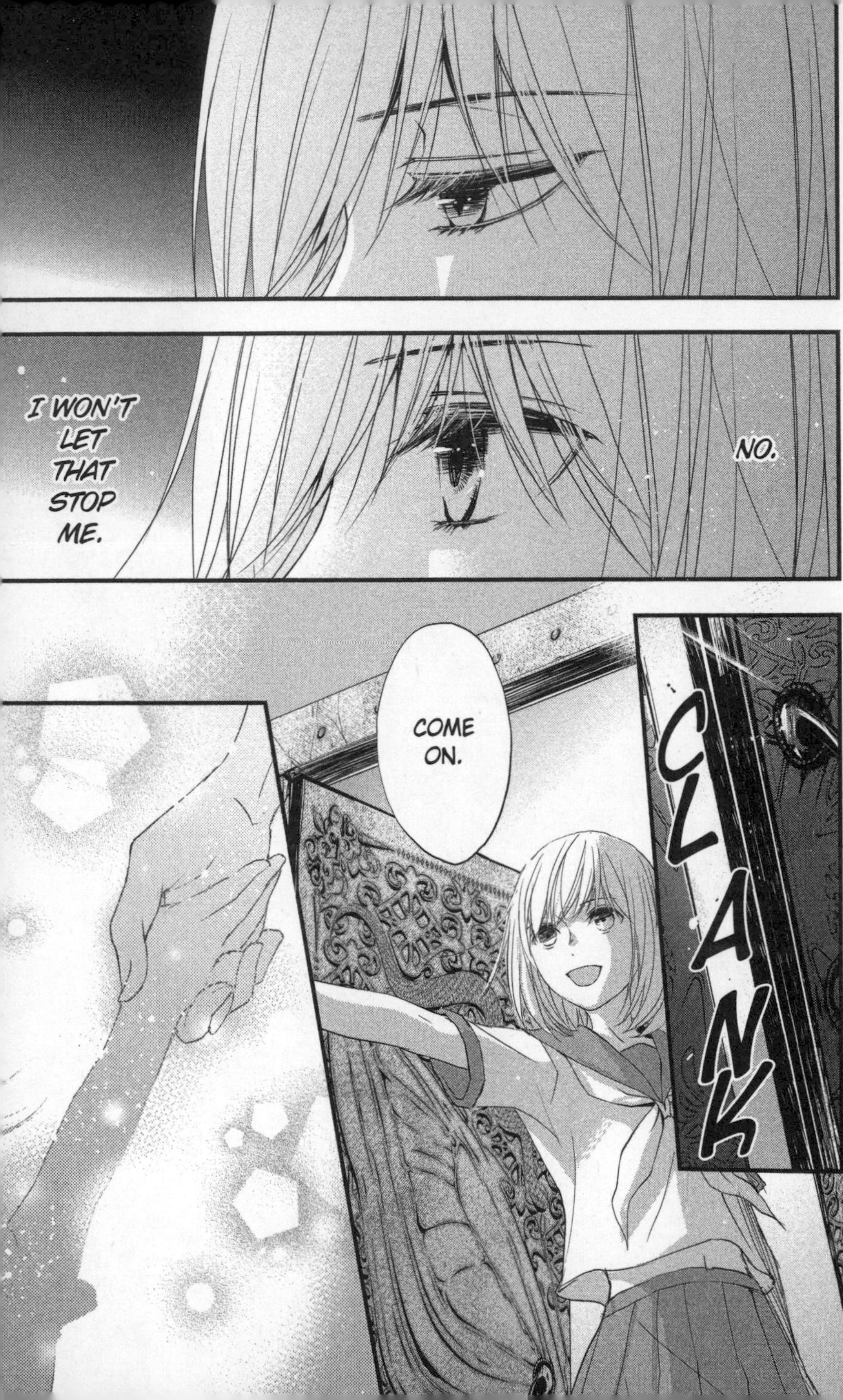
NO.
I WON'T LET THAT STOP ME.
CLANK
COME ON.

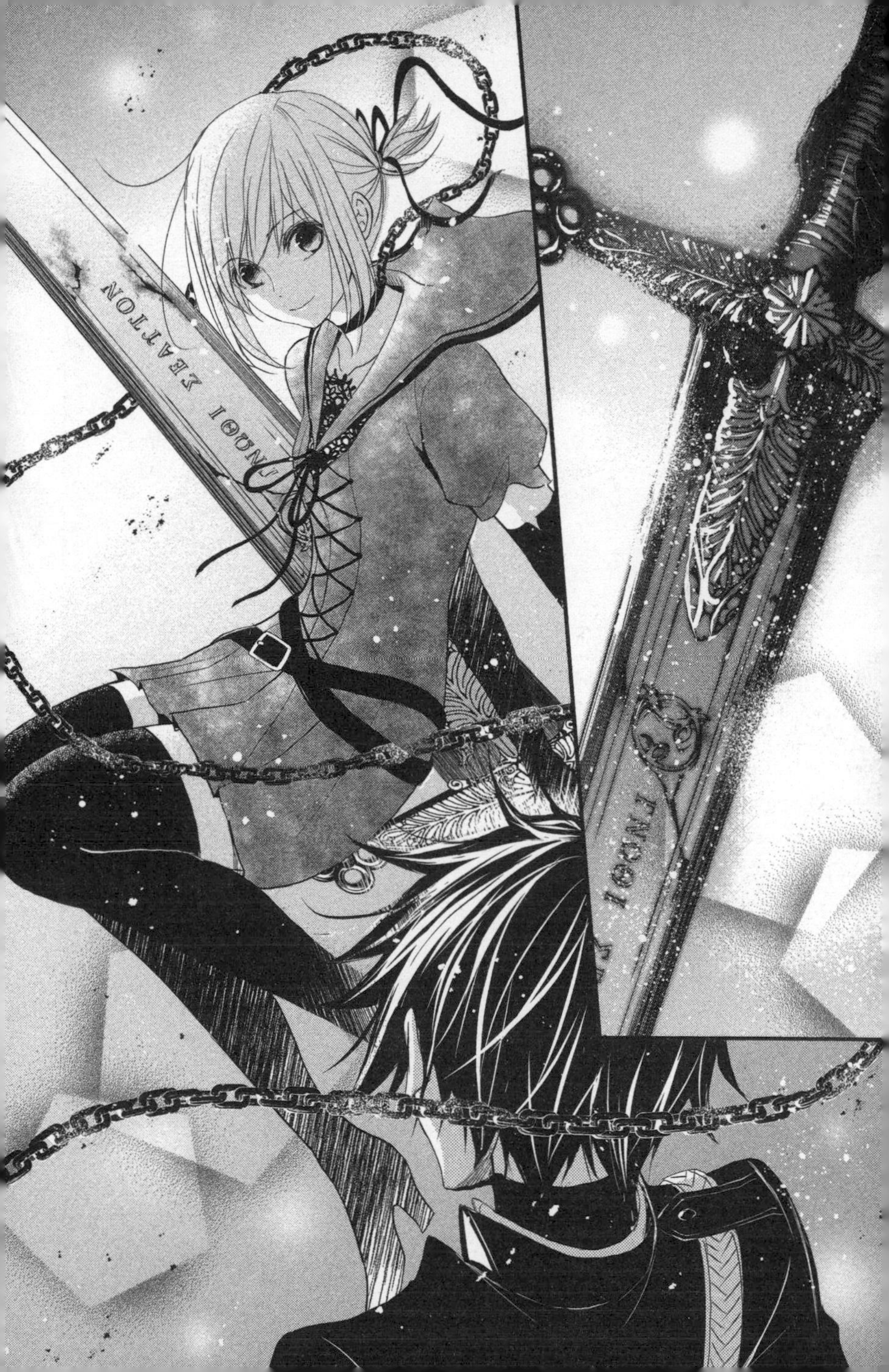

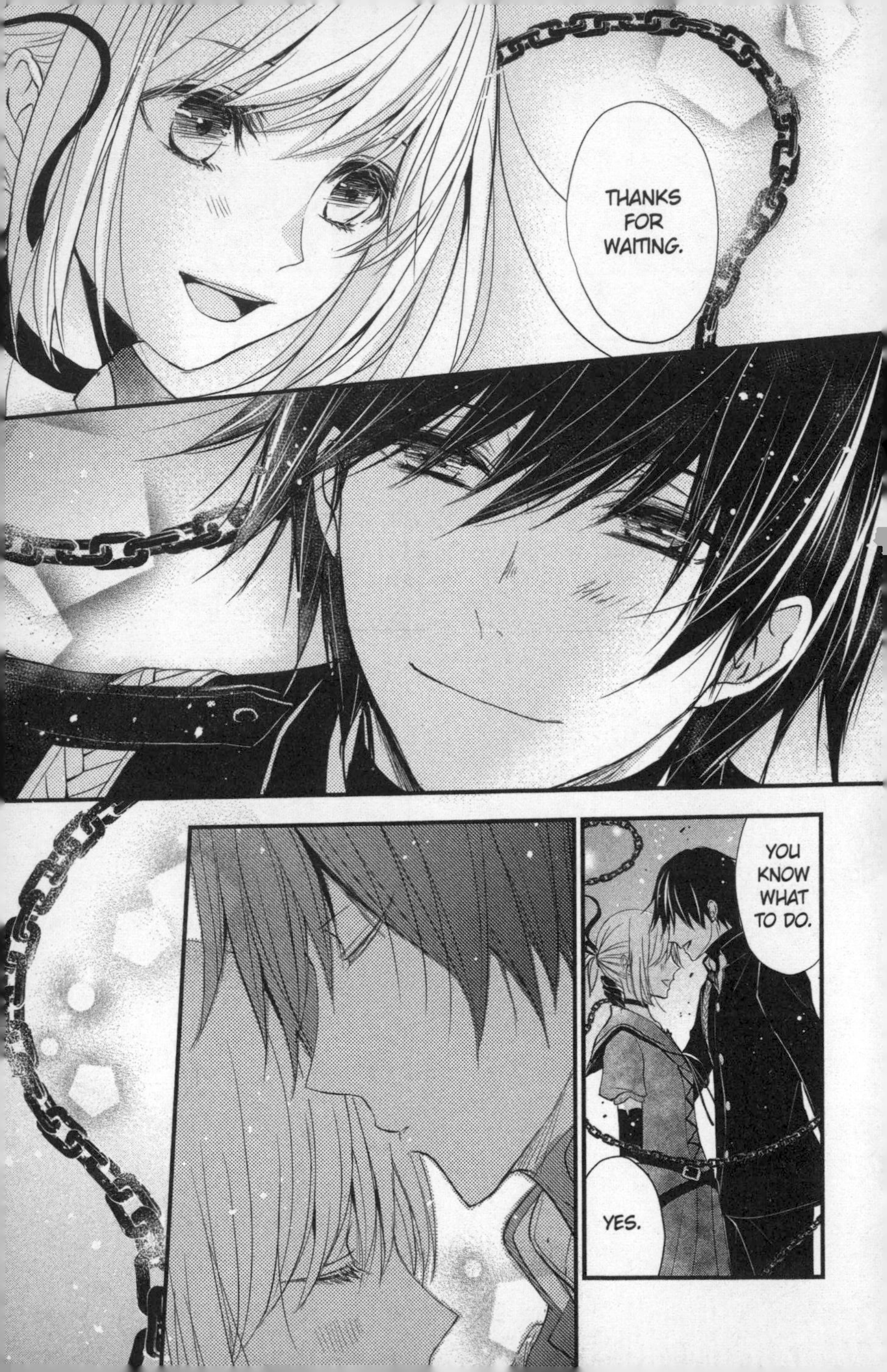
THANKS FOR WAITING.
YOU KNOW WHAT TO DO.
YES.

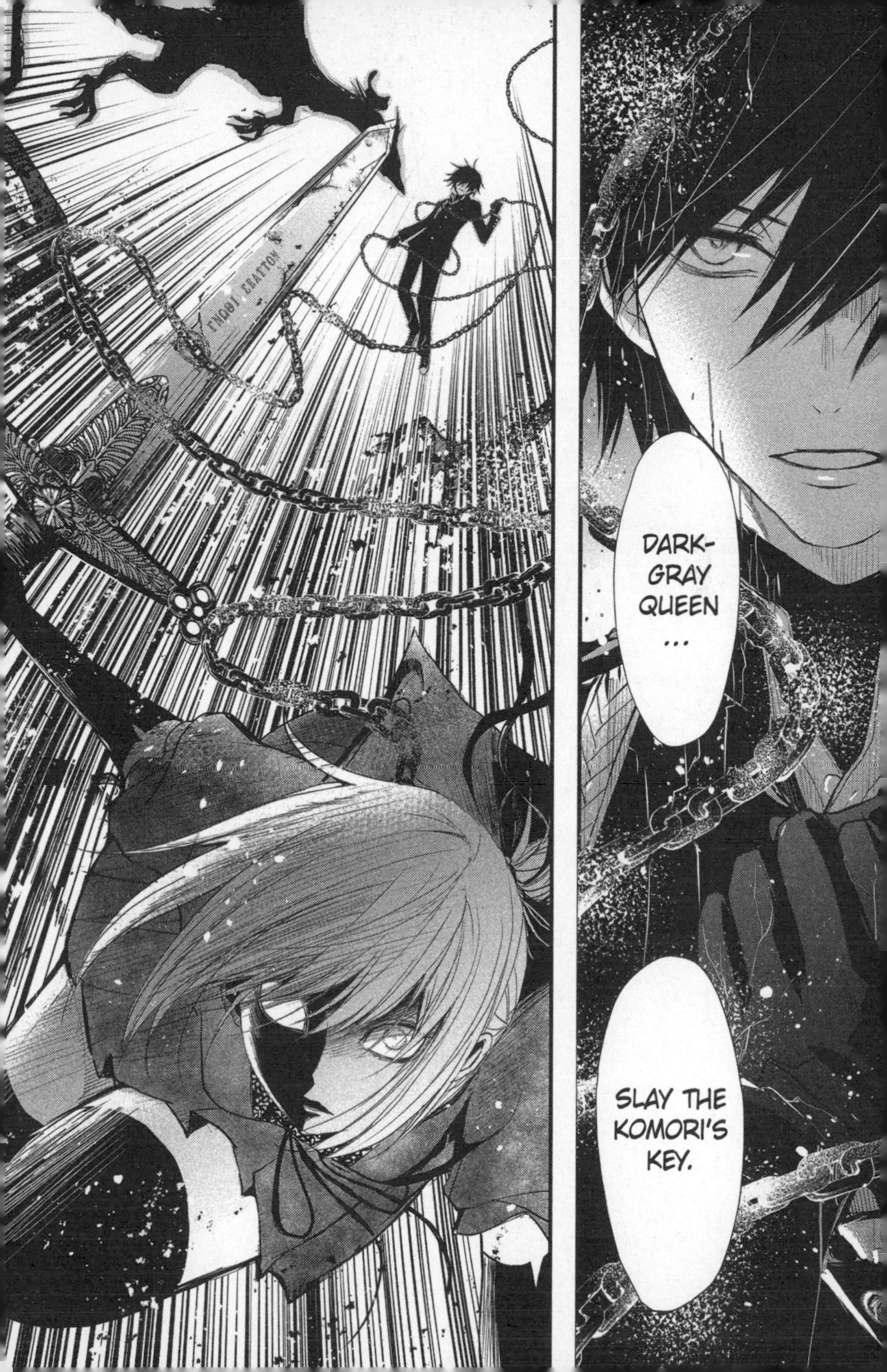
DARK-GRAY QUEEN ...
SLAY THE KOMORI'S KEY.

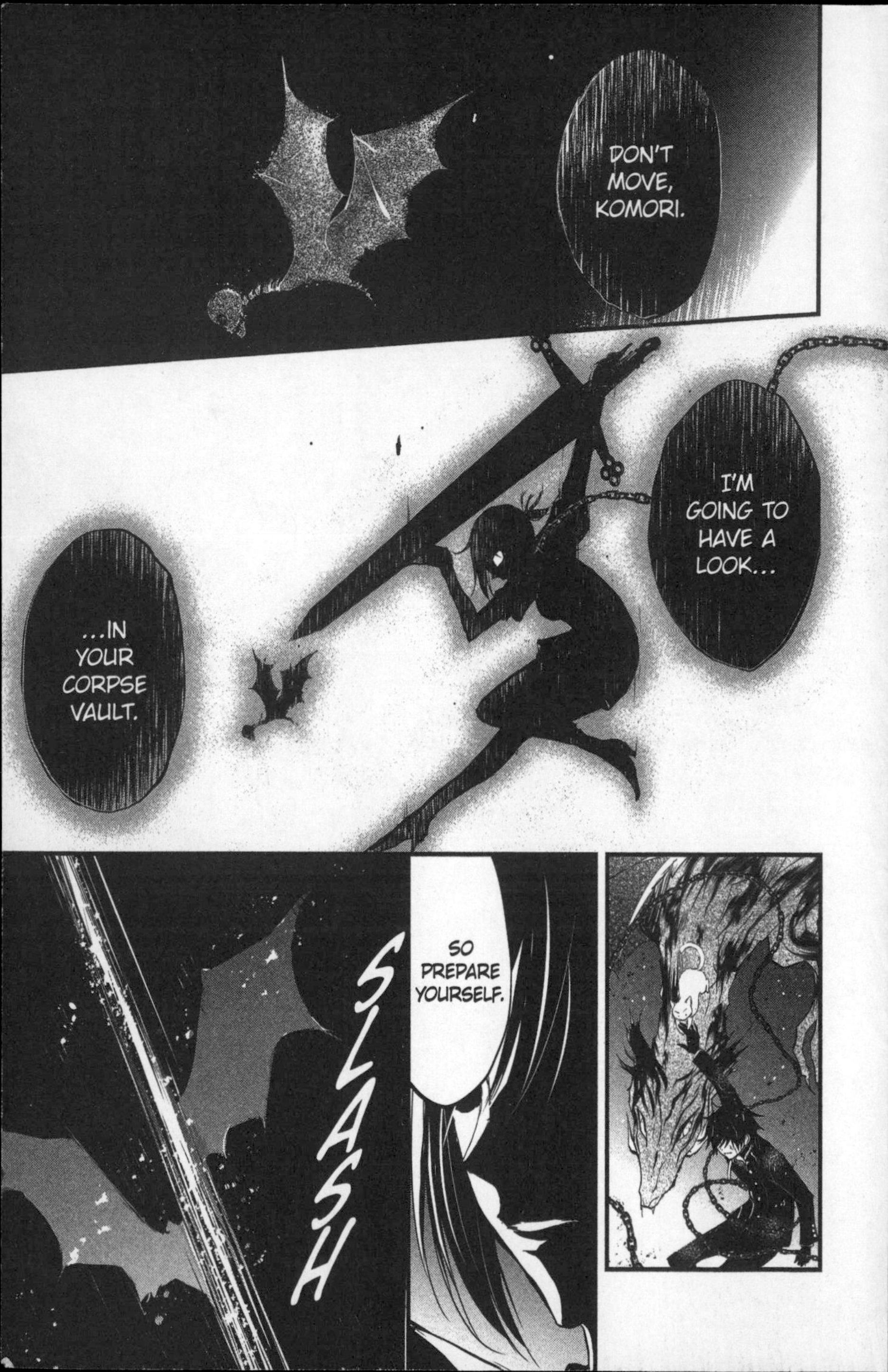
DON'T MOVE, KOMORI.
I'M GOING TO HAVE A LOOK...
...IN YOUR CORPSE VAULT.
SO PREPARE YOURSELF.
SLASH

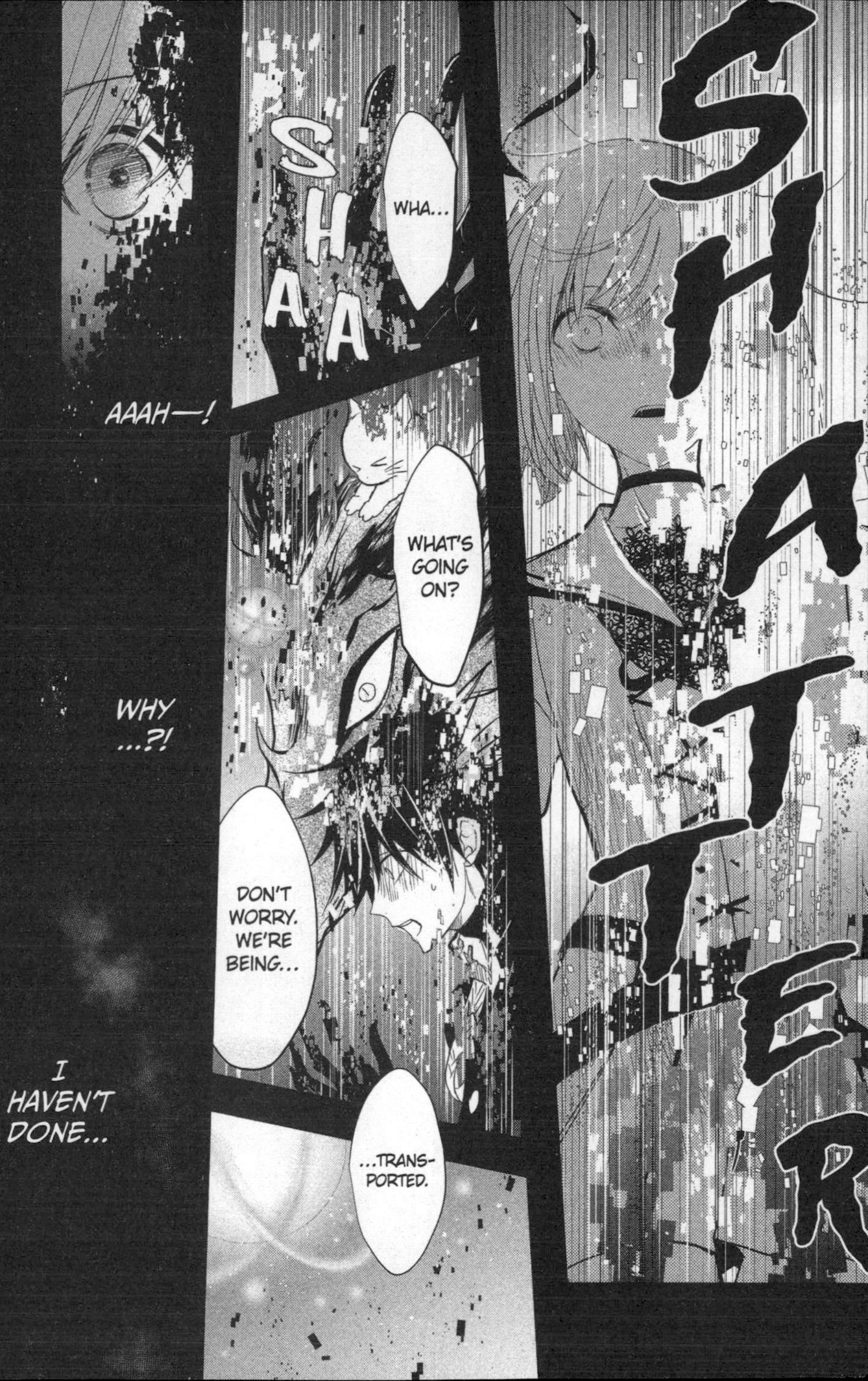
SHATTER
WHA...
SHAA
WHAT'S GOING ON?
DON'T WORRY. WE'RE BEING...
...TRANSPORTED.
AAAH—!
WHY ...?!
I HAVEN'T DONE...

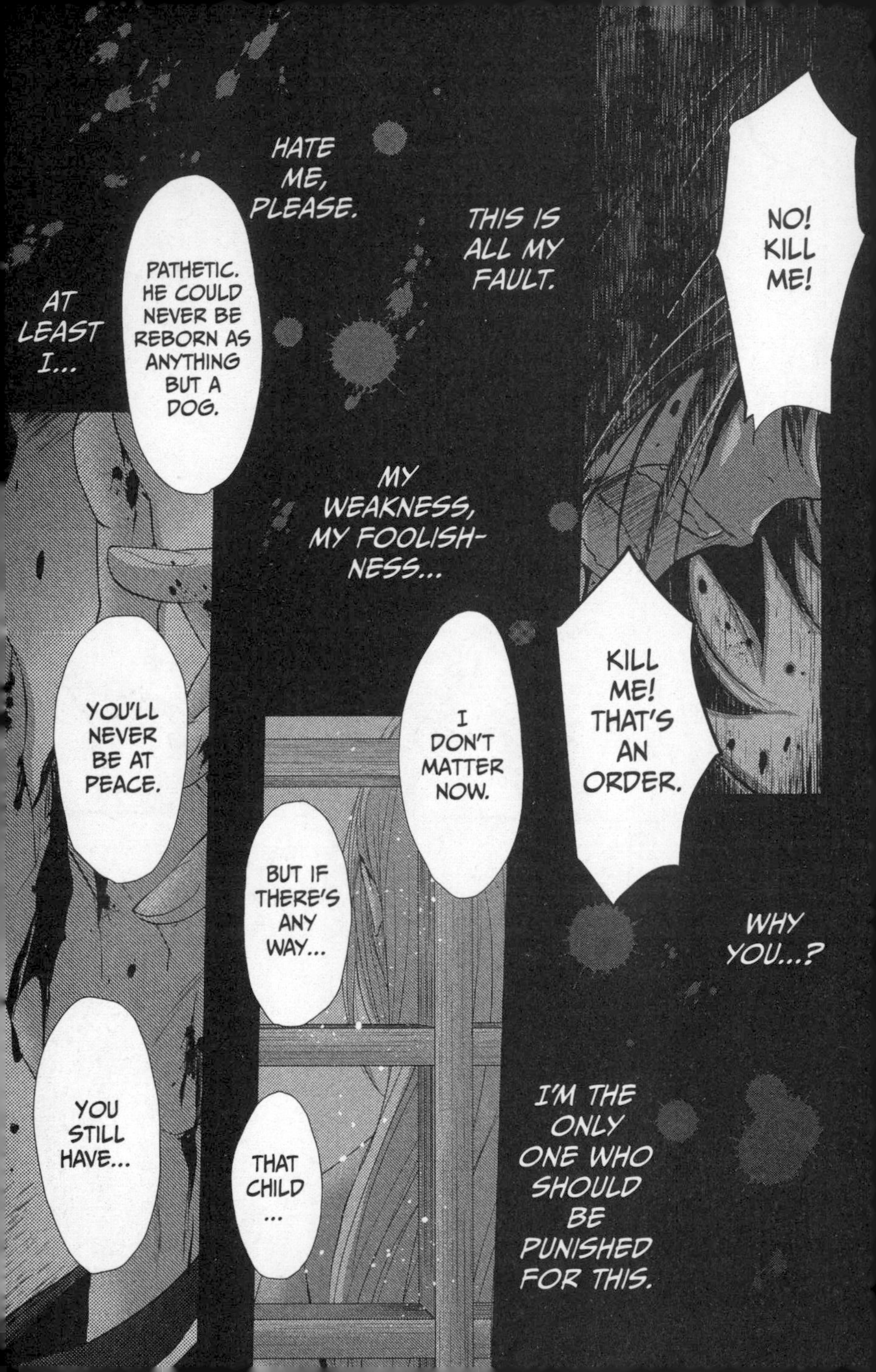
NO! KILL ME!
THIS IS ALL MY FAULT.
HATE ME, PLEASE.
PATHETIC. HE COULD NEVER BE REBORN AS ANYTHING BUT A DOG.
AT LEAST I...
KILL ME! THAT'S AN ORDER.
MY WEAKNESS, MY FOOLISH-NESS...
I DON'T MATTER NOW.
WHY YOU...?
BUT IF THERE'S ANY WAY...
YOU'LL NEVER BE AT PEACE.
I'M THE ONLY ONE WHO SHOULD BE PUNISHED FOR THIS.
THAT CHILD ...
YOU STILL HAVE...

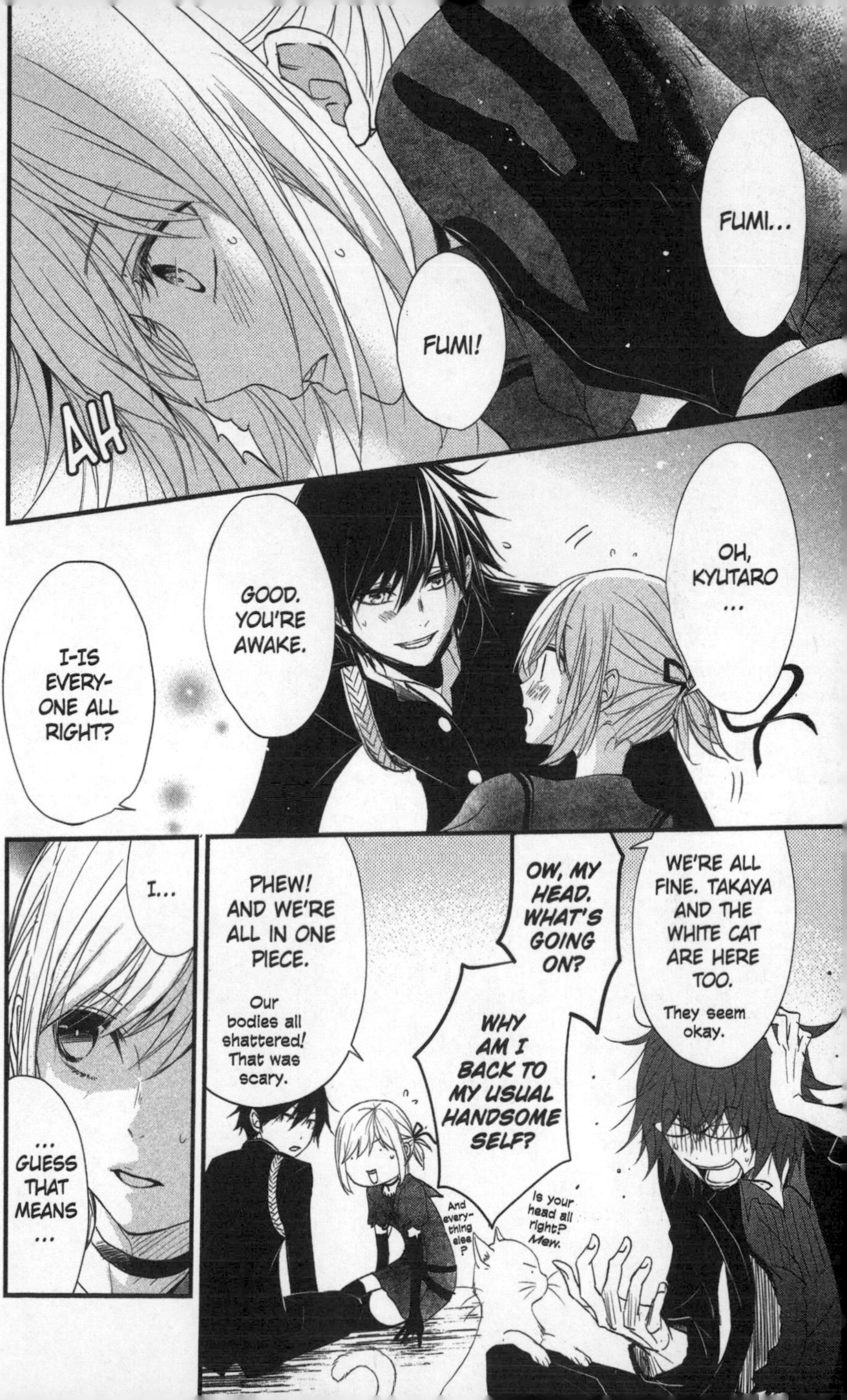
FUMI...
FUMI!
AH
OH, KYUTARO ...
GOOD. YOU'RE AWAKE.
I-IS EVERY-ONE ALL RIGHT?
WE'RE ALL FINE. TAKAYA AND THE WHITE CAT ARE HERE TOO.
They seem okay.
OW, MY HEAD. WHAT'S GOING ON?
WHY AM I BACK TO MY USUAL HANDSOME SELF?
PHEW! AND WE'RE ALL IN ONE PIECE.
Our bodies all shattered! That was scary.
Is your head all right? Mew.
And every-thing else?
I...
... GUESS THAT MEANS ...

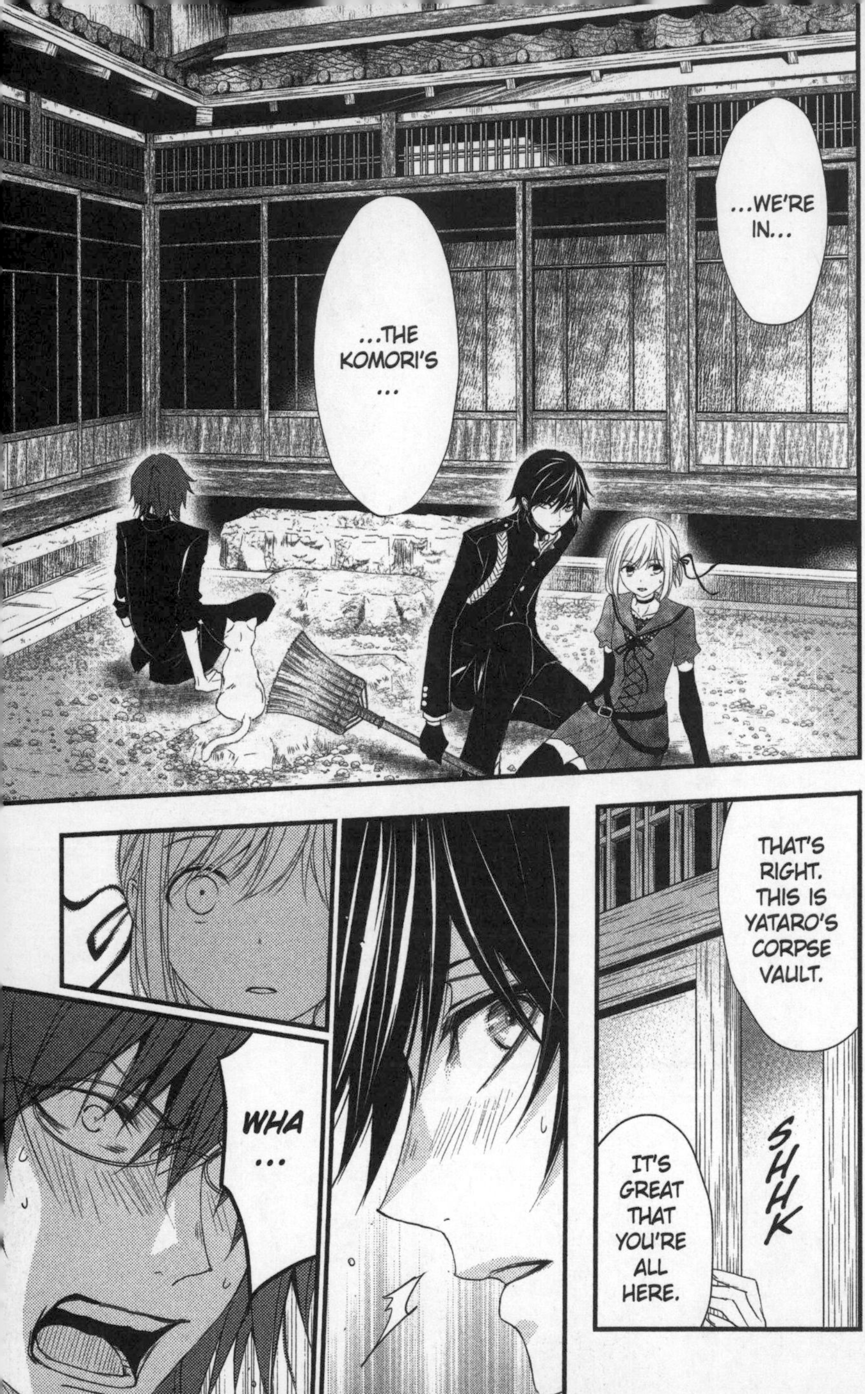
...WE'RE IN...
...THE KOMORI'S ...
THAT'S RIGHT. THIS IS YATARO'S CORPSE VAULT.
SHHK
IT'S GREAT THAT YOU'RE ALL HERE.
WHA ...

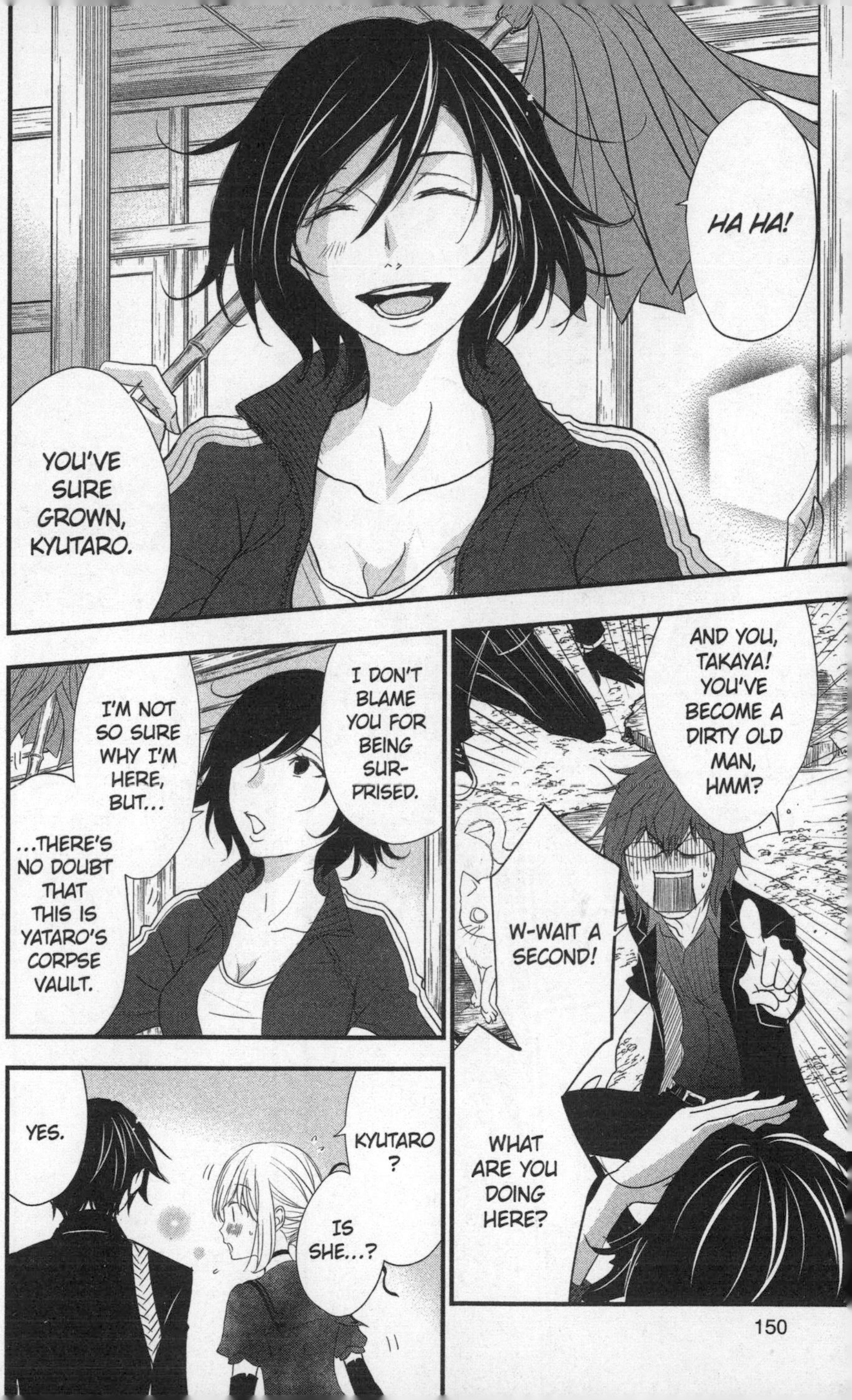
HA HA!
YOU'VE SURE GROWN, KYUTARO.
AND YOU, TAKAYA! YOU'VE BECOME A DIRTY OLD MAN, HMM?
W-WAIT A SECOND!
WHAT ARE YOU DOING HERE?
I DON'T BLAME YOU FOR BEING SUR-PRISED.
I'M NOT SO SURE WHY I'M HERE, BUT...
...THERE'S NO DOUBT THAT THIS IS YATARO'S CORPSE VAULT.
KYUTARO?
IS SHE...?
YES.

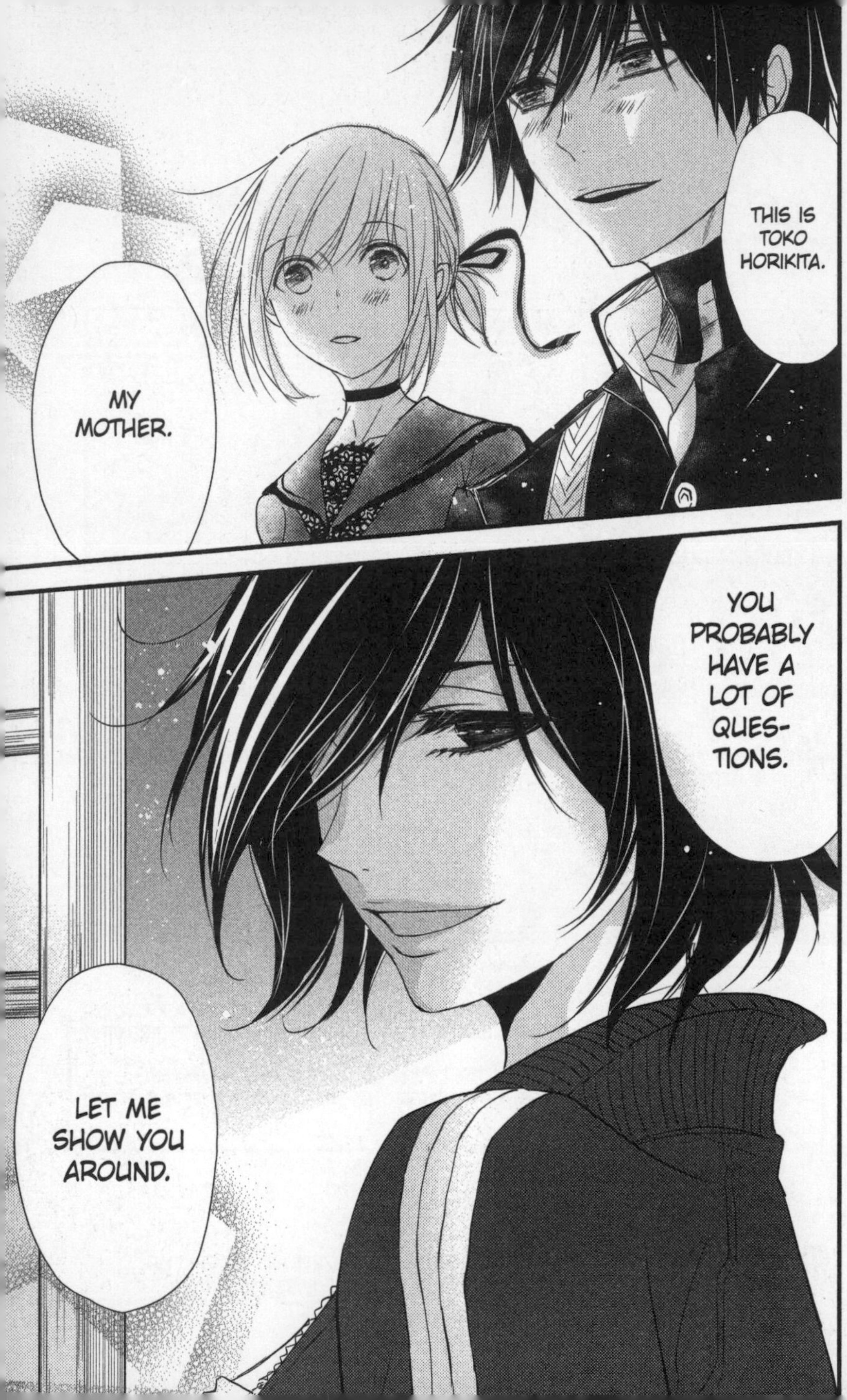
THIS IS TOKO HORIKITA.
MY MOTHER.
YOU PROBABLY HAVE A LOT OF QUES-TIONS.
LET ME SHOW YOU AROUND.

MONTHLY BETSUCOMI SALE DATE NOTICE ON TWITTER

CHAPTER 35

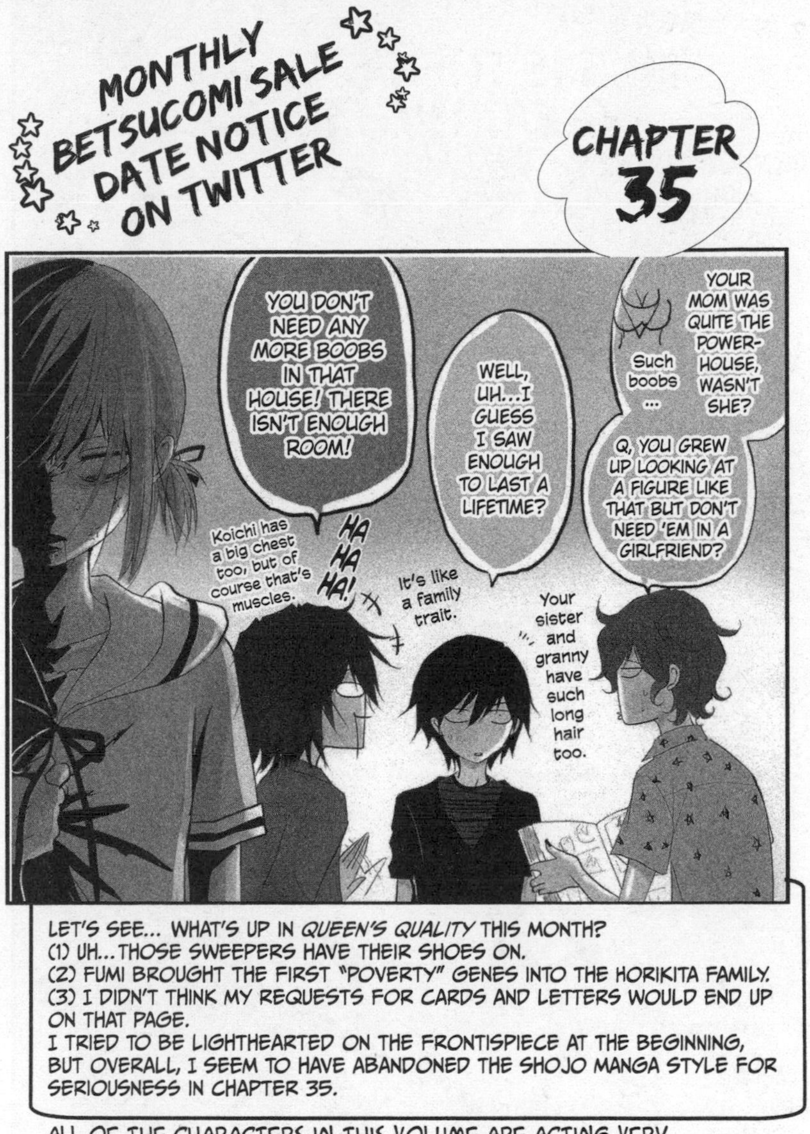
YOUR MOM WAS QUITE THE POWER-HOUSE, WASN'T SHE?
Such boobs ...
Q, YOU GREW UP LOOKING AT A FIGURE LIKE THAT BUT DON'T NEED 'EM IN A GIRLFRIEND?
WELL, UH...I GUESS I SAW ENOUGH TO LAST A LIFETIME?
YOU DON'T NEED ANY MORE BOOBS IN THAT HOUSE! THERE ISN'T ENOUGH ROOM!
Your sister and granny have such long hair too.
It's like a family trait.
HA HA HA!
Koichi has a big chest too, but of course that's muscles.

LET'S SEE... WHAT'S UP IN *QUEEN'S QUALITY* THIS MONTH?
(1) UH...THOSE SWEEPERS HAVE THEIR SHOES ON.
(2) FUMI BROUGHT THE FIRST "POVERTY" GENES INTO THE HORIKITA FAMILY.
(3) I DIDN'T THINK MY REQUESTS FOR CARDS AND LETTERS WOULD END UP ON THAT PAGE.
I TRIED TO BE LIGHTHEARTED ON THE FRONTISPIECE AT THE BEGINNING, BUT OVERALL, I SEEM TO HAVE ABANDONED THE SHOJO MANGA STYLE FOR SERIOUSNESS IN CHAPTER 35.

ALL OF THE CHARACTERS IN THIS VOLUME ARE ACTING VERY SERIOUSLY. TO COMPENSATE, THE TWITTER-NOTICE ILLUSTRATIONS HAVE LEANED TOWARD PRETTY CRUDE HUMOR.

BY "THAT PAGE," I MEAN THE BLOODY SCENE. RIGHT AFTER THE TRAGIC SCENE, I CHEERFULLY ANNOUNCED, "I'VE BEEN LIVING WITH A JAVA SPARROW!"❤

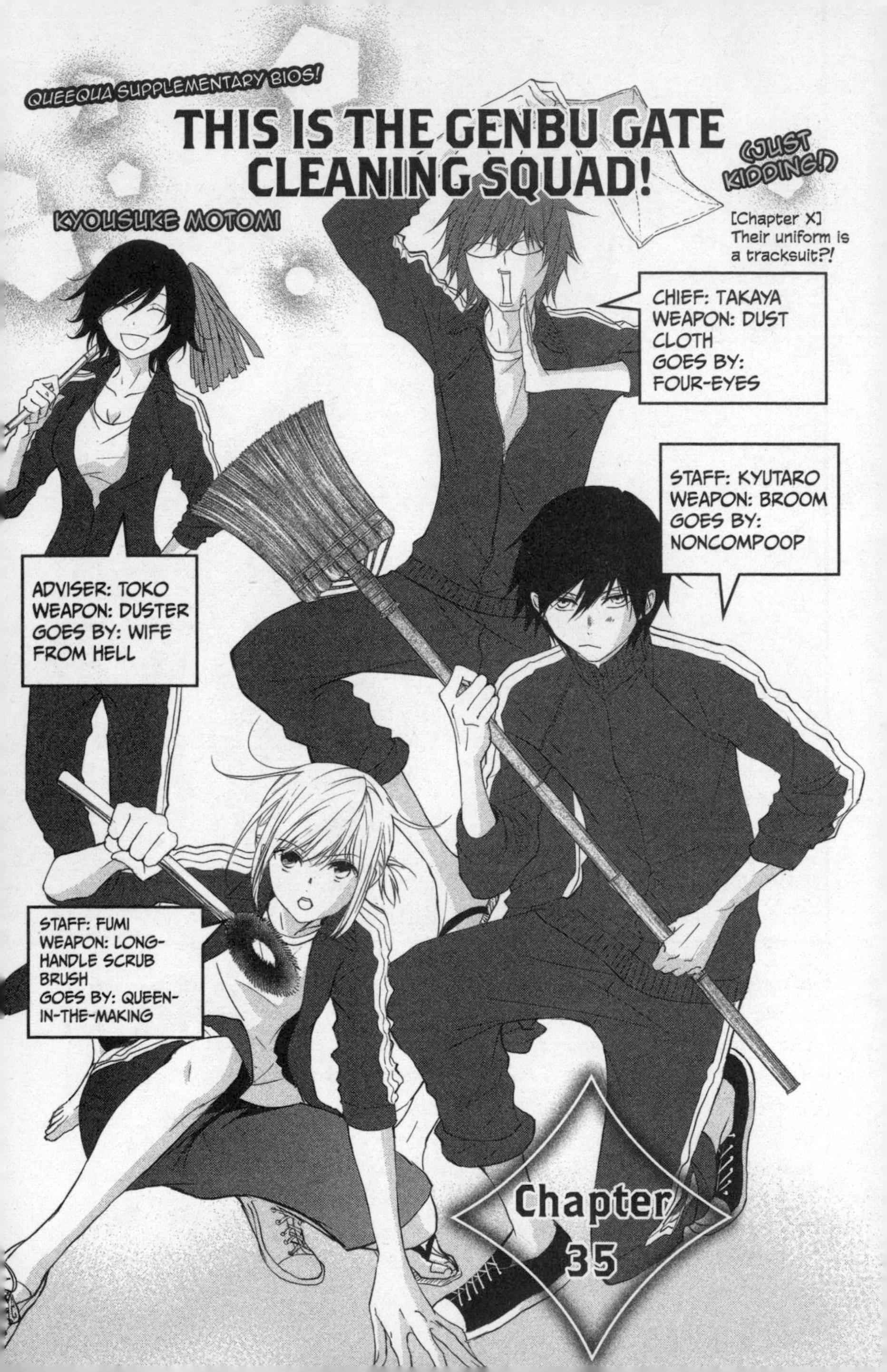
QUEEQUA SUPPLEMENTARY BIOS!
THIS IS THE GENBU GATE CLEANING SQUAD!
(JUST KIDDING!)
KYOUSUKE MOTOMI
[Chapter X] Their uniform is a tracksuit?!
CHIEF: TAKAYA WEAPON: DUST CLOTH GOES BY: FOUR-EYES
STAFF: KYUTARO WEAPON: BROOM GOES BY: NONCOMPOOP
ADVISER: TOKO WEAPON: DUSTER GOES BY: WIFE FROM HELL
STAFF: FUMI WEAPON: LONG-HANDLE SCRUB BRUSH GOES BY: QUEEN-IN-THE-MAKING
Chapter 35

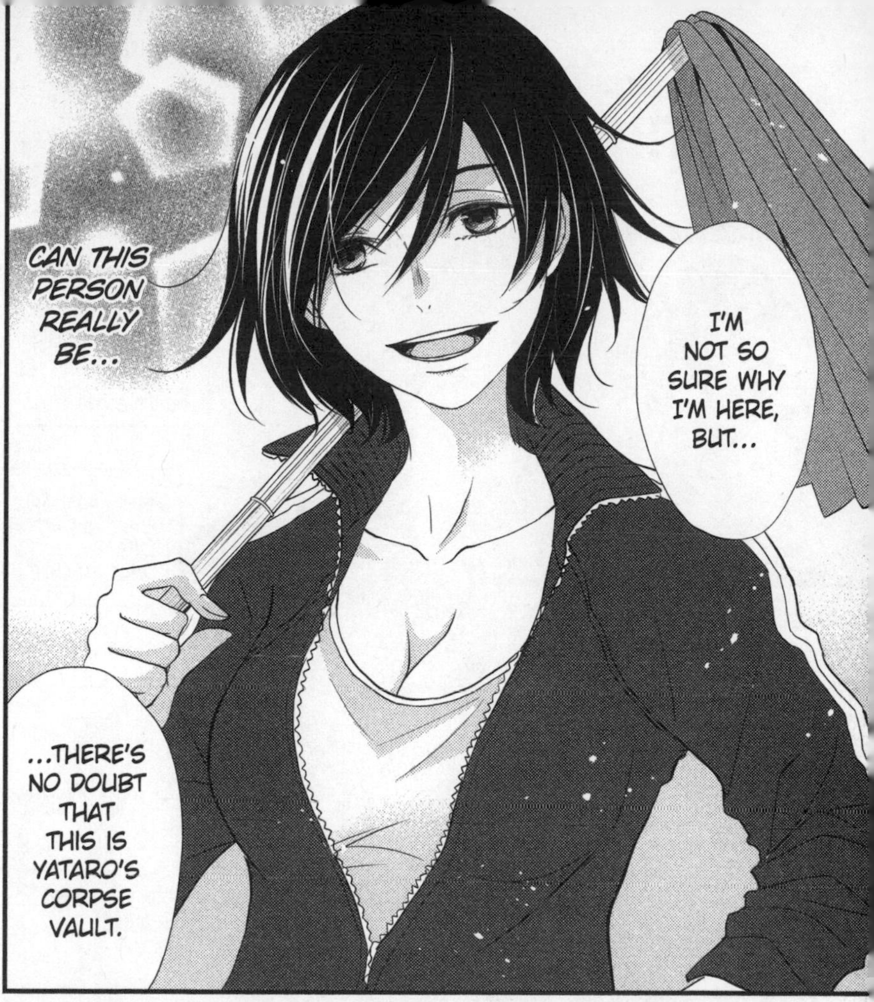
I'M NOT SO SURE WHY I'M HERE, BUT...
CAN THIS PERSON REALLY BE...
...THERE'S NO DOUBT THAT THIS IS YATARO'S CORPSE VAULT.

Lately I've been unable to avoid drawing a lot of big boobs, so I'm doing my best, but somehow they always look smaller than the ones other people draw. I wonder if I have some sort of limiter in my head. Am I somehow incapable of accepting a world where it's okay to have gigantic boobs? Am I afraid people will discover that I've betrayed the small-breasted demographic? I want to be on friendly terms with my breasts.

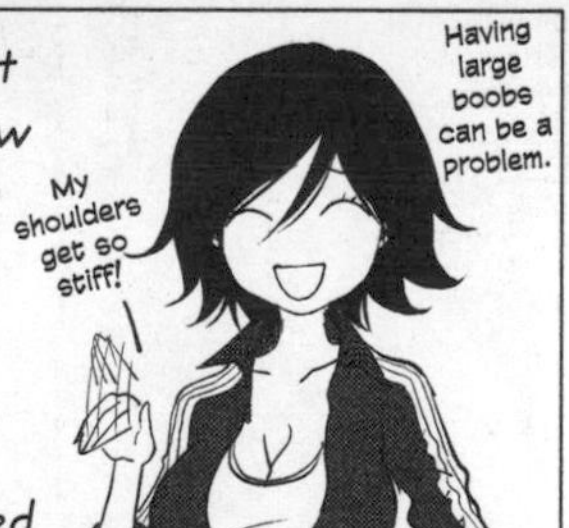
Having large boobs can be a problem.
My shoulders get so stiff!

That's what people who have them say. It's unfair that people who don't have large boobs get stiff shoulders too.

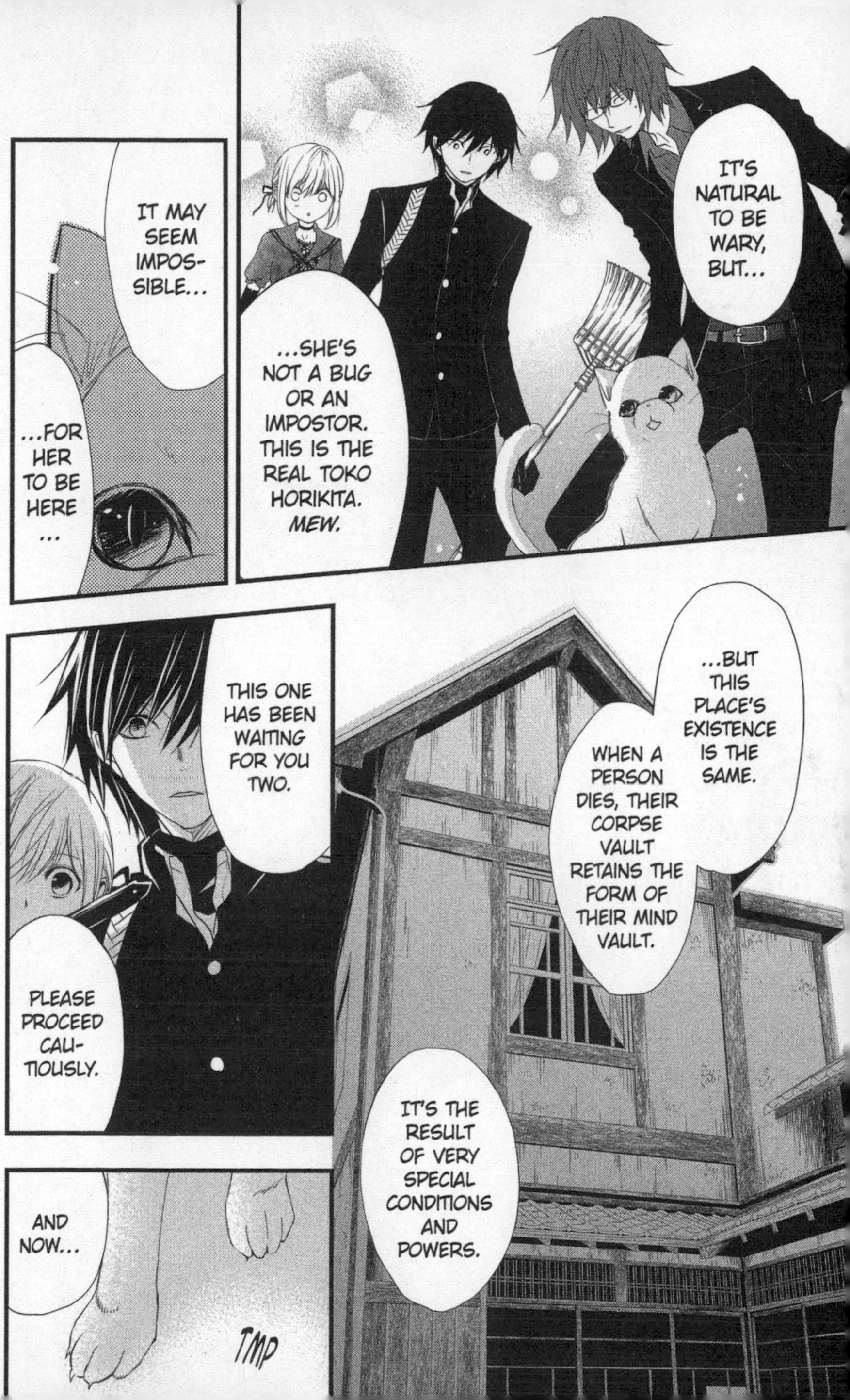

IT'S NATURAL TO BE WARY, BUT...
...SHE'S NOT A BUG OR AN IMPOSTOR. THIS IS THE REAL TOKO HORIKITA. *MEW.*
IT MAY SEEM IMPOS-SIBLE...
...FOR HER TO BE HERE...
...BUT THIS PLACE'S EXISTENCE IS THE SAME.
WHEN A PERSON DIES, THEIR CORPSE VAULT RETAINS THE FORM OF THEIR MIND VAULT.
IT'S THE RESULT OF VERY SPECIAL CONDITIONS AND POWERS.
THIS ONE HAS BEEN WAITING FOR YOU TWO.
PLEASE PROCEED CAU-TIOUSLY.
AND NOW...
TMP

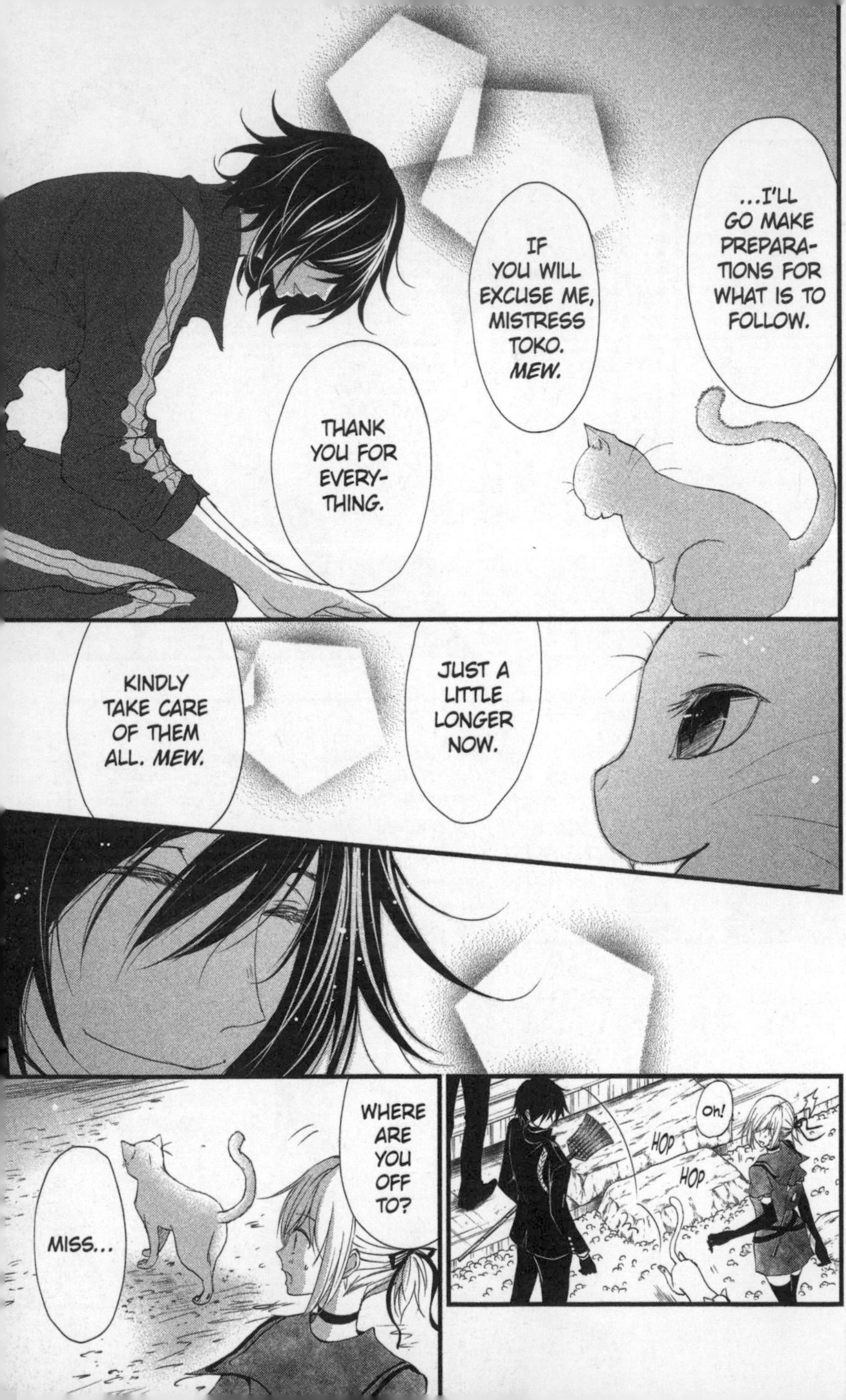
...I'LL GO MAKE PREPARATIONS FOR WHAT IS TO FOLLOW.
IF YOU WILL EXCUSE ME, MISTRESS TOKO. *MEW.*
THANK YOU FOR EVERYTHING.
JUST A LITTLE LONGER NOW.
KINDLY TAKE CARE OF THEM ALL. *MEW.*
Oh!
HOP
HOP
WHERE ARE YOU OFF TO?
MISS...

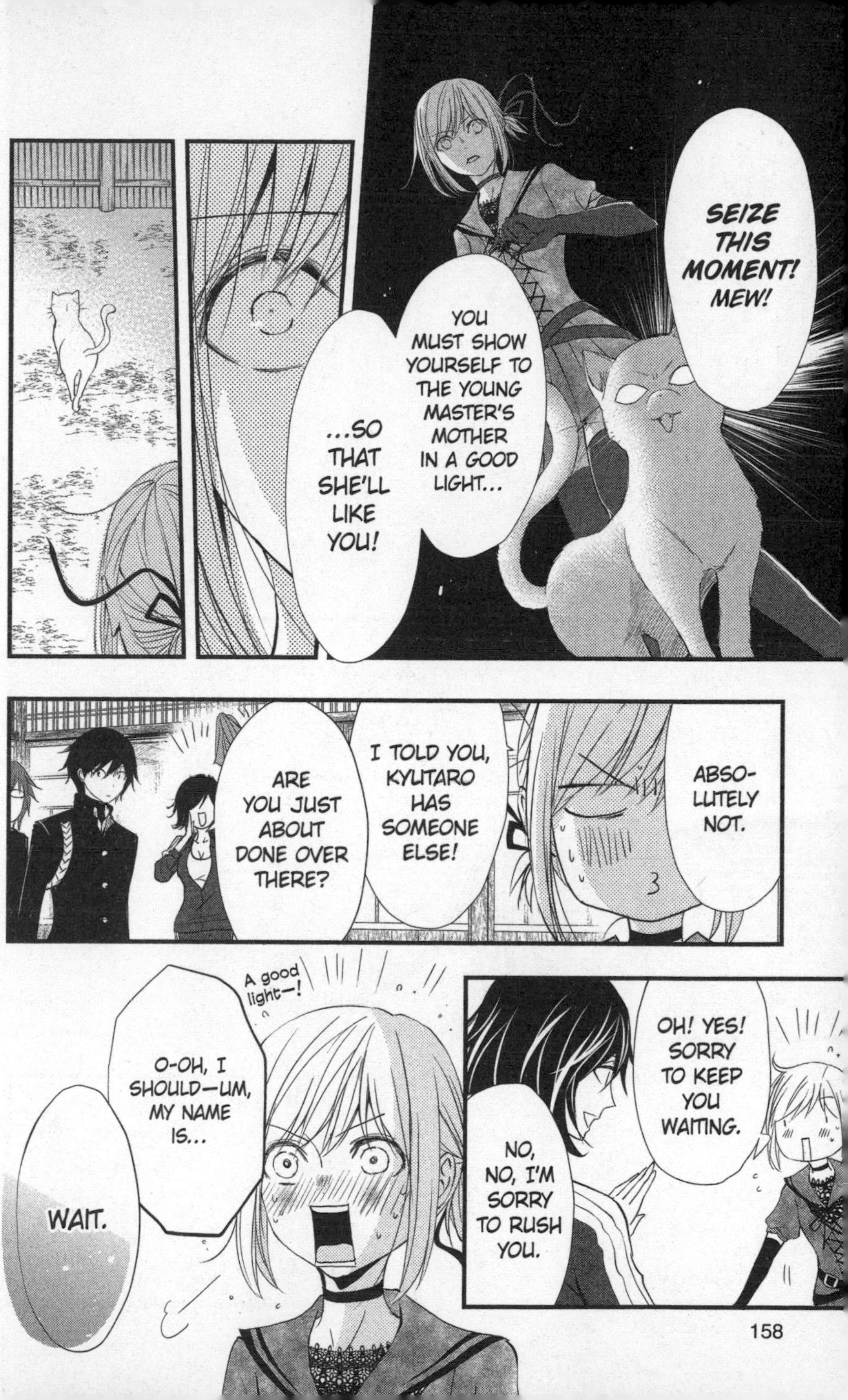
SEIZE THIS MOMENT! MEW!
YOU MUST SHOW YOURSELF TO THE YOUNG MASTER'S MOTHER IN A GOOD LIGHT...
...SO THAT SHE'LL LIKE YOU!
ABSO-LUTELY NOT.
I TOLD YOU, KYUTARO HAS SOMEONE ELSE!
ARE YOU JUST ABOUT DONE OVER THERE?
OH! YES! SORRY TO KEEP YOU WAITING.
NO, NO, I'M SORRY TO RUSH YOU.
A good light—!
O-OH, I SHOULD—UM, MY NAME IS...
WAIT.

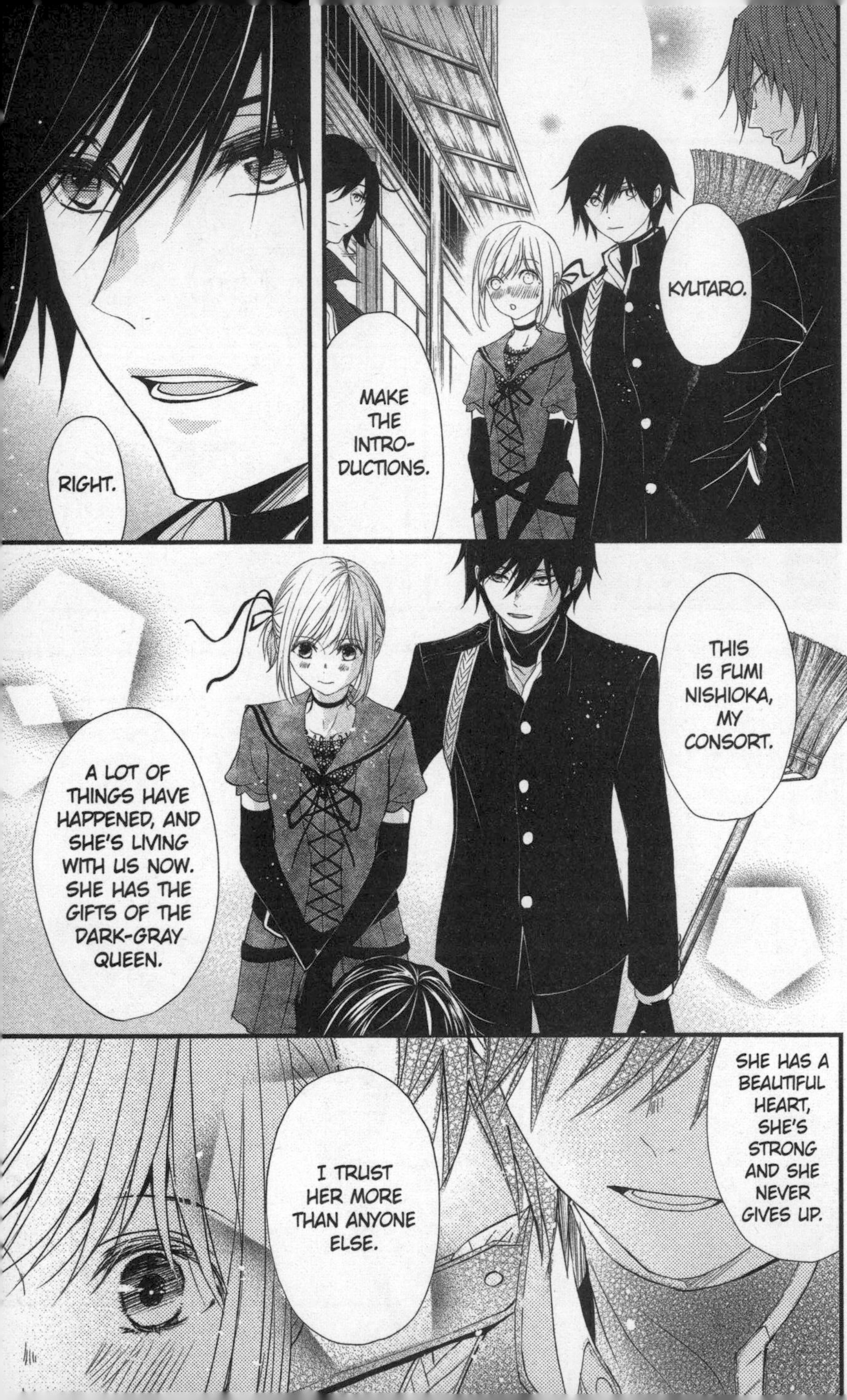
KYUTARO.
MAKE THE INTRO-DUCTIONS.
RIGHT.
THIS IS FUMI NISHIOKA, MY CONSORT.
A LOT OF THINGS HAVE HAPPENED, AND SHE'S LIVING WITH US NOW. SHE HAS THE GIFTS OF THE DARK-GRAY QUEEN.
SHE HAS A BEAUTIFUL HEART, SHE'S STRONG AND SHE NEVER GIVES UP.
I TRUST HER MORE THAN ANYONE ELSE.

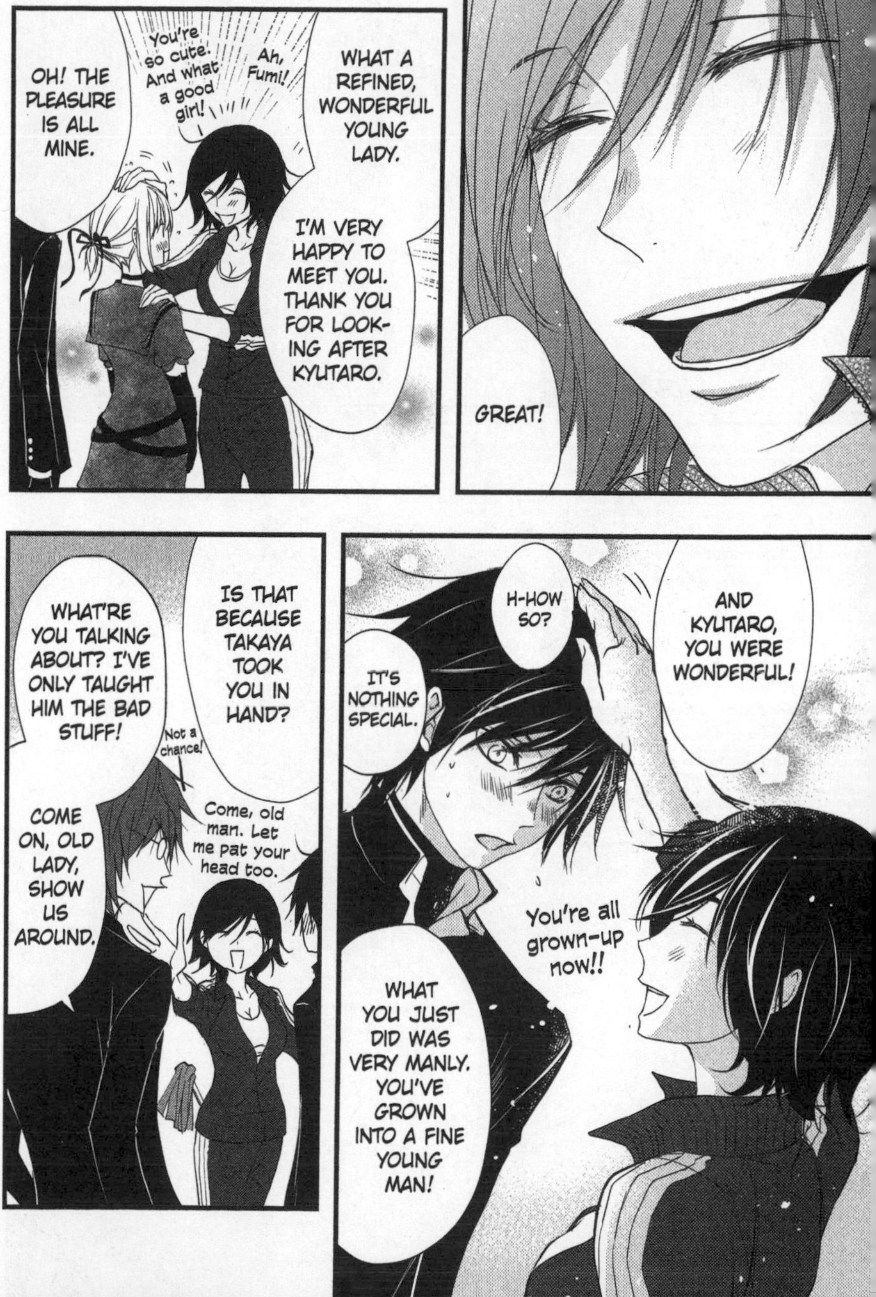
GREAT!
WHAT A REFINED, WONDERFUL YOUNG LADY.
Ah, Fumi!
You're so cute. And what a good girl!
OH! THE PLEASURE IS ALL MINE.
I'M VERY HAPPY TO MEET YOU. THANK YOU FOR LOOKING AFTER KYUTARO.
AND KYUTARO, YOU WERE WONDERFUL!
H-HOW SO?
IT'S NOTHING SPECIAL.
You're all grown-up now!!
WHAT YOU JUST DID WAS VERY MANLY. YOU'VE GROWN INTO A FINE YOUNG MAN!
IS THAT BECAUSE TAKAYA TOOK YOU IN HAND?
WHAT'RE YOU TALKING ABOUT? I'VE ONLY TAUGHT HIM THE BAD STUFF!
Not a chance!
Come, old man. Let me pat your head too.
COME ON, OLD LADY, SHOW US AROUND.

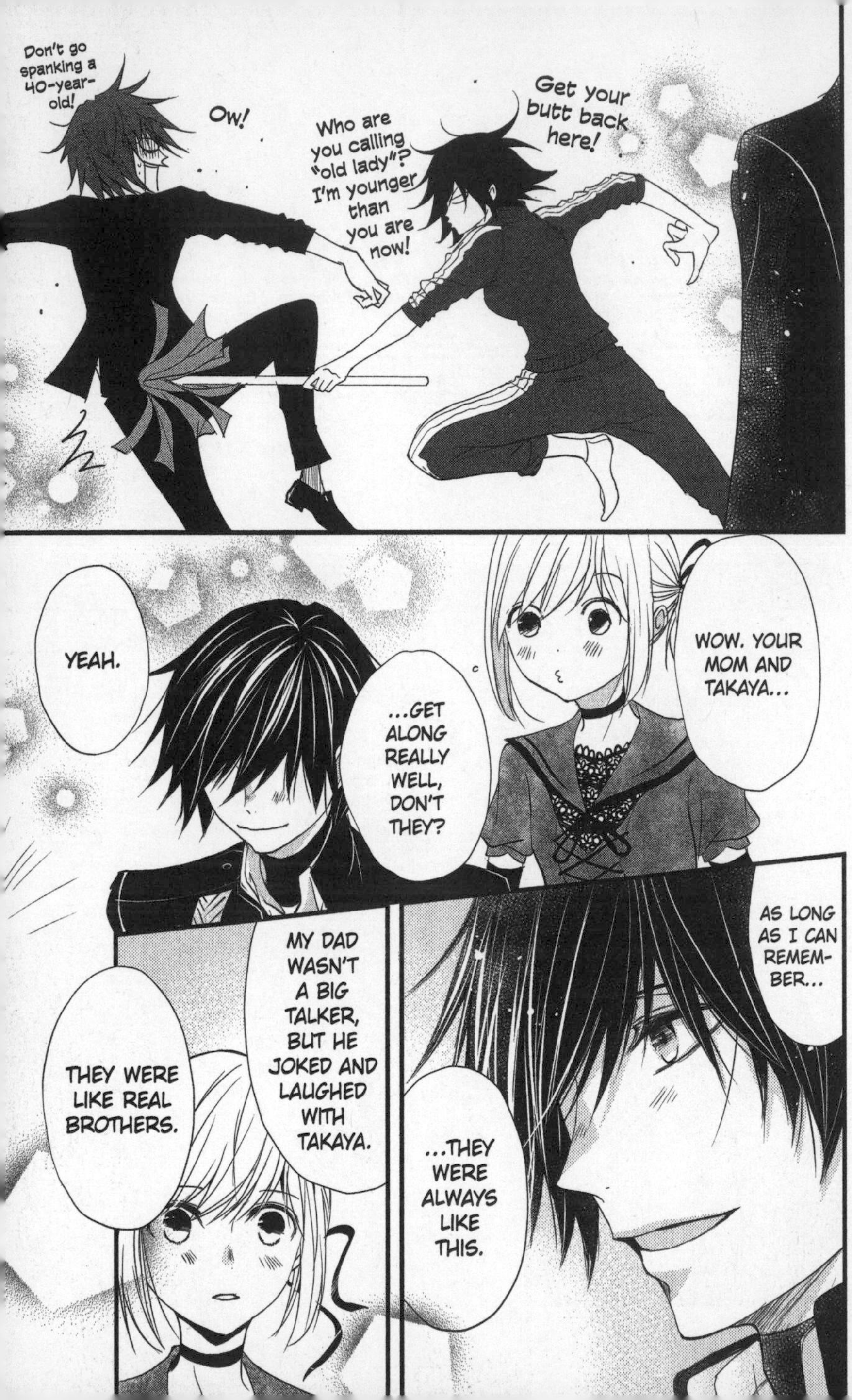
Get your butt back here!
Who are you calling "old lady"? I'm younger than you are now!
Ow!
Don't go spanking a 40-year-old!
WOW. YOUR MOM AND TAKAYA...
...GET ALONG REALLY WELL, DON'T THEY?
YEAH.
AS LONG AS I CAN REMEMBER...
...THEY WERE ALWAYS LIKE THIS.
MY DAD WASN'T A BIG TALKER, BUT HE JOKED AND LAUGHED WITH TAKAYA.
THEY WERE LIKE REAL BROTHERS.

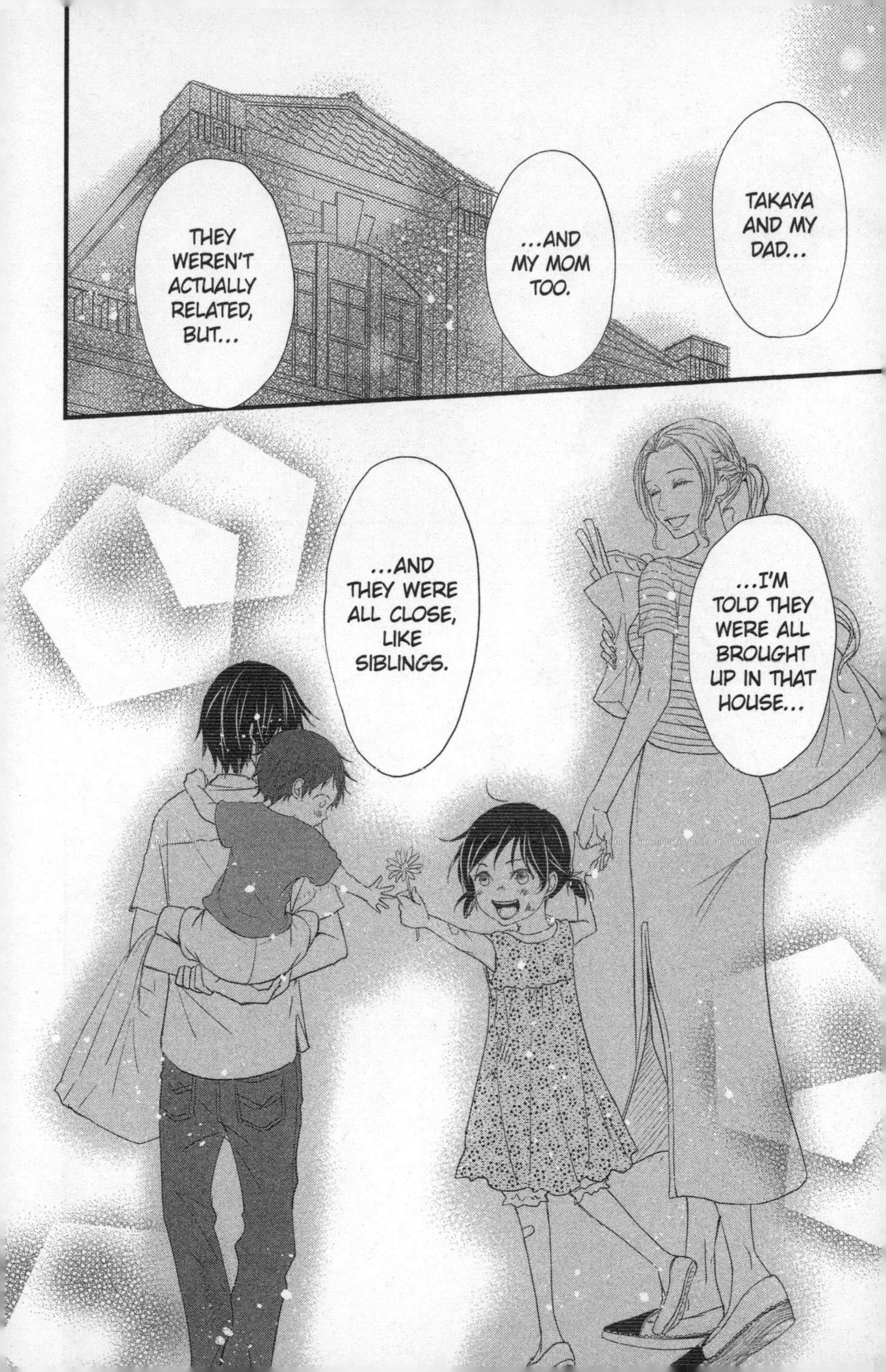
TAKAYA AND MY DAD...
...AND MY MOM TOO.
THEY WEREN'T ACTUALLY RELATED, BUT...
...I'M TOLD THEY WERE ALL BROUGHT UP IN THAT HOUSE...
...AND THEY WERE ALL CLOSE, LIKE SIBLINGS.

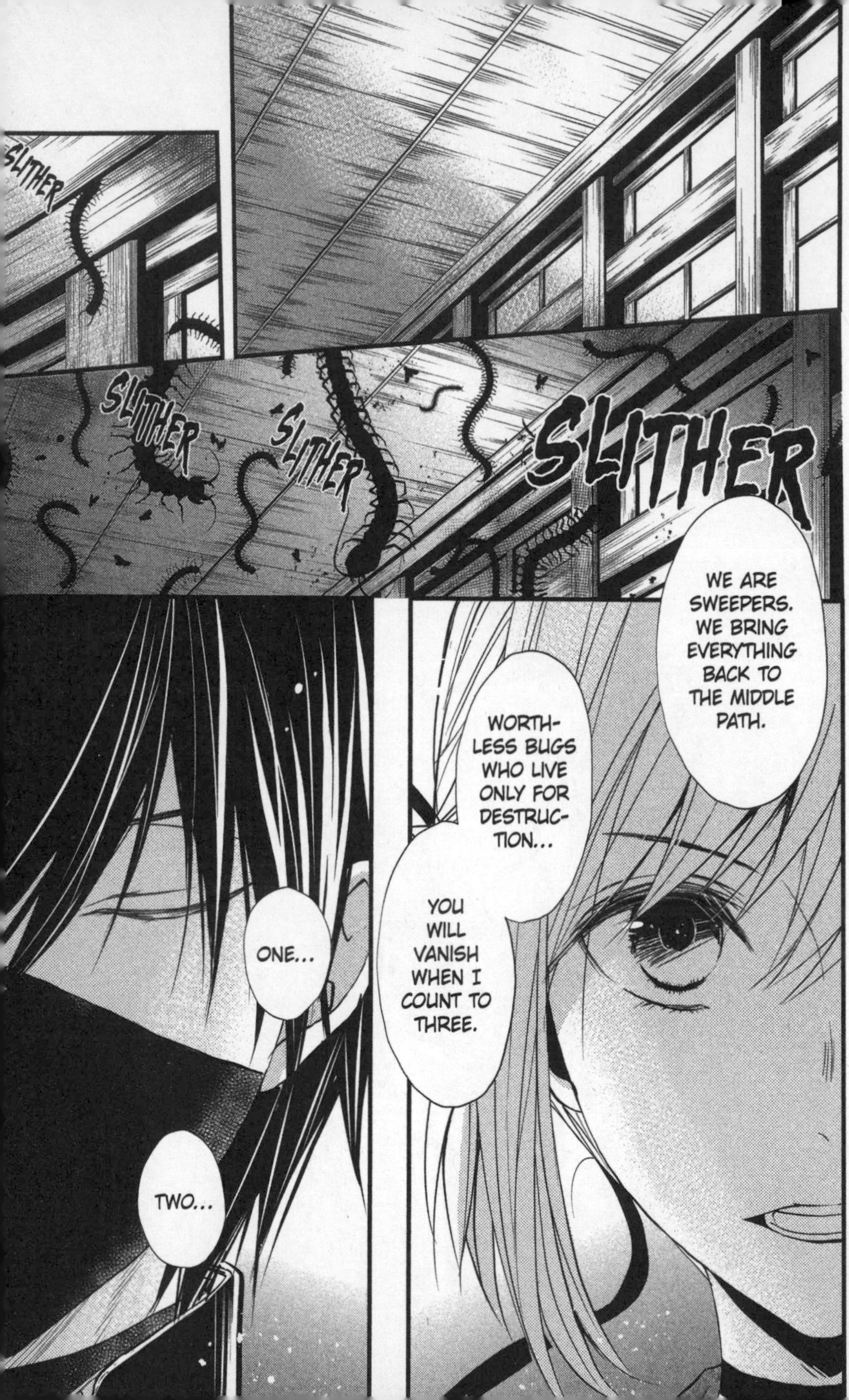
SLITHER
SLITHER
SLITHER
SLITHER
WE ARE SWEEPERS. WE BRING EVERYTHING BACK TO THE MIDDLE PATH.
WORTHLESS BUGS WHO LIVE ONLY FOR DESTRUCTION...
YOU WILL VANISH WHEN I COUNT TO THREE.
ONE...
TWO...

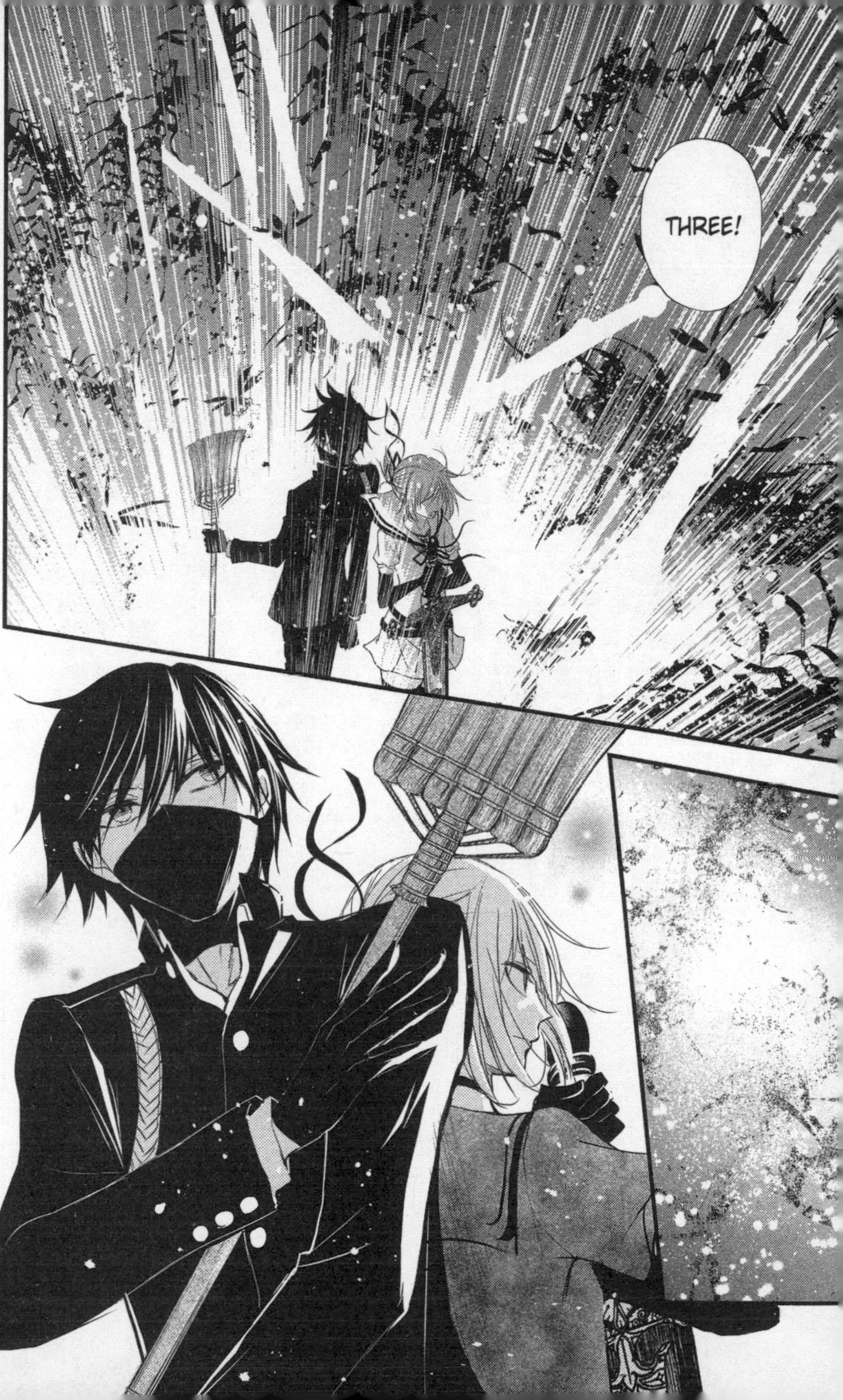
THREE!

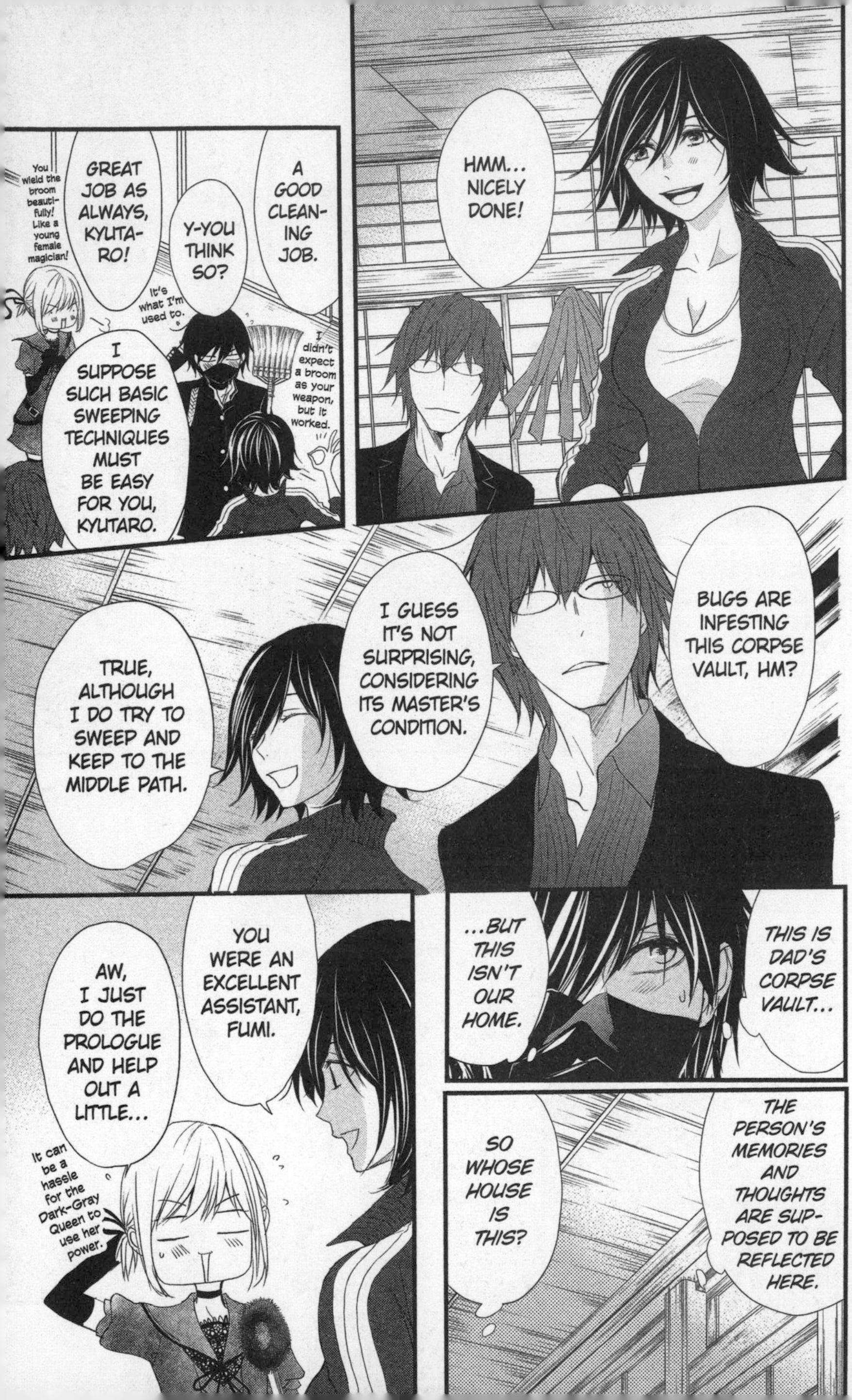
HMM... NICELY DONE!
A GOOD CLEANING JOB.
Y-YOU THINK SO?
GREAT JOB AS ALWAYS, KYUTARO!
You wield the broom beautifully! Like a young female magician!
It's what I'm used to.
I didn't expect a broom as your weapon, but it worked.
I SUPPOSE SUCH BASIC SWEEPING TECHNIQUES MUST BE EASY FOR YOU, KYUTARO.
BUGS ARE INFESTING THIS CORPSE VAULT, HM?
I GUESS IT'S NOT SURPRISING, CONSIDERING ITS MASTER'S CONDITION.
TRUE, ALTHOUGH I DO TRY TO SWEEP AND KEEP TO THE MIDDLE PATH.
THIS IS DAD'S CORPSE VAULT...
...BUT THIS ISN'T OUR HOME.
THE PERSON'S MEMORIES AND THOUGHTS ARE SUPPOSED TO BE REFLECTED HERE.
SO WHOSE HOUSE IS THIS?
YOU WERE AN EXCELLENT ASSISTANT, FUMI.
AW, I JUST DO THE PROLOGUE AND HELP OUT A LITTLE...
It can be a hassle for the Dark-Gray Queen to use her power.

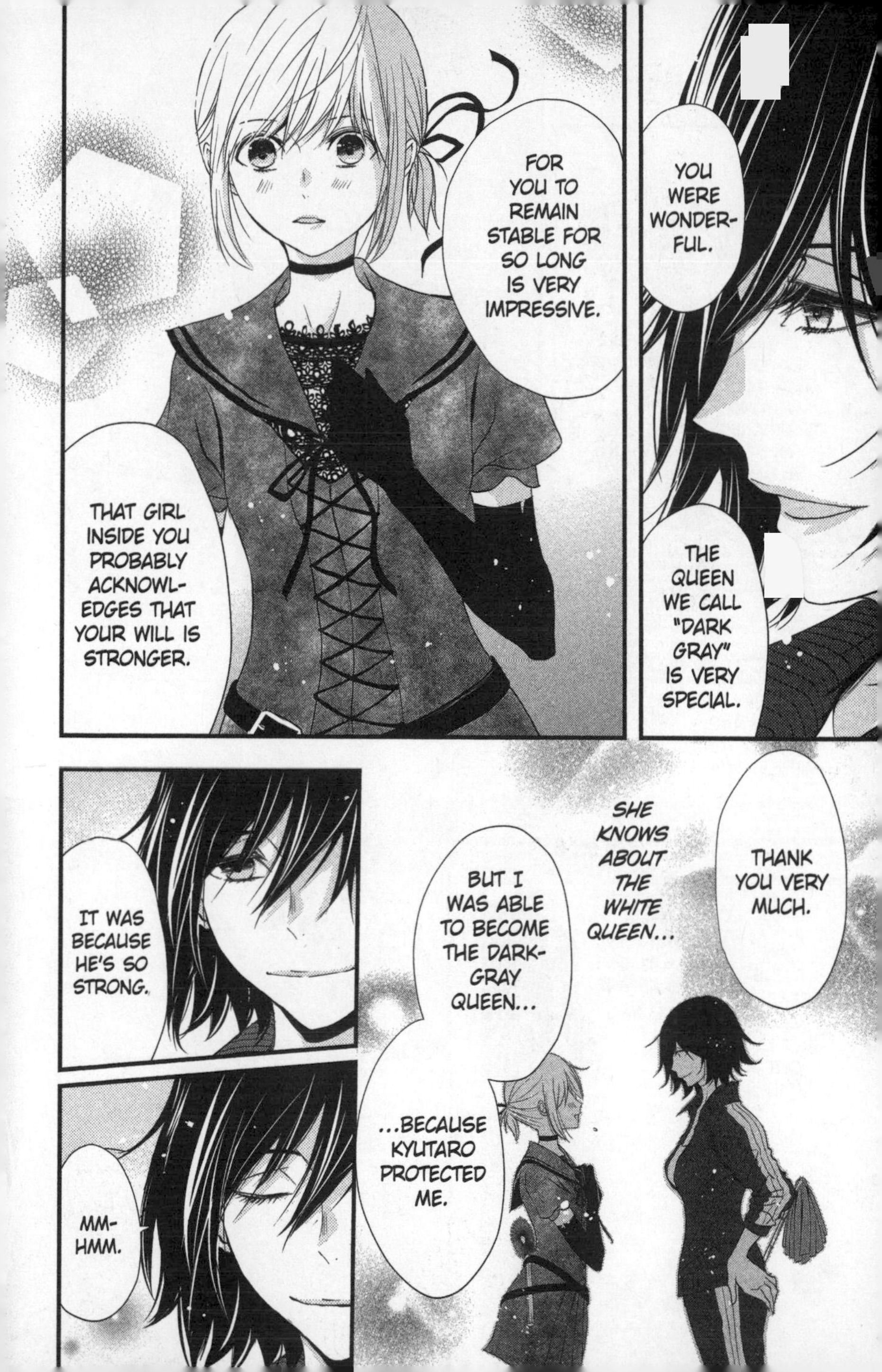
YOU WERE WONDERFUL.
THE QUEEN WE CALL "DARK GRAY" IS VERY SPECIAL.
FOR YOU TO REMAIN STABLE FOR SO LONG IS VERY IMPRESSIVE.
THAT GIRL INSIDE YOU PROBABLY ACKNOWLEDGES THAT YOUR WILL IS STRONGER.
THANK YOU VERY MUCH.
SHE KNOWS ABOUT THE WHITE QUEEN...
BUT I WAS ABLE TO BECOME THE DARK-GRAY QUEEN...
...BECAUSE KYUTARO PROTECTED ME.
IT WAS BECAUSE HE'S SO STRONG.
MM-HMM.

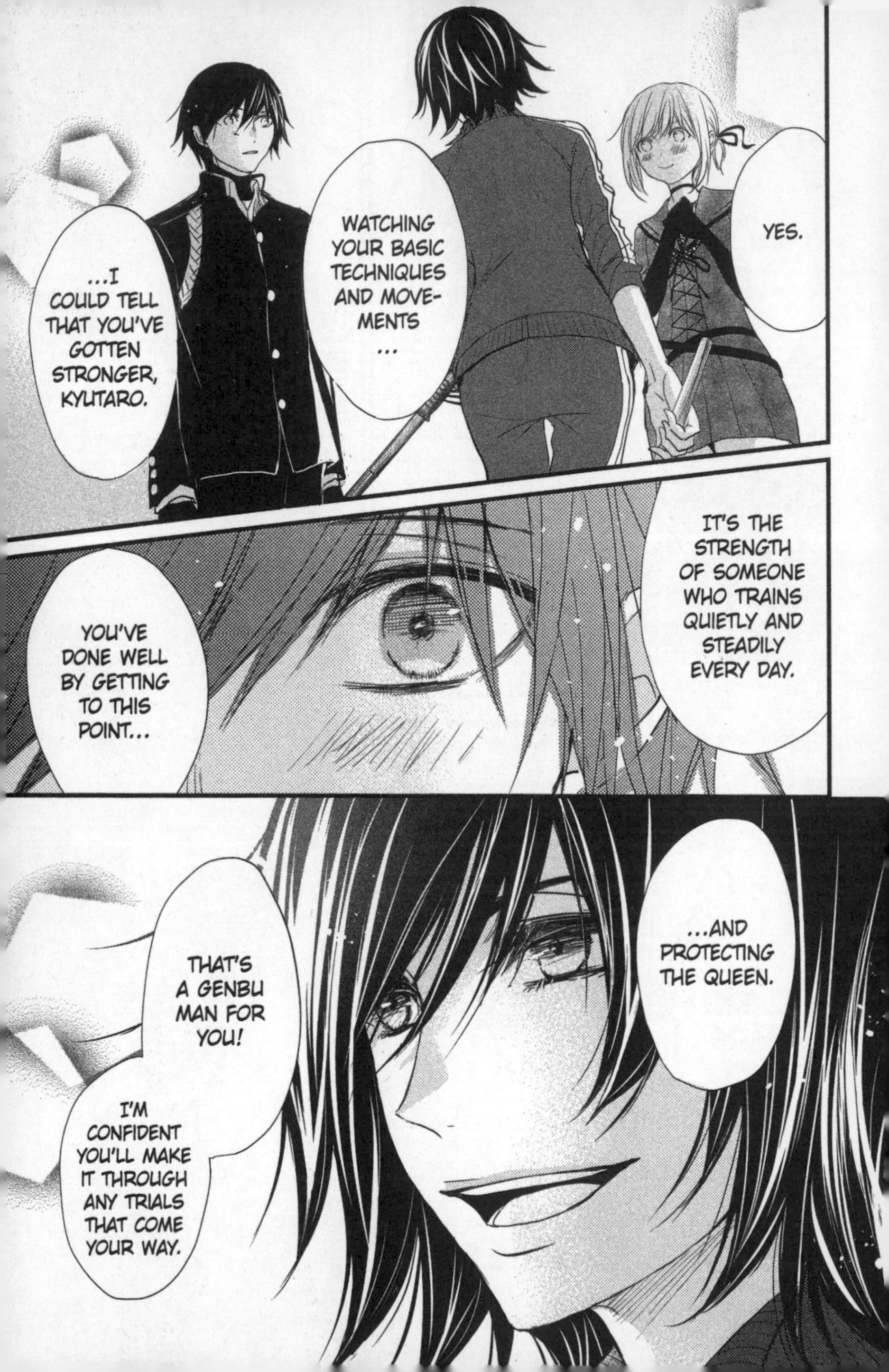
YES.
WATCHING YOUR BASIC TECHNIQUES AND MOVE-MENTS...
...I COULD TELL THAT YOU'VE GOTTEN STRONGER, KYUTARO.
IT'S THE STRENGTH OF SOMEONE WHO TRAINS QUIETLY AND STEADILY EVERY DAY.
YOU'VE DONE WELL BY GETTING TO THIS POINT...
...AND PROTECTING THE QUEEN.
THAT'S A GENBU MAN FOR YOU!
I'M CONFIDENT YOU'LL MAKE IT THROUGH ANY TRIALS THAT COME YOUR WAY.

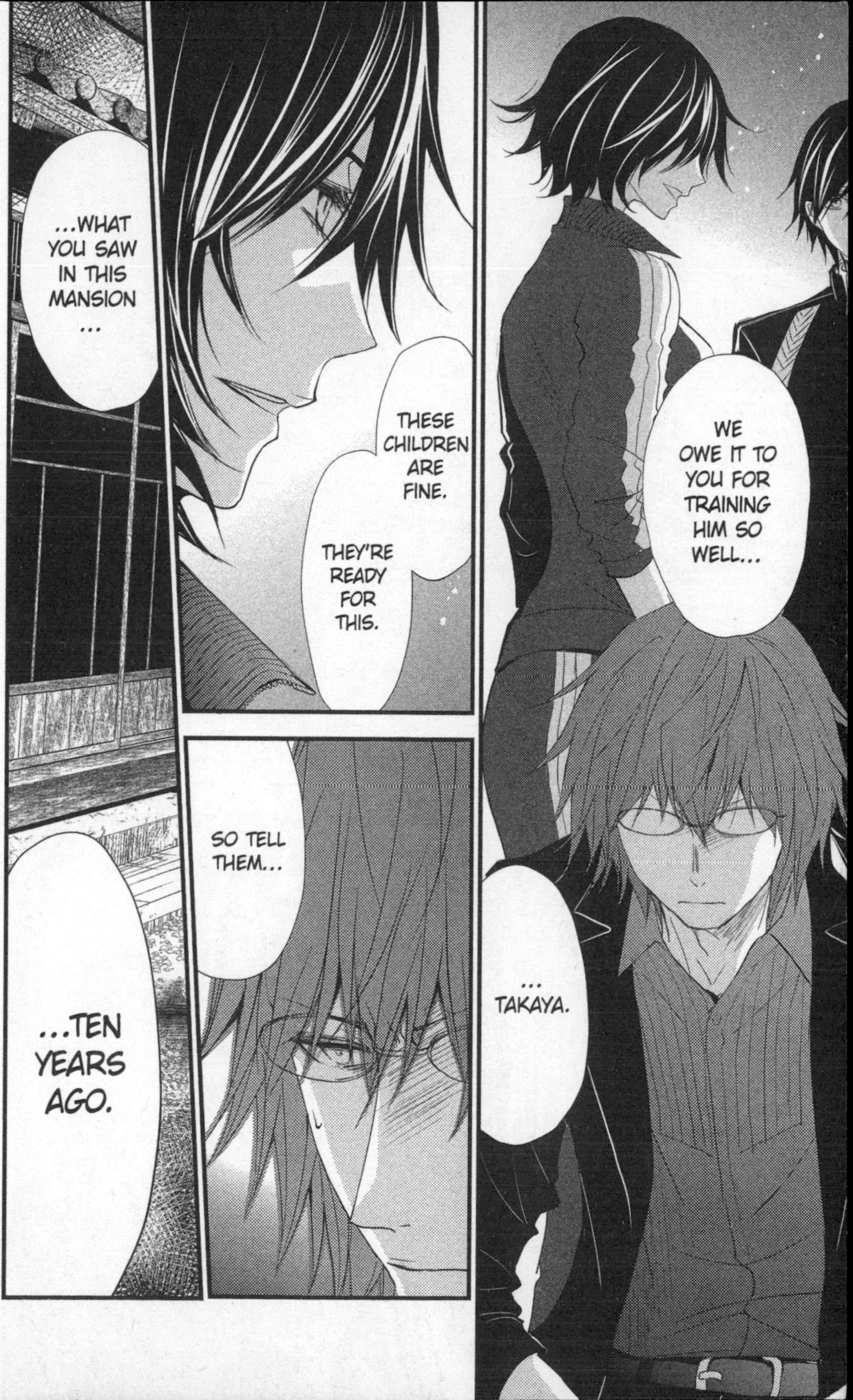
WE OWE IT TO YOU FOR TRAINING HIM SO WELL...
...TAKAYA.
THESE CHILDREN ARE FINE.
THEY'RE READY FOR THIS.
SO TELL THEM...
...WHAT YOU SAW IN THIS MANSION...
...TEN YEARS AGO.

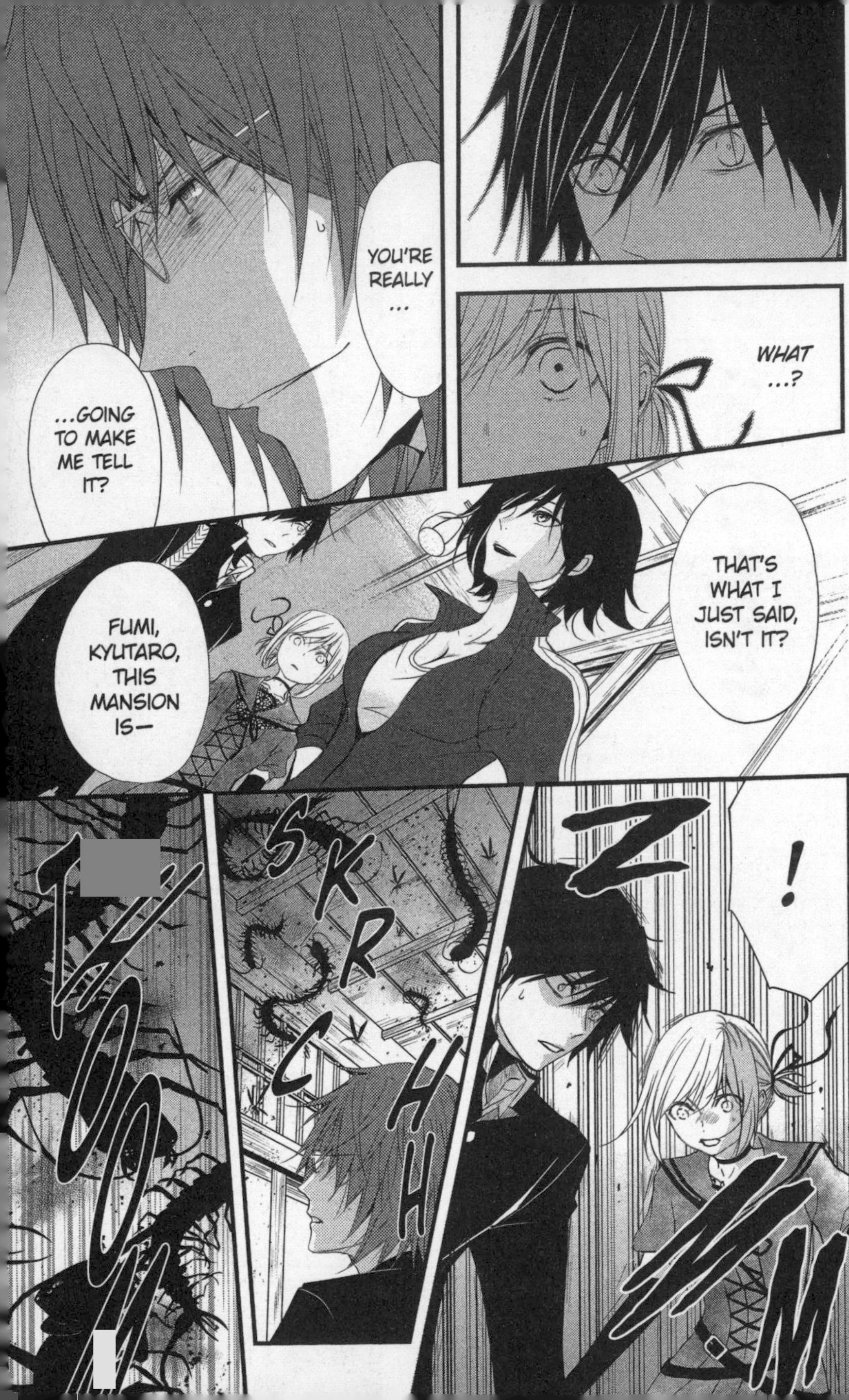
WHAT ...?
YOU'RE REALLY ...
...GOING TO MAKE ME TELL IT?
THAT'S WHAT I JUST SAID, ISN'T IT?
FUMI, KYUTARO, THIS MANSION IS—
!
ZMMM
SKRCHHH
THOOM

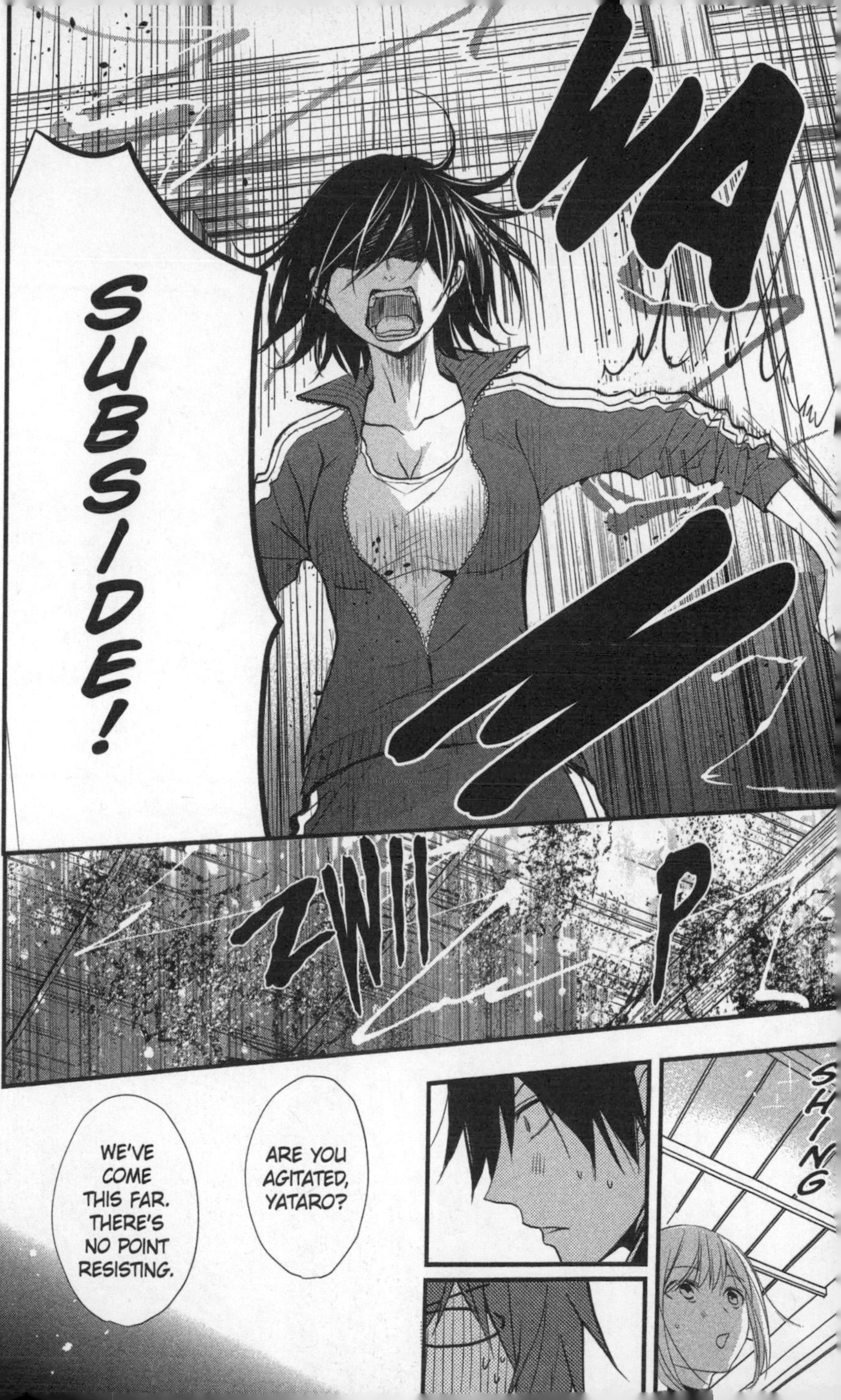
WA
SUBSIDE!
ZWIIP
SHING
ARE YOU AGITATED, YATARO?
WE'VE COME THIS FAR. THERE'S NO POINT RESISTING.

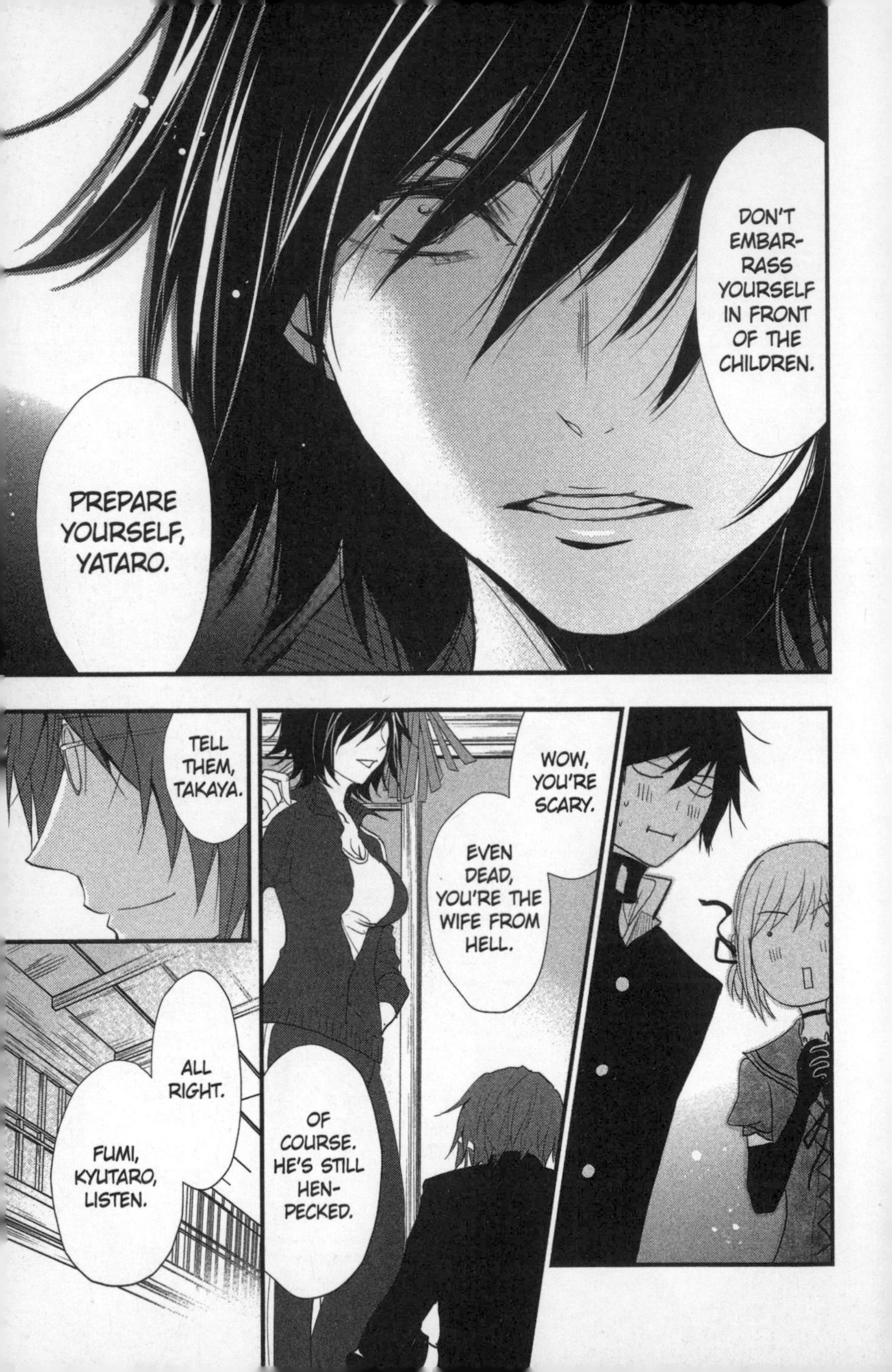
DON'T EMBARRASS YOURSELF IN FRONT OF THE CHILDREN.
PREPARE YOURSELF, YATARO.
WOW, YOU'RE SCARY.
EVEN DEAD, YOU'RE THE WIFE FROM HELL.
OF COURSE. HE'S STILL HENPECKED.
TELL THEM, TAKAYA.
ALL RIGHT.
FUMI, KYUTARO, LISTEN.

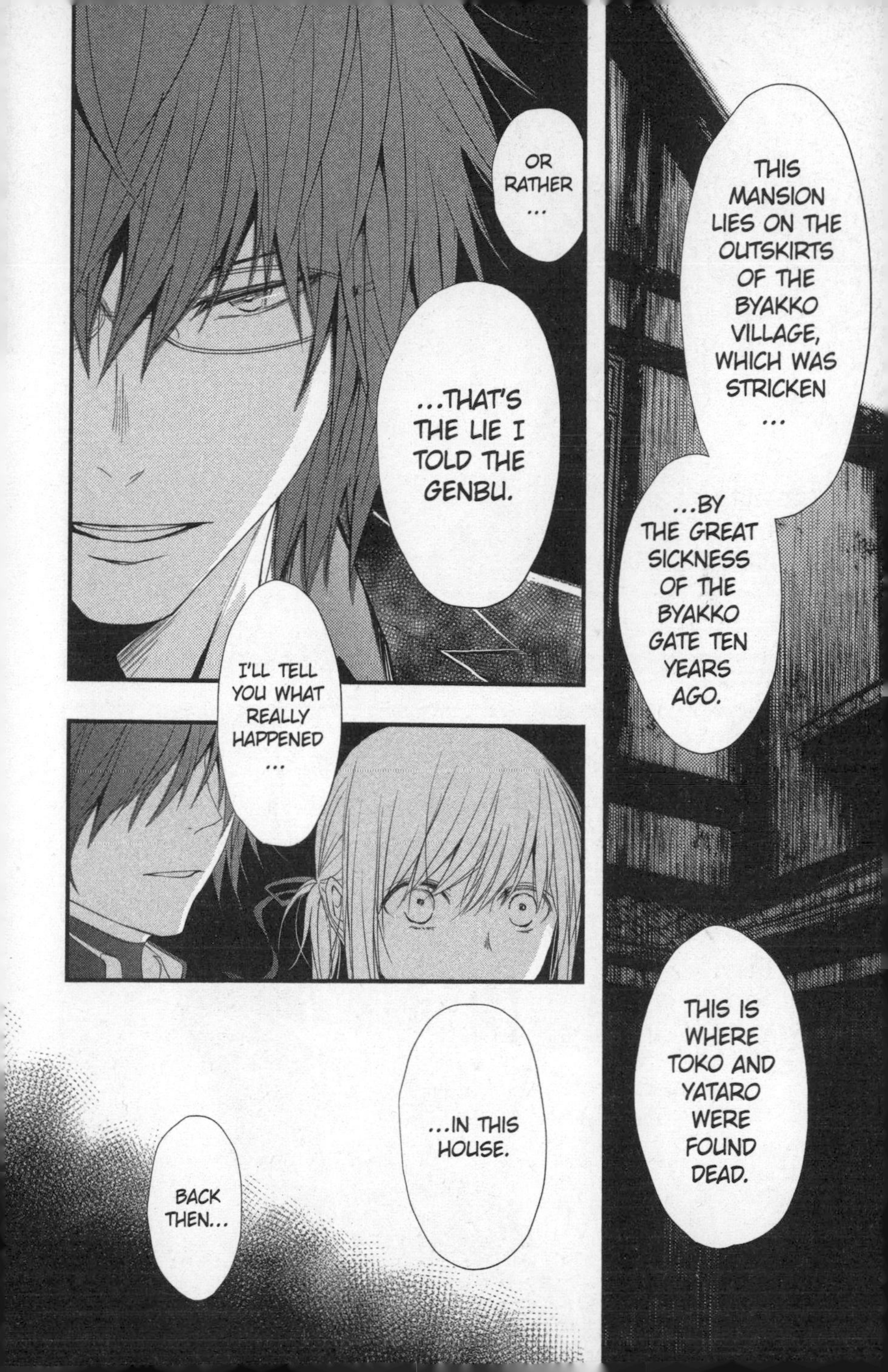
THIS MANSION LIES ON THE OUTSKIRTS OF THE BYAKKO VILLAGE, WHICH WAS STRICKEN …
…BY THE GREAT SICKNESS OF THE BYAKKO GATE TEN YEARS AGO.
THIS IS WHERE TOKO AND YATARO WERE FOUND DEAD.
OR RATHER …
…THAT'S THE LIE I TOLD THE GENBU.
I'LL TELL YOU WHAT REALLY HAPPENED …
…IN THIS HOUSE.
BACK THEN…

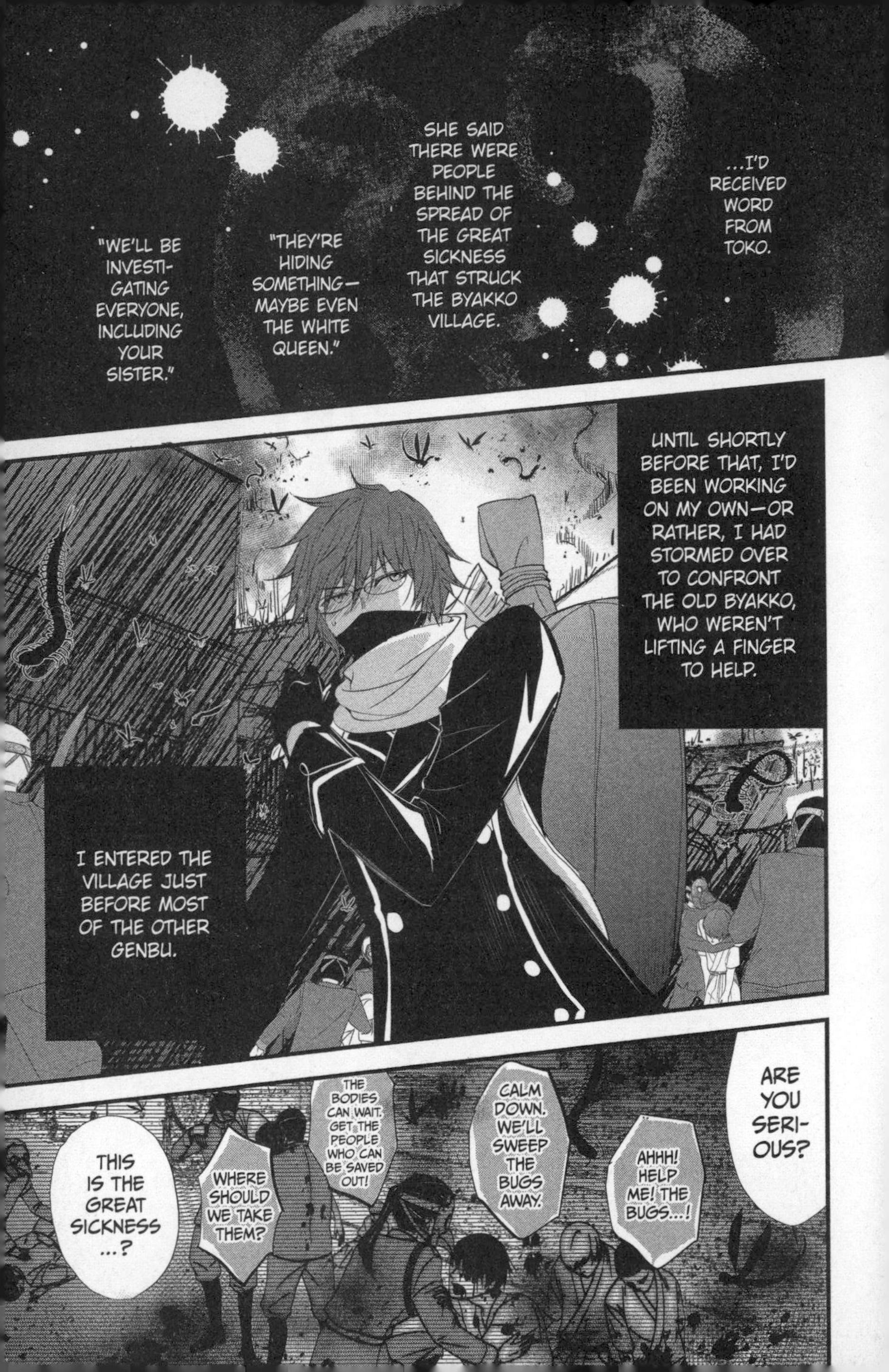
...I'D RECEIVED WORD FROM TOKO.
SHE SAID THERE WERE PEOPLE BEHIND THE SPREAD OF THE GREAT SICKNESS THAT STRUCK THE BYAKKO VILLAGE.
"THEY'RE HIDING SOMETHING—MAYBE EVEN THE WHITE QUEEN."
"WE'LL BE INVESTI-GATING EVERYONE, INCLUDING YOUR SISTER."
UNTIL SHORTLY BEFORE THAT, I'D BEEN WORKING ON MY OWN—OR RATHER, I HAD STORMED OVER TO CONFRONT THE OLD BYAKKO, WHO WEREN'T LIFTING A FINGER TO HELP.
I ENTERED THE VILLAGE JUST BEFORE MOST OF THE OTHER GENBU.
ARE YOU SERI-OUS?
AHHH! HELP ME! THE BUGS...!
CALM DOWN. WE'LL SWEEP THE BUGS AWAY.
THE BODIES CAN WAIT. GET THE PEOPLE WHO CAN BE SAVED OUT!
WHERE SHOULD WE TAKE THEM?
THIS IS THE GREAT SICKNESS ...?

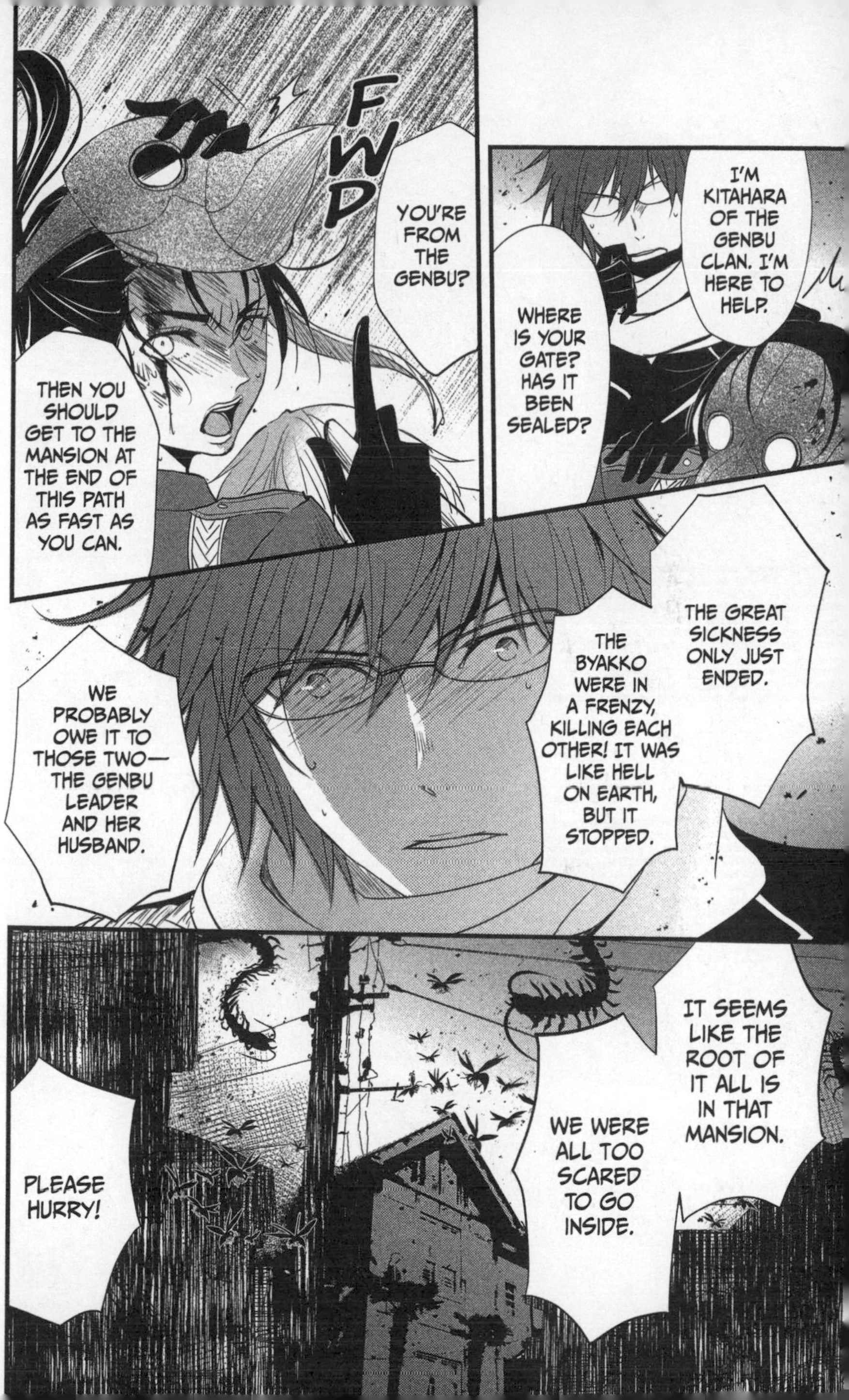
I'M KITAHARA OF THE GENBU CLAN. I'M HERE TO HELP.
WHERE IS YOUR GATE? HAS IT BEEN SEALED?
FWD
YOU'RE FROM THE GENBU?
THEN YOU SHOULD GET TO THE MANSION AT THE END OF THIS PATH AS FAST AS YOU CAN.
THE GREAT SICKNESS ONLY JUST ENDED.
THE BYAKKO WERE IN A FRENZY, KILLING EACH OTHER! IT WAS LIKE HELL ON EARTH, BUT IT STOPPED.
WE PROBABLY OWE IT TO THOSE TWO— THE GENBU LEADER AND HER HUSBAND.
IT SEEMS LIKE THE ROOT OF IT ALL IS IN THAT MANSION.
WE WERE ALL TOO SCARED TO GO INSIDE.
PLEASE HURRY!

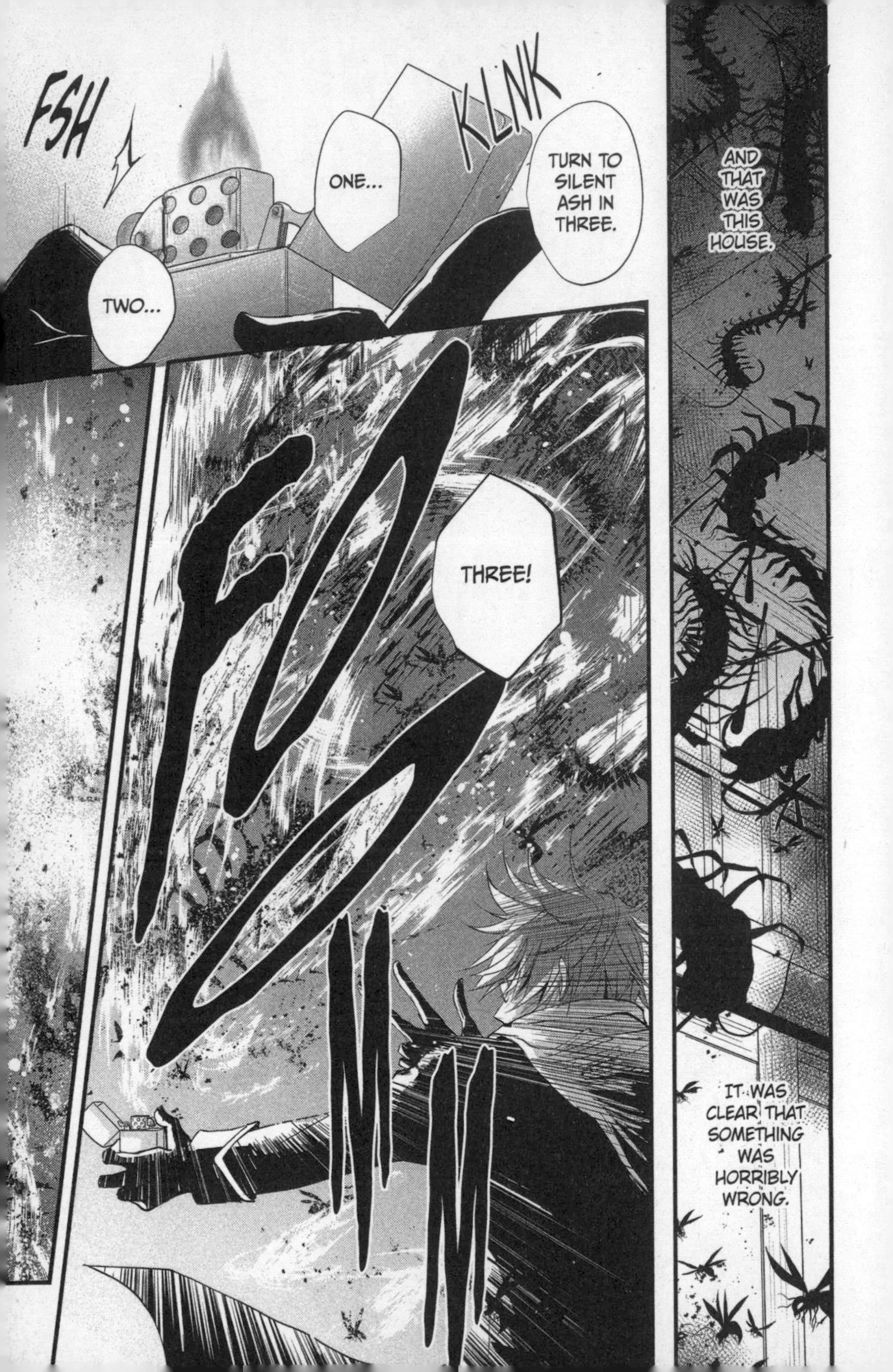
AND THAT WAS THIS HOUSE.
IT WAS CLEAR THAT SOMETHING WAS HORRIBLY WRONG.
KLNK
TURN TO SILENT ASH IN THREE.
ONE...
FSH
TWO...
THREE!

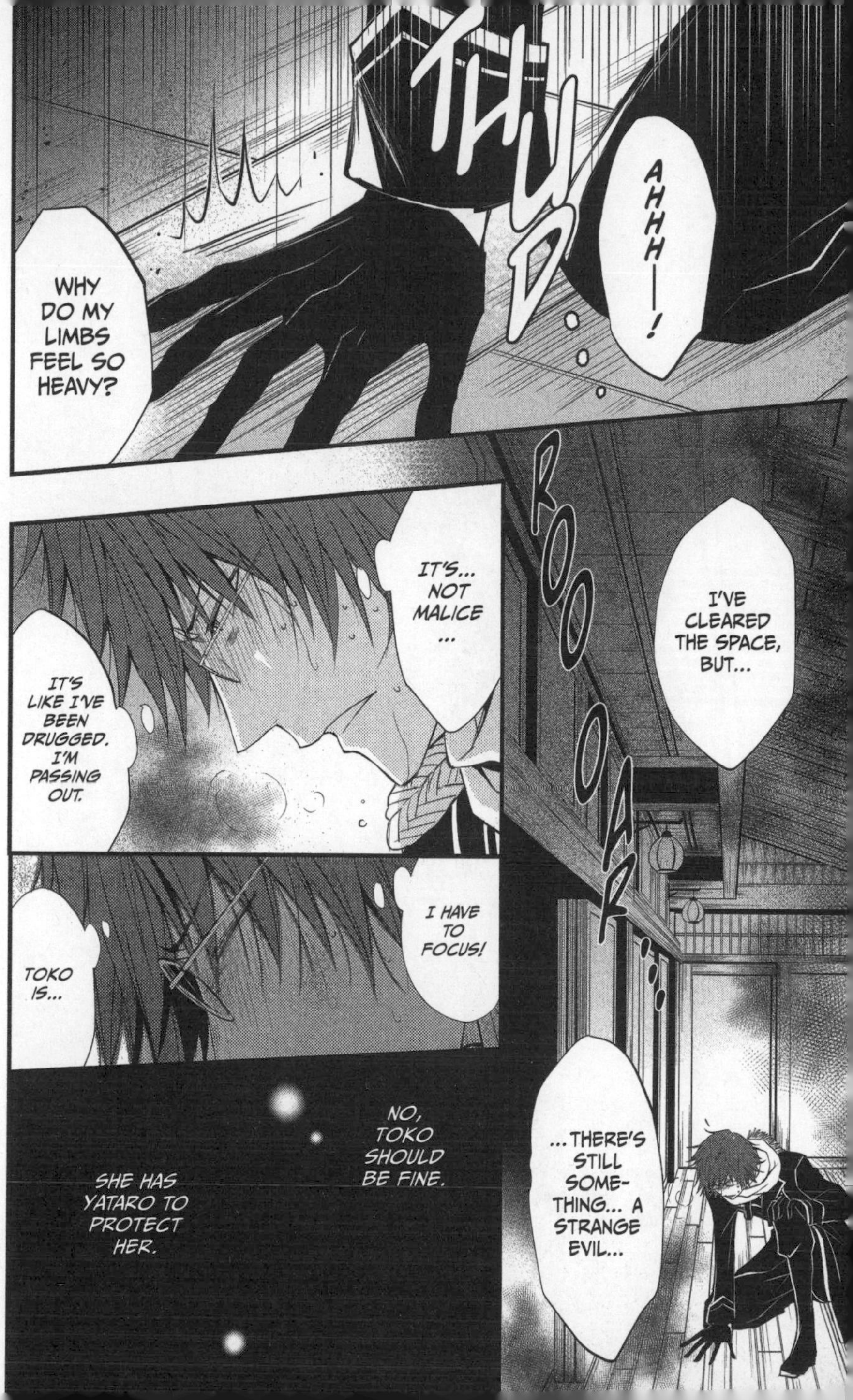
AHHH—!
THUD
WHY DO MY LIMBS FEEL SO HEAVY?
ROOOOAR...!
I'VE CLEARED THE SPACE, BUT...
...THERE'S STILL SOME-THING... A STRANGE EVIL...
IT'S... NOT MALICE...
IT'S LIKE I'VE BEEN DRUGGED. I'M PASSING OUT.
I HAVE TO FOCUS!
TOKO IS...
NO, TOKO SHOULD BE FINE.
SHE HAS YATARO TO PROTECT HER.

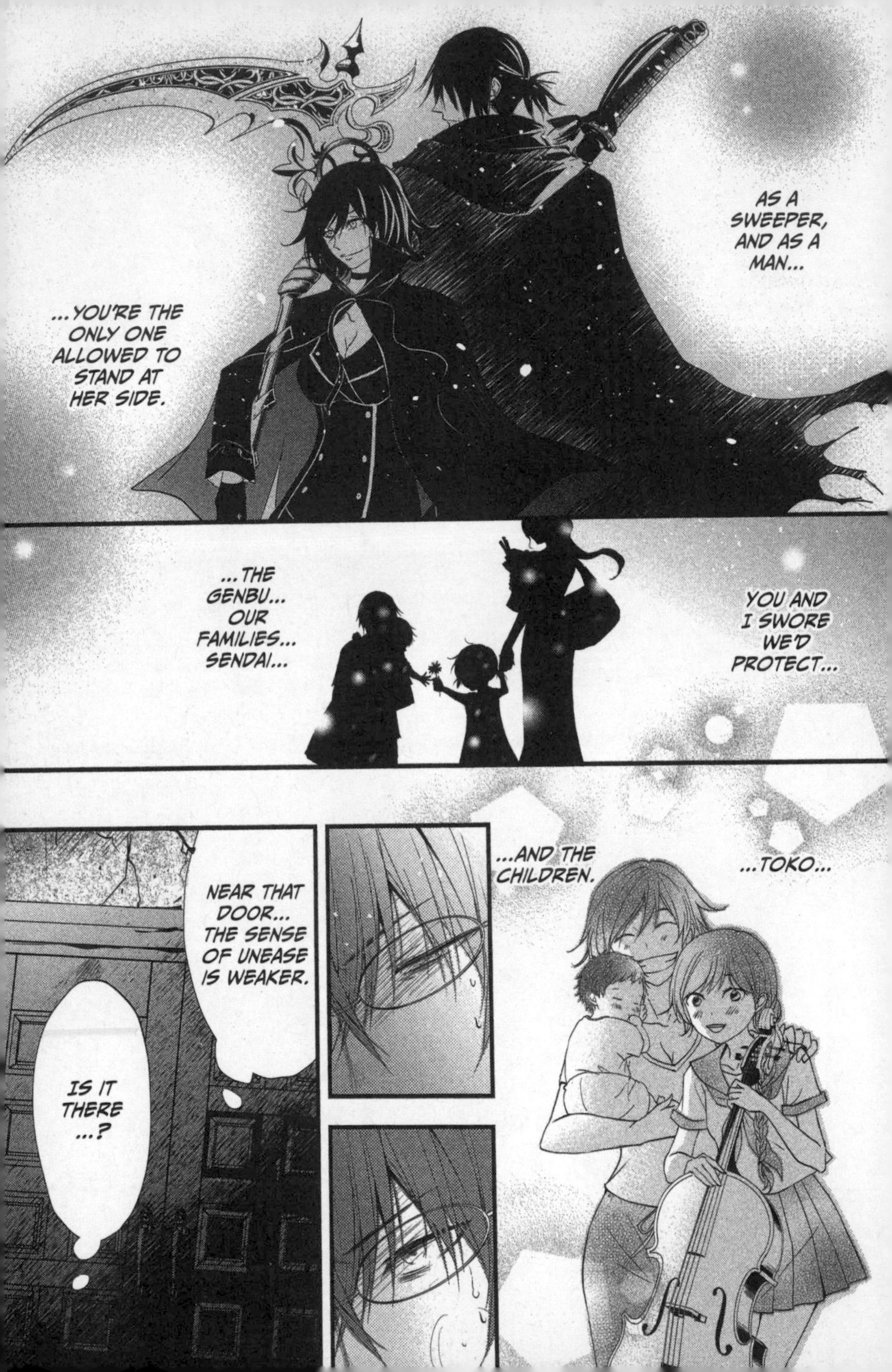
AS A SWEEPER, AND AS A MAN...
...YOU'RE THE ONLY ONE ALLOWED TO STAND AT HER SIDE.
YOU AND I SWORE WE'D PROTECT...
...THE GENBU... OUR FAMILIES... SENDAI...
...TOKO...
...AND THE CHILDREN.
NEAR THAT DOOR... THE SENSE OF UNEASE IS WEAKER.
IS IT THERE ...?

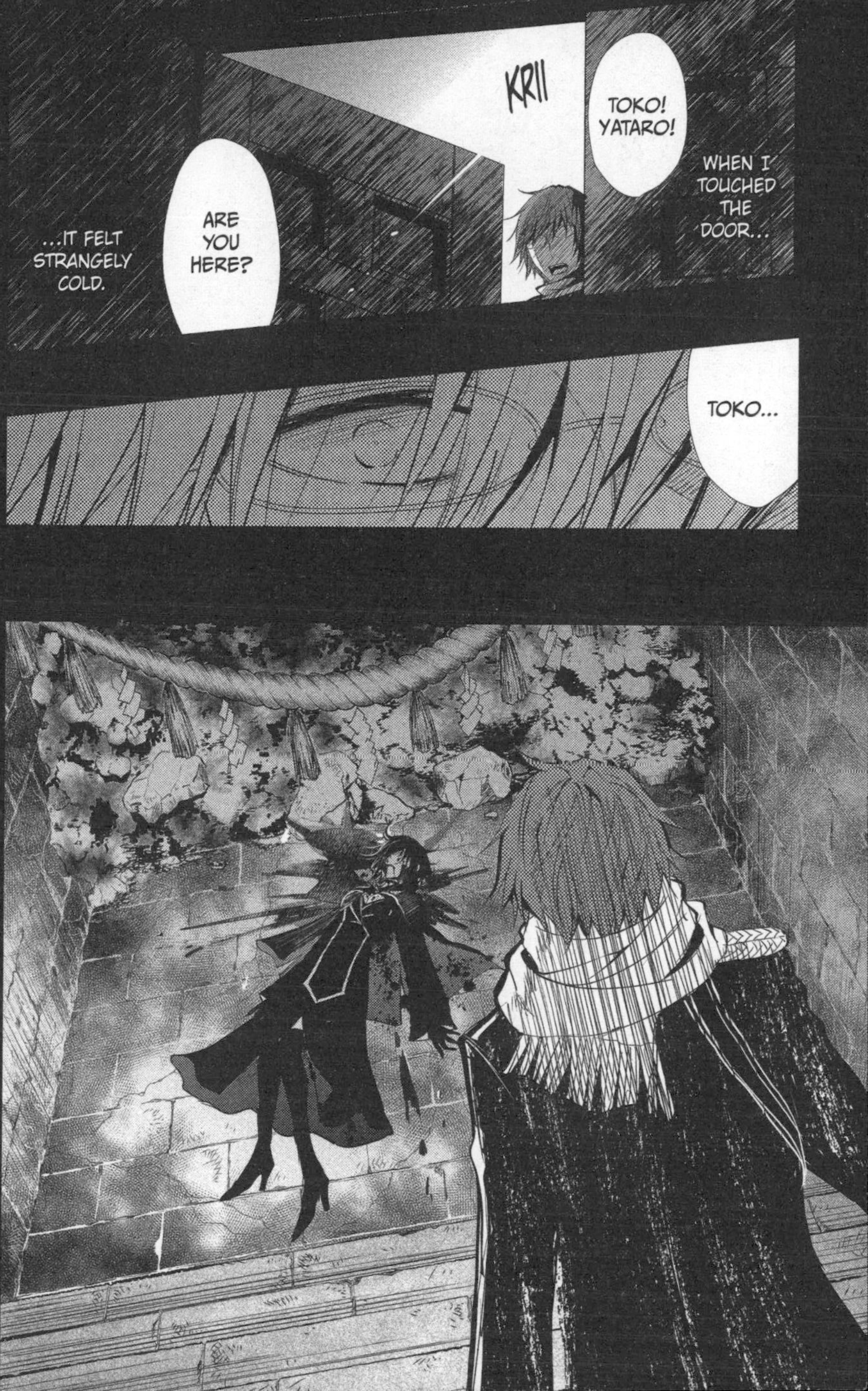
TOKO! YATARO!
WHEN I TOUCHED THE DOOR...
KRII
ARE YOU HERE?
...IT FELT STRANGELY COLD.
TOKO...

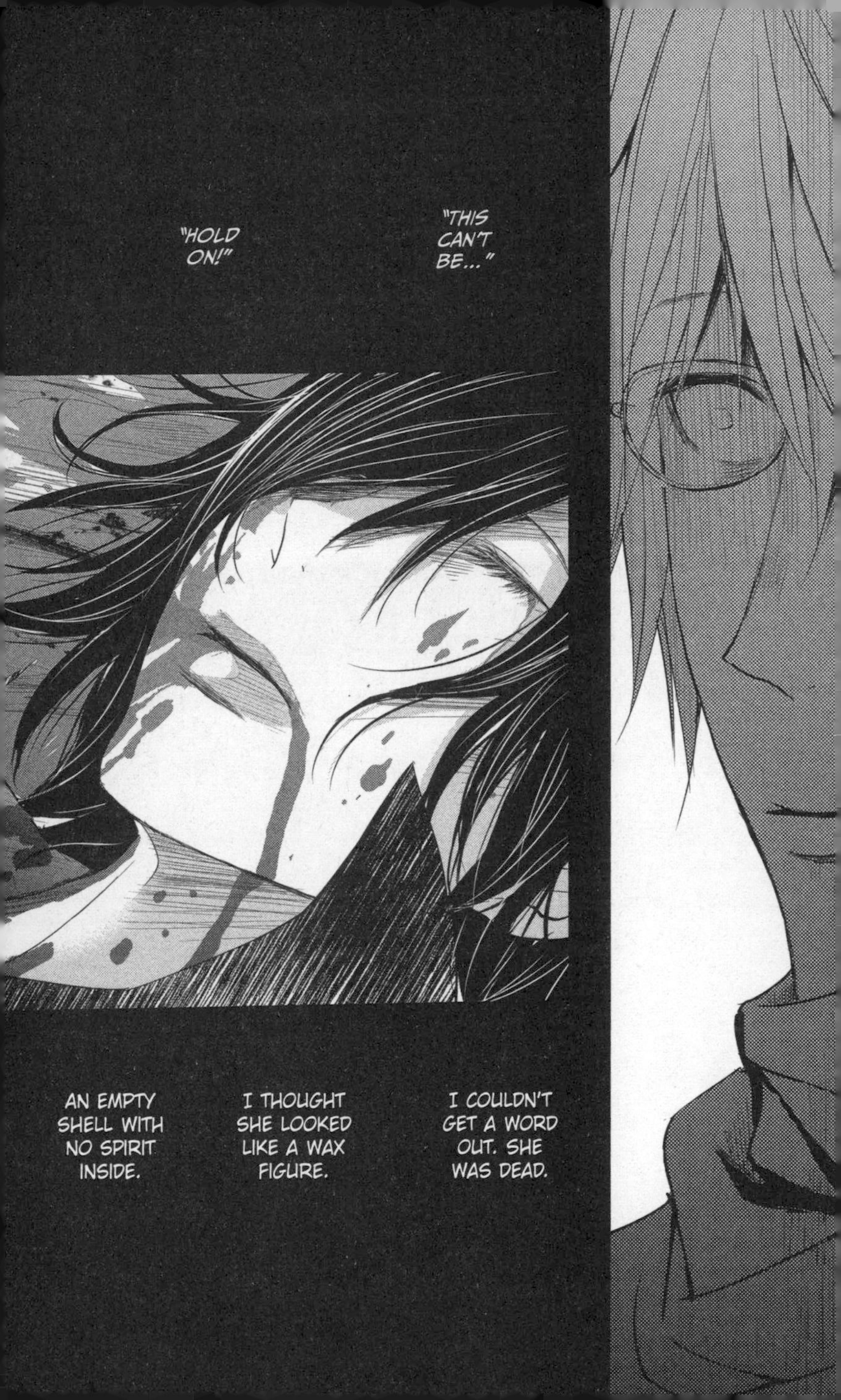
"THIS CAN'T BE..."
"HOLD ON!"
I COULDN'T GET A WORD OUT. SHE WAS DEAD.
I THOUGHT SHE LOOKED LIKE A WAX FIGURE.
AN EMPTY SHELL WITH NO SPIRIT INSIDE.

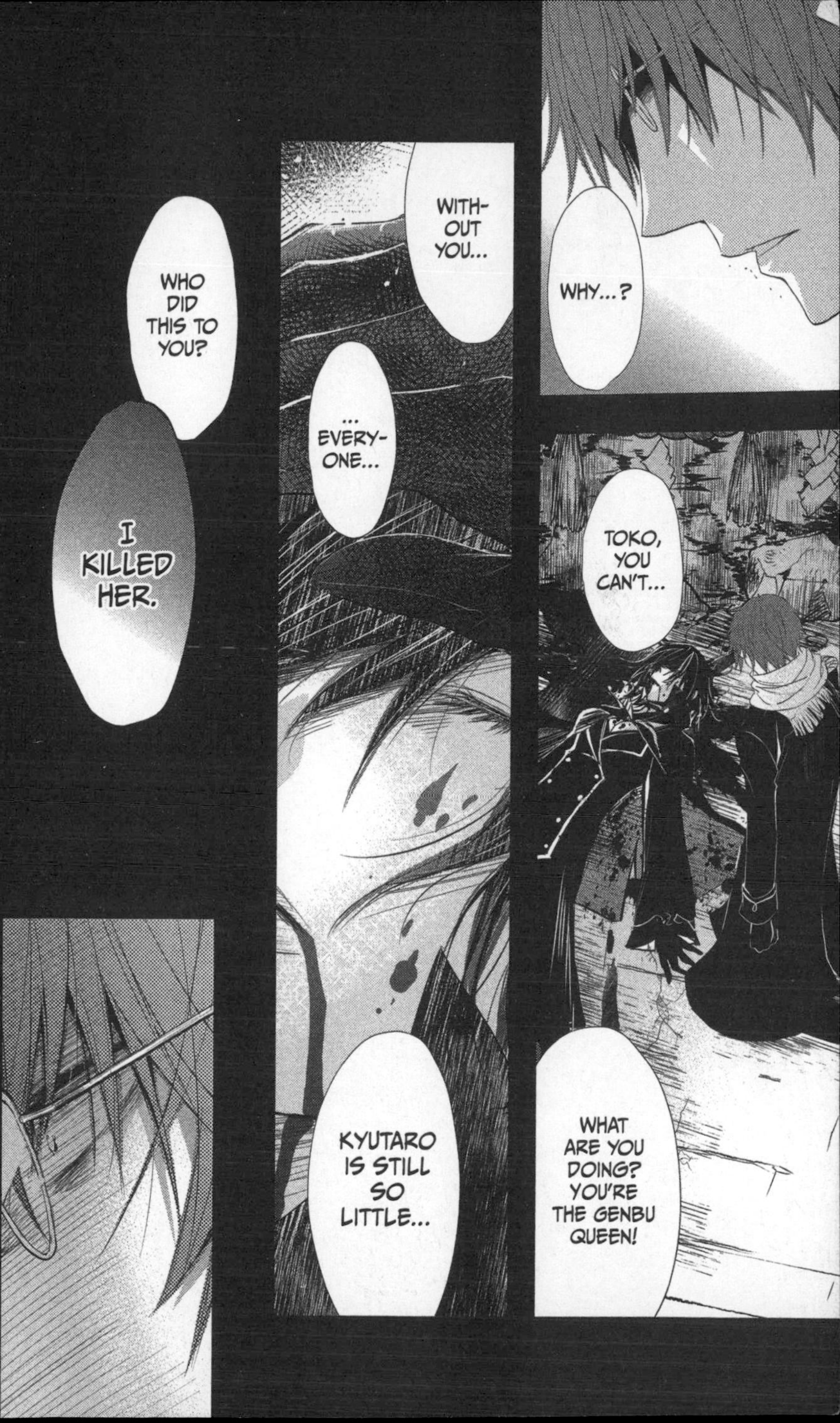
WHY...?
TOKO, YOU CAN'T...
WHAT ARE YOU DOING? YOU'RE THE GENBU QUEEN!
WITH-OUT YOU...
...EVERY-ONE...
KYUTARO IS STILL SO LITTLE...
WHO DID THIS TO YOU?
I KILLED HER.

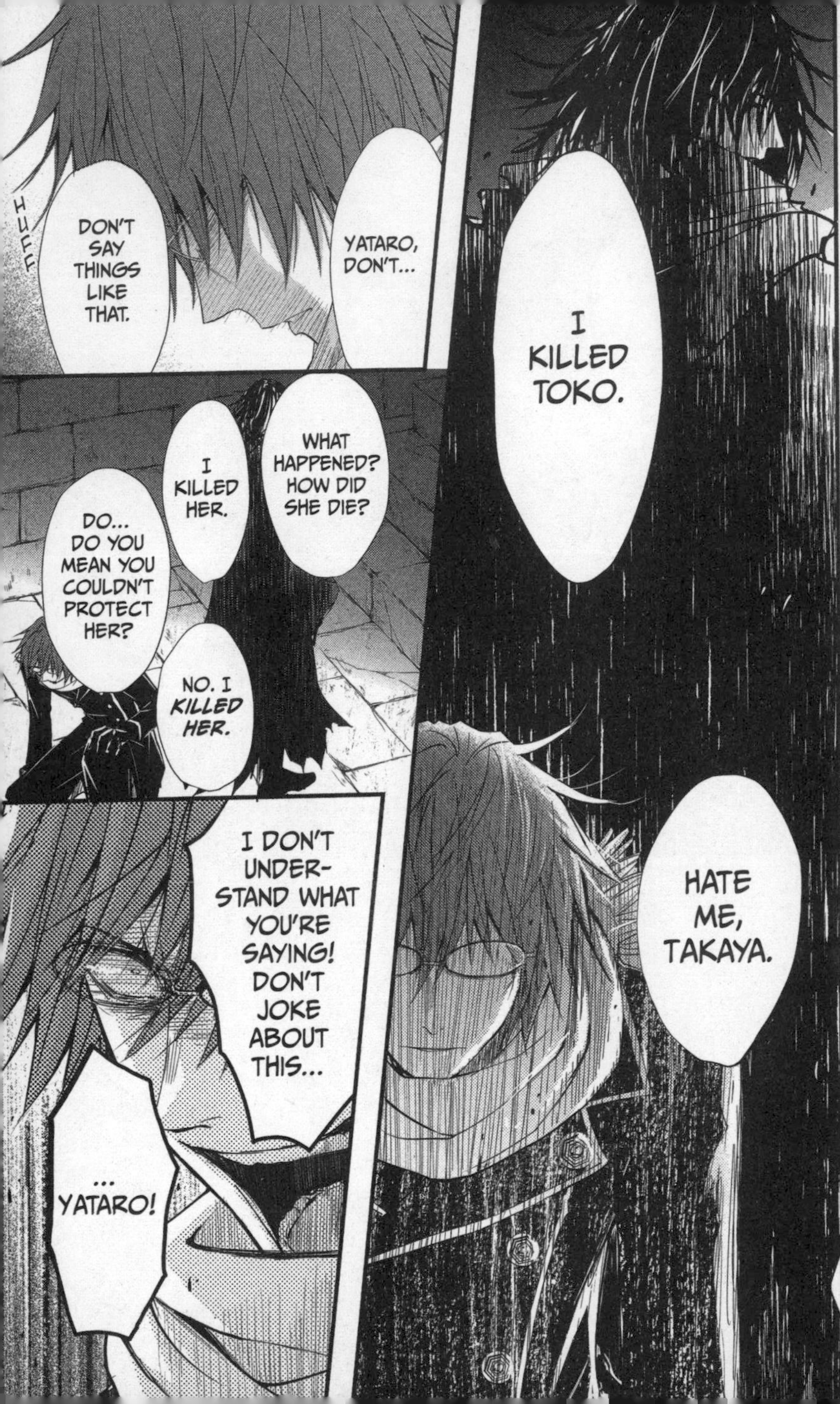
I KILLED TOKO.
YATARO, DON'T...
DON'T SAY THINGS LIKE THAT.
HUFF
WHAT HAPPENED? HOW DID SHE DIE?
I KILLED HER.
DO... DO YOU MEAN YOU COULDN'T PROTECT HER?
NO. I *KILLED* HER.
HATE ME, TAKAYA.
I DON'T UNDER-STAND WHAT YOU'RE SAYING! DON'T JOKE ABOUT THIS...
... YATARO!

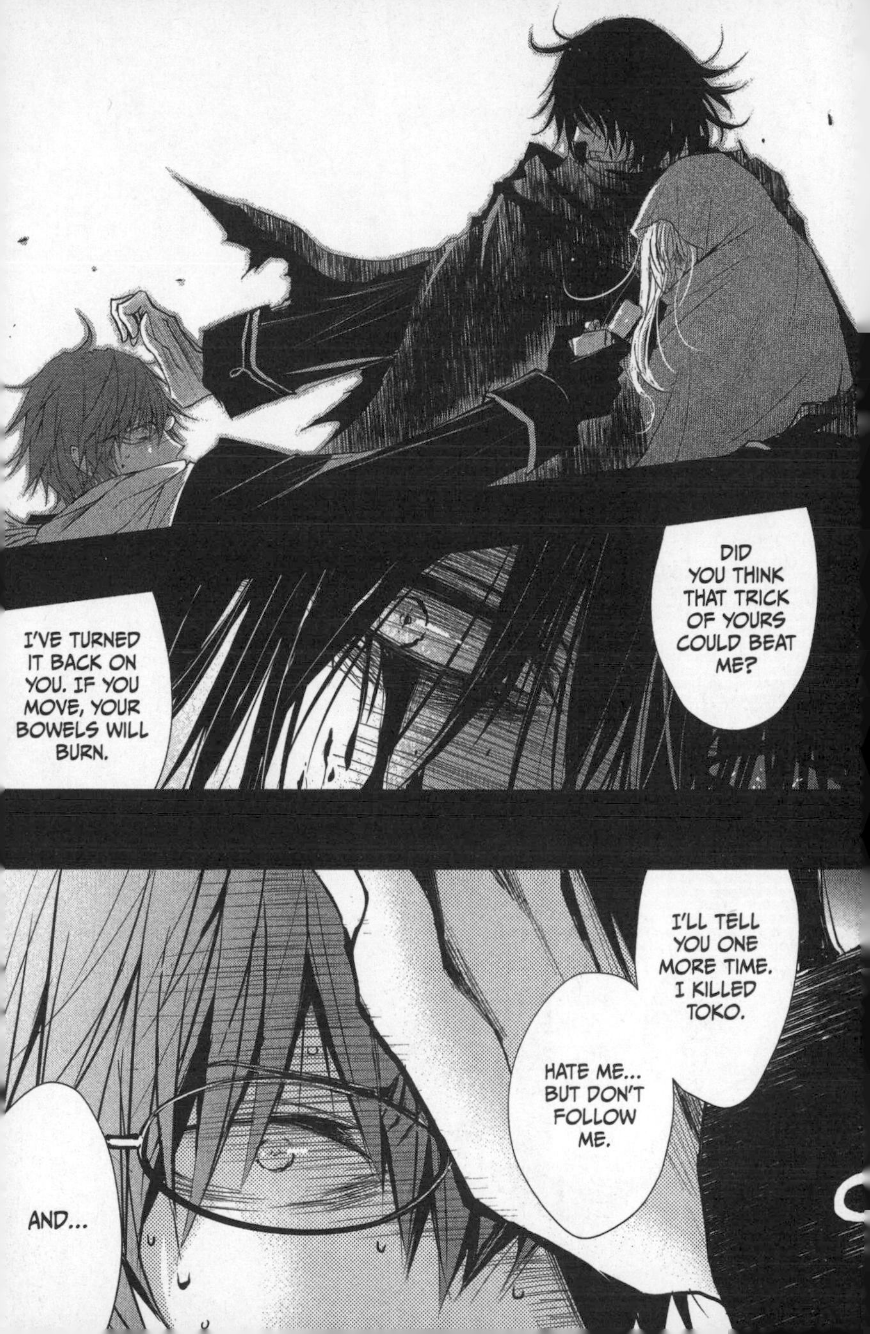
DID YOU THINK THAT TRICK OF YOURS COULD BEAT ME?
I'VE TURNED IT BACK ON YOU. IF YOU MOVE, YOUR BOWELS WILL BURN.
I'LL TELL YOU ONE MORE TIME. I KILLED TOKO.
HATE ME... BUT DON'T FOLLOW ME.
AND...

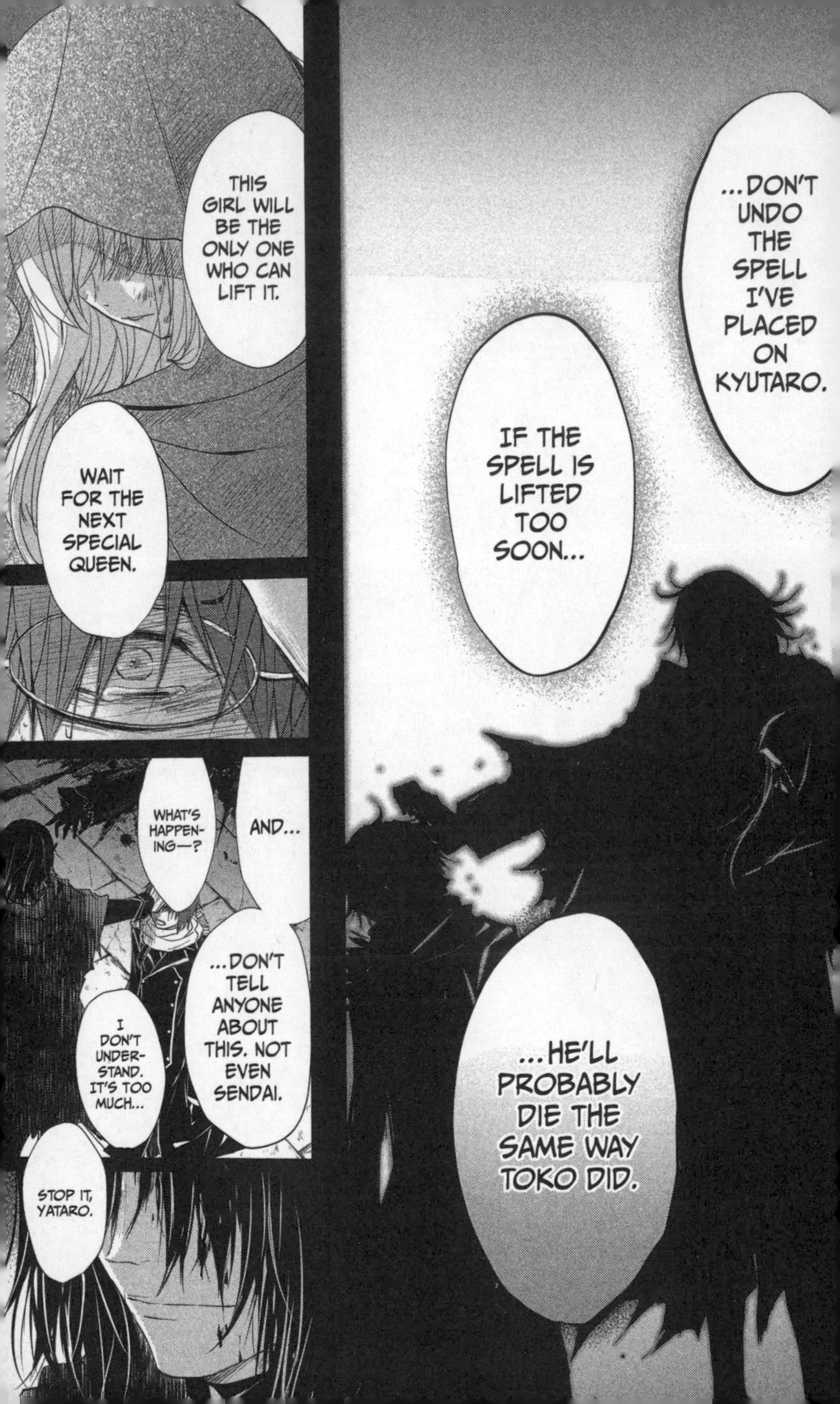
...DON'T UNDO THE SPELL I'VE PLACED ON KYUTARO.
IF THE SPELL IS LIFTED TOO SOON...
...HE'LL PROBABLY DIE THE SAME WAY TOKO DID.
THIS GIRL WILL BE THE ONLY ONE WHO CAN LIFT IT.
WAIT FOR THE NEXT SPECIAL QUEEN.
AND...
WHAT'S HAPPEN-ING—?
...DON'T TELL ANYONE ABOUT THIS. NOT EVEN SENDAI.
I DON'T UNDER-STAND. IT'S TOO MUCH...
STOP IT, YATARO.

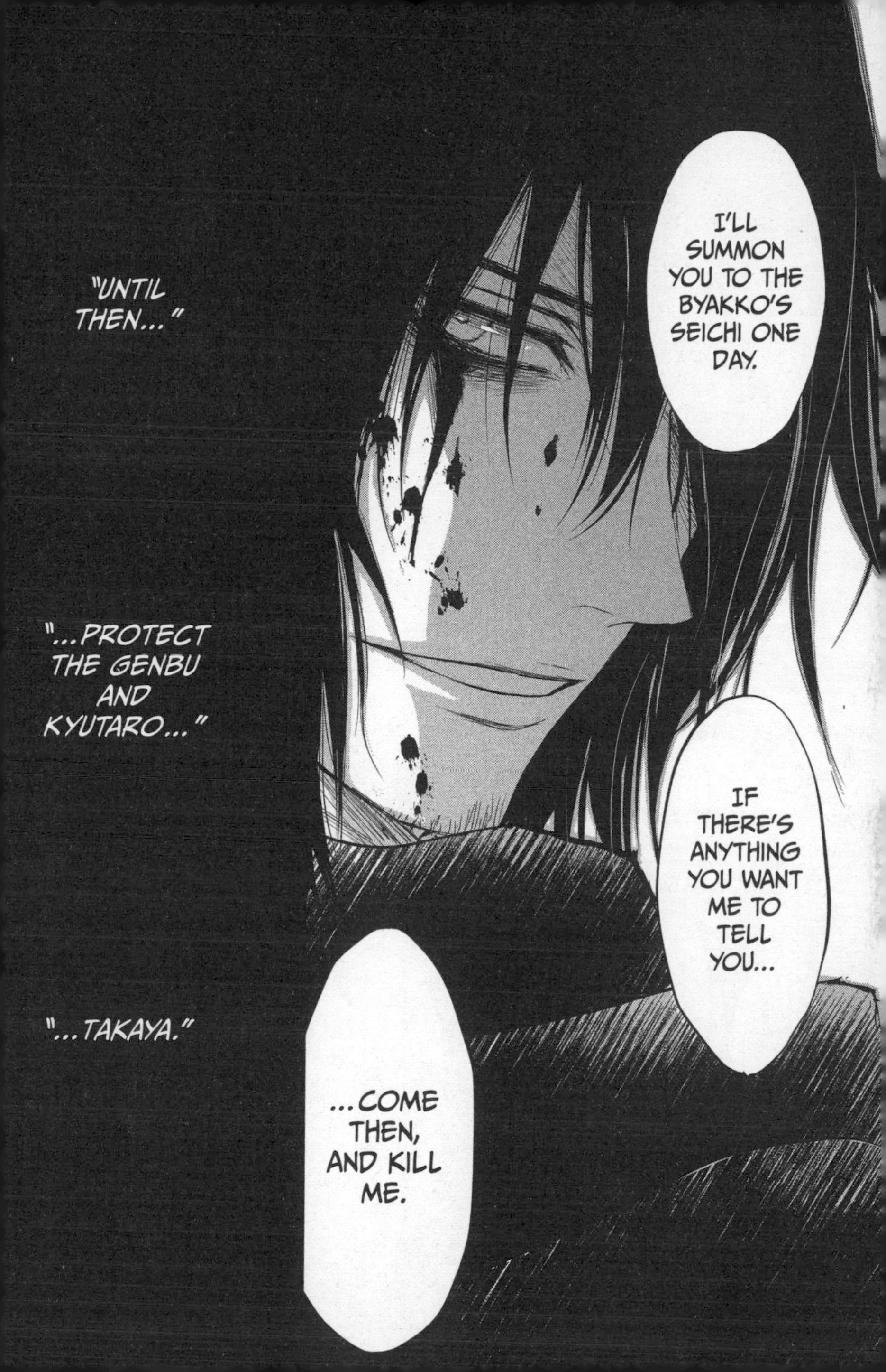
I'LL SUMMON YOU TO THE BYAKKO'S SEICHI ONE DAY.
IF THERE'S ANYTHING YOU WANT ME TO TELL YOU...
...COME THEN, AND KILL ME.
"UNTIL THEN..."
"...PROTECT THE GENBU AND KYUTARO..."
"...TAKAYA."

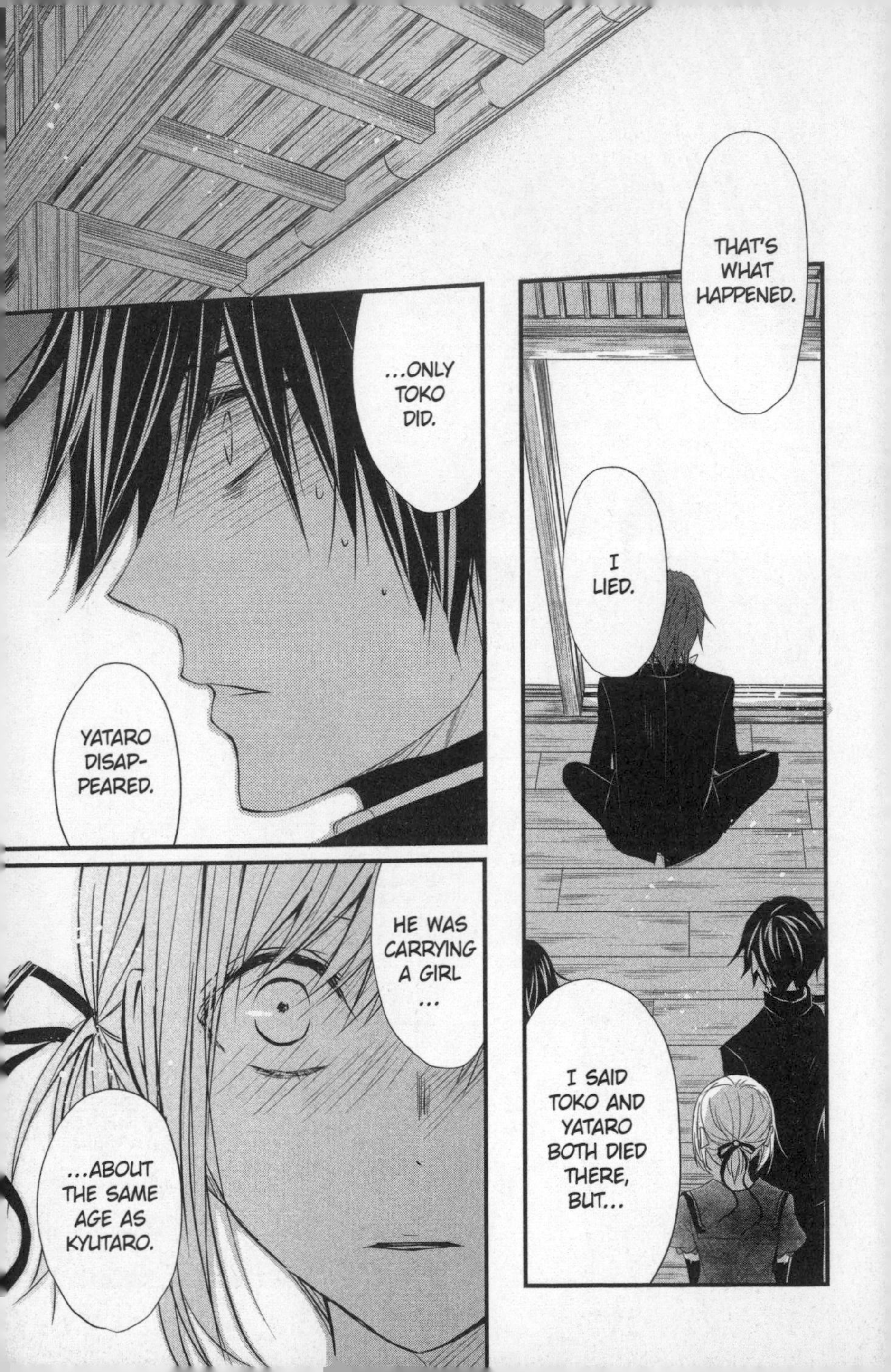
THAT'S WHAT HAPPENED.
I LIED.
I SAID TOKO AND YATARO BOTH DIED THERE, BUT...
...ONLY TOKO DID.
YATARO DISAP-PEARED.
HE WAS CARRYING A GIRL ...
...ABOUT THE SAME AGE AS KYUTARO.

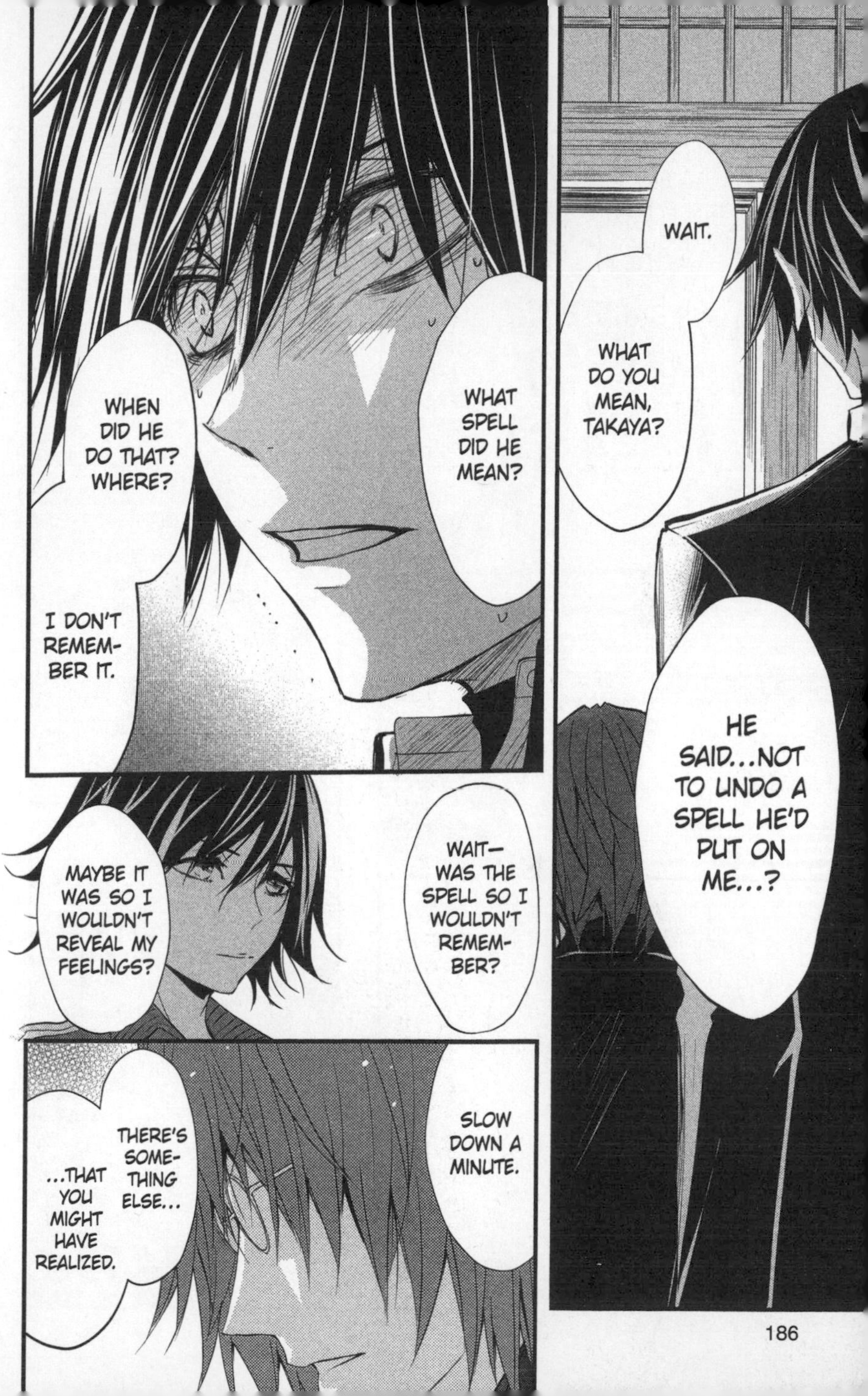
WAIT.
WHAT DO YOU MEAN, TAKAYA?
HE SAID...NOT TO UNDO A SPELL HE'D PUT ON ME...?
WHAT SPELL DID HE MEAN?
WHEN DID HE DO THAT? WHERE?
I DON'T REMEMBER IT.
WAIT—WAS THE SPELL SO I WOULDN'T REMEMBER?
MAYBE IT WAS SO I WOULDN'T REVEAL MY FEELINGS?
SLOW DOWN A MINUTE.
THERE'S SOMETHING ELSE...
...THAT YOU MIGHT HAVE REALIZED.

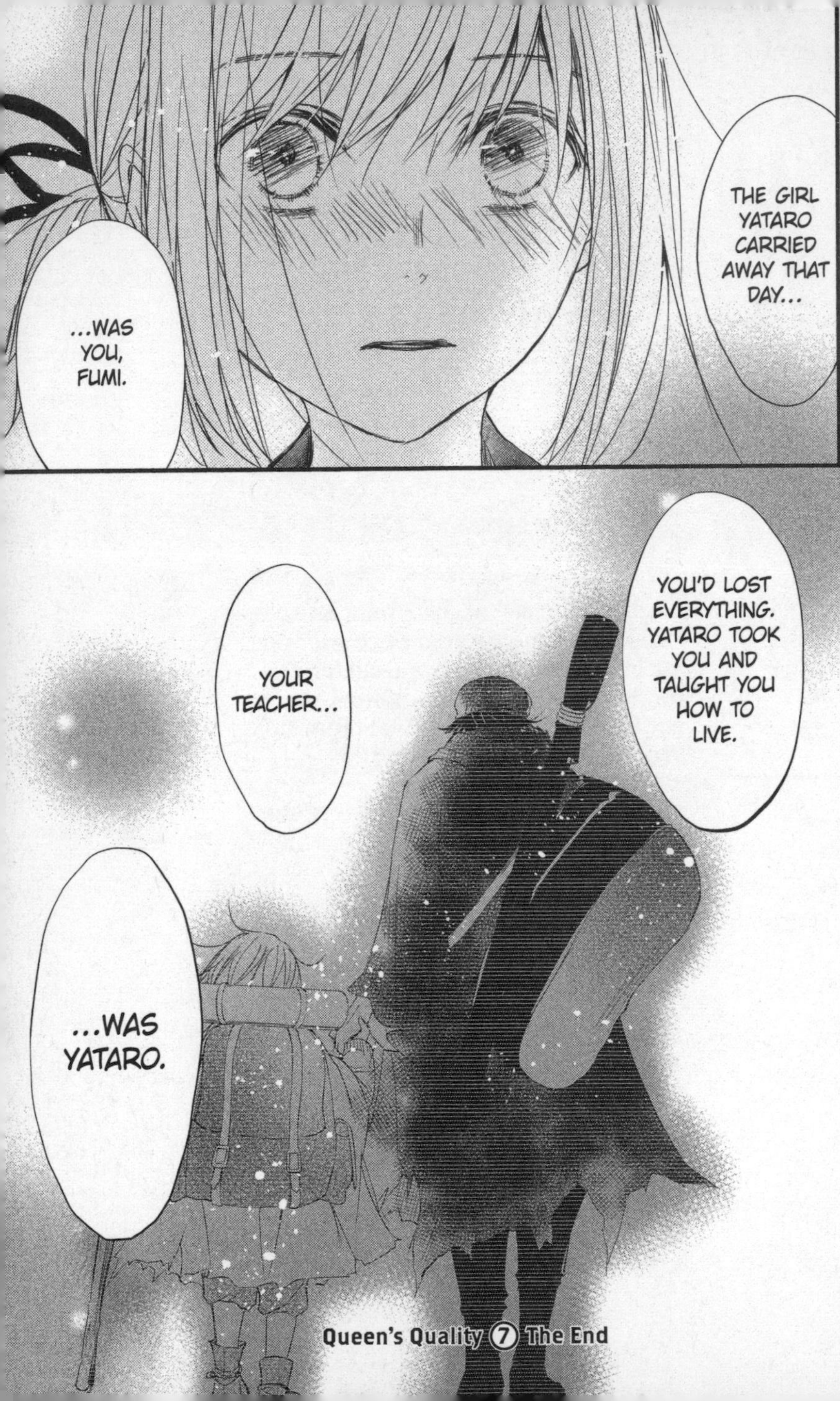
THE GIRL YATARO CARRIED AWAY THAT DAY...
...WAS YOU, FUMI.
YOU'D LOST EVERYTHING. YATARO TOOK YOU AND TAUGHT YOU HOW TO LIVE.
YOUR TEACHER...
...WAS YATARO.

Queen's Quality 7 The End

Around the time volume 6 went on sale,
I was practicing being a pet owner by
raising bean sprouts. Well, my long-
awaited life with a Java sparrow has
finally begun! It's sooo cute! I feel its
impact on my life every day.

—Kyousuke Motomi

Author Bio

Born on August 1, Kyousuke Motomi
debuted in *Deluxe Betsucomi* with
Hetakuso Kyupiddo (No Good
Cupid) in 2002. She is the creator of
Dengeki Daisy, Beast Master and
QQ Sweeper, all available in North
America from VIZ Media. Motomi
enjoys sleeping, tea ceremonies and
reading Haruki Murakami.

Queen's Quality

Vol. 7
Shojo Beat Edition

STORY AND ART BY
KYOUSUKE MOTOMI

QUEEN'S QUALITY Vol. 7
by Kyousuke MOTOMI
© 2016 Kyousuke MOTOMI
All rights reserved.
Original Japanese edition published by SHOGAKUKAN.
English translation rights in the United States of America, Canada, the United
Kingdom, Ireland, Australia and New Zealand arranged with SHOGAKUKAN.

ORIGINAL DESIGN/Chie SATO+Bay Bridge Studio

English Adaptation/Ysabet Reinhardt MacFarlane
Translation/JN Productions
Touch-Up Art & Lettering/Rina Mapa
Design/Julian [JR] Robinson
Editor/Amy Yu

Printed in the U.S.A.

Published by VIZ Media, LLC
P.O. Box 77010
San Francisco, CA 94107

10 9 8 7 6 5 4 3 2 1
First printing, June 2019

viz.com

shojobeat.com

The Water Dragon's Bride

Story & Art by
Rei Toma

In the blink of an eye, a modern-day girl named Asahi is whisked away from her warm and happy home and stranded in a strange and mysterious world where she meets a water dragon god!

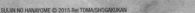
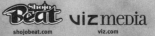

This is the Last Page!

It's true: In keeping with the original Japanese comic format, this book reads from right to left—so action, sound effects and word balloons are completely reversed. This preserves the orientation of the original artwork—plus, it's fun! Check out the diagram shown here to get the hang of things, and then turn to the other side of the book to get started!

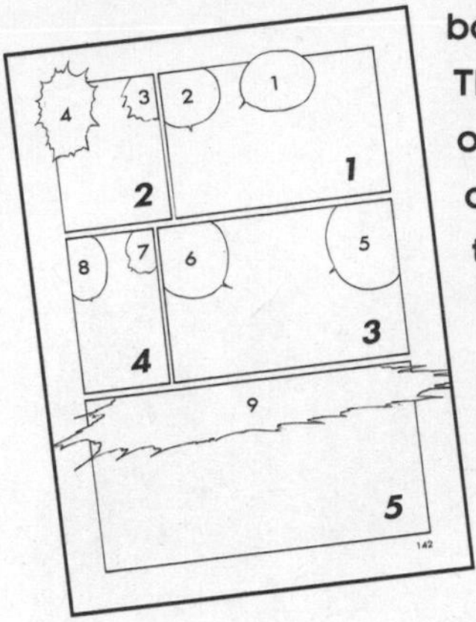
1
2
3
4
1
2
5
6
7
8
3
4
9
5
142

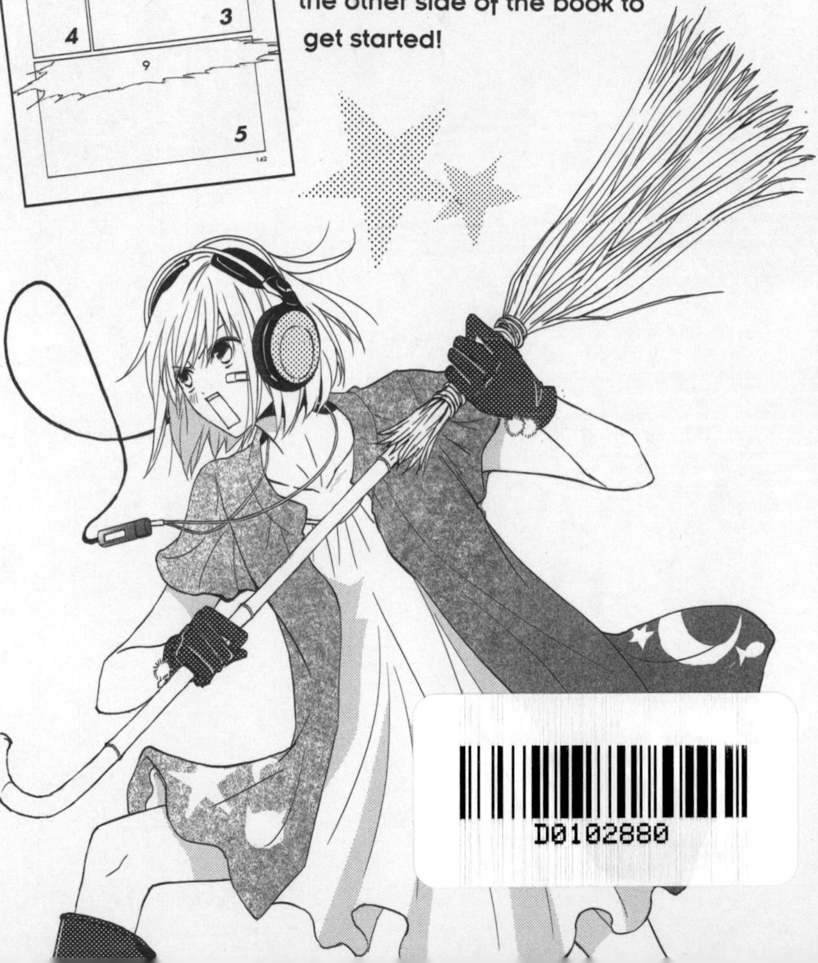